Saul Goodman
— v. —
Jimmy McGill

Saul Goodman
— V. —
Jimmy McGill

THE COMPLETE
CRITICAL
COMPANION TO

Better

Call Saul

ALAN
SEPINWALL

ABRAMS PRESS, NEW YORK

Library of Congress Control Number: 2024941015

ISBN: 978-1-4197-7719-6
eISBN: 979-8-88707-425-2

Printed and bound in the United States
10 9 8 7 6 5 4 3 2 1

Abrams books are available at special discounts when purchased in quantity for
premiums and promotions as well as fundraising or educational use. Special editions can
also be created to specification. For details, contact specialsales@abramsbooks.com or
the address below.

Abrams Press® is a registered trademark of Harry N. Abrams, Inc.

ABRAMS The Art of Books
195 Broadway, New York, NY 10007
abramsbooks.com

To all the doctors and nurses who have taken care of me since Saul Goodman moved to Omaha

Contents

Opening Statement

I still can't entirely believe that this book exists. And I wrote it!

Keep in mind, I've written plenty of books about television before. Some of them, like this one, feature episode-by-episode analysis designed to accompany your first, or latest, binge. One of those, *Breaking Bad 101*, even features many of the same characters who are so prominent on *Better Call Saul*. In most respects, this is very much along the lines of what I do.

But when AMC and Sony announced plans for a *Breaking Bad* spin-off where Bob Odenkirk would reprise his *Breaking Bad* role as sleazy attorney Saul Goodman, my initial reaction was, *That's a terrible idea! Why would they do that?* With all deference to the excellent work on the original show by Odenkirk, and by Jonathan Banks, who would be along for this new ride as unflappable fixer Mike Ehrmantraut, Saul seemed like way too thin a character to support his own series. Hell, for someone who primarily existed as comic relief, he wasn't even the funniest *Breaking Bad* character! (Although Saul was a more consistent source of humor, Jesse Pinkman's comedic highs outstripped anything Saul did or said.)

I went into the spin-off with an open mind, simply because I trusted co-creators Vince Gilligan and Peter Gould, as well as all the other members of the *Breaking Bad* behind-the-scenes team they brought with them to the prequel. While I definitely enjoyed the early episodes, it was more for the craft of individual scenes and performances than for any clear sense of what kind of story *Better Call Saul* meant to tell. The first season of *Breaking Bad* was slow, but never meandering or palpably doubting itself in the way *Saul* was at the same stage. Years later—in interviews you can find elsewhere in this book—both Gilligan and Gould admitted that it took them quite a long time to figure out what *Better Call Saul* even was, that they kept being surprised by where the story was taking them, and that this eventually meant that Odenkirk and Banks were starring in parallel shows that operated under the same title.

Yet for all the trial and error, for all the false starts, abrupt changes in direction, and abundant "Is he Saul now? How about *now*? This time, maybe?"

teases, something was clearly working. Odenkirk, who had no real background as a dramatic actor, was a revelation playing a more multifaceted version of Saul, here still going by his real name of Jimmy McGill. Michael McKean and Rhea Seehorn, respectively playing Jimmy's elitist, mentally ill brother Chuck and Jimmy's best friend Kim Wexler, were so compelling that it felt like the two of them and Odenkirk could carry a legal drama that had nothing whatsoever to do with Walter White. Banks brought even more depth to Mike than he'd gotten to display on the parent series, and Gould and company had great fun mixing and matching new and old cartel characters to keep the non-Jimmy parts of the show gripping.

I'm not sure I could have imagined there being a full book in *Better Call Saul* after the first couple of seasons, though. It had turned out to be much better than I ever expected, but it was still clearly inferior to the show that introduced Saul and Mike, right? As effective as certain episodes and arcs were, *Saul* could never live up to the exploding wheelchairs, acid baths, and other high-stakes drama and action of *Breaking Bad*, could it?

At a certain point, though, two things became clear. The first is that the creative team had, after spending so many years chronicling this fictionalized version of Albuquerque, simply gotten better at their jobs over time. Emotional moments felt richer. Thriller moments felt more suspenseful. The characters—both the ones we already knew from *Breaking Bad* and the ones we met here—felt more nuanced. The penultimate season's "Bagman" was, like the famous *Breaking Bad* episode "4 Days Out," a tale of the show's two male leads struggling to survive being stranded in the harsh southwestern desert. I adore "4 Days Out," and still consider it one of the best *BB* episodes of them all. Yet on almost every technical and storytelling level, "Bagman" is superior. Over the course of writing this book, I rewatched all of *Better Call Saul*, periodically mixing in relevant *Breaking Bad* installments, and I was impressed again and again with how well the *Saul* episodes stacked up against the *BB* ones.

The second is that, while Walter White's rise and fall is superficially more exciting than Jimmy McGill's own moral descent, the darkness of the latter is at least as complex. If anything, Jimmy's transformation into Saul seems sadder than Walt's into Heisenberg, because Gould and company made clear that Jimmy never wanted this to happen, whereas Walt reveled in his newfound power. If the early show told the story of a man who was able to do unspeakably evil things because the world mistakenly assumed he was good, then *Saul* told the story of a man who wanted desperately to be good, only to give in to his worst instincts upon realizing that the world had no faith or interest in the admirable version of him. Which is the greater tragedy? You tell me.

Had *Better Call Saul* turned out to be as great as *Breaking Bad*? Had it somehow, defying all odds and expectations, turned out better? Arguments could be made on both sides, and *Saul* was not without its flaws, particularly whenever the cartel stories seemed to be too concerned with filling in *Breaking Bad* backstory or were simply hemmed in by what we already knew. But the fact that it's even worthy of discussion at all—that a spin-off nobody was too enthusiastic about could plausibly stand shoulder to shoulder with one of the most acclaimed shows ever made, if not stand above it—is incredible. The show I thought *Saul* was going to be, or even the one it was back in its first season, couldn't possibly have merited a book like this. The show it became? I could have written something the size of *War and Peace* and not run out of things to say.

Before we get deeper into laying out an argument in favor of *Better Call Saul*'s genius, I should explain how this book is going to work.

So, what's in here?

The book is primarily made up of essays about all 63 episodes of *Better Call Saul*. Some of them are fairly similar to how they first appeared when I wrote them for HitFix, Uproxx, and *Rolling Stone*. Many of them have been substantially rewritten, and a few started over from scratch. But all are designed to be read after you watch each of those episodes. (Or at random, if you're just feeling nostalgic for the one where Kim makes all those phone calls in the Hamlin Hamlin & McGill stairwell.)

There are also interviews and features I reported and published as the series was airing, along with a brand-new conversation with Peter Gould. The old stories (some in full, some excerpted) will be mixed in throughout the book, appearing at the same roughly chronological point where they did back in the day; the new Gould Q&A comes at the very end.

Is this book for first-time viewers or longtime *Saul* fans?

Like the meme asks, why not both?

Much as the series attempted to both tell its own story and expand our knowledge of *Breaking Bad* history, I've designed these to be completely safe for newcomers to read as they watch, while also trying to make them in-depth enough for people who know every story beat by heart. Many of the original versions of the essays were filled with my predictions of where the story was going—almost all of them incorrect. There is still some speculation in here, because part of the emotional experience of watching *Saul* is wondering about how various familiar characters will get from who they are at this moment to who they are on *Breaking Bad*, and worrying about what might happen to new characters like Kim and Nacho to explain why they never appeared on the other show. Even though I (and many of you) know these answers now, the episodes still draw much of their power from that uncertainty. It felt more important to reflect that than to constantly step out of the narrative of a given episode to say things like, "And this is the first link in a long chain of events that eventually result in Chuck becoming a rodeo clown."*

Can I read this if I've never watched *Breaking Bad*?

You can, though you'll be spoiled on a lot of what happened on the other show. Then again, *Better Call Saul* does plenty of that itself without needing my help. Though largely a prequel, parts of the series take place during and after the events of *Breaking Bad*, and much of the storytelling assumes that the audience knows all about what happened to Saul, Walt, Mike, etc. You can definitely enjoy both the show and this book without sitting through 62 episodes of the earlier series, as I encountered many passionate *Saul*-only viewers during the original run on AMC. It's just impossible to discuss what's happening here without periodically discussing what's to come in the future for Jimmy and everyone else.

If it would please the court . . .

. . . we have a lot of aspects to argue about this case. How does one show compare to the other? Is Jimmy's story darker than Walt's? Are Jimmy, Saul, and Gene all basically the same person, or wildly different characters? Why is Kim Wexler the absolute best? So let's get right to the evidence, shall we?

---

* Don't worry, first-timers: Chuck does not become a rodeo clown. Though I can neither confirm nor deny whether anyone else does.

"Uno"

"Have patience. There are no shortcuts." —**Chuck**

The advice about patience that Chuck McGill offers his younger brother Jimmy can be looked at a couple of different ways. On the one hand, this is a lesson Jimmy obviously needs, since so much of the *Better Call Saul* series premiere involves him trying to take shortcuts to build his legal career, each time landing on his ass like he's still Slippin' Jimmy from Cicero, Illinois.

But on the other, *Better Call Saul* itself has no need to learn about patience, because it's made by the team from *Breaking Bad*, a series whose greatness was built largely on its disdain for shortcuts. That show took its damn time in showing us Walter White's journey from Mr. Chips to Scarface, which made things so much more powerful than if Walt had become Albuquerque's meth kingpin by its fourth episode. "Uno" is lighter in tone and lower in stakes than the parent show was in its own premiere. But it's clear from the start that Vince Gilligan, Peter Gould, and company still know that the only way to tell a story in this world is to take things one careful step at a time.

This means, among other things, that Saul Goodman himself barely appears in the first episode of the show named for him. The bulk of "Uno" takes place in the spring of 2002, nearly six and a half years before Walt entered Saul's office for the first time. In that earlier episode, Saul admitted that his real name was McGill, and here we get to meet the actual James Morgan McGill. He is a reformed con man, struggling to set up his own law practice even as he takes care of Chuck. There are hints of the man we know he will become, but Jimmy feels pretty harmless compared to Saul: a shameless ambulance chaser and small-time hustler, but not an unrepentant criminal mastermind.

Any viewer who puts on "Uno" eager to get more of Bob Odenkirk* with the bad comb-over, tacky suits, and tackier office has to content themselves with what doesn't even qualify as a glimpse. We hear Saul's voice in one of his

---

* Before being cast as Saul Goodman on *Breaking Bad*, Odenkirk was best known as one of the sharpest comedic minds and performers around. As a writer on *Saturday Night Live*, he created Chris Farley's famous motivational speaker character Matt Foley ("I live in a van down by the river!"). He won acclaim as slick Hollywood agent Stevie Grant on *The Larry Sanders Show*, and he and David Cross co-created and starred in the cult-hit sketch comedy series *Mr. Show with Bob and David*.

TV commercials and get a brief flash of color from one of the ads reflected in a pair of eyeglasses, and that's it. We are instead living entirely in the period before and after *Breaking Bad*, with Jimmy McGill at one end and Gene Takovic from Cinnabon at the other.

The opening sequence is a self-contained marvel in the way that so many of the best *Breaking Bad* teasers were. It's a tragic opera in miniature: the slick operator reduced to a quiet corporate drone (managing, as he predicted the last time he saw Walt, a Cinnabon in Omaha, Nebraska, with our first glimpses of the dough being rolled out and formed into buns resembling Heisenberg and Cap'n Cook at work), hiding behind glasses and a mustache that's in many ways even sadder than the one once sported by Walt. (As Gene, he's also stopped trying to disguise his baldness, since it only adds to his new anonymity.) His life is simultaneously depressing and terrifying—like Jesse in Civic Plaza at the end of the "Rabid Dog" episode of *Breaking Bad*, Gene briefly mistakes a shady-looking character as a threat to his life, and you get the sense that this is a regular occurrence, creating a constant Hank-Schrader-waiting-for-the-Cousins level of paranoia. Those six and a half minutes, scored to The Ink Spots' "Address Unknown," tells us all we need to know without asking Gene to say a damn word. The first time we hear Odenkirk's voice is in one of the old ads on a videotape, taken out of a hiding place as a painful but necessary reminder of what Gene used to be—a tiny hint of color in a life that has otherwise gone all gray.

And then, having sated our curiosity about what happened to Saul after he drove off with Ed the vacuum repairman, Gilligan and Gould take their sweet time introducing us to Jimmy McGill.

It's another marvelously elongated sequence, where you can literally hear a ticking clock in the courtroom, while the judge checks his watch in impatience over Jimmy's absence. And Jimmy's fast-talking, long-winded opening argument is just an elaborate set-up for the punch line, where the prosecutor plays a video showing us that the three teenage defendants whose virtues Jimmy just extolled were caught on camera molesting a corpse and sawing off its head. The whole thing is a little wink at the audience: a way for the storytellers to tell us that they, like their new main character, are in no rush to get to the point of the story, and they hope you're entertained along the way.

"Uno" is nearly fifteen minutes longer than the typical *Breaking Bad* episode, and Gilligan and Gould let every scene play out a little longer than you might expect, getting added value out of it each time. There is, for instance, a certain clichéd visual vocabulary that will tip viewers off to when a character driving a car is about to get into an accident. But the sequence where Jimmy hits one of the skateboarding twins—the twenty-first-century Albuquerque equivalents of the kind of slip-and-fall artist he used to be—spends *juuust* enough extra time on Jimmy working the phones to hustle up business that the actual crash is somehow surprising by the time it comes.

This incident later provides Jimmy with inspiration for a way to land a potentially huge client in Craig Kettleman (Jeremy Shamos), a local county official under investigation for embezzlement. Craig's wife Betsy (Julie Ann Emery) is understandably wary of this obvious shyster, so Jimmy recruits the twins to pull their scam on Betsy, allowing him to swoop in and save the day. His pitch to them sets up the most purely entertaining scene of the Albuquerque section of the pilot,* as Jimmy tells them about his glory days in Cicero. It's just Odenkirk, in a skate park, talking under the bright New Mexico sun, but he's so confident and verbally dexterous that it seems clear from this moment that he can carry his own show.

Though Jimmy is not Walter White, this is a franchise where men plan, and their writers laugh. Jimmy thinks he has come up with a foolproof way to land the Kettlemans, but instead the twins wind up crashing into a different medium sandalwood station wagon, and the episode concludes with Jimmy being taken prisoner by none other than Walt's first big nemesis, Tuco Salamanca.

Even more than Mike Ehrmantraut's cameo as the courthouse parking lot attendant†—where he of course won't let Jimmy get out of paying without the full number of parking validation stickers, because Mike believes in an ordered world with rules—it's Tuco's appearance that most firmly places "Uno" into the Heisenberg-verse. This is a very narrow needle the series has to thread, because the Saul introduced on *Breaking Bad* knows the Albuquerque criminal community but did not seem to have been directly involved in the drug game until teaming up with Walt and Jesse. But in the moment, it's a delightful surprise, especially since *Breaking Bad* didn't make nearly as much use out of Tuco as planned, due to actor Raymond Cruz's other commitments at that time.

---

* And the first scene filmed of the series, period.

† A character actor who probably came out of the womb looking world-weary, Jonathan Banks joined the Heisenberg-verse thanks to, of all things, *How I Met Your Mother*. Odenkirk had a recurring role on the hit CBS sitcom and was already committed to making another appearance there when the *Breaking Bad* writers realized they needed Saul—or, failing that, someone working for Saul—to appear in their second season finale, which was filming at the same time as the *HIMYM* episode. Enter Banks, veteran of more than 100 prior film and TV roles. Vince Gilligan was a fan of Banks's work as FBI agent Frank McPike on acclaimed eighties CBS crime drama *Wiseguy*, and jumped at the chance to hire him when casting directors Sharon Bialy and Sherry Thomas suggested Banks.

But there is a whole other world on this show which, so far at least, has absolutely nothing to do with kingpins, explosions, assassinations, etc. In addition to trying to get his solo practice off the ground,* we see that Jimmy has become caretaker for his brother Chuck (Michael McKean†), a brilliant legal mind who has become a hermit, convinced he suffers from electromagnetic hypersensitivity. Chuck insists that the condition is real, and that he will eventually conquer it and return to work at Hamlin Hamlin & McGill, the venerated Albuquerque firm he helped build. Until that day comes, though, he has to reluctantly depend on Jimmy as his man Friday, and Jimmy in turn has to fight with Chuck's partner Howard Hamlin (Patrick Fabian‡) to cash out Chuck for his share in HHM.§ He gets nowhere, and it's clear from the bit of business with the dented trash can, and the cigarette he shares, almost wordlessly, with old friend Kim Wexler (Rhea Seehorn¶), that this is far from the first time he has left these offices consumed with impotent rage.

Establishing that Jimmy is so concerned for his brother's well-being is perhaps the most important thing the pilot does, because it tells us that once upon a time, Saul Goodman was a human being who cared about something beyond acquiring money and sexually harassing his receptionist. To work, *Better Call Saul* needs for him to be a person, not a caricature, and he feels very three-dimensional from the jump.

During Jimmy's visit to Chuck's house, his imperious brother tries to encourage him to not use the family name for his new practice. He acts like this could create confusion between little guy Jimmy and the monolith that is

---

* To make ends meet, Jimmy not only works out of a tiny office in the back of a nail salon, he also lives there. Years later, as Saul Goodman, he will own a bunch of salons and launder his drug money through them. Where Saul drives a top-of-the-line Cadillac, Jimmy has to make do with a battered yellow Suzuki Esteem with a mismatched rear passenger door. And in lieu of Saul's harried assistant Francesca, Jimmy has to play the role of his own secretary, adopting a laughably vague continental accent when answering the phone.

† Between his role as Lenny on seventies smash hit *Laverne & Shirley* and his various acclaimed collaborations with friends Christopher Guest and Harry Shearer, like *This Is Spinal Tap* and *Best In Show*, McKean was best known as a comedic actor prior to getting cast on *Saul*.

‡ Patrick Fabian had spent more than twenty years prior to *Saul* hustling from one guest-starring or recurring role to the next—he played college faculty members on both *Saved by the Bell: The College Years* and *Veronica Mars*—without landing the steady paycheck of a regular, ongoing job. His luck finally hit with this show.

§ *Breaking Bad* established that Saul loves making movie references, and his first scene with Howard features a doozy: Jimmy re-creates Ned Beatty's speech from *Network* about what happens when you meddle with the primal forces of nature.

¶ Like Michael McKean, Rhea Seehorn had mostly worked in comedy prior to this job, though several of her roles were on comedy/drama hybrids, including a multiyear recurring stint on TNT's *Franklin & Bash*, where she also played a lawyer known to come to work with her hair in a ponytail. For more on Seehorn's journey to this series, see page 177.

HHM, but there's also a hint that he's embarrassed to be associated in such a way with the man once called Slippin' Jimmy.

"Wouldn't you rather build your own identity?" Chuck suggests. "Why ride on someone else's coattails?" It would be so easy for the *Saul* creative team to rest on their laurels and coast on all the affection *Breaking Bad* built up over the years. But almost immediately, *Better Call Saul* feels like it's trying to build its own identity, even if we already know several of the players. It's not an adrenaline-fueled wild ride like the *Breaking Bad* pilot (one of the greatest first episodes ever produced for television), nor is it trying to be. Jimmy McGill will eventually partner up with Walter White, but he has his own way of doing business, and so does this show.

SEASON 1, EPISODE 2
WRITTEN BY PETER GOULD
DIRECTED BY MICHELLE MACLAREN

"Mijo"

"Wow, you got a mouth on you." —**Tuco**

The second installment of *Better Call Saul* is really two episodes in one: a long resolution of the Tuco fiasco, followed by Jimmy trying to get his act together to avoid ever being in a situation like that again.

The former suggests a *Breaking Bad* rehash filtered through the personality of the new main character, while the latter suggests something quite different. The episode ends with Jimmy being approached by Tuco's pal Nacho Varga (Michael Mando*), leaving some ambiguity as to which version of the show will be triumphant.

What is clear even at this early stage, though, is how entertaining it is to watch Jimmy try to talk himself out of trouble again and again.

So, yes, the trip to the desert is a vintage Walter White scene, with a Walter White villain—in a nice touch that parallels Saul vs. Jimmy, Tuco is also referred to by a different nickname, the Spanish term of affection *Mijo*—but there is a Jimmy McGill resolution to it. He doesn't have the scientific acumen, the force of will, nor the surprising physical strength of our last Albuqerque leading man, but what he does have, as Tuco notes, is a mouth that is locked, loaded, and ready to spray out a full clip of bullshit at a moment's notice. As he bakes under the New Mexico sun, worrying at various points about his own life and the survival of the skater twins, he's called upon to give the greatest performance of his life to date, relying not only on his gift for gab, but his ability to take any audience member, even one as stupid as Tuco,† where he wants them to go. Same setting, same villain, completely different show. It's a treat.

Jimmy escapes the desert with his skin intact, and with the twins' punishment for disrespecting Tuco's grandma reduced from death to six months of rehab. (Jimmy isn't blowing smoke when he tells them, "I'm the best lawyer

---

* Born in Quebec City into a globe-trotting family that eventually led him to live in five countries across four continents by the time he was in his twenties, Michael Mando had been a working actor in Canadian TV for several years when he caught American notice in the early 2010s, first as Vaas in the video game *Far Cry 3*, then as Tatiana Maslany's drug-dealing ex-boyfriend in the first season of *Orphan Black*, a BBC America original produced in Toronto.

† Tuco's cousins weren't identical twins like these clowns, but with a Salamanca family member present, it's easy to think of the skaters as the pathetic *Saul* comic relief counterparts of Leonel and Marco.

ever.") But you can tell just how badly this experience has spooked him, whether he's puking in the middle of a date or coming to Chuck's house drunk and forgetting to go through all the proper grounding procedures.

It's such a complicated dynamic between the brothers, as is often the case with siblings. Chuck is older, wiser, and more accomplished; he's also mentally ill, and you can tell how much seeing his brother in this state weighs on Jimmy. Jimmy is younger, more reckless, and prone to trouble, but he's the caretaker now, trying to get Chuck to acknowledge that the space blanket isn't actually doing anything for him. We see that both brothers are ultimately lying to one another, and to themselves. Chuck takes off the space blanket, but only until Jimmy is out of the house, while Jimmy won't tell Chuck about the ordeal he endured that day.

Still, the encounter with Tuco, followed by another depressing visit to Chuck, scares, at least temporarily, Jimmy straight, setting up a long montage of Jimmy giving a good-faith effort as a defense lawyer, sparring with Bill Oakley (Peter Diseth) and the other local prosecutors. He never again wants to be in the position of being out in the desert with someone like Tuco, and he doesn't want to let down his brother. As the sequence goes along,* you can see that he has both a knack for this profession and the kind of dogged work ethic Chuck has been telling him about. Peter Gould, director Michelle MacLaren, and the *Saul* editors do a nice job of weaving all these brief interactions into one seamless thing, so eventually Saul's individual arguments on behalf of his sleazeball clients turn into a single long, empty monologue.

That a large chunk of the episode's second half is devoted to this is the kind of set-up a show with this much initial goodwill can get away with. A brand-new series arguably needs more pure story up front to keep the audience engaged. *Better Call Saul*, though, was clearly made with the assumption that a large chunk of its audience would know and love *Breaking Bad*, so the creative team could afford to do basic foundation-laying like this. It's important for us to see our protagonist trying to stay on the straight and narrow before he goes back to Slippin' Jimmy again—perhaps due to his new entanglement with Nacho.

Tuco is our way back into the world of drugs in Albuquerque, but he's not a viable long-term character on this show. He's much too volatile, on top of it feeling like too much of a Walter White crutch this early. Nacho seems much smarter and more cautious, and because he has no history with Walt and Jesse, this show can do anything it wants with him. And the first thing he's doing is

---

* This week, in Jimmy Loves Movies: he uses Roy Scheider's "It's showtime!" mantra from *All That Jazz* to keep psyching himself up in a courthouse bathroom.

providing links to an actual ongoing storyline, since he wants to rob Jimmy's would-be client Craig Kettleman.

"I'm a lawyer, not a criminal," Jimmy insists. It's a wink at one of the most memorable lines from the *Breaking Bad* episode that introduced Saul Goodman, where Jesse told Walt, "When the going gets tough, you don't want a criminal lawyer. You want a *criminal* lawyer." *Better Call Saul* aims to get us to that version of Jimmy McGill, even if he's trying so hard throughout "Mijo" to not be that man.

SEASON 1, EPISODE 3
WRITTEN BY THOMAS SCHNAUZ
DIRECTED BY TERRY MCDONOUGH

"Nacho"

"Nobody wants to leave home." —**Mike**

"Nacho" opens with a flashback set a decade before the events of this first season, as we see how the McGill brothers* reunited after a five-year estrangement, and how Chuck gave Jimmy one last chance to get on the straight and narrow path, rather than go to prison for performing a "Chicago sunroof."†

But the more significant historical development in "Nacho"—for the Heisenberg-verse at large, at least—is that it shows us the original team-up between future collaborators-in-crime Jimmy McGill and Mike Ehrmantraut.

In a manner perfectly befitting the most deliberate and cautious character in the entire franchise, *Saul* slow played this over the first trio of episodes. Mike and Jimmy interact in "Uno" and "Mijo" but entirely in the context of Mike's job in the parking lot. This led to funny moments, particularly Jimmy's "Mijo" rant comparing Mike to a troll under a bridge, but it left Mike feeling even further away from the guy we met on *Breaking Bad* than Jimmy is from being Saul Goodman.

Jimmy and Mike again tangle over Jimmy's lack of parking stickers, and eventually Mike punches out Jimmy to uphold the sanctity of the sticker system. But the mess with Nacho Varga—arrested for allegedly kidnapping the Kettlemans—finally brings Mike out of the toll booth and into the middle of the action. It's a plot that plays off of his history as a cop from Philadelphia, and even more importantly plays off of his history as man with a strict code. He won't let Jimmy skate by without the necessary number of stickers nor will he lie in a police report to help the Albuquerque detectives force Jimmy to flip on Nacho.

Why doesn't he help out some fellow badges? Well, Mike doesn't lie unless he needs to for the job at hand, and his only job at the moment is to count stickers

---

* This season was made six years after Saul was introduced on *Breaking Bad*, yet it's set six years earlier than that first appearance. Even in that 2002 timeline, the show is asking its audience to accept that Odenkirk is playing more than a decade younger than he actually is—and looks. The wigs and makeup that he and McKean wear in the nineties flashbacks, meanwhile, demand a level of buy-in akin to Superman being unrecognizable whenever he puts on eyeglasses. At some point, you just have to go with it.

† The term—used to describe someone defecating through the roof of a car—was coined in the *Saul* writers' room.

and collect parking fees. And just as importantly, Mike doesn't suffer fools gladly, and the detectives' insistence that Nacho harmed the Kettlemans makes them fools in the eyes of Mike, who can see just as well as Jimmy can that the Kettlemans kidnapped themselves. And as a small reward for Jimmy getting something right—or perhaps as the smallest of apologies for putting him on the ground—Mike gives Jimmy the clue he needs in order to find Craig, Betsy, and the kids camped out in the woods on the outskirts of their property.[*]

As partnerships go, this is an extremely minor one. But it creates a genuine bond between the cast's two *Breaking Bad* holdovers and plays so well off of the chemistry Bob Odenkirk and Jonathan Banks built up on the other show. And Mike's comment about not wanting to leave home creates another connection. Neither of them is from Albuquerque and they are only there because of mistakes made in their pasts—an escalating series of petty crimes by Jimmy, and Mike for reasons he's not ready to talk about yet. (On *Breaking Bad*, Hank described Mike's exit from the Philly PD as "dramatic.") They are extreme opposites in temperament and professional style, yet there is a reason they'll still be working together, in one form or another, so many years after this particular encounter.

The rest of "Nacho" is also the closest *Better Call Saul* feels to an episode of television. Among the marvels of *Breaking Bad* was how effectively it built its larger story on a foundation of memorable and distinct individual chapters. The first two hours of *Saul* feel largely like noodling. It's hugely entertaining noodling, thanks to the sheer skill level of all the people in front of and behind the camera, but there is a palpable sense of how difficult the writers were finding it just to define exactly what this show is. With "Nacho," there is a clearer structure, a more obvious done-in-one story—Jimmy has to find the Kettlemans in order to secure the release and forgiveness of the vengeful Nacho—and a broader use of the ensemble.

In particular, the episode finally begins establishing Kim Wexler as a significant part of Jimmy's life. Rhea Seehorn was limited to glorified walk-on duty in the first two installments. Here, she gets a lot more to play with, as the nature of Jimmy and Kim's relationship—business and otherwise—starts to come into focus. It seems they may be more than just friends, given the references to Jimmy doing the "sex robot voice" for her in the past, but it also doesn't seem to have been anything serious. She likes him, he likes her, they are on a similar wavelength when it comes to the work, and she is also smart enough to see through Jimmy's various hustles. She knows almost immediately that

---

[*]   Jimmy Loves Movies: he enters the Kettlemans' tent quoting Jack Nicholson's famous "Here's Johnny!" line from *The Shining*.

there is more to his involvement with the Kettlemans and Nacho than he is letting on and tries pushing him to fess up. In the moment, he avoids having to do this by following Mike's advice, but it's clear that he respects her enough to at least consider the idea of spilling the beans. Odenkirk had years on the other show to build up a great on-screen rapport with Banks, but he and Seehorn have a clear connection even at this very early stage.

Though Jimmy insists at one point that he's no hero, it seems that his actions in these last two episodes belie his words. He could easily have let Tuco murder the skater twins, but he instead stuck his neck out after getting them into that mess. Similarly, he could have sat back and let Nacho rob the Kettlemans—or worse—but instead calls to warn these people who don't even want to hire him. And when the police in turn give him an opportunity to flip on Nacho and rid himself of another problem, Jimmy makes his own life more complicated by acting like a lawyer who believes in confidentiality and being a zealous advocate for his client. Multiple times so far, we've seen him do good things not because he benefits from them, but simply because it seems like he should. Given how pear-shaped things go each time, and given what we know of Jimmy's future, it's not hard to look at this episode as one of the first of many object lessons that will teach him to stop worrying about anyone's interests but his own—whether he's operating solo or with the unflappable assistance of Mike Ehrmantraut.

SEASON 1, EPISODE 4
WRITTEN BY GENNIFER HUTCHISON
DIRECTED BY COLIN BUCKSEY

"Hero"

"You're the kind of lawyer guilty people hire." —**Betsy Kettleman**

Midway through "Hero," Kim confronts Jimmy about the odd PR campaign he's waging—investing the money from the Kettlemans in a bespoke, Howard Hamlin–inspired wardrobe and buying a billboard designed to make it look like Jimmy is part of HHM.

"I'm building a brand," Jimmy insists. "You're ripping off a brand," his old friend replies.

Never let the *Better Call Saul* writers be accused of a lack of self-awareness. They knew going into the series that it would be inevitably compared to *Breaking Bad*, and they clearly knew at this stage of things that leaning too far into those comparisons would do more harm than good. So, yes, Jimmy wound up on the wrong end of Tuco Salamanca's gun for a hot minute, but for the most part, *Saul* is doing everything it can to distinguish both itself and its main character from what everyone thinks of when they think of that other show.

This attempt to zag when everyone expects a zig feels particularly obvious in "Hero." It's an episode bookended by two Jimmy McGill confidence schemes—one in his younger days back in Cicero, the other involving the billboard—both of them arguably more complicated than they need to be, both of them still working through the sheer tenacity, and lack of shame, of the man they once called Slippin' Jimmy.

We open with a nineties flashback to Jimmy running a short con with his friend Marco (Mel Rodriguez) that involves a fake designer watch, a wallet full of cash, and an unsuspecting sap (Kevin Weisman) who has just spent the evening being plied with liquor and charm by James Morgan McGill. The scam seems to offer more risk than reward—what happens if the mark opts to take the cash in Marco's wallet, leaving the Fugazi watch for Jimmy to deal with?—yet Jimmy is able to subtly steer the guy in the right direction to make it work.*

The 2002 business with the suits, the billboard, and Jimmy's temporary perm—he claims he wants to resemble Tony Curtis in *Spartacus*'s bath scene,

---

* Peter Gould: "Our theory was that Jimmy was an absolute master at choosing his mark. In our minds, he spent hours drinking at different bars until he found a mark he was absolutely sure would get greedy at the right moment."

but it clearly furthers the illusion of him being Howard—takes longer to reveal itself. First, there are the Kettlemans to deal with. Betsy still rightly does not trust Jimmy to represent her husband and tries to buy his silence with a small cut of Craig's ill-gotten gains. Jimmy is hurt by Betsy's characterization of him, but the path he takes with the money seems to live down to her expectations.

At first, the wardrobe, the haircut, and the billboard appear to be little more than an overly elaborate way to troll Howard, whom Jimmy blames for his and Chuck's precarious current circumstances. But, in time, the shape of the scheme becomes clear. Jimmy needs Howard to take legal action to have the billboard taken down, which will give Jimmy the opportunity—and, he hopes, the platform from local news—to pretend to be a hero when a worker falls off the scaffold and Jimmy climbs up to rescue him. When the newspapers and TV stations won't bite on the David vs Goliath story, Jimmy improvises and hires a couple of local film students to film him in action. And the stunt goes off without a hitch, which is a significant departure from nearly every Walter White plan, just as director Colin Bucksey and director of photography Arthur Albert shoot the sequence in a way that looks like nothing from the parent show, with Jimmy and the workman appearing so very tiny and fragile way up above the ground.

It's to Howard's credit that he immediately sees through what Jimmy is doing. (And, for that matter, it's to the show's credit that he's portrayed as smart, rather than the cartoonish failson Jimmy tries to paint him as.) The more interesting reaction, though, comes from Kim, who lets out a small but unmistakable smile while Howard's back is turned. Whatever reservations she has about Jimmy's antics, she also can't help but enjoy them.

In the cold open, we learn that Jimmy was using Saul Goodman—as in "S'all good, man"—as an alias long before it became his professional name as the most famous criminal defense lawyer in Albuquerque. The billboard plan is awfully benign compared to the crimes Jimmy will commit when he goes by Saul full time. But Jimmy has people who are wise to him already—including Chuck, who braves the crippling sunlight and nearby power lines in order to steal a neighbor's copy of the *Albuquerque Journal* after Jimmy hides Chuck's to conceal news of the stunt from his certain-to-disapprove brother. We know how convinced Chuck is that his condition is real, and that the world outside his house is a threat to him, yet he's so innately suspicious of Jimmy that he would risk exposure just to find out what his troublesome sibling is up to now.

And perhaps this is the biggest change from *Breaking Bad* so far. Walter White was able to build his drug empire in part because no one suspected—for a very long time—that a beta male high school science teacher could have a secret life as a master meth cooker. Jimmy McGill, though, is operating in a world where his brother, his best friend, and his former boss can all see right through him. We know where his journey will end—or, at least, how he becomes Gene from Cinnabon—but his transformation from Jimmy to Saul has to take place more in plain sight than when his future client went from Walt to Heisenberg.

And odds are, Walt would have no more patience for Chuck's use of the space blanket than Jimmy does.

SEASON 1, EPISODE 5
WRITTEN BY BRADLEY PAUL
DIRECTED BY NICOLE KASSELL

"Alpine Shepherd Boy"

"I'm on the up and up. I will be good." —**Jimmy**

Jimmy spends much of "Alpine Shepherd Boy"* trying to find a professional niche, and the episode itself feels like the *Better Call Saul* creative team is still figuring out what exactly the series is, beyond a showcase for Bob Odenkirk and a chance to bring so much of the *Breaking Bad* team together again.

Like the second episode, this hour is made up of a bunch of interesting individual pieces that don't entirely feel like part of the same whole. After a prologue detailing the immediate, traumatic aftermath of Chuck's sprint to steal his neighbor's newspaper, we spend a long time on Jimmy trying to cash in on the notoriety that came with his billboard "heroics," then get an interlude with Jimmy and Kim dealing with Chuck's hospitalization, then a bit more of Jimmy scrambling for business (inspired by Kim's advice and the only success he had earlier in the hour), followed by Jimmy tagging in Mike to close out the episode with a glimpse of his estrangement from both his family and his former Philly co-workers.

Piece by piece, there's a lot to like here. Each of Jimmy's house calls plays out in the leisurely fashion this creative team does so well. You know, for instance, that there's no way he's actually going to make a small fortune pursuing some wealthy lunatic's desire to secede from America, but that scene takes its time getting to the payoff with the fake money, which only makes the whole thing funnier. The sex toilet is a marvelous dirty joke that keeps going and going, and in a way where you can understand why the dad thinks all the language is appropriate for his son to hear. And the visit to elderly Geraldine Strauss (Carol Herman), whose figurines give the episode its title, is all about Jimmy watching the very slow march of time.

Chuck winds up in the hospital, meanwhile, after being tasered by cops who assume the unusual contents of his home mean that he's cooking meth.† Jimmy and Kim find him there, and Jimmy rushes to turn off every light and

---

*   This episode breaks with the title rubric used for the rest of the season, where every other episode name is a two-syllable word or phrase ending in an "O" sound. Originally, it was supposed to be called "Jell-O," but the production couldn't get legal permission to use the name, which is trademarked by Kraft.

†   If they only knew with whom Chuck's brother will be working in a few years ...

piece of equipment in the room to stop his brother's physical torment. But Dr. Cruz,* while empathetic and willing to hear out the brothers McGill, figures out that the condition is psychosomatic, surreptitiously turning on a monitor without an oblivious Chuck suffering any effects. This allergy to electricity feels real to Chuck, but it's not, and this confirmation brings Jimmy—and, in some ways, the show—to a significant fork in the road. Jimmy could heed Cruz's advice, have Chuck temporarily committed, and let his brother get the help he actually needs, rather than continuing to enable a crippling mental health problem. Even beyond the good it would do for Chuck, it would relieve Jimmy of the burden of caring for him, and of the sense that Chuck is constantly judging him. But doing so would make Jimmy feel like he's failed the brother whose respect still matters so much to him. So he has to believe in the condition just as much as Chuck does, and he has to take his brother home, so they can once again perform the familiar dance where Jimmy promises to be good, and Chuck pretends to believe him this time.

As Jimmy once again craves Chuck's approval, he borrows Kim's suggestion that he go into elder law. And if the senior McGill sibling isn't exactly impressed by it, he seems relieved. It's a specialty that seemingly has much less room for Slippin' Jimmy–style shenanigans, and it's a form of law where the rewards are more emotional than financial—a noble calling for a guy Chuck has a hard time thinking about as noble, no matter how many sacrifices Jimmy has made for him in recent years. And Chuck's response, coupled with Kim's argument and a lack of better options, inspires Jimmy to schmooze his way through a local retirement facility, clad in a full Matlock suit.[†] The same traits that made Jimmy a great con man also make him the perfect guy to charm a room filled with senior citizens—Slippin' Jimmy using his powers for good instead of petty theft.[‡]

This is followed by both a literal handoff, where Jimmy gives Mike one of his business cards, and a metaphorical one, where Mike takes over as protagonist for the episode's final minutes. It's a largely wordless sequence, letting Jonathan Banks's eyes convey what a sad and lonely life in exile Mike has made for himself, and how he is as much of a disappointment to his daughter-in-law

---

* Played with obvious warmth by actor/director Clea DuVall.

† Though he always seemed like a tacky dresser as Saul Goodman, this show is suggesting that he has a very clear sense of how he wants to style himself, even if that sense often involves him copying someone else. Saul's suits and loud shirts must be just as curated as the Howard Hamlin lookalike suit was in "Hero."

‡ The soundtrack, though, provides a reminder that Jimmy is not always to be trusted, as his entrance is accompanied by "Harry Lime's Theme" from *The Third Man*—Lime being a surprisingly villainous character played by Orson Welles.

Stacey* (glimpsed only briefly here) as Jimmy is to Chuck. But before we can really get anywhere with this idea, some of Mike's old police colleagues from Philly turn up for a cliffhanger that suggests Mike might need to use Jimmy's card sooner rather than later.

So, yes, this is more of a grab bag of ideas than it is a cohesive hour in the way that, say, "Nacho" was. But it's hard not to think about what Kim tells Jimmy in the midst of their pedicure date at the nail salon: "Even your lousy days are more interesting than my good ones." At this point, even disjointed *Better Call Saul* episodes are more entertaining than polished ones from most other dramas.

---

* Irish actress Kerry Condon had been working in American TV and film for years prior to *Saul*, including stints on a pair of HBO dramas, *Rome* and *Luck*. A few months after this episode aired, she began providing the voice of F.R.I.D.A.Y., Iron Man's operating system in the later Avengers films, and would go on to an Oscar nomination for her work in *The Banshees of Inisherin*.

SEASON 1, EPISODE 6
WRITTEN BY GORDON SMITH
DIRECTED BY ADAM BERNSTEIN

"Five-O"

"I broke my boy!" —**Mike**

Toward the end of "Alpine Shepherd Boy," Mike tagged in for Jimmy as the show's central character of the moment, and "Five-O" powerfully reflects that shift. With Mike as the focus, and Jimmy popping up only briefly to help Mike pull the spilled-coffee play, the lightness and whimsy of the earlier episodes are replaced by a dark intensity, illustrating the differences between Mike and Jimmy as individuals, and of their circumstances at the moment.

Both are in Albuquerque because they let down family members in the past, but on wildly different levels. Jimmy never did anything to his brother that can't be undone, even if "Alpine Shepherd Boy" suggested that Chuck's episodes can be triggered by Jimmy's shenanigans. Jimmy's getting a fresh start and gets to apply the skills of his old trade to his new one, (mostly) staying on the right side of the legal line even while spewing his trademark line of BS. Mike, on the other hand, lost a son, and in a way that crushes him, because before Matty lost his life, he lost his innocence and his faith in his old man. Jimmy's running from minor sins, where Mike has three bodies on his conscience: the son he couldn't save, and the two dirty cops he executed as revenge.

Any hour focusing on this man at this time would have to be significantly heavier than what *Saul* has given us so far, and fortunately "Five-O" has Jonathan Banks to shoulder that burden. He can be dryly hilarious, but this episode doesn't need his comedy skills. It needs the gravity and overpowering sadness that he brought to the role of Mike Ehrmantraut on *Breaking Bad*. And that in some ways links this episode to the parent show even more than the earlier installment where Tuco dragged Jimmy out into the desert.

Mike's cop days came up in conversation from time to time on *Breaking Bad*, most famously in the "no half-measures" speech he gave Walt, inspired by Mike's failure to prevent a terrible act of violence. Here, he is struggling with the guilt over another such incident, and one much closer to home. It's not just that a pair of crooked cops killed Matty because they didn't trust that he'd stay silent about their crimes. It's that Mike revealed himself to his noble son as a dirty cop, and encouraged Matty to take a payoff from Fensky and Hoffman as a way to stay alive—and it didn't even work. As he puts it to Stacey, "I was the only one that could get him to debase himself like that. And it was for nothing. I made him lesser. I made him like me. And the bastards killed him, anyway."

This entire concluding monologue is devastating not only for its content, but for how Banks conveys Mike's self-loathing without resorting to histrionics. He barely even raises his voice, though the tone of it is higher-pitched and far more vulnerable than we're used to hearing from him. Even in the depths of his pain, Mike Ehrmantraut is a man striving to keep himself, his emotions, and the world around him under control. He failed his son, but he also—in the sort of lo-fi scheming that Mike used so often on the other show—got revenge on Fensky and Hoffman, with minimal physical damage to himself.* And in expressing his crimes—both the legal ones and the paternal ones—to Stacey, he has begun to carve a path for a relationship with Matty's daughter Kaylee,† who is the primary reason for nearly everything he will later do with Gus Fring and Walter White.

It's a much simpler episode, plot-wise, than anything we've gotten previously in the more Jimmy-centric hours. But when you have an actor as powerful as Banks, and when you have a story that says so much about the origins of an iconic character, you don't need anything fancy. Mike prefers to use simple, straightforward methods to devastating effect. So does this first *Better Call Saul* spotlight on him.

---

*   The flashback section of the episode introduces Joe DeRosa as Dr. Caldera, an Albuquerque veterinarian with a sideline in treating human patients who can't risk going to a legitimate doctor, and who seems to have larger connections to the local underworld. Seems a very useful sort of person for a future master criminal to know, doesn't he?

†   Though this season is set six years before the beginning of the *Breaking Bad* story, the three actresses who play Kaylee at various points on *Saul* all look roughly the same age that the character did at the end of the other show. Thomas Schnauz says that there was a little debate about finding a much younger actress, but everyone agreed it made sense to ignore the timeline in this instance, because "the producers wanted to work with older kids to make it easier on production, and to have a better chance of finding kids who could act and interact with Banks."

Better Call Saul Creators on the "Purposely Shitty" Opening Title Sequence

[This article originally appeared on HitFix.com on March 16, 2015]

It's not often that you hear TV producers proudly describe an aspect of their show as looking terrible—and using much less polite language than that—but then it's not often you have TV producers both as talented and idiosyncratic as *Better Call Saul* creators Vince Gilligan and Peter Gould.

The aspect in question is the show's main title sequence, featuring various images from Jimmy McGill's future life as Saul Goodman, all of it presented with the same terrible image quality of early VHS or public access television. I spoke first with Gilligan and Gould—who, I should say, had trouble controlling the laughter at times when using a certain profane adjective to describe the picture quality of those credits—and then with *Saul* assistant editor Curtis Thurber, who put together the different title sequences, about what they wanted and what was necessary to put them together.

How did you come up with the concept for this title sequence?

PETER GOULD: I think we were talking about what kinds of credits were around in other shows. I have to attribute this mainly to Vince and Curtis. One day, while we were cutting an episode, I was sitting there, and you guys started playing with the layers and wondering what shots we had. It started off as a little bit of goofing around, almost. But then pretty soon, the test was the Statue of Liberty, wasn't it, Vince?

VINCE GILLIGAN: You're right. The thought was for that to be it: just have *Breaking Bad* footage of the inflatable Statue of Liberty every week. I think the ultimate impetus behind the way this title sequence looks—specifically, how shitty this title sequence looks—is we look around at other TV shows and see what everyone else is doing. And right now, there's a lot of wonderful title sequences on a lot of excellent TV shows. And they look very well-produced and beautiful and high-class. There's obviously a lot of TLC going into a lot of credit sequences on big hit shows these days. But because that is such a look now for TV, we figured, what could we do different? These titles look so wonderful on all those shows, I know what we can do for sure is make ours look shitty. [*laughs*] I want to stress that our titles are purposely shitty, not unintentionally shitty. It takes a lot of work to be intentionally shitty, and that work is done by the very talented Curtis Thurber, who is really more responsible for them than anybody else. I think the idea is that Saul Goodman is a man who hires the lowest bidder when it comes to making television commercials and such. Even though our show isn't centering on Saul Goodman as of yet, we're riffing off of the later Saul of the *Breaking Bad* years, and the very lowball public-access look of his advertising. We also figured these titles are cheap enough to generate, and therefore, why not have a different set of titles every week? Have a different image every week for all ten episodes.

PG: Actually getting it shitty enough was a challenge. A lot of the process was, Curtis would do something, and then Vince and sometimes I would say, "What if we made it even shittier? What if we made it look like the keying on the titles wavered? How can we make this look worse?" We were both thinking of eighties public access, and how could we make the color combination even more of an eyesore? It was a little analogous to picking out Saul Goodman's suits on *Breaking Bad*, which was one of the most fun things on that show. The titles here really go along with that. It's fun for us to have a little stab at the beginning of each episode of who this guy is going to be. I think, ultimately, underneath it all, that's this guy's taste, and it was fun to have that poke out for twenty-six seconds at the beginning of each episode.

Is there a pattern to how you're assigning them to different episodes? Are you trying to suggest some kind of link with, say, the drawer of cell phones and the episode that follows it? Or is it entirely random and no one should be looking for connections?

VINCE GILLIGAN: There's no real deeper hidden meaning or puzzle to be solved from the images, but there was some thought given to which images seemed the most fitting for which episode.

PETER GOULD: I think that's true for most of them, but I think, certainly, for the last two episodes, there's a certain tone that does go with the episode. I don't really want to give anything away, but there's a certain direction that the show takes in the last couple of episodes, and those two, especially, to me, echo where we're going. There were actually times when we thought not to. We have one that's coming up eventually, that's actually in the desert, and we decided not to use that one in episode two, when we're in the desert, because we wanted to make clear to the audience that this was something separate from the text of the show.

VG: That desert one was a fun one. It was actually shot in our producer Melissa Bernstein's backyard in Los Angeles. Our excellent assistants, Jenn Carroll and Joey Liew, bought a bunch of sand for mixing with concrete at the Home Depot, and Melissa was nice enough to let us spread it out in her backyard. The interesting thing about this imagery is that it can be shot on a cell phone, and the resolution is so good that what we found is we have to get way back, or way up on a ladder for this purposely-shot footage, and then Curtis would zoom in on it, and then magnify it two thousand percent until it looked all grainy and blocky and crappy like eighties video. It's very hard to make modern high-definition video look that crappy. You have to hammer way in on it.

[*We're in the middle of saying our goodbyes when Gilligan pulls a Lt. Columbo and realizes he has just one more thing he wanted to talk about.*]

VG: To talk about the titles, we should also talk about the music. The original idea was to not have music at all, or just have a busy signal.

PG: That's the version that went out to critics. We had a couple of critics say, "I liked that." And I liked it, too—how spare and weird it was. But having said that, as we played with different kinds of music, I think we felt that was a better choice.

VG: [Music supervisor] Thomas Golubi, as usual, hit it out of the park. He found a group in the UK called Little Barrie, and this guy is a hellaciously great guitarist. And he came up with a bunch of riffs. There was one song of his that we really liked and pursued, but for certain legal reasons and Sony rules and regulations, we couldn't use a preexisting song that Sony didn't own. So the band was very accommodating and came up with some licks and some riffs, and then sent them through Thomas to us. One in particular really stuck with us, and that became the theme music. It cuts off very abruptly, the music, as does the title sequence, and that, too, is on purpose. It is meant to be the world's shittiest music ending, along with the purposeful shittiness of the video.

[*At this point, Gilligan and Gould head back to work, and Curtis Thurber comes on the line to explain more about the process of making the titles.*]

What did Vince and Peter say they were looking for when you began work on the idea?

CURTIS THURBER: They wanted to do something that was different from what anyone else in TV was doing. They threw it out to the whole editorial team to be, "What can we come up with here that would mimic what Saul Goodman would have within his means to create, with very little budget, and very little means, and very little know-how of how a professional commercial would be done?" Obviously, our inspiration was from the original Saul Goodman ads, which were done in the same style of public access. We looked up a lot of You-Tube inspiration from even the nineties and public access, some old comedy stuff, even some stuff from *Mr. Show* had the same stylistic inspiration, so there's a Bob Odenkirk connection there.

But basically, we took that and we ran with it. Earliest drafts of it were understandably a little bit comedic, trying to jam so many different Saul Goodman stylistic elements into it. One of the biggest challenges was to refine it and keep going back to the drawing board and being, "How can we take something that's this short and in this style, but make sure it fits with both the comedic and dramatic side of the story they're trying to tell about Jimmy McGill?"

Technically, what was involved in creating imagery with 2014 video technology that looks like crappy 2000s public-access commercials of the kind Saul might have had?
CURTIS THURBER: We intentionally limited ourselves to tools we had in our editing software. We're editing on Avid Media Composer. We could have gone outside the box and brought in Photoshop and After Effects, all these other elements that graphic designers have, or for that matter, that a main title house would be using. We asked, "What can we create by just limiting ourselves to these rudimentary tools?" A lot of which are designed to work on a temporary basis, and in a normal TV workflow, we might temp with some of this stuff and then turn it over to a post-production house, who would re-create things and make them look a little bit flashy. So, for example, just the look of the letters in the frame, there was so much that went into that. The simple request that it look like bad green screen was difficult to achieve in a digital environment. We couldn't just throw green futz on there. I had to go scouring the internet for green screen, but not good green screen, that wasn't lit very well. So when I brought that into the Avid and tweaked the green screen effect, I could get it to still have noise popping up on the screen.

Vince said the fact that it was relatively cheap allowed you to do a new one for each episode. But how much effort was involved in doing them? After you did a few, did it get easier, or was the process of making it look like this really time-intensive for you?
CURTIS THURBER: That part was kind of fun for me. It was presented as a challenge. They weren't sure it would work. At first, Vince and Peter thought we would play with different images, but weren't sure we could come up with enough iconic Saul images, or things that would work that would cue the audience in that this is something that is central to the Saul Goodman character. What they ended up doing was, they shot a bunch of those on set, some of the new ones, like the phone booth. So I took those, but there weren't enough to fill out the entire season. We had also been pulling—not only myself, but I have to give a shout-out to the rest of the editorial team, Skip MacDonald, Chris McCaleb, and Kelley Dixon, who all helped out immensely and threw in a lot of

contributions and ideas—other images from *Breaking Bad* as well to start playing with. The challenge became, "How many of these can we make work?" Ultimately, we ended up with nine that they liked, and we had to go out and shoot one additional. But they were really happy when we were able to get a different one for each episode. So I think it turned out really well. Once we had the template, I wouldn't say it was easy, each one required a little bit of finessing, and the colors had to be futzed. Some of them, we wanted to go for a slightly more realistic look, and some were more over-the-top stylish, but that was just a matter of tweaking an initial pass for it, and they would come in for five minutes and we would lock down each additional title.

So some of these were using old *Breaking Bad* footage, and some were shot specifically for this. How much effort did it take to get the preexisting footage and the new footage shot with this in mind to match visually?

CURTIS THURBER: The fact that we were taking so much liberty with the colorization of it helped everything blend together and look like a seamless set of main titles. There were a few extra challenges to using some of the *Breaking Bad* footage, because it wasn't intended for this purpose. So in some cases, we did have to be more creative with that.

It's a lot of work to make something look this terrible.

CURTIS THURBER: Exactly. Surprisingly so.

SEASON 1, EPISODE 7
WRITTEN BY GENNIFER HUTCHISON
DIRECTED BY LARYSA KONDRACKI

"Bingo"

"Thing you folks need to know about me: I got nothing to lose." —**Jimmy**

In something resembling con-man parlance, "Bingo" pulls a reverse "Alpine Shepherd Boy," opening with a resolution to Mike's problems with the Philly cops before passing the narrative baton back to Jimmy for the rest of the hour. And for a while afterward, life looks pretty damn sweet for our hero.

He has become a modestly successful elder care attorney, loved by the local senior community. Chuck has bounced back from his hospitalization and is now taking deliberate action to build up his tolerance to electricity and sunlight. (Never mind that the condition is in his head; if Chuck thinks he's getting better, then he's getting better.) And between his growing client base and the "retainer" he still has from the Kettlemans, Jimmy has enough cash to consider renting a swank downtown law office with a palatial view—where, he dreams, he and Kim can work as partners, and hopefully in more than one sense of the term.

This glass and steel marvel is as far as is stylistically possible from the strip mall office Saul Goodman will later use as a solo practitioner. But Saul's clientele wouldn't trust a man who worked in such a gleaming tower, and Saul didn't have a colleague—and potential love interest—to impress with his real estate choices. We understand Jimmy won't end up in this space, but for the majority of "Bingo," it's hard not to wish otherwise.

Because the most shocking thing about *Better Call Saul*, seven episodes in, isn't that the show is entertaining. It's that the man whom we all know is going to become Saul Goodman, played by the same actor, with many of the same tics, periodically sharing scenes with Saul's favorite fixer, is so likable, so complex, that how could anyone be rooting for him to move to the strip mall this soon?

"Bingo" is an episode that leans heavily on Jimmy's innate charm and surprising reservoir of decency, and just as heavily on the audience's awareness of the character's future. It's fun to see him on top of the world, schmoozing with the seniors, enjoying the chance to show off the literal high life of this office to Kim, finding his brother taking baby steps toward recovery, and more. It has to feel this good to see him doing so well—we have to root for him as much as we have, surprisingly, so far—for it to then hurt when it all falls apart by the end of the episode, and Jimmy is left behind the door of that wonderful office, screaming with impotent rage.

And of course it all has to fall apart, not only because we know where the story is going, but because we know where it's already been. The only reason Jimmy could rent the billboard that eventually led to his new business model, and the only reason he could even think about putting down a deposit on a workspace this ritzy, is because he took that bribe from the Kettlemans. Everything after is, to borrow a phrase Chuck surely could recite in his sleep, fruits of the poisonous tree. And the poison quickly spreads throughout this episode, until Jimmy has to give up the cash, the chance to impress Kim, and many of his other current dreams.

The unrelentingly awful, delusional Betsy Kettleman* refuses to accept the idea that her Craig should have to serve even a minute of prison time—and, worse, that they should have to give back the money they stole—leading her to walk out on HHM and the sweet deal Kim had arranged for Craig with the DA. Although Kim did her job perfectly, she still gets banished to the HHM "cornfield" as a result. It is a nickname uttered with such indignation by Jimmy that you know he has some firsthand knowledge of the place, and suddenly all he wants to do is save Kim, no matter the financial or emotional cost. With an assist from Mike—who gets to pull off his first full-fledged heist on this series, with the use of an RC truck and a chemical spray that shows up under UV lighting—Jimmy gets back all the money the Kettlemans took, throws his share into the pile, and has Mike deliver it all to the prosecutor, in turn steering the enraged Betsy back to Kim and HHM. Not only does he lose the office deposit, but he mends fences between Kim and Howard in the process, giving her even less of a reason to jump ship to work with him.

When Mike is bagging up all the money, he wonders what Jimmy is doing. "The right thing," Jimmy says, as surprised to hear himself saying it as Mike is to hear it. The very idea of doing the right thing would seem so alien to Saul Goodman as to have arrived in a flying saucer. And as Jimmy melts down inside the office he'll never occupy, it's easy to see how Saul got that way. Doing the right thing hurts, a lot of the time. And what little we knew of Saul Goodman suggested that he was a man who had long ago decided to never let anything hurt or bother him again. The view from the strip mall isn't nearly as fancy, but there's also not nearly as far to fall when something goes wrong, is there?

---

* Throw some flowers in the direction of both Julie Ann Emery and Jeremy Shamos, who have made a hilarious alpha/beta comedy team throughout this season.

SEASON 1, EPISODE 8
WRITTEN BY GORDON SMITH
DIRECTED BY COLIN BUCKSEY

"RICO"

"It's a bit hard to read. Next time, I'd use double-ply." —**Rich Schweikart**

In both the past and the present of "RICO," Jimmy accomplishes something in the legal field that should be impossible for a man of his background and means. In flashback, we see that he managed to get a law degree and pass the bar, without letting Chuck or any of the HHM bosses know about it ahead of time. And in 2002, he uncovers evidence of a widespread scheme of overcharging by the Sandpiper Crossing company against the elderly residents of its retirement communities. This is impressive work, in both timelines, but Jimmy has to take some creative steps to make them happen. To avoid missing his day job in the HHM mailroom, Jimmy takes correspondence school courses from the University of American Samoa.* And when the Sandpiper employees begin shredding documents to stop Jimmy's case before it starts, he has to scribble a demand letter on the only thing he has handy—rolls of toilet paper—and then go hunting through Sandpiper's garbage to find this evidence.

And in both cases, the substance of what Jimmy has done doesn't matter to the members of the legal establishment. All that counts is who he is, and the unconventional way he goes about things. Howard won't offer him a position as an associate. And Sandpiper lawyer Rich Schweikart can barely prevent himself from laughing as he talks on the phone with Jimmy—and he doesn't even know that his opposing counsel is currently hiding in a dumpster, covered in filth. No matter how hard Jimmy works, no matter how resourceful he proves himself to be, it seems that the legal establishment will keep looking down on him like he's someone who belongs with the trash.

It's because of that uphill battle that *Saul* can introduce an idea like the Sandpiper class action suit, without the usual problem with the prequel business. Because we know how and where Jimmy is going to end up, there are certain things that Gilligan, Gould, and company simply cannot do. Jimmy can't get superpowers. He can't run for the U.S. Senate and win. He can't abandon the law forever and move to a developing nation to do relief work. But spearheading a lawsuit that could be worth $20 million, and probably a lot more? The specific

---

*   On *Breaking Bad*, even Saul seems to treat it as a joke that he got his law degree this way. But Jimmy is genuinely proud of what he's done, and makes sure to remind Chuck that the school is fully accredited.

context the show has established for its main character somehow allows that. Jimmy doesn't necessarily have to turn into Saul Goodman for the financial rewards. A rich Jimmy McGill is still an outsider to the Albuquerque legal establishment, still the guy who worked in the HHM mailroom, still the guy who got a law degree through correspondence classes, still the guy whose professional demeanor and methods will always come across to his would-be peers as classless and inappropriate. Saul Goodman is a trash person, but much of the world already thought of Jimmy McGill that way, right?

And by this point in Season 1, the predetermined quality of Jimmy's story and Mike's has turned out to be a feature, not a bug. We know where they will both be six years into their futures. The "what" isn't the important part of *Better Call Saul*. The "why" is.

In Mike's case, the "why" is what we've always known it to be: Kaylee. His determination to provide for her, no matter what, caused him so much trouble on *Breaking Bad*. But in telling us how Kaylee's father died, and showing how much Mike blames himself for that death, it gives so much more weight to his need to give the girl a better life. He's not just your run-of-the-mill grandfather trying to give his sweet granddaughter a college fund; he's a killer who feels responsible for the girl losing the father, who otherwise would have been caring and providing for her. That's powerful stuff, and it casts even more darkness over his decision to revisit Dr. Caldera in search of criminal work. The vet's question about what Mike will and won't do—and Mike's answer— suggests a pretty rich vein to mine about Mike's slow transformation from cop (albeit one who executed two dirty cops who had murdered his son) to the more cold-blooded man we would know on *Breaking Bad*.

Jimmy, though, is more complicated and surprising. The more we've seen of his past and present this season, the more it becomes clear that he really did have a come-to-Jesus moment when Chuck got him out of his last bit of trouble in Cicero. He's had his periodic Slippin' Jimmy moments, but he wants to be a good guy, and wants to play by the rules. Look at him in the flashback that opens the episode: he's the low man on the totem pole at HHM, but he doesn't seem bitter, he is clearly well liked by those around him, and he's gone to all this trouble to become a lawyer because he wants his brother finally to be proud of him.

It's obvious by now that this is not a long con Jimmy is running, but a sincere effort to do right and impress Chuck. But throughout this season, we've seen that the world has no interest in a good-guy version of Jimmy McGill. So far, it's cost him money and a fancy office (and potential partner in Kim). It's put his life at risk from Nacho. It's gotten him overlooked by the Rick Schweikarts of the legal community. And it's gotten him covered in unspeakable waste.* If the world doesn't want him to be good, then eventually he'll have no choice but to break bad, won't he?

In the meantime, though, his good work has had a major impact on Chuck, who eventually gets so caught up in acting like a lawyer again that he briefly forgets about his bogus symptoms altogether, only having the Wile E. Coyote realization moment when Jimmy points out that he's outside (and using his car remote) without any issue at all.

It's yet another quasi-miracle performed by Jimmy in an episode full of them. But we know that miracles can only take him so far. No matter what he tries, or how hard he works, Jimmy is who he is, and his future is his future.

---

* Perhaps the best part of the dumpster sequence is its punch line: Jimmy finally climbs out, having come up empty on his search, and only then discovers that all the shredding is in the far more hygienic recycling bins located just past the dumpster.

"Pimento"

"You're not a real lawyer!" —**Chuck**

Among the many amazing aspects of the final scene of "Pimento"—as powerful in its own way as Mike's breakdown at the end of "Five-O"—is that it hits like a ton of bricks even though you can see most of it coming long before we get there. The episode doesn't really try to hide Chuck's role in screwing over Jimmy, first letting us see him making a clandestine call on Jimmy's cell phone,* then making clear that something is up with Howard through his scene with Kim, and then her scene with Jimmy. And over the course of the season, it's become harder and harder to reconcile the idea of Chuck as an arrogant true believer in the power of the law, with Chuck being okay with the idea of his disreputable brother joining that hallowed profession.†

But even though it's not a total surprise, the venom of Chuck's explanation is still shocking, and Jimmy's reaction is no less painful.

And here's the thing: both brothers are right in a way, even if the end result is very wrong. We understand why Chuck is afraid of Slippin' Jimmy with a law degree, because we've seen on the other show *exactly* what can happen when Jimmy gives in to that hustler side of himself within the legal arena. But at the same time, *Better Call Saul* Season 1 has offered ample evidence that at this stage of his life, Jimmy McGill is sincere in his desire to do things the right way, both to impress his brother and because he has somehow developed a moral compass. But we can add his own brother to the list of people in this world who have no interest in a good version of Jimmy McGill. The irony is, Chuck's reaction can only make Jimmy more dangerous, not less. Had Chuck not placed that call to Howard, Jimmy might have spent a long, fruitful, and honest career as a civil attorney. But we know that's not going to happen, in part because the only family Jimmy has left thinks so little of him. If even Jimmy's brother—whom he has protected and cared for throughout his prolonged illness, and even come up with a way for Chuck to go back out into the world

---

* As I believe the great Russian playwright Anton Chekhov once said, "If you have your hero placing his cell phone, wallet, and keys in someone else's mailbox in the first act of your season, then someone has to take advantage of this by the third act."

† This was something the *Saul* writers needed time to figure out, too. The original idea was exactly what we saw in the first few episodes: Howard as the pompous villain, and Chuck as the wary but ultimately trustworthy ally. But McKean's performance made clear that Chuck would never support Jimmy being a lawyer, and the writing began to subtly reverse the roles of the two HHM partners.

again—can't trust him enough to be good, then who can? And what's the point of trying?

The Mike subplot, meanwhile, offers us a delightful glimpse of Mike Ehrmantraut at his most confident and unflappable. In taking a bodyguard job for "Pryce"—a dweeby pharmaceutical company employee[*] looking to peddle factory-sealed pills to Nacho Varga[†]—Mike gets to calmly disarm an idiot who's toting multiple guns, scare away a giant, collect the entire three-man fee himself, and even impress Nacho with his bottomless reserves of cool. Fun as that is, the most important part of that subplot—and one of the most important scenes of the series so far—comes after Nacho has taken the box of pills and driven away. After explaining why he knew he wouldn't need a gun to deal with Nacho, Mike adds, "The lesson is, if you're gonna be a criminal, do your homework." "Wait, I'm not a bad guy," Pryce objects, leading Mike to clarify, "I didn't say you were a bad guy. I said you were a *criminal*." A baffled Pryce asks, "What's the difference?"

And *that*, boys and girls, seems to be the big question of this series. Mike was once a seemingly good guy who, by taking bribes and kickbacks, was also a criminal. Jimmy's a former criminal trying not to be a bad guy, even though no one seems to believe him. Eventually, both of these men are going to become very serious criminals indeed; but will they be bad guys at the same time?

---

[*] Pryce is played by Mark Proksch, who would soon go on to crack up comedy fans as "energy vampire" Colin Robinson on FX's *What We Do in the Shadows*. Also, while it wasn't intentional on the part of the creative team, it's hard to look at Pryce's nebbishy, extremely beige wardrobe and not draw a line from him to Walter White—and thus to imagine why Mike might have underestimated Walt in some of their early encounters.

[†] Mike points out that Nacho's given name is Ignacio, which is one of the names a fearful Saul Goodman throws out when he's in danger in his very first *Breaking Bad* appearance. Hmm.

SEASON 1, EPISODE 10
WRITTEN AND DIRECTED BY PETER GOULD

"Marco"

"I know what stopped me. And you know what? It's never stopping me again."
—Jimmy

Late in the *Saul* Season 1 finale, Jimmy finally tells his old partner in crime Marco about his legal career. Marco is startled to hear this news, and even more so when Jimmy reveals that this is not an opportunity for him to scam clients, nor is he making a fortune doing it so far. "All due respect," Marco argues, "you're a lawyer, and you're not makin' bank, you're doin' it wrong." Jimmy, struggling to explain his shifting ambitions to his buddy, replies, "I'm building something. It takes time."

Of course it takes time. This is a *Breaking Bad* prequel, part of a franchise defined by its patience and deliberation above all else. Even when the plot is meant to be moving more quickly, the writers can't stop themselves from slowing down, asking questions, taking detours, and making sure they explore every last idea from each phase of the story. As Peter Gould, Vince Gilligan, and all the rest would tell you, they assumed that Jimmy would be using Saul Goodman as his professional name, and working out of the strip mall office, by the end of this episode, if not earlier in the season. Instead, we've all—whether we watch the show or make it—gotten to know and care about Jimmy in such depth that his inevitable transformation no longer feels like a thing to root for, but to dread.

Does that transformation occur in the final moments of this episode? That's a conversation for when we get to Season 2 a few pages from now. But if this is the end of Jimmy, he goes out in a damn blaze of glory.

At first, "Marco" doesn't seem like it will be taking us anywhere near Saul. Early on, Jimmy and Kim walk past the dented trash can in the HHM parking garage—a reminder of so many of Jimmy's early frustrations with his brother's law firm—and he assures her that he's at peace with what he learned about Chuck. It seems, just then, that the *Better Call Saul* creative team will be playing a particularly long game in getting us from Point A to Point Saul. Chuck's betrayal was a brutal blow, but maybe it wouldn't be the one that knocked Jimmy over the edge.

In the very next scene, though, Jimmy has a meltdown while acting as bingo caller at the senior center. As he flees Albuquerque for the friendly confines of Cicero, and lets Marco talk him into running one last scam, and then another, and another . . . and another, it seems as if Saul Goodman might be on the verge of appearing, and the writers are just making sure they don't skip over any steps in that transformation, just as they didn't for that chemistry teacher who wound up employing Saul.

Although we had seen glimpses of Slippin' Jimmy in action, an episode largely comprised of his greatest hits—with Mike, Kim, Chuck, and Howard left on the sidelines back in Albuquerque—feels like exactly what we need before Jimmy's big declaration to Mike in the episode's closing moments. The season to this point has done such a thorough and convincing job of presenting Jimmy as a decent guy, who had learned to reign in his worst impulses far more often than even he might have expected, that we didn't need to just hear about the thrills of the Slippin' Jimmy days. We needed to see it for ourselves.

And boy, did we see it.

The Cicero scenes get to play things both slow and fast, first giving us the entirety of the hustle with the Kennedy half-dollar, then presenting the rest of the week's worth of scams as a giddy, kaleidoscopic montage, scored with jazz sounding straight out of the Rat Pack era, so that we can appreciate how much fun Jimmy and Marco are having, and also how good they are at this. Jimmy has found the law much more satisfying than Marco finds standpipe work, but this is quite obviously the true calling for both of them.

After a decade of staying on the straight and narrow, Jimmy needs more than just Chuck's betrayal and harsh words to knock him off the wagon. He has to go on an epic bender* back among his old haunts, to really soak in that life, so that even when Marco dies of a heart attack, and the dream scenario of a partnership-track job with a large Santa Fe firm presents itself, Jimmy's inclined to instead drive away. With the late Marco's ring on his pinky, giving in to all his most selfish criminal impulses seems the easier way to go.

That's the ring Saul will wear throughout *Breaking Bad*, and you can per-haps look at it like the Precious from *The Lord of the Rings*, corrupting Jimmy and possessing him with the spirit of Marco. (As he peels out of the courthouse parking lot, he starts humming—just as Marco did while waiting for Jimmy to arrive in the alley for their final scam—the classic opening riff of Deep Purple's "Smoke on the Water," before the song itself comes on the soundtrack.) Or you can simply look at it as a reminder of who Jimmy/Saul wants to be, and how much he has to resist the temptation to do the right thing when it could cost him money.

---

* This includes a payoff to an old joke from *Breaking Bad*, where Saul claimed that he once convinced a woman he was Kevin Costner. Here, we see that he wasn't lying to Walt about that—though the woman he tricked is mortified to realize her mistake the next morning.

But it is a high we know Jimmy will chase, whether now or down the road. It's like Marco puts it when Jimmy tries to offer him some cash in lieu of running the wallet scam one more time: "I don't need the money, Jimmy. I need *this*." It's a feeling Jimmy understands well. And when Marco dies before they can bilk one more sucker—his final words: "This was the greatest week of my life"—Jimmy perhaps takes on the burden for both of them.

As Jimmy roars out of the parking lot, he's headed for destinations unknown, in a closing shot that leaves open to question whether Saul Goodman has arrived for real. But if the moniker of *Better Call Saul*'s protagonist remains ambiguous, the series as a whole has very much come into focus over the back half of this season. It no longer feels like it's casting about blindly, hoping to figure out what will work, or even what kind of show this is meant to be. Whatever Jimmy is, and whatever he's trying to become, *Better Call Saul* has already carved out its own identity by now, rather than something aimlessly drafting off of the success of *Breaking Bad*.

"Switch"

"I've been doing the right thing for all these years, and where has it got me?"
—Jimmy

Better Call Saul Season 1 ended with our man roaring down the open road, "Smoke on the Water" blasting on the soundtrack. He had given up the straight life. He was *free*. He was also, it seemed, Saul Goodman, in spirit if not in name.

With "Switch," the *Saul* writers slam on the brakes of their metaphorical Suzuki Esteem and put the series in reverse, backing away as far as possible from the implications of the last scene of "Marco"—even going so far as to insert a brand-new scene into the middle of that previous one to help reorient the narrative.

Before we get there, though, it's time for another visit with poor Gene from Cinnabon and his lonely, colorless life in Omaha. At first, the sequence just seems to be a rehash of what we saw at the start of this series. But it soon expands to underline just what a terrible fate this is for Jimmy/Saul/Gene. He had Ed from the vacuum repair shop set up this new life for him as a way to avoid prison, but he's only traded one kind of cell for another. A truly free man who got locked in the mall's trash room could just open the emergency exit and not worry about the consequences; Gene can never, *ever*, do anything even vaguely sketchy if it might bring him into contact with the police. The time he spends trapped in that room* is a more literal kind of imprisonment, but back when Saul was advising Walt to turn himself in rather than spend a life on the run, maybe he should have listened to his own advice.

From there, we are back in the Albuquerque courthouse parking lot, Jimmy once again pausing on the way to his meeting with the lawyers from Davis and Main. But instead of returning to his car and driving away, he actually goes inside and chats briefly with senior partner Cliff Main, only then getting cold feet, having the conversation with Mike about the Kettleman money, and driving off like a bat out of hell.

It's a clumsy insertion, but a telling one. It shows that the *Saul* writers had second thoughts about letting their protagonist break bad this early, and wanted to explore the idea of Jimmy getting everything he's claimed to want since he passed the bar. It takes the rest of the episode for Jimmy to change his

---

* When he leaves, the camera pushes in on the wall to see that Gene has left a small line of graffiti behind, declaring "SG was here." Even in his new identity, he is still treating Saul Goodman as his true self—or, at least, the self he wishes he could still be.

mind about the job, but it's clear from the moment Ed Begley Jr.* appears onscreen as Cliff that this is where the show is going for now.

There's another motivation for this, well, switch in narrative priorities, and it's just as telling. In 2020, Peter Gould stated that when the Season 2 writers' room opened up, everyone began to realize that Jimmy was doing his pal Kim dirty by blowing off this huge opportunity that she had gone out on a limb to arrange for him. Jimmy's concerns have already shifted from impressing Chuck to impressing Kim, and much of "Switch" is about examining the complicated, ever-evolving dynamics of their relationship, and the ways in which they're beginning to influence one another.

There's a subplot where Mike's part-time employer "Pryce" foolishly lets Nacho find out his real name (Daniel Wormald) and home address, then even more foolishly calls the cops after Nacho robs him of both the drugs and his baseball card collection. But the episode is largely structured like "Marco" was, with Jimmy spending the middle of it trying to avoid responsibility by going back to the grift. And having failed to enlist Kim to go into legal practice with him, he instead enlists her to be his partner in low-level crime.

Their mark is finance bro Ken, played by Kyle Bornheimer. *Breaking Bad* fans will remember him as the jerk with the bluetooth headset who steals Walt's parking space in a Season 1 episode, eventually inspiring Walt to blow up Ken's fancy BMW with its "KEN WINS" license plate. Because Jimmy is a very different man from his future number one client, his assault on Ken is much less explosive, with the only damage being the financial hit of having to pay for an obscenely expensive bottle of Zafiro Añejo† tequila.

Back when Jimmy pulled the billboard stunt in Season 1's "Hero," we saw Kim smiling at it ever so slightly. While she's a rule follower herself, there is a part of her that likes it when Jimmy colors outside the lines. She's at first confused and displeased when Jimmy tries roping her into the scam, where they pose as siblings seeking advice from Ken on how to invest a large inheritance. But then she jumps in with both feet, proving a natural grifter herself. She's quick on her feet enough to not only invent the alias "Giselle St. Claire" (sister to Jimmy's "Viktor with a k") but explain the name as having Boer origins, because they had family in South Africa. And when Viktor and Giselle have walked away, drunk on the tequila and high on the thrill of getting one over on this d-bag, Kim's face positively lights up as she looks at Jimmy and then gives him a long, passionate kiss. It's not just that she went along with this short con.

---

* A veteran character actor, Begley has a long history of co-starring in projects with Michael McKean. (Among other things, he played the Spinal Tap drummer who died in a bizarre gardening accident, in a case that the authorities felt was best left unsolved.)

† This is another *Breaking Bad* callback: the same tequila that Gus Fring gave as a gift to Don Eladio, with a poisonous surprise inside.

It's not just that she turned out to be good at it. It's that this side of Jimmy genuinely excites her, to the point where they wind up in bed together,* and are still flirting when they wake up in her apartment[†] the next morning.

"Wouldn't it be great if we could do that every night?" Jimmy wonders, referring not to the sex, but to the feeling he got when Kim joined him in taking Ken down a peg. "Yes," Kim acknowledges. "But we can't."

But it's Kim's willingness to hop over to Jimmy's side of the fence that in turn convinces him to give her side another try. He no longer cares about winning Chuck's respect, or doing anything for his brother. He still cares deeply, though, about Kim Wexler. He tried to rent an expensive office just so she might agree to work alongside him. He gave up the Kettleman money for her, came back to Albuquerque to meet with Davis and Main for her, and ultimately decides to take the job for her. Kim might be willing to play Giselle as a one-shot deal, but Jimmy recognizes that if he wants her in his life, he in turn has to keep living in her world.

The Davis and Main job is practically everything he wanted when he began taking law school classes and plotting for a way to move out of the HHM mailroom and into the associate ranks. He has money, respect, a fancy office,[‡] an assistant, a company car on the way, and more. He's not technically working with Kim, but their firms will be collaborating extensively on the Sandpiper case, and Santa Fe's only an hour's drive from Albuquerque.

Yet you can see that the place feels every bit as much of a cell to Jimmy as the shopping mall does to Gene. As Jimmy studies his own office, his attention is drawn to the eponymous switch, which comes with a note warning that the occupant should never turn it off. Based on the way the franchise generally structures its stories, this might be used as Chekhov's Light Switch, with Jimmy waiting to flip it until the moment he's ready to blow up his life at the new firm. Instead, he flips it immediately . . . and nothing seems to happen.

But that neatly sums up Jimmy's current circumstance. He has gotten all he dreamt about. Life is good on seemingly every level. Even flipping the switch doesn't signal doom. But you get the sense that maybe he wanted it to.

---

* Is this their first time? "There was no consensus" in the writers' room, according to Thomas Schnauz. "Because of the robot sex voice [in "Nacho"], I believed they had slept together. I think they were a couple and then drifted apart when Kim started her law career, motivating Jimmy to follow in her footsteps, thinking it might change things."

† We see that Kim sleeps in an oversized Kansas City Royals baseball jersey. Kansas City is only a few hours drive from Cinnabon Gene's home base in Omaha, and the Royals have long had an Omaha minor league affiliate team.

‡ The office comes complete with wall art that seems apropos for both Slippin' Jimmy (the figure seems to be falling over) and Walter White (it looks like clothes with an invisible occupant, just as the wind inflated Walt's pants in the opening shot of Breaking Bad).

SEASON 2, EPISODE 2
WRITTEN BY GENNIFER HUTCHISON
DIRECTED BY TERRY MCDONOUGH

"Cobbler"

"You're going to have to make a video." —**Jimmy**

"Switch" had to bend itself this way and that to unring the Saul Goodman bell
that the Season 1 finale had seemingly rung. It's hard to blame the creative
team for wanting to put off the transformation, because Jimmy has turned
out to be just that appealing, and because characters like Kim and Chuck
have added so much richness to the parts of this series that so far have nothing to do with *Breaking Bad.*

Yet it's not hard to understand why that same team might have been
inclined to go full Saul so early. Because as "Cobbler" offers in its hilarious climax, Jimmy McGill giving in fully to the dark side can be damned entertaining.

Since "Switch" was busy walking back the final scene of "Marco," "Cobbler" in many ways feels like the proper beginning of Season 2. For starters,
Chuck returns in all his odiousness. It's impressive how easily and convincingly
the show has reversed our sympathies about him and Howard, and how much
everything Chuck says or does now seems like the height of entitled arrogance.
(It no longer, for instance, feels like a kindness when everyone else puts their
phones and watches into a bin when Chuck comes to the office, but rather an
indulgence on behalf of a smug absentee despot.) The episode opens with him
being taunted, first by the metronome when he can't quite play a classical piano
piece, then with the news, delivered by Howard, that Jimmy has landed a job at
a prestigious firm like Davis and Main. The idea is so foreign to him that when
Howard says Jimmy is working at Davis and Main, Chuck's first impulse is to
ask, "Doing what?" Later, he interrupts a joint meeting between the two firms
to, as he puts it bluntly to Jimmy, "bear witness."

Chuck's arrival completely disrupts his brother's flow, and in turn makes
Jimmy susceptible to a phone call where Mike asks if Jimmy is still "morally
flexible." Jimmy can trigger Chuck's electromagnetism episodes, and Chuck in
turn can trigger Jimmy's moral flexibility episodes. So this is great timing for
Mike, and for Daniel Wormald, who very badly needs a lawyer to get out of the
mess he created with his ridiculous Hummer (which he has to give to Nacho*
in exchange for the return of his baseball cards, plus an extra ten grand).

---

* Mike gets to Nacho through his father, Manuel (Juan Carlos Cantu), an immigrant who runs a local
car upholstery business and seems to have no idea that his Ignacio moonlights for the Salamancas.

Jimmy meets with a pair of local detectives who understandably want to know what Daniel kept in the hidden compartment their uniformed colleagues found when Daniel called them about the burglary. And Mr. Wormald's new attorney provides an alternate explanation with a high, incredibly odd, level of detail: this was not a hiding place for drugs, but for videos Daniel recorded in which he performed the Hoboken Squat Cobbler, a fetish which, as Jimmy explains, "It's when a man sits in pie! *He sits in a pie!* And he ... he ... wiggles around."

Odenkirk has been a revelation as a dramatic actor on this show. But the man rose up through the showbiz ranks as a comedian, and this is the single best piece of comedy he's been given to play so far as this character, by any of his names. And Odenkirk turns it into an opera. Every pause, every glance, every line reading, is perfectly calibrated both to convince these cops and to wring the maximum amount of laughter possible from this material. Jimmy comes across as completely mortified to have to discuss this at all, putting the baffled detectives* in the position of having to keep asking more and more questions about these recordings, and making it seem like this is something Daniel had legitimate reason to want to keep secret from the world. It's a master class, and the funniest *Breaking Bad* universe moment since Jesse thought Walt was going to build a robot.

Once we're done laughing at Odenkirk's verbal brilliance, though, "Cobbler" brings in Kim to point out that when Jimmy had Daniel actually record a Squat Cobbler video, he crossed a significant ethical and legal line. It's one thing for an attorney to feed a bunch of nonsense to the police, and another entirely for him to fabricate evidence. Jimmy sees no difference between the two, nor between this and their recent takedown of Ken Wins. When Kim[†] presses him on it, he seems to back down. But it's obvious how much happier he was making up Squat Cobbler nicknames like "Dutch Apple Ass" and "Simple Simon the Ass Man" than he was sitting in Sandpiper meetings, even before Chuck's arrival. He has a seemingly perfect life, which now includes a top-of-the-line Mercedes to replace the Esteem. But the company car's cupholders are just a fraction too small to accommodate the "World's 2nd Best Lawyer" travel mug Kim has gifted him, and the fit with Davis and Main as a whole feels similarly off to Jimmy. Eventually, he tosses the mug onto the

---

Mike pretends to be a customer looking to spruce up his ancient sedan, and in a very Ehrmantraut kind of move, Manuel tries to talk him out of such an extravagant and unnecessary purchase.

* Full credit to A. Russell Andrews and Troy Winbush for making excellent straight men to Odenkirk's tomfoolery.

† The show keeps riding an emotional roller coaster with Kim, who's giddy hearing the story one minute, nauseous the next after learning one detail too many. Rhea Seehorn does a great job playing Kim's very complicated and rapidly shifting responses to this man.

passenger seat, and it seems like he'll soon start looking for ways to toss the entire job aside.

Because when it comes down to it, Jimmy McGill likes to have fun. And one of the legal jobs he took in this episode was a lot more fun for him than the other.

SEASON 2, EPISODE 3
WRITTEN BY JONATHAN GLATZER
DIRECTED BY SCOTT WINANT

"Amarillo"

"Whatever happened to showmanship?" —**Jimmy**

It would be easy to look at "Amarillo" as an episode entirely reverse-engineered to set up the moment where Geraldine Strauss paraphrases one of the most famous movie lines of all time (from *Sunset Boulevard*), declaring, "I'm ready for my close-up, Mr. McGill."

And if that's all it was, it might be worth it. It is a great, *great* joke, and the centerpiece of an hour that is largely an expanded version of Jimmy Loves Movies.* But the streamlined "Amarillo" is in service of a crucial larger point about where both of our *Breaking Bad* holdovers find themselves. It's about as slow as things have gotten so far—so light on incident that it gets by almost entirely on the charms of Odenkirk, Banks, and Seehorn—while also pointing out that the two very different men have the same basic Achilles heel: a family member who keeps pushing them into reckless behavior that threatens otherwise cushy situations.

Jimmy wants so hard to be good, to prove Kim right and to prove Chuck wrong. But Chuck's mere presence at the office overrides all of Jimmy's emotional and ethical controls, and pushes him into the exact kind of behavior that confirms every one of Chuck's Slippin' Jimmy suspicions. In the previous episode, Jimmy followed a surprise Chuck conference room visit by spinning lies about Hoboken Squat Cobbler and fabricating evidence. When we find him here in the eponymous Texas city, he's not exactly playing by the rules, and lies about it when Chuck inquires at another inter-firm meeting. So his hands aren't exactly clean here. But when Chuck calls him out on the solicitation bylaws, Jimmy can't stop himself from continuing to freelance, not only producing a commercial† without Cliff's permission, but letting it air up in Colorado Springs. He can't stop. He wants to prove himself, but after watching Davis and Main's aggressively dull previous commercial, he knows Clifford

---

* *Ice Station Zebra*, the film Kim makes Jimmy watch, will have a big enough impact on him that he'll name one of his holding companies after it in the Saul Goodman years.

† Jimmy rehires the film students who helped him with the billboard scam in Season 1's "Hero" to shoot the ad. One of the episode's cleverer gags comes when Jimmy shows the completed commercial to Kim, and we realize that the dolly shot Jimmy wanted was accomplished using Mrs. Strauss's stair lift chair, because Jimmy didn't ask the kids to bring a dolly.

isn't likely to approve his more sensationalized approach, and opts to ask for forgiveness rather than permission. Would he do this even without Chuck getting under his skin first? Maybe. Certainly, Jimmy's love of flash is at odds with the hidebound nature of corporate law in general, and of the sample Davis and Main ad he watches in particular. But he also understands his orders, and having Chuck lurking around encourages Jimmy to break them.

Meanwhile, Mike has a simple life he seems content with. He just wants to do right by Stacey and Kaylee, as father-in-law and grandfather, and as a man drowning in guilt over his role in his son's death. Each time he's edged back into the criminal world, it's not been to obtain creature comforts for himself (all he needs is his old portable radio and a pimento sandwich), but out of guilt for not being able to do more for Kaylee.

The episode patiently shows Mike putting in the time to figure out whether Stacey's neighborhood is dangerous, or if she's imagining it. Ultimately, it doesn't matter, nor would it even matter if Stacey were overtly making this up to guilt Mike into helping her move to a nicer place. Mike is all-in with this situation, so her motives are irrelevant. He realizes the gunshots are fictional, but any regret from that discovery is only from his realization that he can't solve the problem by playing cop (and eliminating a genuine threat to the neighborhood), but by playing crook again to make the money that will get them off that street.

Again, it's a pretty thin episode, primarily designed to set up the potential fallout from each man's decision, with Cliff Main being furious with Jimmy about going around him with the ad, and Nacho trying to hire Mike to make someone go away. But it also takes advantage of how well we know these characters, and how thoroughly the two leads inhabit their roles at this point. And it reinforces the idea that, no matter how hard each of them is trying to stay on the up-and-up, it's fundamentally in their nature to do shady things.

SEASON 2, EPISODE 4
WRITTEN BY GORDON SMITH
DIRECTED BY ADAM BERNSTEIN

"Gloves Off"

"That all ya got?" —**Mike**

"Gloves Off" reunites the writer/director team from "Five-O." It's another Mike spotlight, albeit not as overwhelmingly tilted toward him as that earlier one. Given the title, think of it more like a title fight and an undercard. In the former, Mike gets into a physical, entirely one-sided bout with Tuco Salamanca. In the latter, Jimmy and Chuck take off their metaphorical gloves for the most brutal argument we've seen them have to date.

The person Nacho wants to get rid of is, of course, Tuco. We've seen on *Breaking Bad* just how dangerously erratic Tuco can be when he's using too much of his own product, so Nacho's stories about that ring unnervingly true. The plot could easily fall into the prequel problem trap, where Mike spends a long time attempting to do something we know he can't, simply because Tuco is still alive in 2008 to meet Walt and Jesse. Instead, the story digs in a bit deeper on Mike's would-be target, before Mr. Ehrmantraut decides that he does not want to be in the Salamanca assassination business at the moment.

The notion of Tuco staring at his employees as a form of lie detector evokes Larry David using that idea throughout the run of *Curb Your Enthusiasm*. And despite the constant threat Tuco poses to anyone he's around, whether he likes or hates them, the show often treats him as a figure of comedy. Like his cousins and his uncle, he is a fundamentally monstrous person, but he's also ridiculous in a way that they are not. To Domingo,* it's terrifying to have to endure Tuco's gaze while they're meeting at Tuco's unofficial headquarters, the taco restaurant El Michoacáno. To us, it may as well be accompanied by a whimsical bassoon sting. But whether a nuisance or an outright menace, Tuco is a huge pain in the ass for Nacho, who can't risk having his side business discovered.

This leads to Mike making like Walter White, pointing out the flaws in every one of Nacho's suggested plans of attack. Rather than go for a drive-by, Mike decides to lean on his past as a Marine sniper in Vietnam, taking Tuco out from long range. And this brings Mike into the same room as one of the two

---

*   Yes, that's Max Arciniega reprising his *Breaking Bad* role as one of Walt's very first opponents/ victims. Here, he is not yet going by the nickname Krazy-8.

men in the Heisenberg-verse who is as thorough as he is:* Walter White's favorite gun dealer, Lawson. Character actor Jim Beaver slides back into the role with his trademark ease, and as Lawson offers Mike an updated version of the M40 bolt-action rifle Mike used in country, it seems like the beginning of a beautiful friendship. And perhaps it will be. Just not today, as Mike has a change of heart. He declines to kill Tuco, instead opting for a much more complicated and dangerous gambit where he sets himself up to be on the receiving end of a vicious assault from Tuco right as police arrive in response to Mike's own preemptive 911 call.

An incredulous Tuco will later point out that Mike chose a smaller payday with a much higher degree of risk to himself in the process. "You went a long way to not pull that trigger," he observes. In that sense, the episode "Gloves Off" resembles most is not "Five-O," but Saul's very first appearance on *Breaking Bad*. In that one, Walt and Jesse similarly go a very long way—and surrender a significant chunk of change in the process—to avoid having to kill Badger before he rats them out to the cops, with Saul in that case playing the Nacho role as the incredulous observer who thinks murder would have been simpler for all involved.

Walt and Jesse overcomplicate things because they're still in the phase of their criminal careers where they've deluded themselves into thinking they can sell drugs without actually hurting anyone.† Walt will eventually recognize the naïveté of that attitude, and accept that some problem dogs just need to be put down—a lesson that will cost Mike everything. Mike Ehrmantraut, though, is not someone prone to lying to himself. So why does he choose this up-close punishment from Tuco, rather than the neatness and finality of a long-distance kill? He does not offer Nacho an answer in the moment. Certainly, the idea of killing a Salamanca brings with it some potentially huge blowback. But it's also not hard to look at how unhappy Mike was upon arriving in Albuquerque, and how much grief and guilt he was carrying about Matty, Fensky, and Hoffman. He doesn't necessarily regret killing the dirty cops, but he also doesn't feel proud of it. Other people might see no moral difference between a revenge killing and a contract killing, but to Mike Ehrmantraut, the gap between the two is as wide as the Grand Canyon. We know he will eventually kill many, many people for money, but he's no closer to that at the time of this episode than Jimmy is to being the kind of lawyer who might advise his clients to bump off a troublesome underling.

---

* The other is Ed the disappearance expert, whom we know from *Breaking Bad* is not someone Mike has ever met or heard of.

† Other than the end users, that is, but *Breaking Bad* mostly avoided thinking about them.

And speaking of our favorite ethically questionable attorney, the Jimmy section of the episode does an impressive job of once again recalibrating our sympathies regarding the brothers McGill. Chuck's refusal to believe in Jimmy appears to be one of the motivating factors in our man's eventual transformation. But the situation is more complicated than Jimmy breaking bad merely to spite the sibling who expects nothing more from him. On some level, he will always be Slippin' Jimmy or Saul Goodman,* and only some of his behavior with the ad can be blamed on being goaded by Chuck. He knew at the end of the previous episode, for instance, that Cliff was furious about the whole thing, but he didn't warn Kim about it until it was much too late. And we know that Jimmy was itching to do this thing his way no matter what, and declined to ask for permission once he got a look at what the partners had deemed an appropriate ad the last time. Jimmy's a showman. He can be a showman in service to a good cause, but he has a very hard time putting his hustler tendencies aside when they conflict with the rules, and it's a big problem. Chuck is making matters worse with his treatment of Jimmy, but it's like that old saw about hypnotism: he can't make Jimmy do something Jimmy would never do of his own volition.

Jimmy's not completely rigid. However mad he is at Chuck, he still puts in an all-nighter to take care of him after Chuck has another electromagnetism flare-up. Whatever betrayals there have been, and no matter how much Jimmy has come to understand the true nature of Chuck's condition, they are still brothers. And if Jimmy can't see the damage he did to the firm, he's at least genuinely chastened by the harm he may have done to Kim's career. But as Chuck notes, Jimmy's attempt at self-sacrifice—daring to quit the law forever if Chuck will get Kim out of the HHM cornfield—is just as legally questionable as a lot of his other stunts.

Even when Jimmy's trying to be good, he's doing bad. He and Mike have a lot more in common than either man would probably want to admit.

---

*   Again, remember whose initials Gene from Cinnabon wrote on the wall in the season-opening teaser.

SEASON 2, EPISODE 5
WRITTEN BY ANN CHERKIS
DIRECTED BY JOHN SHIBAN

"Rebecca"

"You don't save me. I save me." —**Kim**

When *Better Call Saul* began, the assumption by everyone, both in the audience and on the creative team, was that Jimmy would very quickly begin practicing law as Saul, and that he and Mike would begin having periodic encounters with various *Breaking Bad* characters in the years before Walter White's cancer diagnosis would change all their lives. Instead, the show has put that transformation on indefinite hold, allowing for some *Breaking Bad* cameos, mostly in the Mike subplots, while building the lawyer world of Jimmy, Kim, and Chuck into such a vibrant place that those scenes all but dare the audience to root for the Heisenberg-verse stuff. Why, the show invites us to wonder, would we ask for Gus Fring to turn up when Jimmy McGill and friends are so entertaining?

That dichotomy is on palpable display throughout "Rebecca." The majority of the episode revolves around doings at HHM. It's such an incredible Kim Wexler spotlight that all memory of Mike versus Tuco would be easy to banish, if not for Jimmy jokingly humming the theme from *Rocky* when he gets a look at Mike's purple face. Forget the Salamancas. Forget Nacho. Hell, forget Mike and even Jimmy, who's largely absent from the episode's second half. Much of "Rebecca" seems to be arguing—convincingly—that Rhea Seehorn deserves to be treated like a lead of the series just as much as Odenkirk and Banks.

And then, just as the show has conditioned its viewers to pledge their undying loyalty to the woman with the power ponytail, the episode's final minutes reintroduce Hector Salamanca. And suddenly, the hotel bell we can all hear ringing in our ears as Mark Margolis appears on screen in this familiar role is powerful enough to drown out all thoughts of power struggles at HHM, of Mesa Verde, Chuck and Jimmy's messy history, or any of the rest. All that seems to matter is the return of one of the parent show's most indelible characters.

Ding. Ding. DING.

But we'll get back to him. Let's begin with the episode's breakout star. Seehorn has certainly been put to good use in prior episodes, most memorably when she jumped into the con-artist deep end with Jimmy and Ken Wins in the season premiere. Here, though, she is a woman alone, partially by circumstance, partially by choice. Jimmy's stunt with the TV commercial earns him a justified punishment, in which less experienced Davis and Main associate Erin (Jessie Ennis) is assigned to supervise his every move. But Kim becomes collateral damage, because the HHM partners assume Jimmy told her what he was doing, and that she in turn kept them as in the dark as Jimmy kept his own bosses. For understandable reasons, they can't fathom the notion that Jimmy wouldn't tell Kim, and it puts her in an impossible spot. In the version she lets the partners believe, she made an error in judgment in not warning them and the Davis and Main partners. In the real version, she comes across as the naive dupe of a former con man with whom everyone is rightly angry at the moment. She's worked hard from humble beginnings to get to where she is, and her allegiance to Jimmy has seemingly put all of that at risk. So she accepts another banishment to the cornfield, refusing any and all attempts by Jimmy to fix the mess that he and only he made.

As she puts it—in a line that says so much with so little that it makes "I am The One Who Knocks" seem overwritten in comparison—"You don't save me. *I* save me."

And boy, does she. At least, until she doesn't.

What follows is a master class in montage-building. Seehorn, director John Shiban, writer Ann Cherkis, editor Kelley Dixon, and the song "A Mi Manera" by Gipsy Kings combine for the most riveting three minutes you will ever see involving Post-it notes, rolling phone calls, stairwells, and restrooms. Those three minutes hammer home just how hard Kim is working—over a much longer period of time for her than for us—to find something, anything, that will get her out of doc review. So when she finally lands a meeting with banking chain Mesa Verde, and allows herself a brief celebratory dance in the HHM parking garage, it feels extra sweet. And *that*, in turn, makes it all the more crushing when Howard makes clear that Kim will remain in exile while he and other lawyers handle Mesa Verde's big business. Just watch the way Seehorn's jaw moves ever so slightly as Kim absorbs this latest hit; like the tiny smile she lets escape while watching coverage of the billboard stunt in "Hero," she says so much with barely any movement at all.

That Howard, not Chuck, is the one responsible for her punishment is another reminder that Jimmy often argues for things he knows nothing about, and that human beings are a lot more complicated than he makes them out to be. The episode is named for Chuck's ex-wife Rebecca (Ann Cusack), whom me meet in the opening flashback. Jimmy is still brand-new to Albuquerque, and Chuck is so convinced that Rebecca (to whom he's still happily married at this point) will hate Slippin' Jimmy, he encourages her to tug on her ear like Carol Burnett when she inevitably gets uncomfortable. Instead, Rebecca is utterly charmed by Jimmy and his endless supply of lawyer jokes, and it's a mortified

Chuck who winds up pulling the Burnett move. After Jimmy's gone, Chuck tries telling a lawyer joke himself, and it absolutely bombs. It's the brothers' relationship in microcosm: no matter how smart or accomplished or wealthy Chuck may become, he will always struggle to compensate for the deep gulf in charm between himself and Jimmy.

Eventually, Jimmy's brother and girlfriend come together for a conversation about how much damage that charm can cause. It's an absolutely stunning scene, and a twisty one. It seems to start off as the latest of Kim's humiliations—now she's the coffee girl?—until Chuck invites her into his office to chat about their mutual loved one. Again, the series has really elegantly switched our sympathies back and forth between the four main legal players, and it continues to do so even within the span of this episode. In the flashback, Chuck can't be more contemptuous, or envious, of Jimmy, and this conversation appears headed for another round of Snob vs Slob. But then comes Chuck's story about their father, wonderfully delivered by Michael McKean, which casts a whole new light on the relationship. It's not just that Chuck has spent half his life getting Slippin' Jimmy out of trouble, but that Jimmy's insatiable thirst for the hustle couldn't even be controlled when their father's business was at stake. If I were the one in Chuck's shoes, I imagine I would say something far less kind about my sibling than the words he leaves Kim to consider:

"My brother is not a bad person. He has a good heart. It's just . . . he can't help himself. And everyone's left picking up the pieces."

McKean is so convincing, right on the heels of Seehorn working her usual subtle magic, that all thought of the non-legal part of the series falls away. Or, it does until Hector wanders into Mike's favorite diner* and tries to talk our man into changing his testimony about the incident at El Michoacáno, thus erasing the gun charge that would put Tuco behind bars for the next eight to ten years. Because we are intimately acquainted with Hector, we know that this is the softest, gentlest sell he is capable of making. And because we know Hector, we know the implicit threat to Mike should he decline the $5,000 offer. And while Mike has not seen what we've seen, he is a man who does his homework, and his grimace upon Hector's departure, like Kim's own upon realizing Howard wasn't ready to forgive her, makes clear that he knows how bad his current circumstances are.

And suddenly it feels very exciting to be so deep in *Breaking Bad* country, doesn't it?

---

* Mike's waitress there, Fran, first appeared in the *Breaking Bad* Season 5 episode that introduced Lydia Rodarte-Quayle, where it was clear that Fran (played by Debrianna Mansini) had been happily serving Mike for years.

SEASON 2, EPISODE 6
WRITTEN BY GENNIFER HUTCHISON
DIRECTED BY MICHAEL SLOVIS

"Bali Ha'i"

"You knew what you wanted, but I got in the way." —**Kim**

For the second episode in a row, Jimmy disappears for long stretches of his own series. (Other than his apologetic performance of the episode's title song, from *South Pacific*, on Kim's answering machine, he doesn't appear at all between when he pulls out of the nail salon parking lot and when Kim calls him to announce she has a fish on the line.) And, for the second week in a row, the stories involving Kim and Mike are so compelling that the show does just fine leaving its leading man to suffer off-screen mortification at the whip-cracking hands of Erin Brill.

The Mike subplot leans even further into all things Salamanca, this time bringing in Leonel and Marco—aka "the Cousins," who were such a memorable part of *Breaking Bad* Season 3—as Hector's latest weapons in his campaign to intimidate Mike. The Cousins don't do much, but the image of them glaring down at Mike and Kaylee from an opposing rooftop is chilling. Their presence is all Mike needs to realize he has to find a way out of this mess, agreeing to change his story for the cops in exchange for an extra $50,000* (Hector's original offer times ten). And once Mike starts pushing back,[†] Hector is free to drop the harmless-old-man act and assume the colder and more arrogant persona we remember from the *Breaking Bad* flashbacks to his cartel glory days. It's very much an old home week.

Kim's life isn't in any danger, but she's nonetheless feeling the squeeze from Howard, who continues to treat her coldly even after Chuck has negotiated her release from doc review. (Just check the stony look on Patrick Fabian's face as they march through the HHM offices, and how easily Howard turns on the charm as they approach Kevin and Paige from Mesa Verde, played

---

*   Half of which he of course gives to Nacho, because Mike believes in being paid honestly for his work, even when it's in a dishonest field like this.

†   Where the show has done its best to age down Bob Odenkirk so that he'll look younger than when we met Saul on *Breaking Bad*, no such effort has been attempted with Jonathan Banks. ("They'll always try to make me look younger, but you can't put a silly wig on my head," he told me before the series premiered. "I ain't going to look right.") The fact that he's visibly older is actually working for the character, at the moment because Mike so very clearly feels like he's past the point where he should be pistol-whipping two Salamanca goons who are hiding in his bedroom. The weariness and shakiness only adds to the gravity of a scene, like the one where he washes blood off his hands (and the gun) after chasing away the intruders.

respectively by Rex Linn and Cara Pifko.) Like Jimmy, she's struggling to get appreciation from one of the HHM partners. And, like Jimmy, she now has a pretty sweet offer to get on the partner track at another firm, with Rich Schweikart trying to hire her away to Schweikart & Cokely. And by episode's end, she has finally started to embrace his love of the grift, ending her recent silence by inviting Jimmy to help scam another obnoxious mark. It's at the same restaurant where she had her lunch with Rich, but she seems much happier and more at ease there when she's pretending to be Giselle St. Claire than when she was considering the next step of her legal career.

There's an unfortunate history with twenty-first-century prestige dramas—with *Breaking Bad* among the most infamous examples—of audiences turning against female characters whose only sin is objecting to the morally dubious, if not outright criminal, behavior of the male leads. So it's fascinating to see the *Saul* writers, who were so dismayed by this reaction to Skyler White, trying a different approach with Kim. She objects to certain aspects of Jimmy's con artistry, like when he fabricated evidence with the Squat Cobbler video. But on the whole, she is most attracted to him—and in some ways the most alive—when they are running a grift together. She's not trying to pull him over to the light side of the Force, but rather allowing herself to enjoy the highs of the dark side, just so long as they don't take things too far. (Here, for instance, she decides to keep the $10,000 check* as a trophy, rather than cashing it.)

Is this really the life for her? Jimmy wants so desperately for it to be true, and he'd probably even settle for her being an honest lawyer by day and running harmless cons by night. But there still remains a pretty big gap between tricking some d-bag into paying for your booze, or getting one to write a check you'll never cash, and pulling many of the stunts that we've seen bring Jimmy such joy. And we know that what he does as Saul Goodman is infinitely worse than faking a video with Daniel Wormald. Will Kim happily slip on down there with him, or is this current compromise going to end badly for all involved?

After all, when Jimmy is onscreen, we see him really chafing at all aspects of his current life: not just answering to Erin, but staying in what should be ample luxury at the corporate apartment, and driving around in a much nicer car than his two-toned Esteem. Instead, he finds he can only sleep peacefully back at the nail salon, and he eventually has to take a tire iron to the Mercedes' cup holder so that the travel mug from Kim will fit.

The only question is when Jimmy will feel the need to take a metaphorical tire iron to his entire life with Davis and Main, and whether Kim will still be hanging around with him after he's done with the alterations.

---

* Made out to a company named for Kim's old favorite *Ice Station Zebra*, of course.

SEASON 2, EPISODE 7
WRITTEN BY GORDON SMITH
DIRECTED BY COLIN BUCKSEY

"Inflatable"

"There's no point in me doing this if I can't be myself." —**Jimmy**

Mike's half-measures speech from the *Breaking Bad* episode of the same name has echoed throughout a lot of this *Saul* season, and not just because Mike himself has been suffering no end of headaches over his decision to opt for a half-measure rather than simply killing Tuco.* It's also because both Jimmy and Kim have spent much of this season, and "Inflatable" in particular, struggling to pull off half-measures when it comes to their careers and their relationship.

Jimmy tried with Davis and Main, sort of. As Kim noted a few episodes back, he never really committed to the job, which we know he only took as an excuse to be near her. But he made an effort at times, and even mostly swallowed his pride to endure being bossed around by Erin. But the episode's opening flashback—with a young Jimmy trying hard to talk his father out of falling for a scam artist, before pocketing money from the till himself out of disgust with his old man's gullibility—is a reminder that even when Jimmy really wants to do the right thing, especially for the people he cares about, it's almost impossible for him to avoid cheating along the way.

A cynic could look at the entire Davis and Main stint as a stall tactic from a writers' room who decided in between seasons that they weren't ready for Saul Goodman just yet. But that's really the entire point of the series: Jimmy alternately listening to the angel and devil on his shoulder, trying his best to defy his fundamental nature and the destiny we know he has to embrace eventually. This creative team is all about charting every step of a particular journey, even if the trip can be slow and occasionally travel in circles. If they had just jumped to this point in the season premiere, none of it would have felt as rich or as earned.

---

* With Kim more or less promoted to co-lead at the moment, Mike is back on the periphery of things, feeling disgusted with himself for lying to the cops about Tuco's gun, wanting as little as possible to do with Jimmy, and still keeping an eye on Hector's crew, just in case he sees an opening to hurt them back.

Even when Jimmy knows he needs to leave Davis and Main, he can't do it the honest way* or risk losing his bonus. So he finally—in a hilarious, raucous, heist-style montage (another gem by editor Kelley Dixon, scored to "Son of Scorpio" by Dennis Coffey)—figures out a way to get fired without giving back any of the money he's already received, simply by annoying the hell out of everyone at the firm† while feigning innocence at every turn. It's a nice touch that Cliff Main is completely aware of what Jimmy is doing, but gives in anyway because it's easier than fighting a man well-equipped with loud suits and crazy stunts to wage a sustained campaign of obnoxiousness.

With Davis and Main out of the picture, Jimmy‡ again tries to talk Kim into going into business with him. She doesn't understand why they can't just be a couple, not fully appreciating how much he's driven to be professionally closer to the people he cares about personally: first Chuck, now her. He successfully argues that Kim going over to Schweikart would be a lateral move, putting a bug in her head so that she has a Freudian slip and calls Rich "Howard" by mistake at the end of an otherwise successful meeting. She knows Jimmy well enough to know that actually partnering up with him would be too big a risk to take at this stage of her career. Instead, she rips the business card he made for them in two, coming up with the idea to work side-by-side, but not officially together. But after seeing how this season has gone so far, Kim and Jimmy running separate practices that share the same office feels like just one more half-measure that will end up causing everyone further aggravation along the way.

---

* The flashback to Jimmy's childhood confirms at least part of the story Chuck tells Kim in "Rebecca," but places it in a new context, given Jimmy's futile attempts to warn his father about the con artist. If Mr. McGill is that much of a soft touch once, it's not hard to imagine him playing the sucker many times in the future. Does that justify Jimmy stealing from the family? No, but it's unclear how much he took over the years versus how much their dad foolishly gave away.

† Note that when Jimmy goes to visit Kim at HHM, he's wearing one of his more subdued and traditional suits, rather than one of the loud ones inspired by the inflatable dancing man he passes on the drive to work. He will eventually make those outfits his signature as Saul Goodman, but for now, they're just a tool to get himself out of the Davis and Main job.

‡ When Jimmy is re-recording his outgoing answering machine message to mark his return to solo practice, he abandons the silly continental accent and does it in his normal speaking voice. No more pretensions about what kind of firm he's running. Jimmy is going to be Jimmy, finally.

SEASON 2, EPISODE 8
WRITTEN BY THOMAS SCHNAUZ
DIRECTED BY LARYSA KONDRACKI

"Fifi"

"I need to find a way to do this that's right for me." —**Kim**

"Fifi" gets its title from the B-29 Superfortress that Jimmy uses as a prop for his latest TV commercial. He brings along his favorite local film students,* as usual, and they once again make minor cinematic magic with barely any time or equipment. It feels appropriate to have this triumvirate working together again in an episode that opens with the most lavish *Better Call Saul* movie homage to date: a four-and-a-half-minute sequence where we follow a Salamanca popsicle truck through a U.S./Mexico border crossing, where it is inspected for contraband. It is lovingly modeled on the famous opening shot of Orson Welles's *Touch of Evil*, where Charlton Heston and Janet Leigh made a similar crossing. That one ended in an explosion, while this one concludes peacefully, with the truck sent on its way by border patrol agents who fail to find anything illicit.

Though the *Saul* creative team had *Touch of Evil* in mind as they set up their own border crossing, the idea to actually film it in one take—covering a lot of ground and moving around several tight spaces—came from director Larysa Kondracki. In addition to evoking Welles, the oner underlines just how thoroughly the agents appear to be searching the truck without discovering its true contents. It feels like a magician rolling up his sleeves, or sliding a hula hoop across the levitating woman, as a way to prove there's no trickery involved, even though we in the audience understand that there's much more going on than we can see from where we're looking.

As a result, the opening works not just as a way for Kondracki and *Saul* to show off, but as a reminder of the show's meticulous nature and incremental pacing. Those were hallmarks of *Breaking Bad*, too, but that show tended to use them to build up to moments of extreme violence—sometimes physical, sometimes emotional, sometimes both. *Saul* isn't a show completely without physical violence, but its deepest wounds are on the emotional side of things. And a lot of "Fifi" is about incrementally pushing forward the story of Kim and Jimmy coming to work together (sort of), so we can eventually feel devastated when things go badly between them.

---

* The scripts never give these guys names, always referring to Josh Fadem's character as "Camera Guy" and Julian Bonfiglio's as "Sound Guy."

And they will go very badly. If there was any doubt of that before, the events of "Fifi" should probably put those to rest.

This is primarily a tale of the two McGill brothers, though Kim gets a few moments to impress, first when she convinces Kevin from Mesa Verde to jump ship from HHM, then when Rhea Seehorn flashes that enormous smile (heartbreaking in retrospect) as Kim reveals that she won the meeting. But it's now active war between Jimmy and Chuck, despite Jimmy continuing to nurse Chuck through his latest bout of psychosomatic pain, even after Chuck has helped Howard steal Mesa Verde out from under Kim.* We know that Chuck has sandbagged Jimmy in the past, but this is the first time we've seen him actively do it in an attempt to hurt Jimmy,† and in turn the first time we've seen our hero go full Slippin' Jimmy on his older brother.

What Jimmy does in transposing two digits of the address on every relevant document page is very clever as hustles go. It will look like an innocent mistake a low-level HHM staffer made that didn't get caught until it was too late—the sort of mistake that a single-client shop like Kim's might be less likely to make. But it's not something Kim asked Jimmy to do, or would have wanted. And if he actually succeeds in getting her the business back, it's going to be tainted for her. That huge smile on her face in the dental office is there because she did this, on her own, the way she wanted to—playing it clean. She didn't even engage in the resignation letter shenanigans Jimmy suggested, which are in an ethical gray area but in no way illegal, and she still won out. She wants to do it her way, and now Jimmy has put her in an unwitting position where she's doing things his way.

It's a much subtler stunt than what the production team does with the border crossing sequence, but both serve as potent reminders of how detail-oriented both *Better Call Saul* and its quasi-titular character are—and about how much harm can be done when someone's being as thorough as Jimmy McGill can be when he puts his mind to it.

---

* This is a great showcase episode for Michael McKean, as Chuck demonstrates that Jimmy isn't the only salesman in the family. The difference between the brothers is that Chuck is running a hustle that he wants his client to be aware of—the routine about banking law being a young person's game works because everyone in that conference room understands what Chuck is really saying, and in the most effective context—but there's still a lot of showmanship there from the guy who so often seems envious of Jimmy's gift of gab. It's also a nice touch that Chuck makes like a superhero right before the meeting, throwing off the space blanket like it's a cape.

† Howard never corrects Chuck's assumption that Kim and Jimmy are going to be part of the same practice, rather than simply sharing an office and expenses. It might have turned out to be a distinction without a difference as far as Chuck was concerned, but I also wonder if Howard might have said the bare minimum he needed to get Chuck's full support (if not his physical participation) in the campaign to keep Mesa Verde.

SEASON 2, EPISODE 9
WRITTEN AND DIRECTED BY PETER GOULD

"Nailed"

"But you're the one who made him this way." **—Kim**

Walter White has yet to appear on *Better Call Saul*, but his spirit very much hangs over it—not only because we know that Jimmy and Mike are both doomed to get tangled up in his business, but because we keep seeing them make the kinds of mistakes Walt made all the time on *Breaking Bad*.

This is particularly apparent in Season 2's penultimate chapter, "Nailed," where Jimmy and Mike stage crimes that each man believes will bring harm only to the guilty, but that instead go awry and do grave harm to three innocents. One incident is definitely fatal, as a Good Samaritan gets killed helping the trucker Mike robbed. One is emotionally brutal, as Kim discovers what Jimmy did to steal Mesa Verde back for her. And one ends on a note that could encompass both, when Chuck takes a nasty blow to the head as he collapses in the copy shop while trying to prove what Jimmy did. Walt's criminal turn was predicated on the idea that he could do it without hurting anyone, but it didn't take long for his willful ignorance to drown in the blood of his many victims. Here, two of his future partners learn the same nauseating lesson.

Let's start with Mike, the truck, and the dead Samaritan. For much of this episode, this is peak Ehrmantraut. He's ruthlessly efficient as he takes down the Salamanca truck all by his lonesome, in a way that's stunning to Nacho but makes perfect sense to those of us who know him better. The cash is nice—less for him than for Kaylee and Stacey—but it's clear by the end that his main goal was to hurt the man who would dare to threaten his adorable granddaughter, not only by stealing a quarter million from him, but by putting law enforcement on to the whole operation. But just as refusing to assassinate Tuco had the unintended consequence of bringing the full weight of House Salamanca down on him, Mike's reluctance to kill the truck driver results in a civilian's death instead—while also preventing the cops from getting wise to how Hector* gets his drugs across the border. It doesn't matter that we never so much as see the murdered man; Mike's response to learning the fatal consequence of another half-measure is all we need for it to hit incredibly hard.

The copy shop sequence, meanwhile, leaves things ambiguous about how bad Chuck's injury is, but that is a *bad* sound effect when his skull hits the edge

---

* While Mike is watching the ice cream joint, he sees Hector so full of rage that the kingpin seems on the verge of having a stroke. He takes a pill to calm the symptoms, but given what we know of Tio Hector's future, an incident is coming where his meds can't help (or perhaps won't be available).

of the table—one not dissimilar to when Ted Beneke got paralyzed running from Huell and Kuby on the parent show. But even in the event it's more minor than it appears at the moment, there's still the matter of Chuck having a very public meltdown in front of both witnesses and a co-worker, after already having lost his cool in front of the regulatory commission—both of which were entirely Jimmy's fault. Chuck has his ego, and will go to extremes to prove that he's right . . . but he is one hundred percent right at the copy shop, and the only reason he's wrong in front of Paige and the commission is that Jimmy altered the paperwork while Chuck was too ill to notice. As much as the show has successfully turned our sympathies against Chuck this season—for reasons articulated very well by Kim during the argument at his house—both of those scenes are stomach-churning, because our hero has put his mentally ill brother in a position to at least be embarrassed in public, if not worse.

As for Kim, she's physically okay, but you can see none of this is sitting well with her. She plays ignorant and loyal in the confrontation with Chuck to keep Jimmy* from going to jail. (It's a credit to Rhea Seehorn's continued spectacular work this season that you can tell Kim believes every word Chuck is saying even as she's ripping them all to shreds.) But she's not happy about getting the business back this way, nor about having her career and life tied to someone who keeps casually breaking the law even as he promises her that he won't. At first it seems like Jimmy is getting off lightly with those punches she delivers to his arm. Her warning to him about Chuck, though, is clearly delivered out of a desire to keep Jimmy from sleeping soundly after all the grief he's put her through. But first by covering for Jimmy, then fanning the flames of his own paranoia, Kim inadvertently put him in a position to drive Chuck past the boiling point, setting up the calamitous events at the copy shop.

It shouldn't be surprising at this point that this show, from these creators, can build so slowly and carefully toward the kinds of devastating payoffs that we get in "Nailed." But because it's so much fun to watch both Jimmy and Mike do what they do best, it can still sneak up on you how many awful things can happen when they're operating at peak capacity.

Not unlike their future collaborator.

---

* Before things get especially nasty between the brothers, there's an amusing piece of business—and a lovely visual homage to the cover of The Beatles' *Abbey Road* album—where Jimmy and his film crew scam their way onto an elementary school playground to get a shot of Jimmy standing in front of a giant American flag. Things almost go pear-shaped when Jimmy claims that singer-songwriter Rupert Holmes attended the school, while the makeup artist who's new to the team (played by Hayley Holmes, and referred to in scripts as "Drama Girl") points out that the man behind "Escape (The Piña Colada Song)" was English. The truth is more complicated—though born in England, Rupert Holmes spent much of his childhood in suburban New York—but all that matters is that Jimmy is able to talk his way into another great image for his new commercial.

SEASON 2, EPISODE 10
WRITTEN BY HEATHER MARION & VINCE GILLIGAN
DIRECTED BY VINCE GILLIGAN

"Klick"

"Well, you finally got me where you want me." —**Chuck**

Over the course of its first two seasons, *Better Call Saul* has essentially been two shows squeezed into one. The stories of Jimmy and Mike are joined in their accounting of how each man is traveling down a slippery moral slope that will eventually put them in business with one another, and then with Walter White. But they're often so separate in tone and supporting cast that it's a small miracle Gilligan and Gould are able to make it all feel coherent.

Rarely, though, has the contrast between the show's two halves looked starker than it does throughout "Klick," where Mike is deep in *Breaking Bad* country—to the point where his story for the season doesn't have a proper pay-off unless you assume a certain gentleman of poultry left that note on his windshield—while Jimmy's family drama is almost entirely free of any prequel qualities, where knowing about the other show only vaguely informs what's coming next on this one. Both halves are excellent—the Jimmy/Chuck conflict in particular—but one leans very heavily on *Breaking Bad* awareness, and the other barely at all.

Mike gets to take target practice with Lawson before attempting to assassinate Hector (as payback not only for threatening Kaylee, but for murdering a civilian because of what Mike did) while Nacho and the Cousins watch. This is gorgeous, tense material (who knew that Nacho's stillness would wind up being such a problem for Mike?), directed expertly by Vince Gilligan himself. But it's almost entirely a tease for what's coming next season, which all signs point to being Gustavo Fring.

Season 2 of *Breaking Bad* cleverly hid that year's denouement in the title of multiple episodes, which, placed together, combined to say "737 Down Over ABQ" (aka the plane crash that Walt inadvertently caused). The second season of *Saul* makes it a bit harder, but if you rearrange the first letters of each title, you get "FRINGS BACK." And there is no one else in the Heisenberg-verse who makes sense as the one who would interrupt Mike's plan. (The only other person we know from either show who might have an interest in saving Hector's life is Nacho, and he's there in the shack, oblivious to Mike and his trusty M40 rifle.) But if you don't have a murder board you use to look for hidden clues inside episode names—or if you're among the cohort of *Saul* viewers who never watched the other show—it's a slightly puzzling note to end that story on for the season.

Our knowledge of Jimmy's future* certainly informs aspects of what's happening with Chuck. No matter what evidence Chuck has gathered, Jimmy's not going to prison and he's not getting disbarred, given what comes later for him as Saul. But it's not really essential, because what's happening in the moment is so savage and so emotionally complicated.

It's remarkable how well the show has lived in moral and emotional grays with the two McGill brothers. Jimmy's the more likable one—Ernie provides him with an impromptu alibi because Jimmy's always been nicer to him—but he's also guilty of every crime Chuck has tagged him with regarding Mesa Verde. And even though he risks his freedom and livelihood by running into the copy shop to help Chuck, Jimmy still played a huge role in Chuck getting injured and having to endure another horrifying hospital trip.† As terrible as it is for us to see Chuck endure a condition that feels profoundly real to him, it's even worse because *Jimmy is the one who put him there*. Chuck is the judgmental ass whose suspicions keep nudging his brother into becoming Saul Goodman, but he's also correct about everything Jimmy has done, and the flashback that opens the episode suggests that Chuck has spent most of his life playing second fiddle to Jimmy, despite overwhelmingly being the good son for all those years.

The ambiguity about the brothers even extends to their work. Jimmy has turned out to have a brilliant legal mind, not that Chuck will ever fully recognize it. And in pretending his mental condition has worsened to goad Jimmy into confessing into a hidden tape recorder, Chuck has run a con as elegant as anything we've seen Slippin' Jimmy attempt.

In the end, though, it's hard for the show to not side with Jimmy, despite all his crimes. As he points out in their final argument, he never imagined Chuck would push things this far over Mesa Verde. And he repeatedly risked exposure, and worse, to help Chuck once the situation reached this dire physical and emotional point. Even though he doesn't know about the tape recorder, he still has to know that confessing to Chuck could keep Chuck on this vendetta, and he doesn't care, because it's the best way he knows to peel off the metaphorical space blanket and get Chuck living again.

---

* The final version of the commercial we watched him film over the previous episodes looks very much like a Saul Goodman ad, between the shamelessly jingoistic imagery and the rhyming slogan: "Gimme Jimmy!" instead of "Better call Saul!"

† Gilligan shoots it as something resembling an alien abduction video more than a hospital visit, keeping the camera upside-down for Chuck's time in the emergency room.

Jimmy has made protecting his brother from the world his top priority, while Chuck has chosen to protect the world from his brother at all costs. The show has thoroughly explained why each has come to feel that way, but it's hard not to take the side of the guy whose (fake) name is in the show's title, and who's so damn charming for all of his abundant flaws.

SEASON 3, EPISODE 1
WRITTEN BY VINCE GILLIGAN & PETER GOULD
DIRECTED BY VINCE GILLIGAN

"Mabel"

"For ten minutes today, Chuck didn't hate me. I forgot what that felt like."
—Jimmy

After another sad glimpse of the life of Cinnabon Gene, *Saul* Season 3 picks up moments after Season 2 left off, with Jimmy attempting to reconcile with Chuck after confessing to the Mesa Verde stunt. The emotional explosion is over, and Chuck has gotten what he wanted—more than Jimmy realizes, since Chuck secretly recorded the conversation. So the brothers seem at peace with one another, and quickly set about removing all the space blankets Chuck had duct-taped to the walls as part of the con he was running. But even a calm McGill family moment is only so calm, because of course Jimmy's method of removing the tape by yanking it off the wall annoys the finesse-oriented Chuck, who rolls it off slowly to avoid damaging the wood underneath.

This is the Jimmy/Chuck schism in a (wal)nutshell: one brother opting to do a job as quickly and easily as possible, the other insisting on doing it the right way, no matter how long it takes. And while *Better Call Saul*'s sympathies are almost entirely with the younger brother—despite frequent acknowledgments that Chuck is right about every suspicion he has regarding Jimmy—its methods are almost always on Chuck's side.

Even by the standards of *Saul*—or, for that matter, *Breaking Bad*—at its most drip-drippingly slow, "Mabel" is a deliberate episode. Its parallel Jimmy and Mike narratives each feature a scheme unfolding at a snail's pace, just to make sure we appreciate the patient, clever nature of the men preparing to execute their respective traps.

It's more extreme in the Mike half of the episode, in which more than thirteen combined minutes are devoted to a pair of dialogue-free scenes. In the first, Mike dismantles his station wagon in search of evidence that someone is tracking him. In the second, Mike turns the tables on the people following him by swapping out their tracker for his own.* This should be a ludicrous amount

---

* Because the latter sequence takes place at night, and because Mike doesn't have anyone to explain himself to, it's hard on first viewing to entirely make sense of what happened. The shortest possible version (which, like this entire subplot, isn't that short): using the duplicate tracker Dr. Caldera helps him procure, Mike realizes that the tracker hidden in his gas cap runs on a battery, that the receiver gets a warning when the battery is low, and that odds are greater that the people following him will

of time to simply watch a guy disassemble and reassemble equipment, but it never drags. We know Mike, that he doesn't say much even when he's around people he likes, that he is even more thorough than Chuck McGill dreams of being on his best day. On top of that, thanks to "FRINGS BACK," the between-seasons announcement that Giancarlo Esposito had agreed to reprise the role of Gus Fring, and the obviousness of who might have left the "Don't" note on Mike's windshield, we have a *prettttty* good idea who it was who planted the tracking device in the gas cap. And we know that the man in question is perhaps more detail-oriented than even Mike or Chuck. It would take Mike going to the kind of superhumanly meticulous lengths that an ordinary criminal (or, for that matter, cop) wouldn't to even find the tracker, much less figure out how to turn the situation to his advantage. (Even someone who figured out to open up the gas cap might just destroy the bug then and there, rather than let his unknown opponent continue to keep tabs on his movements.) And, because this matter sure seems to be poultry-related, there's a sense of delicious anticipation to the whole thing: the *Saul* writers are making us wait for Gus* because they know they can, and because they know we enjoy getting a step-by-step glimpse of how Mike (or Jimmy, or Walt, or . . .) manages to complete a single task. Gilligan built *Breaking Bad* atop "the in-between moments," and sequences like these take that approach to extremes without it feeling self-indulgent. Mike is a man at work, and this is everything he has to do to complete the unexpected task at hand.

The Jimmy/Chuck half of the episode isn't quite as patient, in part because we already saw Chuck arrange and spring the first phase of the trap in the Season 2 finale. But there's still more to it, which is made clear when Howard arrives at Chuck's house and points out the many reasons Chuck *can't* use the confession. Chuck McGill is a smug, imperious SOB whose suspicions of his brother's return to criminality are only hastening said return. But he's also very good at what he does, and we see other parts of the plan carefully slip out over the rest of the hour. At first, it seems like he has screwed up by letting

---

simply swap out the whole gas cap (with a new tracker) each time the battery needs changing, since that can be done in seconds, rather than the minute or more it would take to dismantle the cap, swap the battery (or tracker), reassemble the cap, and screw it back in. He puts the duplicate tracker, which he has the receiver for, into the car, then runs down the battery from the original tracker by using it to power his trusty transistor radio. When the battery runs low, he knows the people following him will come to replace it and drive off with what they think is their tracker, but is really his. Once they've come and gone, he hops into his sedan and follows from a safe distance, knowing he can use his receiver to keep tabs on their position. It's not as complicated as, say, Jesse figuring out what Huell did with his cigarettes, but it's still pretty wonky even for this franchise.

* At the end of Season 1, Peter Gould told me that they needed to get Mike deeper into the Albuquerque criminal world before it would make sense to reintroduce Gus: "What crimes has [Mike] committed in Albuquerque so far? So far, he facilitated one drug deal, armed with a pimento sandwich."

Ernie go anywhere near the tape recorder, but as we see from the satisfied look on his face, this is of course part of the whole scheme. Chuck knows from past experience that Ernie's loyalties are more to Jimmy than to him, and thus that Ernie will go tell Jimmy about the tape, which is now locked in a desk drawer and would require a blatantly illegal action for Jimmy to get his hands on.

The duct tape scene is fascinating because it feels completely honest in the midst of Chuck trying to out-hustle his hustler brother. Chuck even warns Jimmy at the end, "Don't think I'll ever forget what happened here today. And you will pay." And before that, the detente between the brothers doesn't feel like part of the scam. They have a complex relationship, those McGills. Both have done things to hurt the other, things that might seem unforgivable, yet there's a familial bond neither seems to entirely want to break. Jimmy is still hungry for Chuck's acceptance. Chuck in turn is able to compartmentalize the part of him determined to drum Jimmy out of the law business from the part of him that appreciates what's been done for him during his ailment. And for brief periods, Chuck can genuinely enjoy being in his brother's company, recalling childhood books and night lights before being reminded of all that's transpired between them of late, and all the jealousies and grievances he's harbored for a lifetime.

But just as Chuck is plotting to destroy the career of his brother, Jimmy can't let go of his resentment for the way Chuck has treated him for their entire lives. Instead of coming out in the presence of Chuck, though, Jimmy unleashes his repressed anger at Captain Bauer, the Air Force officer whom Jimmy conned in "Fifi" so he could film part of his commercial in front of the World War II bomber.* Bauer's a relative stranger, and his gripe with Jimmy is completely legitimate. Yet the high-handed indignation with which he scolds our title character can't help evoking similar sentiments expressed by Chuck McGill. And for a moment, Jimmy starts having a conversation with his brother rather than the angry man standing in front of him. It's a mark of just how much Chuck is in Jimmy's head at all times that he would let himself get so distracted while trying to get this crewcut out of his office before any real damage can be done.

The utter melancholy of our latest visit with Gene from Cinnabon only underlines what a terrible fate Jimmy's brother is steering him toward. Season 1 showed us that Gene is completely alone in his new life, while Season 2

---

* Bauer is played in both appearances by TV veteran Brendan Fehr. A different actor was initially cast in the role but got violently ill on the day of the "Fifi" shoot. Fortunately, NBC hospital drama *The Night Shift* was also filming in Albuquerque at the time, and Fehr's character on that show was a military veteran with the appropriate hairstyle. He rushed over and got into wardrobe, and then returned for this second episode a season later.

literalized the prison-like nature of the situation by locking him in a back room at the mall. The teaser in "Mabel," though, goes deeper, illustrating how becoming Gene has forced our man to turn his back on everything that made him Saul Goodman—or, for that matter, Jimmy McGill. Gene is anonymous, reserved, getting along fine with his employees, but not the life of the party he always fancied himself as. And when his lonely lunch break happens to intersect with a shoplifter's attempt to evade both a mall cop and a real cop, he finds himself forced to turn rat just to stay invisible himself. In that moment, he could perhaps stay silent and hope that the kid makes a clean getaway while his pursuers are looking elsewhere. But given the guy's clumsy inexperience, the odds are much higher that he'll be caught, and then the officers might wonder why a mall store manager in good standing wouldn't help them catch a criminal. Ed the disappearance expert may do excellent work, but the identity of Gene would probably not stand up to close scrutiny, and our man knows he can't do anything to invite it . . .

. . . but it so obviously pains him to meekly assist law enforcement that he's unable to stop Saul Goodman from making a brief return from the dead, just long enough to warn the kid to shut up and ask for a lawyer. This is the exact wrong thing he should do in the moment. While odds are that no more comes of it beyond the mall cop calling Gene "asshole," the chance that he's exposed himself to something much worse, and the internal struggle between Gene and Saul/Jimmy, does such a number on him that Gene passes out minutes later:* a response to the enormous stress and misery he endures every day by being someone he's not. Once upon a time, Slippin' Jimmy loved slippin' into another role. But that was always temporary, and usually with the promise of a payoff at the end of it. Cinnabon Gene isn't a con, though; it's his life, and a life he's been consigned to through a combination of his own terrible choices and the almost violent mistrust visited upon him by his brother over the years.

It's bad enough knowing that the mostly well-meaning Jimmy McGill will soon become the amoral Saul Goodman. But to know that both men end up as . . . *this* feels particularly tragic. By the standards of what happened to many other people in Heisenberg's orbit, it may not seem so awful. But understanding what we now do so well about Jimmy/Saul/Gene, this at times appears to be a fate worse than death.

---

* The fall looks not unlike Chuck's copy shop collapse late in Season 2, albeit without Gene's skull striking the counter on the way down.

SEASON 3, EPISODE 2
WRITTEN BY THOMAS SCHNAUZ
DIRECTED BY VINCE GILLIGAN*

"Witness"

"Can I help you?" —Gus Fring

Continuing to treat patience as perhaps the greatest virtue of all, *Saul* Season 3 follows up the two lengthy Mike-at-work sequences from "Mabel" with an episode that in many ways feels even more meticulous. But instead of demonstrating Mike's thoroughness, this time the goal is to build anticipation for the grand re-entrance of Mike's future boss.

Like the Season 2 letter jumble promised, Fring's back! But "Witness" makes the audience wait for him for quite some time.

After a teaser establishing that Chuck has hired a private investigator to stay in the house while they wait for Jimmy to make a false move about the incriminating tape, we're back in Ehrmantraut country. Over about nine minutes—again, an unheard-of amount of time for a TV episode to devote to a sequence where barely anyone talks—we watch Mike follow the goons who are unwittingly carrying his own tracking device, then follow the next man up in the organizational ladder as he goes about his rounds, then continue on to that man's final stop, which is gradually revealed to be the flagship restaurant of Los Pollos Hermanos, the fried chicken chain established as a front business by our old friend Gustavo Fring.

And then, after a stopover in lawyer world, where Jimmy impulsively hires Francesca Liddy† from New Mexico's Motor Vehicle Division to work as his and Kim's receptionist, "Witness" continues to take its sweet, finger-licking-good time getting us to the Chicken Man. Mike recruits Jimmy, who is not on the radar of this organization, to go inside the restaurant and keep an eye out for what the courier does with his bag on his morning visits. This sequence runs more than five minutes between the time Jimmy walks in the

---

*   After helping to break the Season 3 stories with Peter Gould and the rest of the writing staff, and directing that year's first two episodes, Gilligan ceded showrunner responsibilities for *Saul* entirely to Peter Gould, so he could focus on developing other projects. (One of which turned out to be the *Breaking Bad* sequel film *El Camino*.) He would return periodically to direct and help break stories, but this was the end of his day-to-day involvement in the show until the final season.

†   That's Tina Parker, reprising her *Breaking Bad* role as Francesca, whose disposition while in the employ of Saul Goodman is decidedly less upbeat than what we see here.

door and when we can first glimpse Giancarlo Esposito's* familiar trim silhouette slightly out of focus in the background, and more than seven minutes from Jimmy's entrance to when Gus speaks the first words we've heard from his mouth since Walter White and Hector Salamanca blew off half of that mouth on the other show. In between, all that happens is Jimmy and other customers ordering food, and Jimmy getting the lay of the land without trying to make his interest in the courier too obvious.

This should feel tedious or, even worse, like obnoxiously showing off. Instead, Thomas Schnauz's script and Vince Gilligan's direction throughout feel delightfully tense. The episode evokes the old Alfred Hitchcock line about how surprise is having a bomb explode under a table without warning, while suspense is showing the bomb under the table at the beginning of a scene, then making the audience wait for the moment when it will explode. In this case, the bomb is Gus, whose stature and ability are such that he seems about to completely blow up the power dynamic in the Mike half of the show. And "Witness" takes great pleasure, and demonstrates great filmmaking craft, in building the tension of exactly when and how Gus will appear, and also whether there will be a rewriting of what we knew on *Breaking Bad* about Saul Goodman not knowing Gus at the time he hooked Walt up with him.

The whole scene is wonderfully assembled, starting with that big sweep around the restaurant, which both reacquaints us with the place and leaves us wondering if the camera might just whiz right past Gus himself. Then we're watching Jimmy watching the man with the backpack, and everyone else, for such a long time that it's fair to wonder if this will become another tease. And when Gus finally speaks, it's at an unexpected moment where we're watching Jimmy dive through the trash can in the event the backpack guy dumped something there. When last we saw Gus, he was in pieces, and now he is being reintroduced in piecemeal fashion: first as a blurry background figure, then as an off-screen voice, and finally as the superhumanly polite, fastidious, secretive man himself.

It's not quite the master class in making the audience hold its breath that Gus's arrival at the Super Lab in the "Box Cutter" episode of *Breaking Bad* was,

---

* Esposito first gained attention as a member of Spike Lee's repertory company of actors, most notably as the abrasive, idealistic Buggin' Out in 1989's *Do the Right Thing*. Born in Copenhagen to an Italian father and a Black mother, Esposito was cast as many ethnicities, and many wildly different kinds of characters, in the busy quarter century of work before he landed his signature role as Gus Fring. As Peter Gould recalls, the *Breaking Bad* producers were pleasantly surprised that an actor of Esposito's stature was willing to audition. When they watched his tape, they didn't even recognize him at first, but, "His interpretation was so different from anyone else's, in that he was just so restrained, and so quiet that you just couldn't take your eyes off him. As soon as we laid eyes on him, he was the guy."

simply because the stakes here are nowhere near as high. But it's a similar example of how Gilligan and company use their powers of manipulation for good, not evil. And it manages to create an encounter between this show's title character and its huge new addition without violating what we've been told is the history between the two men, or forcing the show to retcon it so that Saul was lying to Walt at the time when he framed his knowledge of Gus as, "I know a guy who knows a guy . . . who knows another guy." Jimmy McGill can have met local businessman Gustavo Fring without having any idea that he's one of the region's biggest drug traffickers. He sees the cheerful and solicitous middle manager, not the cold and steely kingpin who reveals his true face only when no one is looking.*

As beautiful as the reveal of Gus himself is, the earlier shot of Mike driving away from his surveillance of the restaurant, with the camera slowly pulling back to reveal the Los Pollos Hermanos sign for the first time, is at least as artful, if not more. Again, we have a pretty good idea who's been bugging Mike, and the glimpse of the restaurant itself is a huge clue just in case. But for now we know more than Mike does, and the patient unveiling of the sign, and this confirmation of our suspicions, feels as if it should be accompanied by an orchestral fanfare and the dropping of a curtain. *Saul* could have gotten to the sign, and Gus, much more quickly, but the occasion warrants a proper buildup, the presence of both the sign and man felt so much more exciting and cathartic as a result of how Schnauz and Gilligan made us wait for each.

The Gus story also gives us something of a Mike/Jimmy role reversal since Mike has to use Jimmy as *his* investigator lest he risk exposure inside the restaurant. It's a fun tweak on their usual relationship, and a good excuse to put the show's two leading men together for a few minutes, even as their story arcs are diverging more and more.

Jimmy's half of the show, in fact, is where the bigger "Witness" events happen, relatively speaking. Yes, it's huge to see Gus again, but that story is still in set-up mode, and the more relevant meeting of Mike and Gus hasn't even happened yet.

As was implied in the "Mabel" scene where Chuck smirked after Ernie listened to the recording, the plan here is to nail Jimmy for the cover-up, rather than for the original crime with Mesa Verde. Howard explained in the premiere that the tape was inadmissible in any kind of court or hearing and wouldn't even help them win Mesa Verde back, but Chuck created it solely as bait to get Jimmy to do something stupid. "Howard, I know my brother," he

---

* And in a neat inverse of his introductory shot: now Gus is in the foreground, while Jimmy's car is barely in focus, recognizable only because we know what the Esteem looks like.

boasts, and while he's proven instantly wrong on the specific point he was making about Jimmy making his move at night, he is proven right overall beyond his wildest dreams when Jimmy doesn't just storm into the house without permission, doesn't just use force to vandalize both Chuck's locked desk drawer and the cassette itself, but threatens to burn Chuck's house to the ground, all while Howard and David the detective (the eponymous witness) are listening from the next room.

This is a huge jackpot Jimmy has stepped into, against both Kim's better judgment and his own. He knows this is a terrible idea—even if he couldn't conceive of his straight-arrow brother running one con on top of another, given his disbelief and rage that Chuck ran the first one at all—and so he stays at work, trying to remove the masking tape from his fancy new office logo (an abstract mash-up of Kim's last initial and his) in the painstakingly slow way Chuck tried to teach him with Chuck's improvised foil wallpaper. He has tried to do everything in his life of late the right way, and even the Mesa Verde stunt was him doing a bad thing for what seemed like a good reason, since he felt Kim had been unfairly squeezed out of the account by her big ex-firm. But Chuck McGill does, indeed, know his brother, and knows that Jimmy can only resist his worst impulses for so long—even if much of Chuck's own recent behavior and refusal to believe in Jimmy's goodness has led to their current circumstances. Soon enough, Jimmy is back to yanking the tape off the wall, leaving a blur in his perfect jagged line* as he rushes out to meet his doom, so wounded about what Chuck has done that he can't think straight, and so indignant that he would not only threaten to burn down the house, but throw some especially dark shade at his brother about why Rebecca left him.

Chuck would seem to have Jimmy dead to rights here, having played this out so carefully that even Mike Ehrmantraut would be impressed. But we know from *Breaking Bad* that Jimmy is still practicing law six years later in Albuquerque, just under a different name, and his ads are so ubiquitous around town that there would be no way for him to be doing it without Chuck's knowledge. But even though we understand that Jimmy/Saul will wiggle out of this somehow, a line has been crossed. There's no going back from this, and the likable elder-law attorney we've come to know so well will soon be turning into the guy who will one day do business with Gus Fring that goes much deeper than the matter of a wristwatch in a garbage can.

---

* Though, as Kim points out, the line was already "a little crooked," which seems about right for her man.

SEASON 3, EPISODE 3
WRITTEN BY GENNIFER HUTCHISON
DIRECTED BY JOHN SHIBAN

"Sunk Costs"

"You know, Jimmy has a good heart." —**Chuck**

Sometimes, *Breaking Bad* or *Saul* cold opens reveal what they're about before the main title sequence plays. Others are more abstract, only coming into clear focus later on. "Sunk Costs" begins with one of the latter type, a series of lingering images at a desert road intersection south of the border, where a pair of badly faded old sneakers hangs from a cable, swinging idly above a bullet-riddled Stop/Alto sign, a Los Pollos Hermanos cargo truck passing through right before the sneakers' laces finally fall apart after a long period of enduring friction and sun damage, sending the shoes floating through the air like Walter White's khakis. The images are pretty, but in the moment, it makes no more sense than, say, the *Breaking Bad* episode that opened with Jesse's car bouncing up and down outside of Tuco's hideout, or the one where we saw poor Drew Sharp collecting spiders in the desert.

By episode's end, the image is more or less complete. The sneakers were thrown up there by Mike* as part of a convoluted but clever plan (more on that in a bit) to get one of Hector Salamanca's trucks stopped at the border, and have simply hung there ever since, long enough to be bleached by exposure to the sun, and for this particular drug route to be taken over by Mike's new enemy-of-his-enemy Gus Fring. How far into the future is this? Well, we know that Gus's empire is still in business six years after the events of this episode, and we know how the Gus/Hector rivalry ends (and then ends again), if not all of the steps on the way there. The transition from one of Hector's ice cream trucks to Gus's chicken trucks is happening, and now we're getting to watch exactly how that happened.

With the Mike/Gus half of the show, we have pretty much the entire big picture. All that's left are the individual details, like when and how Hector winds up in a wheelchair (a chair not much fancier than the one we see in the free clinic where Gus's personal physician helps Mike procure the "yea big" package of drugs he needs to pull off the sneaker stunt) and Mike's rise from

---

* According to Gennifer Hutchison, this was not a repeat of the famous roof pizza shot from *Breaking Bad*, where Bryan Cranston actually managed to fling the thing onto the roof of the White house. The final scene is a mix of Jonathan Banks in motion, stunt work, and special effects. "Those wires are high!" she says.

Fring organization outsider to Gus's number two man above the likes of Victor and Tyrus. And it's a lot of fun to watch, from the way director John Shiban shoots the first meeting between Mike and Gus with as much majesty as the desert outside Albuquerque has to offer, to the way Jonathan Banks keeps being able to deliver entire monologues' worth of emotional information in the way he flexes his jaw—first when he realizes that Gus has him boxed in on the matter of Hector, then after he has made the tricky shot necessary for the sneaker plan to work. The sneaker scene isn't quite as elongated as some of the other Mike process sequences from this season, but it's a smart plan, nonetheless. Mike keeps firing the M40 into the air to convince Hector's men that the shots are from nearby hunters, so they won't even notice the sound when he finally shoots at the sneakers, contaminating the truck enough that the customs dogs will be alerted.

Where the series has more narrative wiggle room—and where, perhaps not coincidentally, it's at its most dramatically interesting at the moment—is in what happens to Jimmy between now and when Walt and Jesse walk into his office. We know a lot, including the fact that Chuck won't be successful in getting him disbarred. But there are many ways to get there, and a lot of them involve the state of his relationships with both Chuck and Kim.

By this point in the series' run, *Saul* fandom had largely turned on Chuck as a pompous villain. The show aims for more ambiguity with his behavior, since he's ultimately correct about what Jimmy will do with a law degree, even if Chuck's own actions help push him there. But his first scene in this episode is about as odious as he's ever been:* so secure in his victory over Jimmy that he can afford to play the role of the protective older brother, delivering one patronizing theory after another about how Jimmy is much better off this way. He's feeling his oats so much, in fact, that he doesn't even seem to notice that he's standing out in the harsh New Mexico sunlight, with no space blanket to protect him, without ill effects of any kind, even as Jimmy explains that Chuck will likely die alone the next time he has a bad attack, given their estrangement. For a moment in his conversation with the new prosecutor, it seems Chuck might be softening toward his brother, but it's all just part of the whole scam, as he nudges her in a direction that would keep Jimmy from serving any prison time, but surely result in his disbarment.

It's a chastened Jimmy who sits on the curb, smoking an ancient cigarette while waiting for the police to come. It's a chastened Jimmy who tells Chuck

---

* Chuck also fires Ernie even though Ernie *did exactly what he needed him to do* for the hustle to work. Yes, on paper Ernie's loyalties being to Jimmy creates trust issues for Chuck, but HHM is a really big firm; assign the poor guy elsewhere and give him a pass as thanks for the huge favor he unwittingly did you!

how he'll die, not out of spite, but out of sadness that their rift has led to this point, because despite it all, he still cares for his brother far more deeply than Chuck cares for him. It's a chastened Jimmy who doesn't want Kim representing him at his arraignment and seems embarrassed to talk to her about it at all. Gone, for the moment, is Gimme Jimmy the showman, or Slippin' Jimmy the con artist, because he knows how badly he blew this, and how much it can hurt not only himself but the woman he cares about. Bob Odenkirk does some wonderfully small, calibrated work as Jimmy tries to make this right without troubling anyone further. Even the apologetic speech he gives Kim seems on paper like the kind he's delivered many times over the years—usually to Chuck—but his heart's not really in it. That Kim is so cool to him—not cruel, but not making any effort at all to engage after being sent away during the arraignment—for most of the episode only seems to increase Jimmy's mortification.

Kim should, by this point, know better when it comes to Jimmy, but she cares about him too much—and still has a weakness for his shenanigans, as evidenced by the return of their Viktor and Giselle pseudonyms in the closing scene—to let him flail about on his own, even if that's what he wants. Near the end, she cites the eponymous fallacy of sunk costs, where you keep pouring more and more resources into a mistake rather than admitting failure and moving on. But that's just her covering for her genuine and inescapable feelings for her boyfriend and business semi-partner, and Rhea Seehorn and Odenkirk's chemistry is particularly palpable in that tender moment.

That scene concludes with one of the most distinct, lovely, and perhaps very telling images of the entire series so far, as the two partners (in every way but the official one) appear as silhouettes up against the glass blocks outside Kim's office,* holding hands in a way that makes their bodies appear to be spelling the letter M. *Saul* doesn't do images like that by accident, and that happens to be the first letter of the McGill family name—a name we know our main character will be abandoning sooner or later. For now, though, he's Jimmy McGill, and he's more complicated and compelling than any of us could have expected.

---

* When he asks a worried Francesca to drive him to the car that got left behind at Chuck's after his arrest, Jimmy assures her it's not always like this at the office. By the time of *Breaking Bad*, she'll be so used to craziness and extra-legal shenanigans that she'll have no problem at all extorting Walter White for $25,000 even as Saul has bolted to hide out for the remainder of the Walt/Gus war.

"Sabrosito"

"Perhaps in the future, you will consider working for me." —**Gus**
"Could be. That'd depend on the work." —**Mike**

As Mike has gotten deeper into cartel world over the last season and change, it's worth asking a simple question: Why is he still working as Saul Goodman's investigator six years from now, when he has a very busy, lucrative, and low-profile job as Gus Fring's number two man? Will we eventually see Jimmy/Saul do him such an important favor that Mike will feel indebted to him for years? Will Gus encourage him to maintain the relationship so Mike can be better plugged into what's happening in Albuquerque's criminal underbelly? Will Mike need some kind of front job to disguise some of his income? Or does Mike Ehrmantraut, deep down in places he doesn't like to talk about at parties, like this guy enough that he'd look for excuses to hang out with him?

Many of those theories are improbable—Mike has a police pension to live on and squirrels his Gus money away for Kaylee, and he's not a good enough actor to hide his feelings about Jimmy—but "Sabrosito" offers us a more plausible theory: Mike never really wanted to work for Gus, took the job because the money was just too good, but liked having an opportunity to occasionally not feel like a drug kingpin's enforcer.

We get hints of this over the course of a fascinatingly bifurcated episode. For much of its run, *Saul* has been split into the Jimmy show and the Mike show, with occasional intersections. With "Sabrosito," it's instead the Gus show and the Jimmy show, and there's barely any cutting back and forth: a half hour with Gus, then a half hour with Jimmy, with Mike popping up in both halves. (There is one Gus/Mike scene in the second half, but it's brief.) Mike isn't thrilled to be involved with either man. He refuses to accept the cash that Gus wants to pay him for the sneaker stunt, and is only working for Jimmy again as a quid pro quo for Jimmy doing recon at Los Pollos Hermanos (and barely speaks to him at all while focusing on his diner breakfast). But going undercover as a handyman at Chuck's house at least feels closer to police work than when he's robbing drug shipments and playing desert sniper. Plus, the specific undercover role has a bonus: "Nice to fix something, for once."*

---

* Mike finally meets the other McGill brother, albeit in a circumstance where neither man can take each other's true measure. In many ways, Mike has much more in common with Chuck than with Jimmy,

Mike is extremely wary of going into business with Gus Fring—and he's right to be, given what we know about how all of this ends for him. It's not just about being conservative and safe, but about the fact that, even as someone who went vigilante to kill a pair of dirty cops, he still considers himself separate from these drug dealers for whom he does occasional work. That separation is easier when you're a freelance bodyguard for an amateur like Daniel Wormald, harder when an obvious professional like Gus is trying to bring you into the fold. When Mike spends an evening with Stacey and Kaylee, even Stacey can see that something is wearing on him. His involvement with Nacho put his family in danger, got a civilian killed, and put him into contact with heavyweights like Hector and Gus. This isn't the life he seems to want, even if he's so obviously good at it that the careful Gus would offer him a job after only two meetings.

"Sabrosito" is the first time Mike's side gig as Saul's investigator starts to make sense. This is a situation where the writers are having to reconcile decisions they made long ago without realizing what would happen down the line: Mike only exists in the first place because Bob Odenkirk was busy when the *Breaking Bad* Season 2 finale was being filmed, and somebody had to help Jesse with the immediate aftermath of Jane's death. It wasn't until later that Gilligan and company decided that Mike was also working for (and was ultimately loyal to) Gus. So that is now a problem for *Better Call Saul* to solve, however that ultimately happens.

Having Mike appear in both halves of the episode does a better than usual job of unifying the two worlds of *Saul*, even as the episode is so blatantly cleaved down the middle. The Gus half feels more or less like the show that many *Breaking Bad* diehards seemed to want when *Better Call Saul* was first announced: a more straightforward prequel, set firmly in the drug game, with lots of criminal intrigue, a plethora of Walter White villains* and henchmen, and a more direct link to the rise and fall of Heisenberg. It's certainly fun to see Don Eladio and Juan Bolsa again, to see Gus trying to outplay a man like Hector who respects none of the rules of the game, and to see Gus, like Walt, have to protect his secret identity through the elaborate and very sincere-sounding lie he tells his employees after Hector and his men invade the restaurant.

---

since the two older men share a similar determination to do a job the right way, or not at all. Yet Chuck's patrician manner might ultimately be more of a turnoff to Mike than Jimmy's shamelessness.

* The episode-opening scene brings Don Eladio, Hector, and Juan Bolsa together for the first time since we saw them in the flashback from "Hermanos," the *Breaking Bad* episode where Hector executed Gus's partner Max. Director Thomas Schnauz frames a lot of moments to evoke shots from "Hermanos." And, as was the case in that earlier episode, Hector is still convinced that Gus and Max were lovers, dismissively referring to Los Pollos Hermanos as "The Butt Brothers."

Certainly, it's not hard to imagine a full-on *The Chicken Man Cometh* approach to the material working, even just for the telling little moments like Gus tossing the tin foil ball into the trash can. It's a show-off move he would never even consider if anyone else were around to see it, because it flies against both of his assumed identities as the impeccable and polite restaurateur* and as the colder drug lord. That one move suggests that the "real" Gus is someone else entirely, who has been hidden from view of the world because it would be bad for both businesses. There is so much the show could unpack here, if it was of a mind to do so.

And yet even with all of that, the show just feels more vibrant when Kim pops up midway through, working the phones again as she tries to find the repair company Chuck has contracted to fix the door. There's less potential for explosions or magic bullets or decapitated heads on tortoises, but there's so much life in Jimmy and Kim's relationship—and the way that they're essentially playing Viktor and Giselle as they prepare to undo Chuck's hustle with one of their own—so much electricity in every encounter between the brothers, and so much more room for the series to maneuver overall, because it's less bound by things we know from *Breaking Bad*. When Jimmy and Kim march out of the courthouse together, matching each other stride for stride with the confidence of having successfully baited a hook with Chuck, it's even more exciting than when Gus appeared at the edge of the frame while Jimmy was at Los Pollos Hermanos.

It's easy to understand why Mike doesn't like Jimmy McGill. But it's also becoming easier and easier to understand why he might want to keep a toe in this guy's world even as he takes a different job for Gus. Mike's a grump, but even he has to see at least some of the appeal we can in being on Jimmy's side of things.

---

* The fire station Gus is visiting (akin to his glad-handing of the DEA and local law enforcement on *Breaking Bad*) is the same one where Walt will leave baby Holly at the end of "Ozymandias."

SEASON 3, EPISODE 5
WRITTEN BY GORDON SMITH
DIRECTED BY DANIEL SACKHEIM

"Chicanery"

"I am not crazy!" —**Chuck**

Following an episode split evenly between cartel world and lawyer world, "Chicanery" takes place entirely in the latter arena. Mike, Gus, Nacho, and all the other major criminal players take the episode off,* while we get a convincing argument for how riveting *Saul* can be when it's just about Jimmy McGill and the two people he cares most about in all the world. Nothing blows up, no one gets shot, and there aren't any long montages of Mike disassembling heavy machinery. But it's arguably the best, most exciting, most satisfyingly plotted episode of the entire series to this point—and would be even if Jimmy and Kim's plan hadn't required the services of our favorite snoring pickpocket, Huell Babineaux.

It's a pretty efficient hour, taking place almost entirely in one room at the courthouse. As Kim explains it to the representatives of the state bar association, what the matter comes down to is a dispute between brothers: one brilliant and cultured and respectable, but also resentful and petty and arrogant and cruel; the other a well-meaning charmer with a weakness for doing what is easy over what is right. Jimmy and Kim aren't disputing the facts of the case, because they can't: another copy of the cassette tape exists, and Howard and the private investigator witnessed Jimmy's crimes. All they can do is get the bar committee to view his actions in a more flattering context than the one Chuck is presenting.

And that's where the fun, and drama, begins.

Like most of Jimmy's best cons, the hustle that he and Kim run on Chuck is built on a foundation of truth. Jimmy does care deeply for his brother—far more than his brother cares for him—and he did make that confession as a way to pull Chuck out of the spiral he seemed to be in after the copy shop incident. And Chuck's condition *is* a mental illness—Jimmy has seen more than enough evidence of that in the past—that the world has indulged him in because he's rich and smart and charismatic enough to keep them from questioning the true nature of his "sensitivity." All of this is true. It's also true, of course, that

---

*   Mike is at least alluded to, as the friend who points Jimmy to Dr. Caldera, who in turn hooks Jimmy up with Huell.

Jimmy did alter the Mesa Verde documents so that HHM would lose the account to Kim, that he still has no regrets about this serious crime, and that with his background, his attitude, and what we know about his future, he has absolutely no business being licensed to practice law in this or any other state. But all Jimmy and Kim* have to do is make the committee see Chuck for what he is: a mentally ill man obsessed with preventing his brother from practicing law, no matter what.

The chicanery of the title involves layering cons on top of cons, because Chuck McGill is understandably conditioned to expect a certain degree of hustle from Jimmy at any time. The arrival of Chuck's ex-wife Rebecca,† for instance, is greeted smugly by him because he assumes Jimmy is doing a variation of the Frankie Pentangeli gambit from *The Godfather Part II*, where Michael Corleone foiled Frankie's attempt to testify against the family by bringing Frankie's brother over from Italy and into the courtroom, unnerving the duplicitous wiseguy into silence.

Jimmy *is* running the Pentangeli to a degree, because he knows Rebecca's presence—and her discovery of the condition that Chuck went to great lengths to hide from her, with Jimmy's assistance—will agitate Chuck and make him more primed to explode when evidence is presented of what the condition actually is. But she's there primarily to trigger that condescending response from Chuck—to convince him that he's once again two steps ahead of his brother, that Chuck's brilliant legal mind will always be more powerful than Jimmy's con-man brain, and that if Chuck is prepared for a hustle to come, it can't possibly work.

For that matter, that's what the stunt with Huell's nimble fingers,‡ Jimmy's cell phone battery, and Chuck's breast pocket is all about. Jimmy primes Chuck by doing the more obvious, elementary version: a cell phone hidden in

---

* The episode builds, as it should, to a showdown between the brothers. But it's fascinating to see how committed Kim is to this defense strategy, since she knows what Jimmy did with the documents. She never lies in the hearing, never tries to claim that Jimmy didn't do something that he did. But she's also ready to push the outer edge of the ethical envelope, until it's just at the point of ripping, to pursue a rigorous defense of her client. It's not quite what Saul Goodman would do, but it's closer than we might have expected Kim Wexler to get when we first met her. She cares for Jimmy, and he's rubbing off on her, enough for her to do this, rather than playing things straighter.

† The episode opens with a flashback to Rebecca returning to Albuquerque after what appears to have been an amicable split with Chuck. He wants to keep his condition—which arose after the divorce, and perhaps because of it—hidden from her. (This makes Jimmy inviting her to the hearing yet another betrayal of one sibling by the other.) To maintain the ruse, Chuck claims the power company mistakenly turned off his electricity because of a transposition of numbers in an address—the exact same move Jimmy used as part of the con to steal Mesa Verde out from under him.

‡ Actor Lavell Crawford lost more than 100 pounds after the end of *Breaking Bad*, making this version of Huell not only younger, but noticeably svelter.

his own jacket when everyone else had allowed theirs to be confiscated. Only it's a phone without a battery, because *of course* Chuck would have noticed the battery, given his electromagnetic hypersensitivity. It makes Jimmy look desperate and weak, and lets Chuck feel in utter domination of his kid brother . . .

. . . and *that* is when Jimmy reveals the trick hidden inside the other trick. Chuck has to be both exasperated and utterly assured of his victory to explode the way he does when Jimmy presents Howard (his longtime partner), Rebecca (the woman he still deeply loves), and the committee (the representatives of the institution that he has just referred to as "mankind's greatest achievement") with incontrovertible evidence that he does not suffer from some rare, exotic, largely undiscovered but totally legitimate physical ailment that will one day be studied in medical texts just like HIV or diabetes, and that the hypersensitivity is all in his head. Chuck is convinced the hearing is about to end in utter humiliation for Jimmy, but instead he's the humiliated party, and he responds with an explosion of ancient grievances that—while almost certainly true in every instance—serves to paint him in exactly the light that Jimmy and Kim intended: as a sick, irrational, bitter individual whom Jimmy was only trying to help.* And, for that matter, as someone who seems no more fit to continue practicing law than he insists Jimmy is.

It's not just the case that's ruined in this moment, but Chuck McGill himself. You can see it on the faces of the committee members, Howard, and Rebecca. He might not get disbarred, might not get committed, might not suffer any disciplinary action at all for that outburst. But his reputation is forever altered now and made worse because he has spent so much time and energy trying to convince the world that his condition is real, and that his brother is a no-good hustler. He protested too much, for too long, and now it has all come back to make him look very small, very petty, and very sick in a way that he cannot abide looking.

It's a stunning moment, beautifully shot by director Daniel Sackheim, who keeps pushing the camera in until Chuck is ranting about nine-year-old Jimmy stealing from the cash drawer, then pulls way back out to make Chuck look as tiny and weak as he feels after realizing what he's just done to himself— with help from the brother he once again underestimated.

Yet it doesn't play like a joyous triumph for our heroes because *Saul* is a smarter and more nuanced show than that. This is a cruel thing Jimmy has done to his brother—who, again, is a condescending ass, but is also *right* about

---

* This is less a case of Jimmy Loves Movies than *Better Call Saul* Loves Movies: In addition to the implied *Godfather Part II* reference with Rebecca, Chuck's meltdown is very much modeled on Humphrey Bogart's Captain Queeg rambling about strawberries and imaginary keys in the climax of 1954's *The Caine Mutiny*.

so much of this, including Mesa Verde—and Jimmy and Kim both know it's cruel, and knew it would be even as they were doing it. It's the only way Jimmy can keep practicing law after the stunts he pulled, and Chuck has been inviting this level of comeuppance. But still . . . he's Jimmy's brother, and Jimmy loves him despite all of what's happened. It's a victory, and a tragedy, all rolled into one, and an incredible payoff to an episode that just lets the tension build and build as we wait to see exactly what the plan was, until it all explodes right when we can't take it anymore.

Sackheim closes the hour by focusing on the hearing room's red exit sign. To everyone else, this is something we pass every day without noticing. And earlier, it was something that Chuck insisted wouldn't bother him, as the only electrical object in the room that couldn't be turned off (due to the fire code). Here, though, in this moment of abject mortification, the sign seems impossibly large to Chuck, its electrical hum the only thing in his ears, taunting him all the more because he now has such overwhelming evidence that its effects on him aren't real. It's all he can focus on, just as "Chicanery" so potently forces out all thought of the parts of *Better Call Saul* that don't involve the brothers and their partners.

It's been so much fun to spend time this season at Los Pollos Hermanos, to see Jonathan Banks and Giancarlo Esposito do what they do so well together, and to be surprised by additional *Breaking Bad* cameos. But there was a reason Vince Gilligan and Peter Gould decided to make Saul, and not Mike or Gus, the main character when they began building this spin-off. And Bob Odenkirk, Rhea Seehorn, and Michael McKean have more than justified that decision. The drug lord side of the show is wildly entertaining. The Jimmy McGill side is special, and "Chicanery" is an instant classic.

SEASON 3, EPISODE 6
WRITTEN BY ANN CHERKIS
DIRECTED BY KEITH GORDON

"Off Brand"

"That guy has a lot of energy." —**Kim**

Prequels are bound by the what, but not always by the when, why, and how. Certain events are inevitable, but the way they happen makes all the difference between the bad prequels and the good ones. Two and a half seasons in, *Better Call Saul* has already made its case as one of the greatest prequels ever—depending on how you define *The Godfather Part II*, or Vince Gilligan's treasured *The Good, the Bad, and the Ugly*, it might be *the* greatest—and a lot of that comes from how clever Gilligan, Peter Gould, and company have been in adding compelling, surprising context to developments we all know about already.

The show's most important point of inevitability, given the name and how its protagonist started out, is Jimmy McGill's transformation into Saul Goodman. It generated theory after theory from all the *Breaking Bad* fans who had happily come to the new show. How would it happen? When? Why? Would it be when he put on Marco's fateful pinky ring at the end of the first season? Would Chuck's quest to drum his brother out of the legal profession lead to a name change as a compromise? Would *this* be the week? How about this one?

Leave it to this ever-surprising series to introduce its title character in a manner no one could have possibly expected: as a moniker Jimmy improvises while filming a last-second ad for his new business producing local television commercials.

We've seen in the past that Jimmy likes the phrase "s'all good, man," and also that he takes enormous pleasure in writing and producing his legal ads, so it all fits with what we know. But it's a hilariously obscure and low-key way to introduce the name and the persona, especially with the way Rhea Seehorn plays Kim's stunned reaction to this man her boyfriend has become— temporarily, she thinks, even if we unfortunately know better.

"Off Brand" actually lays the groundwork for a lot of the transformation from Jimmy McGill—dutiful brother, happy elder-care lawyer, a man who tries to do things the right way as much as he can—into the more unapologetically slick and amoral criminal lawyer we first got to know so well. When Rebecca stops by Jimmy and Kim's office to plead for Jimmy's help with Chuck, Jimmy

Customer Service: 1-800-759-0190
customer.service@hbgusa.com

BILL TO:
AB FREE/REVIEW -
PUBLICITY ADULT
ACCOUNTING DEPARTMENT
100 5TH AVE

SHIP TO:
TONY MAGILO
7 SAMANTHA DR

CUST #: 19703332

NEW YORK, NY 10011

MORGANVILLE, NJ 07751

3750

ORD'D	SHIP'D	ITEM	TITLE	PRICE	DISC
1	1	9781419777196	Invoice# 76533049 Order Ref# 250109018668/001 SAUL GOODMAN V. JIMMY MCGILL	$.00	0

PO# 1001

EXT. TOTAL: $.00

is cruel and cold in dismissing the idea that he owes his brother anything anymore. And where we've always seen Jimmy as someone who genuinely enjoys spending time with his elderly clients, the montage of him calling all of them to explain about his suspension suggests even his patience has limits, at least when so many of these conversations are packed into such a small window. The twelve-month suspension from practicing law is a relatively short sentence, given his crimes, but it's a long time for him to think about exactly who and what he wants to be when his law career resumes. When he and Kim stand outside the office discussing whether to give Francesca her two weeks' notice, Jimmy insists, "As far as I'm concerned, nothing's changed." But it has. He can't be a lawyer for a year, and even if the commercial business turns into a thriving enough concern to cover his half of the rent and Francesca's salary, it's easy to see Jimmy in twelve months deciding that he'd like to be Saul Goodman as a lawyer, too, and maybe take some criminal cases instead of drinking tea with a lot of nice but long-winded seniors.

Saul's first appearance comes at the end of an episode where most of the characters are pondering what to do following recent setbacks. After the riveting courtroom theatrics of "Chicanery," "Off Brand" is a more relaxed, piece-mover sort of episode that allows us to catch up with the whole ensemble, including its least-used member.

In terms of screen time, Michael Mando has been the biggest victim of the show's unexpected decision to slow roll the arrival of the true Saul Goodman, with Nacho disappearing for long stretches of each season. After a brief cameo when Hector invaded Los Pollos Hermanos in "Sabrosito," Nacho finally gets some extended time here, particularly as the centerpiece of the pre-credits sequence where he has to lay a beating on Domingo on Hector's orders. Later, he dozes off while working a sewing machine at his father's upholstery business, not noticing until the needle pierces his hand. He is overextended and miserable with this life—and with this cruel and unreasonable killer overseeing his every move—and things only get worse later when Victor pulls a gun on him while he tries to take more than Hector's agreed-upon share of drugs from Gus's supply. Nacho's a tough guy—he reduces Domingo, who as Krazy-8 will be absolutely terrifying to Walt and Jesse in a few years, into a quivering puddle even before he starts hurting him—but the look in his eyes as he walks out of Gus's desert facility is that of a man who is in no way comfortable with having a gun pointed at him, particularly for carrying out the stupid, bullying whims of the boss he hates.

When Hector—right after insisting that the upholstery business will become his new front, whether Nacho wants it or not (and he of course does not want it)—nearly has an attack in the wake of news that Tuco got into a fight that will extend his prison sentence,* he drops one of his pills on the floor, and Nacho makes sure to conceal it until Hector has left. Mike was right when he told Nacho that assassinating Tuco would only bring unwanted attention from the rest of the Salamanca clan—and, as we've seen, moving Tuco out of the way just meant Nacho would have to deal directly with Hector. But if Nacho can poison Hector in a way that makes it look like he just had a massive stroke? Well, who could possibly blame Ignacio Varga for that?

It's a good showcase for an underserved character, making Nacho feel vital to the plot again after his various absences, and right at a moment when a lot of the more famous players find themselves at a crossroads. Gus, for instance, goes looking for a new front business of his own, exploring a laundry facility that we all know quite well as the location of the Super Lab from *Breaking Bad*—and is scouting it with no less than superhumanly anxious Madrigal executive Lydia Rodarte-Quayle. We never saw the two interact on the parent series—Laura Fraser's first appearance was in the season after Gus died—but we know that Lydia was a major player in the operation, and it's nice to see that twitchy lady's face again.

Chuck is also struggling to find a new path. Howard pushes him to look forward, rather than continuing to dwell on his feud with his brother and his failure to get Jimmy disbarred. For the moment, Chuck seems to be mostly focused on learning more about his condition, first holding on to a battery from the infamous tape recorder to remind himself of how real the pain feels, then venturing out to call Dr. Cruz at the hospital.

Mike, meanwhile, is trying to stay clean after his recent flirtations with Gus, attending Stacey's grief support group, and reluctantly agreeing to help build a new playground at the church. When Stacey says Matty told her about the carport Mike built at the family home back in the day, Mike seems to have no memory of this. He has seen and done a lot of terrible things as both cop and freelance criminal, and perhaps has simply forgotten about something benign and peaceful he did decades ago that made a lasting impression on his son. We know that Mike is handy enough to become a full-time contractor if he wanted to. It would be a much less lucrative profession than the one he's eventually going to take with Gus, but also a much safer one, and he'd probably enjoy it a lot more than riding herd over Victor, Tyrus, Walt, Jesse, and the many other people he'll have to deal with in Gus's world.

Similarly, Jimmy McGill loves making these ads. For that matter, he really liked being an elder-care attorney until recently. Either path would

---

* This will keep Tuco behind bars until shortly before he meets Heisenberg.

probably be an easy and secure one for him to travel, to stay with Kim, to avoid ever becoming Gene from Cinnabon.

But we know that Mike's not going to pour concrete forever, just as we know that Jimmy is going to stay Saul Goodman, but in a different role. Again, we know the what, and even some of the why, but there's still a lot of entertainment to be had with the how of it all.

SEASON 3, EPISODE 7
WRITTEN AND DIRECTED BY THOMAS SCHNAUZ

"Expenses"

"We can make it zero." —Jimmy

One of the most surprising parts of *Better Call Saul*—both for the audience and for the people writing the show—is how lovable Jimmy McGill turned out to be. Saul Goodman was a charming scoundrel, but he was still a scoundrel. But we've seen a fundamental core of decency and commitment in Jimmy that's made him more interesting than anyone expected, and has kept the show from transitioning him into Saul far longer than planned. Jimmy's still a con man on some level, and he still bends many rules and breaks a few—albeit often with noble motives, like the felony he committed to get Kim the client he felt she had rightly earned. But he took care of his brother even after learning of Chuck's betrayal of him at HHM, he goes to incredible lengths to support Kim, he usually enjoys talking to and helping his elderly clients, and he puts in absurd amounts of time and effort to get jobs done when they need doing right. He's a good guy fighting an internal battle against going back to being bad, and even though we know he's destined to lose in the end, he's held on remarkably well to this point.

But he's also had things relatively easy until now. He didn't have many material needs—felt more comfortable living in the back of the nail salon than he ever did in his corporate apartment—he had the support of Kim and Mike* and even Howard to varying degrees, got a bunch of money from the Davis and Main job, and found an underserved market in the local elder community. He wasn't always thriving, but even at his lowest, he was doing okay. And it's easier to be good when you're not truly struggling.

In "Expenses," though, he's struggling. It's a vintage "in-between moments" kind of *Breaking Bad/Better Call Saul* episode, pausing the action to deal more thoroughly with the repercussions of Jimmy and Kim's relative victory at the disbarment hearing. Jimmy's not going to prison, but he still has to

---

* Couple of things to note about the Mike half of the show: (1) Daniel Wormald returns, as Nacho enlists his help to slip Hector some fake nitroglycerin pills, which would kill the boss without drawing too much attention from the cartel or the Cousins. (2) Anita, Mike's new friend from the grief support group (played by Tamara Tunie), talks about how painful it is to never truly know what happened to her husband because his body was never found. Years later, when Mike is on the verge of killing Lydia, she pleads with him to leave her body in the house, so her daughter won't have to struggle with a similar lack of closure. Before Mike changes his mind and lets her live, he seems willing to grant the request.

do community service, and that eats into the time he needs to drum up business. He's not allowed to practice law for a year but can't get a refund on his expensive malpractice insurance policy—and later finds out that his rates will skyrocket when his suspension ends. And the commercial production business, which seemed a plausible and fun way for Jimmy to pay the bills while serving out the suspension, hasn't really taken off due to the hesitancy of small business owners to pay for his services.

As this iteration of "Saul Goodman," he isn't yet the man we knew from *Breaking Bad*, nor is he Slippin' Jimmy; he's fast-talking, but not an outright hustler. He believes in this product and thinks it's mutually beneficial to him and his clients, because we know how easily he could relieve them of their money if that was all he cared about. But you can see the pressure he's feeling start to sour what's inherently good about him. The parks department supervisor docks him time for talking on his phone, which makes Jimmy resentful of a situation he had come to accept as his own responsibility; he later turns the man's taunt on a poor delivery guy who complains about the tiny tip that's all Jimmy can afford. And when he takes Kim out for a night of Viktor and Giselle grifting, he can't help but take it all seriously, especially when the arrogance of one of their potential marks starts to remind him too much of Chuck.

Kim is alarmed to witness this, but she's in a bad emotional place in general. Financially, she's far better off than Jimmy, but she can't as easily cast off thoughts of what they did to Chuck to get to this point. When Paige at Mesa Verde laughs about the whole thing as if Chuck got what he deserved, it only puts Kim further on edge, leading to a wildly unprofessional outburst as they go over her compliance paperwork. Paige is easygoing enough to let Kim get off with an apology, but Kim can't let her own actions go—not just in that conference room, but at the hearing.

"As far as I'm concerned," she confesses, "all we did was tear down a sick man."

Jimmy doesn't quite see it that way, as his life spirals further and further from his hopes. The opening shot of him leaning against the brick wall is reminiscent of him in "Amarillo," but rather than a dazzling white suit and Stetson, he's in jeans and a ratty sweatshirt, just waiting for the other offenders to join him.

And when the insurance company rep not only doesn't give him any money back from the now-superfluous policy, but informs him that his premiums will go up 150 percent due to the suspension, he doesn't slink out, but instead decides to pile on Chuck some more, by telling the rep—in between some convincing fake tears—about Chuck's breakdown before the committee, just to make sure Chuck's premiums go up, too.

It's a nasty little trick, and one he takes far too much pleasure in. It was one thing for Jimmy to publicly humiliate Chuck as the only way to avoid disbarment, or worse; that was self-defense, even if Jimmy committed the various crimes that got him into that jam in the first place. In this case, though, Jimmy gains nothing, save for the satisfaction that Chuck shares in this particular part of his punishment. Even if you're an inveterate Chuck-hater, this doesn't seem at all the kind of thing the Jimmy McGill we've come to know and like would do to his brother.

When Jimmy showed Kim the commercial at the end of "Off Brand," he assured her that "Saul Goodman" was just a name. At the moment, this is true, given that most of the things we've come to think about from the Saul persona have yet to fully emerge. But there are lines we know Saul Goodman will cross that Jimmy McGill at this moment in his life simply wouldn't. Actively hurting his brother this way, trying to rope Kim into a real grift rather than a harmless one . . . these take him closer to being Saul Goodman than the name itself.

SEASON 3, EPISODE 8
WRITTEN BY HEATHER MARION
DIRECTED BY ADAM BERNSTEIN

"Slip"

"You believe me, right?" —**Jimmy**

I happened to interview Peter Gould* a few days before "Slip" first aired. Among the things we talked about was the odd structure of Season 3. In another season of *Saul,* or *Breaking Bad,* or most modern serialized dramas, "Chicanery" would have been the finale. It's the climax of Chuck's attempt to drum Jimmy out of the legal profession, and it sets both brothers up on entirely new arcs that the episodes since then have been dealing with, at a pace that the show more generally uses at the starts of seasons rather than at this late point.

Gould noted that he and Vince Gilligan have never been great at planning (most of the best-received stories on *Breaking Bad* were conceived of after the writing staff had painted itself into a corner). So rather than focusing on season structure, they try to follow what the characters would do, and when they would do it. There was only so long they could put off the bar hearing, and that in turn has meant a pivot into each McGill dealing with the ramifications of it, even if it feels like the season is starting over again with only a few episodes remaining, with most of the characters—even on the drug side of the equation— still finding their way. You wouldn't expect an hour this late in the year to have as its showpiece scene a guy trying to throw a pill bottle into an open blazer pocket, right?

But in focusing first on what the characters would be doing rather than worrying about making the tension build and build from one episode to the next, Gould, Gilligan, and company also get to make these in-between moments feel so rich and lived-in and authentic that the structure is surprising, but not disappointing. It's not where you might expect the story to be at this point, but it's so satisfying, dramatically, that it's hard to care about that.

Even more surprising is the way the two brothers' stories have diverged in the weeks since "Chicanery." In that hearing, Jimmy won utterly, and Chuck lost utterly—not only failing to get his brother disbarred, but being exposed publicly as mentally ill and in denial about it—yet you wouldn't think that to look at them through the course of "Slip." Though he hated it at the time, Chuck

---

* Look for excerpts from that—a joint conversation with Gould and Michael McKean—on page 93.

has now been forced to accept the true nature of his condition, which means he can finally get proper treatment for it, rather than the quackery of camp stoves and space blankets. Dr. Cruz has put him on medication and given him exercises to use when he's out in public. The treatment approach follows the old saw about the first step to solving a problem is admitting that you have it. The condition still *feels* real to Chuck, but he's able to push against it, to buy groceries and walk happily out in the sunlight, and to talk with Dr. Cruz about his hopes for the future. Chuck will always be thought of by the audience as an insufferable and manipulative elitist. But there's a vulnerability and openness to him here, wonderfully played by McKean, suggesting a version of him who might be easier to be around. He'll never be loved, but he feels human enough for it to sting when Howard arrives to tell him about his malpractice insurance and perhaps bring all of Chuck's new dreams crashing down on him.

The episode opens with another glimpse of Jimmy's days hanging out with Marco in Illinois, with the two of them searching for hidden treasure in the ruins of the McGill family grocery store. It's yet another opportunity for Jimmy to air his version of the family history—to Chuck, their dad was a saint destroyed by his younger son's thievery; to Jimmy, his dad was a sap destroyed by his insistence on playing by rules no one else really follows—in a way that nicely sets up the moral descent he takes in the episode's later scenes.

Both Jimmy the elder-care lawyer and Saul Goodman the commercial producer are fast talkers with a gift for pushing people into doing things they don't initially want to do. But he's not an outright grifter in either incarnation. He believes his services can genuinely help his clients and is even proven right here when ABQ In Tune sees a surge in business following the airing of the pro bono commercial he made in the previous episode. But just as he feels his father always got screwed over for trying to do the right thing, he's dismayed to find the brothers* trying to renege on their handshake deal because one has realized how much money they can save by cutting out the middleman and buying ad time on their own. They're not necessarily wrong that Jimmy, desperate to escape his contract with the station, is overcharging them for a service they don't entirely need. (One ad would do them just fine for quite a while.) But they also had an agreement, and Jimmy honored his end while they are weaseling out of theirs. Jimmy has tried *so* hard for *so* long to do the right thing to impress his brother, to impress Kim, and also because there's arguably more good in him than bad. But is it any wonder that he would go full Slippin' Jimmy on the twins† to ensure he gets his money no matter what? And, once that succeeded,

---

*   Played by identical twin comedians Randy and Jason Sklar.
†   A good slip-and-fall man, like a good pro wrestler, doesn't escape his stunts unscathed. They're scripted, but the injuries are still real.

is it all that shocking that he would try to further combine his legal and con-man skills in order to get himself and one of his fellow community service workers out of having to pick up trash?

He's still not full Saul yet, but you can also see him stepping—or slipping—more and more into those shoes with each passing episode. Yet he's still his father's son, and his insistence on contributing to his half of the office expenses is starting to drive a wedge between himself and Kim. Their conversation while he's playing the Ritchie Blackmore guitar is among the least warm exchanges they've had, and she follows it by deciding to take on oil rig owner Billy Gatwood as a new client, despite her previous insistence that she would devote all her time to Mesa Verde (though Kevin seems fine with making an exception for his pal Billy). Perhaps she's worried Jimmy won't actually be able to hold up his end, and it would be better to have the extra income. Or maybe she's throwing herself into work as a distraction from a relationship that's starting to falter, as well as memories of the awful thing she and Jimmy did to Chuck. Either way, it's one more thing to keep them apart at a time when Jimmy McGill could *really* use frequent reminding of his own humanity.

It's easy to see parallels, meanwhile, between Jimmy's father and Nacho's, even though Nacho has far more respect for Manuel than Jimmy did for his dad. Nacho is putting himself at grave risk trying to kill Don Hector, but it's the only way to save, at minimum, his father's business, and probably his father's life. So risk he shall. The business with the pills is a pretty classic *Breaking Bad/Saul* piece of sweating the details—literally, once Nacho busts the air conditioner to ensure that Hector won't be wearing his jacket when it's time to swap out the medicine—and showing just how hard it is even for an experienced criminal to pull off a specialized trick like this.* And by showing us just how difficult it was for Nacho to do the swap once, we're primed to feel on edge for the moment when the plan succeeds and he has to swap the pills back again before the police or someone else in the cartel can check them to see why they didn't work.

It's also not hard to find parallels between Jimmy's dad and Mike. Mike has never been a saint, but we've also seen him trying to do things the right way, even as he keeps being tempted by the money he can make for Kaylee by working on the other side of the fence. Working for Daniel Wormald led him to Nacho, which put Tuco and Hector and the Cousins into his life, which led to a truck heist that left the Good Samaritan dead and Mike with $200,000 in cash he can't give to his granddaughter. "Slip" sees him belatedly dealing with both problems, first by identifying the Samaritan's body in the desert near where he

---

* If only Nacho were acquainted with Huell...

robbed the truck, and alerting local authorities to provide closure for the man's loved ones, then going to Gus Fring for help laundering the cash. He presents it as a one-time transaction and offers Gus a hefty percentage for his trouble, but Gus doesn't want Mike's money: he wants Mike Ehrmantraut himself. Their handshake signals the start of an alliance that will last years, create fortunes, ruin lives, and end with the men on either side of it killed by Walter White.

Slippin' Jimmy was never big on violent crime and the risks that come with it, and he would not approve of the nasty ends that both Mike and Gus will come to a few years from now. But he also wouldn't begrudge a man trying to make as much as he can, while he can, given the way the system seems built to screw over the little guy who—like both Papa McGill and the Good Samaritan—does things the right way.

The *Better Call Saul* Braintrust Knows Why You Hate Chuck

[Originally published on Uproxx.com, June 9, 2017]

Because *Better Call Saul* toggles back and forth between Jimmy McGill's law career in the years before he changes his name to Saul Goodman and Mike Ehrmantraut's slow immersion into the Albuquerque drug world, there's no real consensus among the show's fans about which half they prefer. Some are gripped by Jimmy's moral descent, and his relationship with Kim Wexler; others are in it for the *Breaking Bad* prequel of it all and will take all the familiar cameos they can get. But there is one thing pretty much everyone who loves the show can agree on:

They *hate* Chuck McGill.

This comes as no surprise to both Michael McKean, nor to *Saul* co-creator Peter Gould. I sat down with both men* to discuss the roots of the Jimmy/Chuck feud, what it's like for McKean as a *Breaking Bad* fan to be part of a show set in the same universe, and a lot more.

Overall, is the experience of watching this—because you were making it, you've read the script—different from when you were watching *Breaking Bad*?

MCKEAN: Oh, yeah. I read the scripts, obviously, and I even read the stuff I'm not in. There's an old actor saying: "Blah, blah, blah, my line, blah, blah, blah, my line." It's not that. I read it, but I also know when I'm reading these long, block scenes with Jonathan Banks, I have no idea what he's doing. And I look forward to also not knowing what he's doing when I see it until it pays off, because I know how these guys work. Of course, the stuff I work on, I get to learn and I get to know, but the stuff with Jonathan and Mando's story, all that stuff, it's a nice surprise. I'm a fan. I would be a fan even if I weren't in the show. I'd probably be a bigger fan.

GOULD: I don't know; you have to watch yourself.

---

*   Author's note from almost a decade later, probably better off skipped by any first-time viewers: I conducted this interview without having seen the season's last two episodes. You will see some artful dancing around what both McKean and Gould knew was coming. Left on the cutting-room floor of the original article was a moment where McKean felt I was asking too much about Chuck's future, and politely but firmly suggested I keep watching the show to find out. But even in this version, you'll see a moment or two where McKean slips a little, notably in the Ed Begley Jr. discussion.

M: Yeah, I do. I'm stuck with that.

G: I just know I personally can't watch myself or listen to myself, which is why I won't ever listen to any of this. There was a teaser that you did that I just loved. Season Two where you were playing the piano, with the metronome. The origin of that was really, "What's it like to be Chuck? We know how hard he is on Jimmy. How does he treat himself?" That was fascinating to me. Of course, you played beautifully.

M: Thanks to a little movie magic, yes.

G: You played beautifully, but also just that moment when you make a mistake—

M: I begged them to make it a guitar. I can actually play the guitar.

G: We don't believe in actually using the actual talent.

M: Yeah, you gave the guitar to [Ed] Begley, for God's sweet sake. He's a drummer! Don't you know anything?

G: We should have known, absolutely.

And they haven't put you and Begley together yet, right?

MCKEAN: No, we never did. Nope.

GOULD: Not yet.

M: Our relationship is, for forty years, we've been set up for the same parts: "Give me a tall, blonde guy who can hit a joke." Begley is one of my best friends, and one time it was down to the two of us for a pilot, which wasn't particularly good, but, hey, it's a pilot. This was about five years ago. We realized it was down to the two of us. Ed just said the best thing to me: "Look, no matter what happens, it'll be in the family."

What was the experience of doing "Chicanery"—the Captain Queeg scene in particular?

MCKEAN: It was long. It was over thirty pages of dialogue in that scene. It was a chore to learn it, but thanks to these guys everything has been pretty clear to me. I've had fewer questions making thirty hours of this than I've had doing almost anything I've ever done, which only ran for ninety minutes or two hours at a time. They've always been very clear to me. And we watched the characters grow up together. We watched the relationship starting as this very simple thing: Chuck is somebody that Jimmy is taking care of back when Saul Goodman was caring about other people, more than just all the cash in those oil drums. It was always very clear to us. These guys called me and said, about episode nine of the first season, "You know what? There's going to be a little change-up here. We're going to reveal something about Chuck that you maybe didn't suspect." I was delighted, because it helped me be the protagonist of my story, you know? Chuck was never going to be the protagonist of *Better Call*

Saul. It's just not the case. But every character should be the protagonist of his own story. It was wonderful.

GOULD: This cast prepares extensively. You may get the impression, it's television, there's not a lot of rehearsal. There isn't. I would love that, personally, if we did, but we don't. It's not a practicality of the way we work. With this particular script, which Gordon Smith wrote, we worked extra hard to have the script finished and in its final form to the cast early, because we knew that you guys were going to need a lot of preparation. I remember I had to, for various reasons, drop by Bob's house in Los Angeles. It was a week or so before when the episode started shooting, and there I walked in. There's our cast gathered around Bob's dining room table, all with their scripts, running the lines for these scenes. It made me feel so good, and it made me feel so terrific to know that these folks who are so brilliant were all turning their intellects and putting every bit of thought into every word. Which, of course, also is something I think about as we revise the scripts as we work through the story, because we know our cast is really, really smart. They are going to think about the script in ways that we would never dream of. So we try to think of these things from as many angles as we know how in order to give you a script that makes sense to you, that's coherent.

You've said in the past you tried not to really think about the mental illness aspect of Chuck, because as far as Chuck is concerned, this is a real thing he's experiencing. From the moment when Jimmy reveals the battery through these next episodes, how has that changed the way you play the character?

MCKEAN: Well, obviously it means that he has to weigh something he had not considered before. Whenever you have to do that in your life, it changes things. When you're dealing with Chuck, you're dealing with a person who is not really capable of saying, "This changes everything." Couldn't say it to Rebecca. He wouldn't even let her in the door. With Clea DuVall's character, he found a person, a professional. It was like hiring a lawyer: he found someone he could be one hundred percent honest with. That doesn't happen automatically. Episode eight, that was as close to being a human being as we've seen Chuck, because he had to face something. It didn't make it go away. It would have taken us out of reality if the next morning Chuck woke up and said, "Thank God. I have learned the error of my ways. It was all in my head, and now I'm fine." Life doesn't work that way and neither do these guys.

GOULD: I just know my own experiences with therapy. The dream is that you have a breakthrough moment, and then suddenly that changes everything. The truth is that you can have all the insights in the world, but living them out day to day, moment to moment, is really tough. It's a lot of work. I love the fact that Chuck arguably has, to my eye, a breakthrough moment there. A moment where he's willing to admit the thing that he hasn't been willing to consider before, as Michael says, and now the question after that is, is he going to be able to follow up on that?

M: The last line in *Portnoy's Complaint*, which is basically one long session with the shrink, and then the shrink has one line at the end. He says something like, "Oh, Mr. Portnoy, now we can begin." That's kind of what life is.

Michael, when you've encountered fans of the show, what do they generally tell you their feelings are about Chuck?

MCKEAN: They make it clear that they like me, and that they really don't like Chuck. There is no other response but: "Okay. I'm onto something here. We're good." But there are people who seem to understand him without approving of him. I think it became pretty clear that there was something about the parents, about Mom in particular. On some level, and he's overstating it, Chuck does blame Jimmy for the father's early death, as well. Chuck made Mom proud; Jimmy made Mom laugh. You can't buy that, you know? You can buy her pride by working hard, but if someone seems to be loved more than you are, and you can't explain it and it doesn't make sense, then the world's a little bit crazy and you might have to go a little crazy to keep up with it. I don't know whether I'm reading too much into it, but this is just something it's always felt like to Chuck. It's like that thing where you go to a movie that everyone's crazy about, and you see it on the screen, and you know it stinks. Your question is, "Is it me? What's wrong with everybody? Is it me?" Well, Chuck doesn't have the "Is it me?" He knows it's not him. He knows it's everybody else. I'm simplifying a complicated person, but that's just in order to talk about it a little bit.

Well, are each of you surprised by the universality of that kind of audience dislike of Chuck?

MCKEAN: No.

Is that what you would have expected going in?

MCKEAN: I think it makes sense.

GOULD: I hate to go back to *Breaking Bad*, but we learned on *Breaking Bad*, once a viewer is in somebody's corner, they really tend to stay in their corner. So if anybody [on the show] opposed Walter White, the audience hated that person. Especially, and I think most egregiously, in the case of Skyler. But the truth is, it takes a lot to pull yourself away from the first impression of the character, even though we who work on the show may see things very differently. I have a lot more sympathy for Chuck than I think most of our viewers do.

M: But I think that shows in the writing, you know? Because you haven't written a villain. Never.

G: As you've seen in episode eight, Chuck goes to places that I wasn't expecting. As the season goes on, I'll be interested to see whether the audience changes their view of him in any way.

The thing is, Chuck is right. He makes it a self-fulfilling prophecy with the things he does to Jimmy, but he's right about what Slippin' Jimmy with a law degree can become.

MCKEAN: You know, Dean Wormer [in *Animal House*] was right to try and shut down Delta House. They were a bunch of screw-ups. But nobody roots for Dean Wormer.

GOULD: We argue about this in the writers' room, would Jimmy have become Saul Goodman if Chuck had greeted him happily into the legal profession? And I think in the end we can all blame our families for who we become. That's not completely inaccurate. But on the other hand, you also have to take responsibility for your actions. These are the questions that make good drama, at least in my book.

Michael, you like to act in the moment and not think about what's coming, but you know what's coming, at least for Jimmy/Saul. Is it hard to keep that out of your head in these scenes where you're talking about what he can become?

MCKEAN: No, because I have to think chronologically. I can't get ahead because Chuck can't see the future. I can read the future once they deliver a script to me, but that's different. I don't have to really remind myself because it's there every day. Life comes at you fast and death comes at you last.

Peter, have you thought through yet where Chuck is during the events of *Breaking Bad*? Is that something you guys know?

GOULD: We talk about all those questions. About where Chuck is, where Kim is. We talk about these things endlessly in the writers' room. I often say we go brick by brick and scene by scene, which is true enough, but we also can't help talking about it. So where does this go? And how did this end? We definitely talked about it a lot. We have strong theories.

Strong theories but not a definitive answer yet?

GOULD: We know a lot. We asked ourselves a lot of questions at the beginning of Season One, and I despaired of ever having the answers. The fundamental question of the show is, "What problem does becoming Saul Goodman solve?"

I never thought we'd get there, and then here we are at the end of Season Three, and the clouds are beginning to part. Although, there's a sadness to that, because Jimmy becoming Saul Goodman is a loss. I'm going to miss Jimmy.

Michael, as a fan of this series and this world, would you be interested in seeing a version where we get the *Rosencrantz and Guildenstern Are Dead** take on the *Breaking Bad* years, or an extended time in Omaha?
MCKEAN: Oh, yeah. Absolutely. I love Gene in Omaha. I loved the first episode in the season that expanded Gene. You could take the lawyer out of the man, or can you? It was lovely.

Michael, you got to do a scene a few episodes back with Jonathan, but it's not really Chuck interacting with Mike, because it's Mike undercover. Do you ever find yourself thinking, "I wish that there was some way that Chuck could wander into Los Pollos Hermanos"?
MCKEAN: Banks is amazing and fun. He's a horrible human being, but . . . No, I adore him. It was exactly the right way to do a scene with Banks, you know? I always wanted to. I never saw how it could happen, and then I read that script, where he opens the door and it's Mike, and I'm like, "Fuck. All right. Actually, I like that." It was great. I got to spend the day with Jonathan and we had a lot of fun. I also got to play Chuck, the guy who knows everything, being absolutely oblivious to what's going on. It was really fun.

---

* A play by Tom Stoppard where the events of *Hamlet* are seen through the eyes of two minor characters from the original Shakespeare play.

SEASON 3, EPISODE 9
WRITTEN BY GORDON SMITH
DIRECTED BY MINKIE SPIRO

"Fall"

"I can't be partners with someone whose judgment I don't trust." **—Howard**

We knew that, sooner or later, warm-hearted elder-care attorney Jimmy McGill would become cold-blooded defense lawyer Saul Goodman. Again, the "what" has never been in question; *Better Call Saul* has instead been playing with the when, why, and how of it. And what we've seen across Season 3 is that Jimmy's moral descent—like that of his most famous future client—isn't a matter of just one event, one huge decision, but rather a series of incremental incidents and choices that slowly, painfully transform the guy we root for into the guy we enjoy but are appalled by.

Recent episodes have slowly but surely separated Jimmy from the people and things that were keeping him on the good path. He and Chuck went to war, and after Jimmy won, he wanted nothing more to do with the brother whom he'd always tried to impress. The short-term suspension has separated him from the clients he felt such empathy for, as well as the steady income that protected him from the temptation to con again. Jimmy's prideful insistence on not taking handouts (another trait he holds in common with Walter White) has forced him to relentlessly hustle in a manner that has driven a wedge between himself and Kim—who, with Chuck out of the picture, is Jimmy's last tether to any desire to do things the right way—as has her insistence on taking on more work.

Jimmy is isolated and he is desperate, which is a very bad combination for a man inclined to take shortcuts, legal or otherwise, whenever possible. Even with the matter of his ad buy at the TV station resolved thanks to his Slippin' Jimmy stunt in the previous episode, he still needs money, and it seemed only a matter of time before he would remember that he was due for a huge payday from the Sandpiper case.

We haven't really heard about Sandpiper since Jimmy quit the Davis and Main job last season. But that potential windfall has been hanging out there in Jimmy's future since he brought the case to HHM. That amount of money—$1.16 million, according to Jimmy's mental math at the end of the opening sequence—is big enough that the show had to deploy it at just the right moment, and in just the right way. If Cliff Main were to simply call Jimmy out of the blue and reluctantly tell him his check was in the mail, that would have no dramatic weight, and would also make Jimmy so financially comfortable that there might not be much of a story for him for quite some time. By making him hustle for it—cruelly isolating class representative Irene Landry (Jean Effron) from all her friends at the retirement home to manipulate her into pushing for an earlier and smaller settlement*—the story becomes less about what the money can do for Jimmy than what Jimmy does for the money, and the moral depths to which he'll sink to pursue his own ends. He does nothing illegal here, and perhaps once Irene agrees to settle, fences can be mended with her neighbors. But Jimmy knows this is wrong. You can see it on his face as he prepares to swap out the usual bingo balls for the ones he doctored to match Irene's card:[†] he pauses for just a moment, considers how sad and lonely Irene looks, before doing it anyway, because he needs her to change her mind for his own sake.

Jimmy is hanging by a very thin thread in "Fall," but so are most of the show's major characters, who are trying to go it alone in desperate circumstances, and suffering as a result.

When Hector refuses to accept Don Eladio's order for all drug smuggling to run through Gus's operation—and when the fake pills have enough of a placebo effect to quell the angry old man's latest heart episode—Nacho finds himself with no choice but to warn his father about what's coming, and to confess that he's working for the Salamancas again. The "again," and the way that Michael Mando plays Nacho's shame at the admission (along with the disappointment on Juan Carlos Cantu's face as Manuel assimilates this new information), tells us all we need to know about the history between father and son, and the very passionate fight they must have once had about Nacho associating with such scum. And what's particularly brutal about the scene, beyond how drawn and tired and afraid Nacho looks, is that he may have confessed this, and gotten himself kicked out of his father's home, for nothing, because he can't get Manuel to agree to trust him and stay calm when Hector and his people approach him. Nacho insists this will all be over within a few weeks, and the condition that Hector is in during the Heisenberg years suggests some kind of medical mishap is coming. But will it come fast enough to save the upholstery business and Nacho's dad?

---

* As Howard points out, Jimmy is motivated by self-interest. But it's unclear if he's right when he says that the difference in payout to the plaintiffs would be negligible, and that the two law firms are dragging this out just to pad their own bottom lines while preventing a group of senior citizens from getting access to the money while they can still do something with it. Both things—Jimmy needing cash ASAP, and the two law firms delaying things more for their own sake than for that of their clients—can be true, and it leaves a little moral wiggle room to what Jimmy does to the class as a whole, even if there's no excusing the misery he inflicts on Irene.

† *Better Call Saul*: a show filled with murderous drug kingpins and ruthless con artists, yet one of the darkest moments of the entire series involves an old woman failing to get any applause when she wins at bingo. Lots of shows can make you choke up when somebody dies; few could make something that small seem so big.

The disbarment hearing, meanwhile, continues to create aftershocks for Chuck and Howard. Chuck doesn't lose his coverage from Jimmy's stunt with the malpractice insurance agent, but it makes HHM's premiums so onerous that he may as well have, which leads Howard to try to push his mentor and partner into finally retiring. Chuck McGill is even more prideful than his brother, though—the only character in the franchise with more self-destructive pride is Walt, and the gap's not that big between the two. Rather than transitioning into academia, or getting to write that book about the Commerce Clause, Chuck instead threatens to sue HHM for the money he's owed as a name partner. We know from the show's earliest episodes that Howard can't pay that—he indulged Chuck's extended absence because it was much cheaper than buying him out the way Jimmy wanted—but we also know that even with Dr. Cruz's treatment, Chuck can only bluff so much, as we see right after Howard leaves how much pain Chuck is in from using the blender. If the brothers were still on speaking terms, Jimmy would be the ideal sidekick in this operation. But he's not, and it seems like Chuck is going too far, too fast, for this stage of his recovery.

The episode ends not on any of those desperate men,* but on Kim Wexler, dazed and confused as the paperwork she so carefully organized—for a presentation that she admitted to Billy Gatwood had to be *juuuuust* right in order to solve his problem before the tax burden became too heavy—flies through the desert air in the wake of the single-car accident she gets into because she has worked herself to the point of distraction. The car can be fixed, the papers reprinted and collated, and perhaps the meeting can be rescheduled with no harm and no foul, since Kim has a pretty good excuse so long as nobody asks too many questions about the nature of the accident. But Kim is—like her boyfriend, like her ex-boss, and like Nacho Varga—asking more of herself than she's capable of giving at the moment, and bad mistakes are being made as a result.

Kim doesn't die in the crash, but if she screws up the Gatwood deal, that will blow back on her work with Kevin at Mesa Verde. Nacho may save his father's life but sever their relationship in the process. Chuck may be able to outmaneuver Howard, but at the cost of significant physical and emotional pain. And Jimmy may get his Sandpiper money ahead of schedule, but at the cost of another piece of his own humanity.

He's not Saul Goodman yet, but he's much closer than we want him to be, dammit.

---

* The one major character who is relatively secure in this one—in part because he has a very powerful person backing him up—is Mike, who gets to meet Lydia Rodarte-Quayle for the first time and comes to realize both how powerful Gustavo Fring is and how much this man seems to value their new association.

SEASON 3, EPISODE 10
WRITTEN BY GENNIFER HUTCHISON
DIRECTED BY PETER GOULD

"Lantern"

"In the end, you're going to hurt everyone around you. You can't help it. So stop apologizing and accept it, embrace it." —**Chuck**

This is the story of two brothers: one good, one not so good. Or, at least, one the world believed to be good, the other much less so.

And it's a tragedy. For both of them.

The good brother devoted his life to the rules. He studied them, he followed them, he built a whole career and ideology around them. He was successful and widely respected, but he rarely felt as loved as the not-so-good brother, for whom the rules were an inconvenience to be stretched, or shattered, or ignored altogether. Everyone knew the other brother was no good, but they loved him anyway, and that included the good brother, who cared for him as a boy and bailed him out of repeated troubles as a man.

And it's there that the tale of the two brothers becomes truly complex, and tragic. Because the not-so-good brother suddenly, after all these years, decided that the good brother was worth imitating, and he did everything he could to be good, down to choosing the same rules-honoring profession. And he genuinely meant it, even if he was never destined to be as big a stickler as the good brother. But the good brother—suffering from a mental illness that he refused to acknowledge as such, and waited on hand and foot by the now somewhat-good brother—had become so curdled with resentment from decades of watching his sibling slip and fall through life, with no real consequences, that he refused to believe in this conversion. In fact, he went so far out of his way to hamstring this career change that he spoke his suspicions into existence: the harder he leaned on his brother, the more his brother felt he had to push back against the rules just to survive. Eventually, things grew so tense and ugly between the two that the somewhat-good brother had to publicly humiliate the good brother in a last-ditch attempt to stop the good brother from taking his career away. The good brother finally reckoned with the reality of his illness, and briefly seemed to be making progress with it. But in the end, it was just too much to bear, and he destroyed first his beautiful home, and then his own life, using a lantern—very much like the one he once used to read to his younger sibling—to burn the whole place down with himself inside.

That's the worst part. But almost as bad is that, before he spiraled into madness and decided there was no way out, the good brother said the worst possible thing he could say to the somewhat-good brother, who had always craved love and respect, and from his honorable sibling most of all:

"I don't want to hurt your feelings, but the truth is, you've never mattered all that much to me."

And the somewhat-good brother was then destined to become not-so-good again, and then worse, and worse, and worse until he fulfilled every fear the good brother ever had about him, tearing apart lives as easily as he broke all the rules to which the good brother had dedicated every fiber of his being.

The End.

"Lantern" is the conclusion of Chuck McGill's story, but it also feels like the beginning of the end of the Jimmy McGill story. Technically, there's still much more to come—the name change, the shift into criminal law—but nearly everything keeping Jimmy from becoming the man we first met on *Breaking Bad* is gone. And the earlier line from the McGill brothers' final conversation, about how Jimmy needs to just embrace all the bad things he does, will prove prophetic.

Whatever blame Chuck deserves for his role in transforming Jimmy into Saul—and he deserves quite a bit, even if the choices, ultimately, are all ones that Jimmy made—he is once again correct here, even if he can't comprehend exactly how correct. In time, Jimmy will embrace his bad side and stop apologizing for it. If Saul Goodman ever looked stressed in his dealings with Walt and Jesse, it was over danger to himself, not others. We only saw him, of course, when he was dealing with Walt, Jesse, or Mike; it's possible that even in that era, he still had vestiges of the humanity that we've seen throughout these three wonderful seasons—including in this finale, where Jimmy makes the most self-sacrificing move we've ever seen from him. But viewed from the outside on *Breaking Bad*, Saul seemed to have taken Chuck's advice to heart. He was loving his life and not fretting about the consequences of any of it.

Throughout this series, three things seemed to be tethering Jimmy to the light side of the Force: (1) Love of his brother and craving for Chuck's respect, (2) Ditto and ditto for Kim, and (3) His affection for his elderly clients. By the end of "Lantern," Chuck is in the process of committing suicide, and Jimmy's good deed for Irene Landry salts the earth for him in the elder-care field.

The latter move recalls a question Peter Gould and the *Saul* writers have asked themselves many times: "What problem does becoming Saul Goodman solve?" Now we are dangerously close to that answer. Jimmy even tells Kim that he'll have to find a new business model when his suspension ends. He already has some criminal defense experience. And with the Sandpiper money again postponed indefinitely, he will need to hustle for all he's worth to make a living. And a change of name—to one already heard on local TV—wouldn't be a bad idea under those circumstances, given how much his former clients are reportedly badmouthing the moniker of Jimmy McGill.

So Jimmy has lost his brother, and in a way where he will never be able to make peace with him. (As he puts it to Kim, "I'm not good at building shit. I'm excellent at tearing it down.") He's lost his entire client base, and the love of a community whose belief in him also seemed to inspire him to be good. All that's preventing him from becoming Saul Goodman is Kim. And even with a devotion to her that only increases in the wake of her car accident, that just doesn't feel like enough anymore. The series has very deliberately avoided showing them being physically affectionate much of the time—it's almost startling to see her kiss him as they leave the office they briefly shared—in a way that could even lead a newcomer who hadn't seen every episode to be surprised by the fact of their couplehood. The Viktor and Giselle game stopped being fun for her when she realized that Jimmy could use it (and surely has in the past) to put a serious financial hurt on someone. Their victory over Chuck in court has only left her drowning in guilt and working herself nearly to death to push down those feelings and cover for Jimmy's financial difficulties post-suspension. Even though she pulls herself back from the edge by recommending Billy Gatwood take his business over to Rich Schweikart, something is still not right with her. There's an emotional distance between her and Jimmy, even as she tells him of her great admiration for Atticus Finch, and surely neither of them will take the news about Chuck well, perhaps turning on each other for their respective roles in his awful end.

But the focus is primarily on sending off Chuck, and the finale does it right, in meticulously painful fashion.

Chuck's deconstruction of his own cure, and of his big and beautiful house, is a cracked mirror of the centerpiece sequences from the season premiere where Mike dismantles his car looking for the tracker, then figures out how to turn the tables on Gus's men.* In both situations, we are watching

---

* The finale's other major piece of business involves Hector working himself into the catastrophic heart episode that will leave him wheelchair-bound and unable to speak. It's a rare case of a plan working out perfectly for someone in the *Breaking Bad* universe—mostly perfectly, since Nacho still has the rift with his father—in that Arturo and then Gus arrive before Nacho has a chance to just shoot Hector and face death for it, and Hector even does him the service of spilling the fake pills onto the ground, allowing Nacho to slip the real ones back into the bottle he hands the paramedic. The more interesting man in the scene, though, is Gus, not just because his gaze lingers on both the pill bottle and Nacho, but because he actually works hard doing CPR to try to save the man he hates most in all the world. He told Mike that a bullet would be too good for Don Hector, but he has no way of knowing the living hell Hector is about to face as a prisoner inside his own body;

brilliant men being exhaustively, obsessively thorough in their pursuit of a problem that they *know* is there. But Mike Ehrmantraut is a profoundly cautious and wise man who is ultimately proven right when he thinks to check the gas cap, where Chuck McGill is, sadly, a very sick man too consumed by his own illness*—which has wrapped itself around a level of pride that has already proved to be self-destructive in other areas—to stop, or to seek help from Dr. Cruz.[†] He just keeps digging and digging, prying and smashing and breaking, until he comes to decide that the stray voltage will never go away, that he'll never get better—and that, having burned bridges with his ex-wife, his partner, and his brother, there may not be a life worth living even if he can get his condition under control again. Mike Ehrmantraut is built for the show that *Better Call Saul* is becoming (and the one that spawned it); Chuck has no place there.

It's an episode filled with callbacks—twisted to suit present circumstances—to Chuck's difficult life on the series. Again, Howard gathers the entirety of HHM into the atrium to applaud Chuck, but this time it's for a bitter farewell that pleases neither man, and that a resentful (and cash-poor, since he's paying Chuck out of his own savings) Howard doesn't even stay for the end of. In the teaser, we actually see young Chuck reading *Mabel* to young Jimmy and understand how close the brothers used to be and how protective Chuck once was of Jimmy. And Jimmy has frequently warned Chuck about the fire hazard of living in a house filled with books and papers, and with gas lanterns and camp stoves in place of their electrical equivalents.

Even though Kim survives her crash mostly unscathed, and even though Jimmy actually does a very big and difficult kindness for Irene, this is a dark, dark episode of *Better Call Saul*, that for much of its running time dares to put us inside the head of a character who is very much not well, and whom most of the audience rightly loathes. It's not a sympathetic farewell to Chuck, who verbally destroys Jimmy in what both men seem to recognize will be their final conversation, even before the mania cruelly grabs hold of Chuck and refuses to let go. But it's an empathetic one. I don't like Chuck any more than I did going in, but I understand him, and felt for him as he tore his home and life apart until all that was left was fire.

---

this seems either Gus wanting to be the one to kill Hector no matter what, or Gus still being concerned about appearances with Juan Bolsa and the rest of the cartel.

* This plays out exactly as Jimmy predicted when he sat on the curb in "Sunk Costs." Under other circumstances, he would have been there for his brother in this moment of crisis. But Chuck ensured that would never happen again.

† *Better Call Saul* Loves Movies: The creative team frequently looks to the classic French heist film *Rififi* as inspiration for Mike's various wordless exercises. Chuck tearing apart the house instead recalls Gene Hackman's similar breakdown in the paranoid seventies classic *The Conversation*.

Yes, becoming Saul has to solve a problem for Jimmy. But Saul Goodman is more than just a change in name and specialty. He's a very different, far worse man from the one we've watched these past three seasons, and it was going to take something beyond a shift in professional circumstance to make the transformation as complete and terrible as we know it must be. Jimmy's been walking a knife edge for most of the series, and he has to plummet deep down off it to truly become Saul. Chuck dying in such gruesome fashion, and not long after that cold farewell talk, goes a long way toward accomplishing that, while also creating even more dread about what might have to happen to Kim Wexler in order to make the transformation complete.

RIP, Chuck McGill. At least he didn't live long enough to see all his worst fears about his brother come true.

Bob Odenkirk's Not Looking Forward to Being Saul Goodman Again on *Better Call Saul*

[This article originally appeared on Uproxx.com on June 23, 2017]

How did you find out about Chuck's fate?

First Michael told us in a casual way, because he had gotten a call, and then everybody was talking about it on set, and then a few hours later I got a call from Vince and Peter, who are very considerate and very sensitive about these big choices in the story. They were thinking that they were breaking the news to me. I think they didn't realize how Michael would be able to handle it. Michael's done so much stuff, and so many different jobs. While it was such a wonderful part for him, and he did it so well, and I think he would've liked to carry on doing it for years to come, he's also a writer himself, and he knows that story has to be paramount, and this had to happen in this story. He took it like the kind of experienced actor that he is. Look: there's things about this show that are inevitable. You have to be a grown-up about it. It's gonna end at a certain point. I don't really know right now, but sooner rather than later, it's gonna end, and the character's going to become Saul, who's kind of a shitty guy. He's going to go from being a dimensional, empathetic character to a shallow asshole. And that's the journey that we all agreed to. It's a big deal, but these are things we're all knowing are coming down the pike.

With the way you describe the transition from one to the other, if there winds up being an extended period of time where you're playing the Saul of *Breaking Bad*, are you looking forward to that? Or are you going to miss playing this guy you're playing right now?

This is a more rewarding part than that. So, yes, I would miss the part that I'm playing now. I don't think there is an extended period of time that we'll be enjoying Saul's ridiculousness. I think there will be a story to tell there, though. We're not quite there yet. With Chuck gone, that is one of the two big things that are connecting him to humanity, and the other being Kim. When those pillars fall away, he's in free fall. We're fairly close to that. And then there's some story to tell as Saul. Also, frankly, I would like to see what happens to Gene. I hope they'll give some story to him. I think they will. They're talking about it. So I don't know how much time is left, but I will and do already feel bad about saying goodbye to the very likable and, I think, good-hearted Jimmy McGill.

Rhea says she has speculated about where Kim is during the events of _Breaking Bad_, while Michael has said he never liked to think about Chuck's future. Is this something you've spent a lot of time speculating about?

I feel like Kim has to be out of Jimmy's life for him to have to be Saul. I don't know if she has to be gone from the earth. But I also feel like for him to behave as Saul—let's say she lives across town and she can see his billboards and stuff, I think that would be an embarrassment to him. So I don't know what happens to her that he carries on becoming this guy in such a public way. Maybe she just rejects him, and it's his way of making her feel bad. I don't know. This will be interesting to see what happens. These guys are good writers. All the desires and motivations will be acknowledged in some way. But I'd be shocked if they are together, Kim and Jimmy. The weird thing is, if Chuck had lived, becoming Saul would be a great way to fuck with him. Putting your billboards up all over town, that would be a great way to wave that in his face and make him embarrassed.

You referred earlier to Jimmy being a much nicer person than Saul is, but in the season's ninth episode, what he does to Irene feels like one of the worst things anyone has done to anyone else on either this show or _Breaking Bad_. How did you feel when you saw that in the script?

Terrible. It felt terrible. I called Peter Gould, and I said, "Goddammit, man. This is sad. All that's left is for me to go shopping for lime-green socks, and this is Saul now." And he goes, "Well, two things. One, this is the story we said we were going to tell," so kinda tough shit. And secondly, he said, "It's not entirely true that he's all the way there now." But in some fundamental way, in the telling of that little story, that was a big break for this guy into becoming a mercenary, selfish actor in the world, and something he wasn't really entirely before. It bummed me out. Because when we play these characters, you do have to do the things they do, and you have to come up with your mental justification for it, and try to play it as the choice that you justify. It's shitty to play a shitty person. It sucks to play someone who is being a jerk.

Peter has said that the writers didn't expect to like Jimmy as much as they do, and Vince recently said that if they had known going in it would be this tragic, he would have been less excited to make it, even though he loves what the show is now. How would you have felt when they approached you

a few years ago if you had known this is what the show was going to become?

I think I would have been more intimidated. I was lucky to be able to approach every scene as a fresh thing without some big fear of what was to come, or some template being laid down for this emotionally fraught character and this intense personal inner struggle. If somebody had said, "That's what you're going to be playing out," I would have said, "Boy, I'm not sure I'm up for that. I've never done it." I might have said, "I don't think I can pull it off without more comedy in it."

Was there a point where you began to accept that whatever they threw at you, dramatically, you could handle? Or are you still not at that point?

I feel more confident after all that they've given me to do. I'm not ever doing anything entirely alone. I've got Michael McKean or Jonathan Banks or Rhea Seehorn across from me, and that helps immensely, just as in *Breaking Bad*, having Bryan Cranston or Aaron Paul in a room with you giving focus or direction. One of the great things about acting is there's a Zen-like quality to it. All you're ever doing is the moment that you're playing. And that makes it less frightening. I've been a writer and I think with writing, you feel more of this fear and concern about managing the entire piece that you're doing. Whereas with acting, however much it's intimidating you, it's an activity that you're only ever doing moment to moment, and that makes it a little less intimidating.

In the first season, you were in ninety or even ninety-five percent of the show, and these last two years, it's been a much more even split, and almost two separate shows: Jimmy McGill the lawyer, and Mike Ehrmantraut the drug enforcer. Beyond your workload being lighter, how has it been watching the show evolve into these two separate but related things?

I love it. The dynamics of the show are one of the unique, amazing things about it. I hope that we can meld the two. They're gonna have to come together, and I think it can be done. I think these guys are definitely up to the task, but it will be neat to see that happen, and I think it will happen in the next season now. So I'm looking forward to that. But I agree with you, there is a bit of a big divide between the two stories and the tone and the temperature of the two stories. I think we're pulling these two things off. I talk to fans, I get feedback, and I feel like this weird, strange, juggling act of the show, everyone's game for it.

I've said it before, and it's a weird kiss-assy thing to say, but I mean it: the audience is a big part of whether what you do works. We have this amazing audience that was groomed by *Breaking Bad*, and by watching that show and knowing what to look for and how to watch it. Because we've got this awesome platform to launch from, that dialed everyone in to an extent, people have let us do this. But however good our work is, or how hard we work, you've gotta give it up to the audience for giving us a chance. When I say that, part of it is, people on our side of this thing, there's a lot of talk about the audience: "People won't like this, people won't tolerate that." There's a lot of conjecture about what the viewers will tolerate or like. But we don't fuckin' know. It's all guesswork, it's all using your gut. I would have said this show was too offbeat, idiosyncratic, and closely observed to win the affection that it's won. I would've under-estimated its appeal by a lot, if we'd known what we were doing beforehand, but we didn't. Nobody knew what we were doing. We had no idea what we were setting out to do; we just started doing it.

A Candid Conversation with Vince Gilligan on *Better Call Saul*

[This article originally ran on RollingStone.com on August 3, 2018]

It took you and Peter a while to figure out what the show was. At what point did you say to yourselves, "Wait a minute, this is actually good? This isn't just a folly that we've done, to keep everyone together?"
We would never put anything on that we had worked less than a hundred percent on. Having said that, I didn't know it would come together. I knew it would be the product of a lot of hard work and a lot of talent, in front of and behind the camera. I thought that at worst, we would create something that was admirable and a perfectly legitimate attempt at a show. But I didn't realize it would be as successful as it is in terms of a fully jelled world, a full totality of creation . . . one that is as satisfying as it is.

When we first started concocting the idea of doing a spin-off, we literally thought it'd be a half-hour show. It'd be something akin to *Dr. Katz*, where it's basically Saul Goodman in his crazy office with the styrofoam columns and he's visited every week by a different stand-up comic. It was basically, I guess, legal problems. We talked about that for a day or two. And then Peter Gould and I realized, we don't know anything about the half-hour idiom. And then we thought, okay, well, so it's an hour . . . but it's going to be a really funny hour. I said, "*Breaking Bad* is about twenty-five percent humor, seventy-five percent drama. Maybe this will be the reverse of that." Well this thing, especially in Season Four, is every bit as dramatic as *Breaking Bad* ever was. I just didn't see any of that coming. I didn't know how good it would all be. I really didn't.

It's amazing how hard it was to get it right.
The question we should've asked ourselves from the beginning: "Is Saul Goodman an interesting enough character to build a show around?" And the truth is, we came to the conclusion, after we already had the deal in hand [and] AMC and Sony had already put up the money, "I don't think we have a show here, because I don't think we have a character who could support a show." He's a great flavoring, he's a wonderful saffron that you sprinkle on your risotto. But you don't want to eat a bowl full of saffron, you gotta have the rice, you know? You gotta have the substance.

And it dawned on us that this character seemed so comfortable in his own skin. Peter and I do not possess those kinds of personalities. We thought, "Regardless how much comedy is in it, how do you find drama in a guy who's basically okay with himself?" So then we thought, "Well, who was he before he was Saul Goodman?"

Because the show is named *Better Call Saul*, we thought that we had to get to this guy quick or else people will accuse us of false advertising—a bait and switch. Then lo and behold, season after season went by and it dawned on us, we don't want to get to Saul Goodman . . . and that's the tragedy.

If we had thought all of this from the get-go, that would have made us very smart. But as it turns out, we're very plodding and dumb, and it takes forever to figure this stuff out. Which is why we're perfectly matched for a TV schedule versus a movie schedule, because you got to get it right the first time when you're writing a movie. It took us forever to get it right.

Have there been any specific times you can think of where, in the course of making this show, you had an idea; you're starting to do it; and then [writers] Tom Schnauz or Genn Hutchison or somebody says, you can't do that because it contradicts this thing you did on *Breaking Bad*?
I'm sure that it's happened many times. I'm trying to think of an exact example.*

Going in, did you expect to be featuring as many *Breaking Bad* characters as you have? Did you assume at some point we would get to Gus, for instance?
We always assumed we'd get to Gus—I think we thought we might get to him quicker. Just speaking for myself and no one else: I thought we'd have gotten to Walt or Jesse by this point, as sort of the first fan of both shows. I'm greedy to see all of these characters. I thought we would see plenty of *Breaking Bad* characters. I didn't know we'd dig as deep for some of them as we have.

When you say you expected to get to Walt and Jesse by now, how did you expect to use them?
I thought we would have touched base with them already. But having said that, it makes perfect sense that we haven't yet touched base with them. Just being in the writers' room, you realize that there's a lot to do before that happens—if and when it does happen. I don't even want to promise that it will. It's like what I was saying a minute ago: you play the cards that you've dealt yourself. There's no point in cheating in solitaire. That's a weird analogy, but ultimately, a pretty good one. You can cheat in solitaire, but there's nothing satisfying about cheating in solitaire.

---

* I checked with *Breaking Bad* vets Schnauz and Hutchison, and they said it mostly comes up involving characters who exist on *Saul* and met for the first time on *Breaking Bad*. Ted Beneke, for instance, was briefly considered as someone Jimmy could have tried to make a commercial for last season— then everyone remembered that Saul Goodman was part of the scam involving Ted's "Aunt Birgit."

And the analogy holds when you get to the writers' room with *Better Call Saul*. You can change the character's history, you can have it be that Walter White never comes into it, but it wouldn't ultimately be satisfying. And when you play the cards out correctly and you see that it's time to bring Walter White in, for instance, it's a wonderfully satisfying moment. If you force it, if you cheat the cards, if you bring them in just because folks are demanding it or expecting it, and you kind of bullshit the character's way into the show, it's just not going to satisfy anybody. I believe that in my heart.

Has the show evolved and become good enough to the point where it doesn't need Walter White?
Maybe. I mean, it would be satisfying to see Walt. Not to see him shoehorned in—that would not satisfy me. But to see the character properly arrive at a nexus point with *Better Call Saul*. That'd be wonderful . . . [though] it's very possible it won't happen if it doesn't feel properly arrived at. And yes, I believe that *Better Call Saul* is so much its own creation now, its own thing. It absolutely stands on its own.

We're enjoying this overlap between *Breaking Bad* and *Better Call Saul* that we're continuing to arrive at. But there's a version of the show where you don't see it as *Breaking Bad* stuff at all. Where, for instance, we leave out Mike Ehrmantraut, because he barely ever interacts with Jimmy McGill anymore. We could just stick with the Jimmy McGill story: him, Kim Wexler, Howard Hamlin, all of that stuff. We could have a perfectly satisfying show. But we feel like we're giving the fans two shows for the price of one. It really does feel like two TV shows in one now.

The beauty of it is, some people are always going to love *Breaking Bad* more. But I run into people every day now who say *Better Call Saul* is their favorite of the two. I love hearing that. I don't know where I fall personally on that scale, that continuum—I try not to choose. I don't have children, but this is as close as I'll ever get to having children. I find it hard to choose between them. But I'm just glad they both exist.

But, when you embarked on this, and you and Peter are just banging your heads against the wall asking what the show was, could you ever have imagined the idea that someone would come up to you and say they like *Saul* better?
We both wanted it to not be *AfterMASH*.* That's about as high as we had set our sights: we wanted to not embarrass ourselves. We wanted our spin-off series to

---

* A *M*A*S*H* sequel series that's widely accepted to have the biggest gap in quality from the parent show to the spin-off.

not take anything away from the original, to not leave a bad taste in the mouth of the fans of the original. "Let's hope it's more *Frasier* than *AfterMASH.*" Our rational, realistic goals for *Better Call Saul* were simply that it wouldn't suck and it wouldn't embarrass us. It didn't rise much higher than that, to be honest.

It's worked out a little bit better than that.
I'm so glad. I never thought anyone would come up to me and say, "I like *Better Call Saul* better than *Breaking Bad.*" If you had asked me before we started, "Would that bother you if someone said that?" First of all, I would have said, "That's never gonna happen. And yeah, it probably would bother me." It doesn't bother me a bit. It tickles me. I love it.

"Smoke"

"Well, Howard, I guess that's your cross to bear." —**Jimmy**

The thing about Saul Goodman—and the reason Vince Gilligan and Peter Gould had such a devil of a time figuring out how to build a show around him—is that he's at peace with his life. He's not as openly or proudly malevolent as many of the other major players from the Heisenberg-verse, but he's also not particularly troubled by the things he is an accomplice to. The capacity for guilt, or the desire to do the right thing for its own sake, got left behind along with his real name. The Jimmy McGill we've been watching for the previous three seasons is a far from perfect man, but there's a strain of decency in him that would make him so appealing to Kim, and that would drive him to blow up his elder-care practice to undo the damage he caused to Irene's reputation. He takes shortcuts, and he relishes the prospect of separating obnoxious rich bros from their money, but there's more good in him than bad.

How does that guy we've been watching for the previous three seasons become the carefree monster-enabler we met on *Breaking Bad*? What kind of seismic event must have caused him to cast aside all his best qualities in order to more easily enjoy a criminal attorney's life?

How about the gruesome suicide of his revered older brother, as a result of various offenses Jimmy perpetrated against him? Think that could do the trick?

Jimmy spends much of "Smoke" in shock over news of Chuck's death, and his understandable belief that the events of last season's "Chicanery" led to it. This is a muted, closed-off Jimmy, struggling to come to terms with what happened to his brother and the thought that he might be to blame. It's as quiet and understated as Bob Odenkirk has ever been in the role (even more than when he's Gene from Cinnabon, whom we'll get back to in a moment), and it perfectly fits what we know about Jimmy's complicated but ultimately loving and worshipful feelings about Chuck.

But we know more about what happened to Chuck, and by the end of the episode, so does Jimmy. Poor Howard Hamlin*—whose transformation from

---

* Thomas Schnauz recalls that the writers began to ask before this season whether Howard had an ongoing place on the show without Chuck. "If there's ever an indication that we didn't know the overall plot of the show, that was it," he says. But, "We had to decide on cast and getting actor deals

smarmy villain to utterly sympathetic supporting player has been as thorough as it's been surprising—comes over to Kim's apartment to not only share his belief that Howard's death wasn't an accident, but to clarify that Chuck actually got over the bar association incident fairly quickly, and that it wasn't until their falling out over the malpractice insurance premiums that Chuck began the spiral that ended in his death.

We of course know that the premiums only spiked because Jimmy ratted Chuck out to the insurance agency in a fit of pique over the cost of his suspension, and this is too much for him to handle. The thought of Chuck dying because Jimmy publicly humiliated him was bad enough, but Jimmy could always justify his actions as protecting himself after Chuck manipulated him into confessing and then destroying the tape. Had it stopped there, Chuck might still be alive and returned to his treasured practice of the law. But Jimmy didn't let it stop there, and his outing of Chuck to the insurance rep gave Jimmy no benefit other than schadenfreude.

As Jimmy comes to understand the true, and truly indefensible, reason his brother killed himself, something in him breaks. It's the something that has made us like him so much over these three seasons, the thing that has made us all fear the moment when it goes away and he becomes Saul Goodman for real. In that moment, Jimmy McGill realizes that the only way he can deal with this horrible understanding is to turn off his fundamental kindness and let Howard take the blame for it all. In that moment, more than ever before in this show, he is Saul Goodman, utterly untroubled by the decisions he's made and the people he's hurt, whistling without a care in the world as he checks the fish tank and makes coffee, just like Walter White whistled after Drew Sharp's murder. (And Kim looks just as dismayed to witness this as Jesse Pinkman was to see that.)

It's such a small moment in isolation, but *Better Call Saul* has turned out to be a master class in how to turn small things into something emotionally huge. That ability is on display throughout "Smoke." In lesser hands, the premiere would just be a housekeeping episode dealing with the aftermath of Chuck's suicide and Hector Salamanca's stroke, but it feels like so much more because these great storytellers know how to mine each little detail for all it's worth.

Take, for instance, our latest black-and-white glimpse of Gene Takovic. We're picking up right where Season 3 left him, having passed out in a panic over giving legal advice to the shoplifter. He's taken to the emergency room, in

made early, and our love of Patrick made us think, *Sign him and we'll figure out a way to keep Howard in the show,* which really helped us focus on Jimmy's psychology and how he felt about Chuck's death and how Howard was dealing with it versus Jimmy."

a visit that briefly resembles the time we saw Chuck in the ER after his copy shop fall. Though he's soon allowed to leave, the admissions clerk reminds us of how every moment of Gene's existence is fraught with the possibility of being discovered, arrested, or worse. For a normal person, a typo on a hospital admissions form would be something to laugh about, or at worst a bureaucratic headache; for Gene, it's a potential extinction event. You can feel that dread right along with him, and even more when the cab driver taking him home turns out to have an Albuquerque Isotopes air freshener and seems to squint in recognition at Gene. Because the show so far has allowed only one Gene appearance per season, it means a terribly long wait to find out if he's in as much trouble as he believes. And that in turn only puts us inside his paranoid head even more.

The air freshener also provides us with a link to the Mike and Gus half of the show, as Mike is watching an Isotopes game when he decides he's going to earn his laundered money by becoming a security consultant for Madrigal Electromotive. This is another vintage Mike Ehrmantraut heist story—or in this case, a reverse heist, as he breaks into Madrigal's Las Cruces facility to warn company security that it can be done—defined by how little he says and how easily he accomplishes what he sets out to do. It's unclear at this moment exactly what his game is, other than arranging another meeting with Lydia in a very public way, but it's also a welcome respite from the grief of the Jimmy story, as well as the tension of what's happening with Nacho and the other cartel players.

The Nacho subplot is another classic "in-between moment." It would be so easy to jump from Hector having the stroke to even the next day, so we could get a sense of what the new status quo is between Gus's crew and the Salamancas. Instead, we watch Nacho trying to find the right opportunity to dispose of the placebo pills with Gus and the others watching him. It's not strictly necessary, plot-wise, especially since Gus already seemed suspicious of Nacho in the Season 3 finale. But there's value in a refresher course on just how thorough Gus's operation was even pre-Mike (Victor uses another gas cap tracker to follow Nacho to the bridge where he ultimately dumps the pills). And it helps us understand just how deep a hole Nacho has dug for himself. Like the hospital interlude with Gene, it puts us right inside Nacho's head. The cartel half of the show is operating at something of a handicap compared to the Jimmy half, because we know more about what's to come for these people. Anything that's done to help us better empathize with the characters going through these motions—particularly someone like Nacho, who never appeared in *Breaking Bad*—does a world of good.

The patience on display in that first attempted pill disposal scene is also present in how the Jimmy portion of the episode begins. We get more than three dialogue-free minutes to watch Jimmy and Kim sleep—a sleep haunted by burning embers that they'll only find out about after they wake—and to watch Jimmy putter around the kitchen, listen to jazz, make coffee for Kim, and check the classifieds for a job to pay the bills for the rest of his suspension. Three minutes is a very large amount of screen time to devote to something so little, but it's fascinating to watch. Not only is it well directed by Minkie Spiro (even when *Saul* is slow, it's nice to look at, which goes a long way), we know that these are Jimmy's last peaceful moments before those dreams of floating ash become the nightmare of Chuck having died in a fire, and Jimmy having to reckon with his role in that. It's as emotionally fraught as the onscreen action is mundane.

Does Jimmy's brutal response to Howard's confession, and his upbeat demeanor afterward, mean he's gone full Saul Goodman, never to turn back? That feels too easy, especially since this show has already featured a half-dozen potential Saul Goodman "Eureka!" moments that proved only temporary. But this is by far the closest we've ever felt to Jimmy becoming Saul. Given how much we've grown to care for Jimmy, it's the kind of moment we've been dreading, and "Smoke" delivers it with as much craft as we hoped, and as much pain as we feared.

How Kim Wexler Got Her Power Ponytail

Rhea Seehorn, as you will see even more in the archival *Rolling Stone* feature that appears on page 177, is the kind of actor who puts a *lot* of thought into every detail of the characters she plays. So when I reached out to her while writing this book to ask for a brief synopsis of how Kim's trademark ponytail was created, and by which member of the *Saul* hairstyling team, I was not surprised when the response was this long, this detailed, and this insightful about what the ponytail says about who Kim is:

> The fabulous Trish Almeida and I collaborated and discussed the hair, as we were beginning to concoct who this character might be. We knew Kim was a woman competing in a mostly male world, and while she would not be interested in suppressing her femininity, she would not lead with sexuality. (I never let her flirt to get something.) She also was trying to wear a "uniform" to help her fit into a world that I thought was one that she did not come from—both financially and academically—so both clothes and hair needed to be a polished armor that was highly professional, but practical.

> The final piece was that we all discussed single working women we were around growing up, ones that were working overtime to get a foot into the middle class and away from where they'd come from. And we all agreed that those women, in the real world, rarely change their hair, jewelry, or purses. Usually have just a few black and blue interchangeable jackets/pants/skirts. Costumes (Jennifer Bryan) and I felt that her clothes should look like she bought them herself at Marshalls or T.J.Maxx, and not tailored (this evolved and changed when she started to earn money).

> Trish and I thought the makeup and hair should appear as though she could do it herself, quickly, and repeatedly. The one little added thing Trish suggested, was just a *slight* curl to the ponytail. It gave it some shape, and also seemed to add just a little subtle message that even though Kim wouldn't want people to know by her outward demeanor, she is really trying to do this/get this/succeed/fit in/move up. It's not a totally natural hairstyle that took no effort at all.

> We took all of this to Peter Gould and Vince Gilligan for their feedback, and showed them some test pictures, as well as a few other hairstyles. They agreed with us and went with the pony.

Very subtly, Trish would curl it just a bit more when Kim had very important meetings or events that she would feel she needed even more "armor" at. Vince and Peter definitely picked up on that, and really enjoyed it becoming almost a barometer of Kim's state of mind over the seasons. I also enjoyed being very specific in the choice that Jimmy is the only one she lets her guard/ hair down in front of. (Except the flashback, delivering office mail scene.)

And Trish, Peter, and Vince were very thoughtful in the choices we made for her hair when she breaks her arm. It was pulled back in a sloppy low barrette—something we felt Kim could probably do with one hand, and/or just a small amount of assistance from Jimmy. The only exception being Chuck's funeral. We decided that Kim would splurge on a hairdresser for that event, out of respect, but also because she's aware that it will be a very public showing.

Vince and Peter would definitely discuss with Trish, and me, what they thought Kim's pony should be like in each and every episode, and sometimes scene to scene. And the wonderful hair designers that worked with us for the later seasons (Ruth Carsch, Jennifer Bell, and Rita Troy) also became close watchers and keepers of the ponytail! And ALL of the hairstylists told me that the perfect pony is one of the most deceptively difficult styles to do—let alone one that has such a life of its own!

SEASON 4, EPISODE 2
WRITTEN BY THOMAS SCHNAUZ
DIRECTED BY MICHELLE MACLAREN

"Breathe"

"And when is it over for you?" —**Manuel Varga**

Toward the end of "Breathe," Jimmy calls Mike to arrange a caper involving the expensive Hummel figurines he saw in Mr. Neff's office during his job interview.[*] This is a callback both to his elder-law work in Season 1's "Alpine Shepherd Boy" and to the idea of Jimmy and Mike as occasional partners, before *Better Call Saul* had so clearly become two largely separate shows operating under the same title. As Mike gets deeper into the cartel world, while the writers do everything they can to delay Jimmy's transformation into the amoral Saul Goodman, the two halves feel further apart than ever. "Breathe" mainly takes place on Mike's side of things,[†] albeit with him largely sidelined in favor of more dancing between Nacho and Gus. But the Jimmy side provides a lot of vivid moments while we're there.

Jimmy remains in the same jaunty mood in which we saw him at the end of the season premiere. He's still the breakfast maestro,[‡] eager to find a job to help pay the bills and get out of Kim's hair now that the apartment has become her office. And he easily talks his way into a copier sales job for which he has no on-paper qualifications. We've seen Slippin' Jimmy sell things far more useless than a high-end copy machine, but he can't exactly walk into Neff's office and say, "Hey, I'm a con man, so I'm perfect for this gig!"

He comes shockingly close to saying exactly that, but only after he's gotten the job and realized how little he wants it, scolding his befuddled would-be employers by pointing out how easily they let themselves be snowed by a man they never properly vetted: "I could be a serial killer! I could be the guy who pees in your coffee pot!" Why does Jimmy do this? Self-loathing in the wake of Chuck's suicide? The same allergy to the straight life that led him to blow up

---

[*] In case there was any doubt about whether the wig Bob Odenkirk wears is meant to be Jimmy's actual hair or a toupee, this episode confirms that it's supposed to be real. Right before he goes in for the interview, Jimmy is alarmed to find some loose hair strands in his palm. This sets us up for the inevitable Saul Goodman comb-over as he gets into the thick (or thin) of male-pattern baldness.

[†] Mike's meeting with Lydia at the Hotel Chaco clarifies what he was doing in Las Cruces in the season premiere: playing security consultant for Madrigal is a way to backstop any investigation into the source of his laundered money. It's yet another way to stress that Gus doesn't seem to be in Mike's thoughts yet, but it's having that side effect nonetheless, even as it makes Lydia jittery as usual.

[‡] Walter White Jr. was already impressed with Saul Goodman just from the ads. Imagine if Flynn knew what an ace this guy was with his favorite meal of the day.

the sweet job with Davis and Main? Jimmy's at such an emotional crossroads that even he doesn't seem entirely sure about what he's doing, or why. Because as soon as he's stormed out of Neff's office, he places a call about the next job on his list, and later seems enthusiastic with Kim about some of the other leads.

Kim has an even bigger, and more easily understood, outburst in the episode. As executor of Chuck's estate, Howard breaks down exactly how Chuck chose to shaft Jimmy: a $5,000 inheritance—just big enough to prevent Jimmy from contesting the will, but not even big enough to float him for very long during this period of unemployment—and a seat on the board of the scholarship Chuck is setting up with money that Jimmy won't get. Between that final insult, the promise of whatever cruel sentiments exist in the letter Chuck left for his brother, and Howard's confession at the end of the premiere, Kim has completely had it with both her living ex-boss and the dead one. Rhea Seehorn is amazingly raw in this scene—the muscles in her neck seem on the verge of bursting out of her skin as Kim lists all the humiliations Chuck has visited upon Jimmy from beyond the grave. Kim's protective streak toward her boyfriend leads to the most tender and intimate scene she and Jimmy have shared in quite a while, even as we've long since grown used to them as a couple who are close but not usually physically affectionate.

Those scenes are fantastic, but "Breathe" is primarily concerned with cartel business, as Gus and Nacho each plot their next moves in the wake of Hector's debilitating but nonfatal stroke.

It's a tremendous episode for Michael Mando, who seems wearier and wearier with each successive scene. Removing Hector from the board was supposed to solve all of Nacho's problems, but it hasn't. His father still barely speaks with him. The Cousins have come back across the border to guard their revered uncle and stare daggers at anyone around him. Arturo has opted to step into the power vacuum and run the local operation, and he turns out to be infected with the same macho posturing as Hector and Tuco, forcing an armed standoff between Nacho and Victor over an extra kilo from Gus's supply. By the time the pistols have been put away again, the look on Nacho's face is sheer exhaustion as he ponders an eternity of working for cocksure idiots like this.

Moments later, he's out of the impulsive frying pan and into the calculating fire, as Gus emerges from nowhere to asphyxiate Arturo with a plastic bag, then blackmails Nacho with the knowledge of what happened to Don Hector's pills. It is, like many of the Chicken Man's moves, swift, brutal, and thorough. He owns Nacho now. Gus is in some ways an improvement as a boss over any of the Salamancas. But Nacho is less a new employee to Gus than a tool to be used and then discarded in his long-simmering revenge plot against Hector, Juan Bolsa, and Don Eladio. Every time Victor is on screen serves as a reminder of how Gus can treat underlings who have served him long and well; just imagine what can happen to an outsider like Nacho should his utility cease.

This material is tense and well-crafted, but there can be an unavoidable air of puzzle-solving to these stories. Jimmy has a professional destination he has to arrive at just as much as Gus does. But he has a much bigger personal journey to take along the way, where Gus is basically the same man who first sat across a table from Walter White. To get the Gus equivalent of the journey that Jimmy's been on, we would have to pick up in 1989 right after Hector murders Max, to see how Gus rose from that low moment and built himself into the kind of man who could destroy his enemies within twenty years. But that's a very different show from this one. Giancarlo Esposito is still fantastic, and the Gus plots still tense. But it's a more limited role than what his longtime co-stars get to do.

When the series began, there was a charge to the Jimmy/Mike scenes not only because of the chemistry between Odenkirk and Banks, but because each encounter seemed to be pulling Jimmy closer to *Breaking Bad* territory. At this point, even the suggestion of them reuniting is exciting, because it would force Mike to spend more time in the uncharted territory that is the Jimmy McGill show.

SEASON 4, EPISODE 3
WRITTEN BY GORDON SMITH
DIRECTED BY DANIEL SACKHEIM

"Something Beautiful"

"You were meant for better things." —**Gus**

Early in "Something Beautiful," Jimmy is stunned to have Mike turn down his offer to steal the Hummel figurine out of Neff's office. He has no idea that Mike's laundered drug money makes the reward for a job like this not nearly worth the risk. And he's too swept up in the thrill of being back in Slippin' Jimmy territory to see what Mike so clearly can: that this is an unhealthy response to Chuck's death.

With Mike out of the picture, "Something Beautiful" (reuniting the writer/director team from "Chicanery") turns into something of a *Freaky Friday* edition of *Better Call Saul*. For once, it's Jimmy trying to pull off a heist (albeit doing it in his usual brazen and sloppy way), while Team Gus winds up running the grift, in a far more ruthless fashion than Jimmy would ever consider. Things are so topsy-turvy this week that it's not even Mike (who vanishes from the episode after the Jimmy meeting) linking the two halves together, but friendly criminal veterinarian Dr. Caldera, who introduces Jimmy to backup thief Ira* and patches up the wounded Nacho.

Gus was running a long con on the cartel for much of his time on *Breaking Bad*, so this isn't wholly new territory for him. But it's nonetheless fun and fascinating to watch his team play this particular short con, which makes it look like a rival cartel murdered Arturo and wounded Nacho. (If Nacho survived with only a few bruises, it might have aroused suspicion from the Cousins and Juan Bolsa. The gunshot wound absolves him of that, in painful fashion.)

There are only two downsides to the way that story unfolds in the hour. The first is that Victor and Tyrus seem so efficient and thorough already that the organization barely seems to need Mike. The second is the macro issue with the Mike/Gus half of the show, and the way it's constrained by what we know of *Breaking Bad* and can at times feel less like a story in its own right than a very lavishly produced Easter egg. On the one hand, I yelped with delight at the realization that Gale Boetticher was about to appear—and singing Tom Lehrer's "The Elements," no less. On the other, there's only so much the show

---

* Ira (played by Franc Ross) will later run Vamanos Pest, the extermination company Walt, Jesse, and Mike buy as a front operation near the end of *Breaking Bad*.

can do with Gale, and not just because *Better Call Saul*'s run overlapped with David Costabile having a full-time job twirling his mustache on Showtime's *Billions*. There's a timeline for when Gus will finish building the Super Lab, when he'll have Gale running it, when Gale self-destructively convinces Gus to bring in Walt to run it, etc., etc., etc. All of those events are far enough off in these characters' futures that even Gus seems aware that his visit to Gale's classroom is a fun diversion that can't lead to much more at the moment.

As has been the case throughout the early stages of this season, it's left to Nacho (and Michael Mando) to give this story the gravity it needs in order to be more than just a *Breaking Bad* bonus feature. For us, a lot of this is about filling in the blanks, but for Nacho, it's his *life*—a life perpetually in danger because of choices other people keep making for him, going back at least to Mike refusing to assassinate Tuco. Unlike Caldera, he can't unilaterally declare that he's done with the cartel, which means he's likely to continue being a pin cushion for Gus, the Cousins, and anyone else with more juice than he has in this rising civil war.

While Team Fring is operating like a well-oiled machine, Jimmy's own return to crime is all too human and fallible. Ira is able to easily bypass Neff security, but Mr. Neff himself is temporarily living at work, fallout from a gift his wife found very insensitive. (In fairness to him, it does sound like a swell vacuum cleaner. But still.) It's a tense, funny sequence, with Ira doing a better job of staying hidden in such a small space than you'd expect from a man who's not exactly Pinkman-sized. We know Jimmy has criminal skills beyond grifting (though his previous record of vandalizing automobiles involved going in though the sunroof, not the door), and he's able to distract Neff long enough for Ira to slip out with the expensive figurine.

It's an exciting minor triumph for Jimmy—at least, for this version of Jimmy who no longer worries about staying on the straight and narrow to win his older brother's approval. In a poignant twist, it's followed by Kim finally giving him the letter from Chuck. It's not the imperious rebuke she might have feared, but in some ways, it's worse: a letter clearly written during Jimmy's days in the HHM mailroom, before his law career turned him back into a threat that Chuck felt the need to eradicate. It is, from what we know about the McGill siblings, one of the few times in their lives when they were getting along. But those good feelings were based on a very specific set of circumstances, particularly Chuck's need to feel superior to his troublemaking kid brother. Jimmy thriving in the mail room was a perfect outcome for Chuck, but an unsatisfying one for Jimmy, and his desire for more than that led to the unraveling of their relationship, and of Chuck's life.

It's no wonder that Kim is crying by the end of the letter. That Jimmy seems utterly unmoved by it speaks to how swiftly he's come to suppress all feelings about his brother, and to a degree about the life he was trying to build to impress Chuck. He hasn't exactly been a Boy Scout across the series to date, but orchestrating a break-in and theft is a line he wouldn't have crossed a season or two ago. Chuck's gone, though. Jimmy briefly felt some guilt about his role in that before extinguishing those feelings altogether in order to function. But if Jimmy was being good at first to please Chuck, and then Kim, eventually we saw that he liked doing it. At times, particularly with his elderly clients, being good made him feel fantastic.

But we've also seen, in both flashbacks with Marco and the occasional appearances of Viktor and Giselle, how much pleasure he takes in separating suckers from their money. He's riding high after he rescues Ira from Neff, and earlier he's incredulous that Mike wouldn't want to go along on such a simple caper. Jimmy ends the episode standing in a half-open doorway, wanting to go to Kim to offer comfort, but unsure of how to do it. He's at a personal crossroads. Go one way, and he rides out the suspension, finds a new specialty now that he's toxic to senior citizens, and he and Kim build a simple but happy life together. Go the other way, and . . . well, this is one of those situations where our knowledge of where the story is going is both feature and bug. It gives every scene of Jimmy slippin' into Saul extra dramatic heft, but it's sad to watch. Walter White is the more direct cause of so much of the collateral damage on *Breaking Bad* than Saul is, but watching Jimmy's transformation is already starting to hurt a lot more than seeing Walt become Heisenberg, because we know how capable Jimmy is of being the good guy Walter White always mistakenly claimed to be.

SEASON 4, EPISODE 4
WRITTEN BY HEATHER MARION
DIRECTED BY JOHN SHIBAN

"Talk"

"All wrapped up in your sad little stories, and feeding off each other's misery."
—**Mike**

Even by Heisenberg-verse standards, the advancement of plot in *Saul* Season 4 has been pretty slow. Gus has made several moves in the aftermath of Hector's stroke, and Kim did give Jimmy the Chuck letter only one episode after receiving it. But on the whole, all our major characters have been in more of a stasis state than usual. Jimmy is looking to fill the time until his suspension ends, while also trying to realign his moral compass in the wake of Chuck's death. Kim doesn't quite know what she wants to do when she grows up, but she's pretty sure it's not overseeing Mesa Verde's perpetual expansion. Mike has been content playing grandpa, doing the crossword, and making occasional spot checks on Madrigal facilities. Even Nacho, caught up in the plottiest corner of the season so far, is pretty much stuck in narrative quicksand, struggling to get out while gradually sinking deeper into the spot Gus and the Salamancas put him in.

Team *Saul* has long been great at making scenes where nothing seems to be happening into something fascinating to watch. Case in point: Jimmy trying to keep himself busy and entertained while managing a cell phone store with no customers. The sequence couldn't be more explicitly about tedium, but because it's put together with such care, and because we know Jimmy so well and are invested in him, the mere act of him bouncing a CC Mobile ball against the front window* becomes fun and interesting.

We're reaching the point in the season, though, when even well-crafted depictions of boredom risk making the entire show boring, or at least frustrating. We don't need Walt and Skyler to wander into the cell phone store, but we need *something* to be happening in the here-and-now for these characters.

Fortunately, "Talk" not only turns out to be about the way everyone is stuck in neutral but starts to get them going again.

---

* Jimmy Loves Movies: this sequence rings very much of Steve McQueen in *The Great Escape* throwing a ball against the wall to stay sane every time he's sent back for another stint in solitary confinement.

Kim is probably the furthest away from her next move,* but her visit to Judge Munsinger's courtroom at least makes clear that she wants a next move, because Mesa Verde just isn't doing it for her anymore. Ethan Phillips expertly plays Munsinger's reaction to Kim's midlife crisis, making it clear even before he says it that she is far from the first lawyer to wander into his courtroom looking for a renewed sense of purpose. The bit about the plot of *The Verdict* neatly cuts two ways. It illustrates how unreasonable Kim is being in looking for a grand case to rekindle her love of the law. But that lesson is also being delivered by a man who shares a fictional universe with Gus Fring, Walter White, and the man who will be Saul Goodman. Both of these shows manage to have their cake and eat it, too, in this way: depicting the tedious, step-by-step nature of various jobs, legal or otherwise, but using those steps to get to larger-than-life plot points.

Jimmy, meanwhile, continues to run *from* things more than he's running *to* anything. He doesn't want the CC Mobile job, but he takes it as an excuse to put off Kim's attempt to force him into therapy to talk about Chuck. Under ordinary circumstances, this would be a decent way to kill time for the remaining ten months of his suspension since Jimmy's a natural salesman who enjoys interacting with strangers. But the store is so dead, he could probably turn it into a meth cookhouse without Robbie from corporate noticing. A meeting with Ira to divvy up the proceeds from the Bavarian Boy sale provides him with more cash than he was expecting, and also with an inspiration to drum up business at the store, by targeting criminals in constant need of a new phone number. This is a wink at Saul Goodman's drawer full of cell phones, but also an excuse to have Jimmy interacting even more frequently with Albuquerque's criminal element. Emotionally, he's already reasonably close to being Saul Goodman, but the logistics of how he'll get into that field of law and build up such a big client base haven't been in focus. This starts to do that.

Nacho seemingly makes a lot of progress this week. He hasn't healed much from the gunshot wound yet, as he has to operate a gun one-handed (racking the slide by wedging the pistol between his legs) and keeps falling down from the sheer effort of standing and moving. Yet he's able to help the Cousins when those maniacs decide to wage a two-man assault on the Espinosas' motel fortress in broad daylight, without a plan. (The incredulous look on Michael Mando's face as Nacho realizes what they're doing is a thing of beauty, as is the choice to show most of the raid from his POV outside the fence. It's a

---

* Because Kim is essentially one-handed at the moment, she can't pull off the power ponytail. She still does a pretty good job, all things considered, but the fact that her hair isn't perfect contributes just as much as the sling and the facial bruises to making clear how off she's been since the accident. As with so many things about this show, the strength is in the tiny details.

way to save time and money, sure, but it also adds to the legend of the Cousins as these unstoppable killing machines, leaving much of the specifics to Nacho's imagination, and ours.) The massacre is a success, but so high-profile that Leonel and Marco have to head back to Mexico to lay low for a while, freeing Ignacio for the moment from his two most terrifying babysitters. And his ability to put the pieces together about Gus staging this whole scam, in order to take over the Espinosas' territory, winds up impressing the Chicken Man, who speaks in tender, paternal fashion to him after, rather than in the imperious tone he had previously taken. But among the sentiments expressed in that gentler voice is that Nacho has more work to do, which is enough to send our man over to his father's shop to ask for help. Seeing the sorry physical state of his son is enough to finally thaw Mr. Varga's cold heart, but it feels like a sad and hopeless circumstance for both.

And then there's Mike Ehrmantraut, who bookends the episode after being largely absent from the last two. We open with a lovely but bittersweet pastoral flashback to Matty as a little boy watching a young Mike lay cement,* as riveted by the sight of his daddy doing a basic task as we tend to be. (Matty would be an ideal viewer of this show.) That's followed by an abrupt cut to Mike in the grief support group, everyone looking at him with horrified expressions that don't at all match the happy memory we just witnessed. It's not until late in the hour that we realize that the support group scene is a glimpse of another part of the episode: Mike exposes group member Henry as a fabulist who has invented a dead wife so he can be part of the group, then accuses Anita and the others of being narcissistic wallowers who can't see what's obviously right in front of them.

It's a cruel, sad moment. Mike may not have enjoyed the group itself, but he cares deeply for Stacey, and we see earlier in the hour how close he's grown to Anita.† Mike is mostly content in retirement, and the laundered drug money is enough to cover Stacey and Kaylee's needs. This would be a good life for him, certainly more than the one we know *Breaking Bad* has in store. But the thing about the peaceful life is that it's so much easier to think about Matty's death, and about Mike's failure to prevent it. There's an extraordinary moment before Henry enters the group meeting where Stacey talks about how much it hurt her to realize she went through a whole day without thinking about Matty. She's the one talking, and crying, but the camera is rightly focused on Mike, his nostrils flaring, his lip twitching, his eyes getting subtly but unmistakably redder, as we

---

* Presumably for the carport that Matty told Stacey about years later.
† Anita works at Cradock Marine Bank, which has popped up a few times on both *Breaking Bad* (it's where money was deposited for Mike's guys and Kaylee) and *Better Call Saul*. The name goes back to some *X-Files* episodes Vince Gilligan wrote; Fox Mulder has an account with them.

are reminded of just how much pain he carries with him all the time, and especially when he's forced to confront it directly.* What had been a fun game with Anita earlier in the day becomes salt in the gaping wound in Mike's heart, as Henry's invented wife and fake grief turn into an insult he cannot tolerate in this moment. It's a bad thing Henry is doing, but also something of a victimless crime. In exposing him, Mike lashes out at a roomful of people who are experiencing genuine grief just like he is. It's hard to imagine him going back to that place, or even sharing another meal at his favorite diner with Anita, who under other circumstances could have been an outstanding companion.

Gus calls Mike during one of his Madrigal inspections and pretends when they meet that he's upset Mike concealed his past history with Nacho. But Mike, like Nacho, can see through Fring's bluster to what the meeting is really about: a job. And at this moment in his life, Mike Ehrmantraut could very much use a job to take his mind off his dead son and how empty his life feels without him.

It is significant narrative progress for Mike, and for Season 4 as a whole. Emotionally, though, it's a bad direction for him to be going, and that would be obvious even if we didn't know where this partnership will eventually lead him.

But that's the no-win scenario of this show, isn't it? The faster the story moves, the closer we are to terrible things befalling almost everyone. Maybe slow isn't so bad.

---

* Jimmy and Mike are incredibly different people in most ways, but both demonstrate a clear aversion to therapy in this episode.

SEASON 4, EPISODE 5
WRITTEN BY ANN CHERKIS
DIRECTED BY MICHAEL MORRIS

"Quite a Ride"

"I'm gonna be a damn good lawyer, and people are gonna know about it."
—Jimmy

"Quite a Ride" is the first episode of *Better Call Saul* to genuinely feature the title character. Sure, we've seen Jimmy use the name Saul Goodman before while running cons or selling local ad time, but this is more than just the name: this is the guy we met on *Breaking Bad*, literally during the events of *Breaking Bad*. We are in Saul's strip mall office, somewhere in between "Ozymandias" and "Granite State," as Francesca is frantically shredding documents that are evidence of his criminal exploits, while Saul is packing up all the cash he has on hand before reaching out to Ed the disappearance expert. Saul's face is still beat up from where Jesse hit him after figuring out what happened to Brock, and Francesca* is very far removed from the sweet and optimistic lady whom Jimmy and Kim originally hired in their shared office. (Just as she did to Walt at the peak of his war with Gus, she is able to coolly extort money from a desperate Saul to do him a small favor.)

None of it is information we really need to appreciate Saul's story on *Breaking Bad*, but it's nonetheless startling and incredibly powerful to be hurled back into this era, and to be in the company of this man, after three and a half seasons of spending time with Jimmy McGill, with occasional glimpses of Gene Takovic. But why now? Why open this particular episode with a *Breaking Bad* flash-forward, after Gould and Gilligan have spent so long delaying so much as a glimpse of Saul Goodman's early career as a criminal defense lawyer?

Maybe it's because "Quite a Ride" offers the bookends to that career, in reverse. It opens with the end of the eponymous ride and closes with Jimmy McGill plotting out the beginning of it, on the verge of being Saul in everything but name.

Now, we've all cried wolf before on this issue, in part because the show has done the same. But you don't need to have a flip phone broken over your head to see what's happening throughout "Quite a Ride," an episode that is

---

* To which lawyer does Saul send Francesca? It sounds like Saul says, "Tell *him* Jimmy sent you," which would rule out Kim (and perhaps point to Howard, or someone else). But the line in the script is the more ambiguous "Tell 'em Jimmy sent you," which still puts her in play.

laying down the foundation for all things Goodman in the same way that Mike and Gus are interviewing engineers who can help them excavate the space needed for the Super Lab.

Jimmy's plan to sell burner phones to criminals starts out as a way to alleviate the boredom of his new job, and to make some extra cash off the books. But it soon becomes clear how desperately he craves the street life—as beautifully and aptly described in the song of the same name by Randy Crawford, which plays over a crackling montage, edited by Skip MacDonald, of a tracksuit-clad Jimmy moving merch at Jesse Pinkman's old hangout, the Dog House. It doesn't help that Kim's new sideline as a criminal defense lawyer, on top of her regular work for Mesa Verde, gives her precious little time to spend with him. (Even when they're physically in the same room of the apartment, every shot is framed to make Jimmy look alone.) But this itch he needs to scratch goes much deeper than his girlfriend's own midlife crisis. After he gets mugged by the kids from the laundromat (recalling the bruises on Saul Goodman in the teaser), he laments, "What the hell is the matter with me?"* These words could signal a man who has been scared straight from a life he has been lucky and talented enough to escape from, but it's not. It is Slippin' Jimmy being offended that his con-man edges have grown dull enough for punks like those to think they could rob him in the first place. It's a criminal recognizing that he never really wants to be anything else.

Kim's tender manner with him as she cleans his wounds does briefly seem to break that spell, and Jimmy even ends the scene by suggesting that he'll call the shrink she wanted him to see. But that moment of enlightenment lasts only long enough for him to run into a ruined Howard Hamlin at the courthouse. When he sees how little a top-tier, expensive therapist has been able to help Howard, he abandons the therapy plan, and tears up the paper with the phone number on it like it's another burner phone he needs to get rid of before he gets caught and has to actually talk to someone about his problems. Instead, it's his PPD supervisor who inadvertently plays psychoanalyst for him, as his routine questions about Jimmy's future plans force our man to articulate the path we've always unfortunately known he'll go down. He'll be a lawyer—and his desire to keep working with Kim, on top of his own criminal contacts and impulses, will make the choice of specialty for him—and he'll be a well-known lawyer, at that. Maybe even, though he doesn't say it, the kind whose face is on bus benches (the sort featured in this week's opening credits) all over town?

---

* In an episode overflowing with nods at the parent show (see also the bouncing car outside the Dog House with hydraulics), the phrasing here echoes the most important line of "Ozymandias," when Walt asks Skyler and Walter Jr., "What the hell is wrong with you? We're a family!"

Between the cold open, the scenes at the laundromat that will be home to the Super Lab,* and all the other Easter eggs (Walt liked to snap flip phones in half, too), the entire episode is a blinking neon arrow pointing to Saul Goodman's impending, tragic arrival. In the muddled early days of this series, nothing would have made me happier. Now? Well, I know it has to happen. But as we are perilously close to losing the Jimmy McGill we've come to love, it hurts, in a way I couldn't possibly have imagined when *Better Call Saul* began.

---

* Construction on the familiar location is about to begin, and Mike and Gus are as thorough as always, flying their European engineers into Denver and making them travel hooded to Albuquerque so they won't even know where this lab is unless they're the chosen one. That they choose the engineer who makes the job sound almost, but not quite, impossible over the one who makes it sound much too easy, also speaks to how careful and risk-averse they are. Werner Ziegler (played by Rainer Bock) may take a long time to get the job done, but he seems a much safer bet to actually do it, given all the restrictions Gus is placing on him.

SEASON 4, EPISODE 6
WRITTEN BY GENNIFER HUTCHISON
DIRECTED BY ANDREW STANTON

"Piñata"

"I need to be moving forward." —**Jimmy**

If "Quite a Ride" was offering us bookends of Saul Goodman's law career, then "Piñata" appears to be doing the same for Jimmy McGill's. We open back in Jimmy and Kim's mailroom days, when Jimmy's difficulty comprehending one of Chuck's big legal victories—and his recognition of how dazzled Kim, Howard, and everyone else at the firm is by it—inspires him to step into the HHM law library. We've long known that Jimmy went into the law in an attempt to impress Kim (success!) and Chuck (whoops!), so the scene is no more strictly necessary than the previous episode's glimpse of Saul and Francesca shredding documents post-"Ozymandias."* But like that scene, it offers a valuable emotional counterweight to the steps Jimmy takes in the rest of the episode on the road from criminal lawyer to *criminal* lawyer.

We see that criminal law isn't even on his mind when we return from the opening credits. Kim, struggling to do Mesa Verde work when all she cares about are her pro bono clients, comes across Jimmy's sketches for a potential new Wexler & McGill logo, and it contrasts her banking law work with him doing bankruptcy law.† When he learns that his very first elder client—and star of his one and only commercial for Davis and Main—Geraldine Strauss has died in her sleep, his conversation with her nephew is both a reminder of how good he is at connecting with clients, and an opportunity for him to grieve and cry in a way he never allowed himself to do for Chuck. After the prior episode's criminal shenanigans at the Dog House, he seems relatively snapped back into the do-gooder Jimmy we fell in love with around the time he first met Mrs. Strauss. (Note that when he brings up her Hummel figurine, it's not an

---

*　Speaking of future Saul Goodman associates, Gus's speech to Hector about the coati he trapped and kept around to watch it suffer is a stellar bit of acting from Giancarlo Esposito, who's often at his best when his voice is as soft as it is here. And it sets in motion the mechanism for how Gus's story will eventually end on *Breaking Bad* as a result of him not letting his nemesis just die. It gives us a bit of insight into Gus's background—he grew up poor, and the battle with the coati, when Gus was only seven, gave him his first lesson on how ruthless one needs to become to survive in difficult circumstances—and Esposito owns these kinds of moments.

†　This actually seems like a solid specialty for him, with elder law off the table. It still gives him the kind of interpersonal contact he thrives on, even as there's room for a certain amount of con artistry in helping desperate clients conceal assets.

attempt to scam it off of the nephew, but to make sure it ended up where she wanted it to go.)

Jimmy is still on a precipice here, still plotting a good—if slightly more outsized—life as Kim's professional and romantic partner, and he's achingly close to getting it ten months in the future. The problem is that so much of his plan depends on Kim, and she has her own life and desires to worry about, even as she has no idea that she's the last barrier separating him from the terrible future we know is coming. In an attempt to satisfy her lucrative responsibilities to Mesa Verde and her emotional investment in the pro bono work, she belatedly agrees to join Schweikart & Cokely as a partner, figuring that she can do both jobs with a larger team around her.

It's a great move for her, and one that feels entirely in keeping with the journey she's been on at least since the start of this season, if not going back to when she found out how Jimmy helped her land Mesa Verde. But it's the worst possible news Jimmy could hear. He still respects and cares for her enough to tell her to take the job.* But we see in the immediate aftermath of her announcement that the entire foundation of his world has been pulled out from under him, providing Slippin' Jimmy an easy path to slip on out and cause trouble.

After a stop at the downsized wreckage of HHM—where he still has enough decency to give Howard a tough-love pep talk in an attempt to fix what he did to this place he used to care so much about—Jimmy spends his paltry inheritance from Chuck's will on a pallet of burner phones. He is all-in on what Mrs. Nguyen dismisses as a get-rich-quick scheme, but which he understands is a reliable shortcut to get his own firm set up, since he won't have Kim working alongside him anymore. And where he went into his first night as a burner salesman impulsively, here he is a con man with a plan to make sure the three punks from the laundromat don't keep causing him problems.

Jimmy's revenge on these kids—hanging them upside down as human piñatas to be threatened by his masked batmen†—is both a thrilling sequence and an unsettling one. It's by far the hour's biggest showcase for the talents of very special guest director Andrew Stanton (*Finding Nemo, WALL-E*), in both the way he shoots the thieves' disorienting upside-down POV, and the way that one of Jimmy's assistants drags a baseball bat along the warehouse floor like he's Marco Salamanca preparing to chop off a DEA agent's head with a silver axe. After this junior crew smugly took all of Jimmy's money the last time, it's

---

*   When Kim says of her PD work, "I like it, and I'm good at it," it's hard not to think of Walt and Skyler's final conversation, where he finally admits to her his true motivation for becoming a criminal: "I did it for me. I liked it. I was good at it. And I was really . . . I was alive."

†   Said batmen: the ever-reliable Huell, plus the aptly nicknamed Man Mountain, who was so scared of Mike back in Season 1's "Pimento."

momentarily satisfying to see them utterly powerless and frightened—willing to not only lay off of Jimmy in the future but spread the word to warn off other potential muggers. At the same time, this is Jimmy McGill, relatively good guy and less than a year away from returning to the practice of law, using hired goons to abduct and terrorize three kids so they'll stop disrupting a quasi-legal business venture. This is a gangster move, and a far worse crossing of any legal or ethical threshold than that time he told the Albuquerque detectives about Hoboken Squat Cobbler. This is exactly what it means to break bad.

Earlier in the hour, Kim confronts Jimmy about his reluctance to go see the therapist, even after he had promised to do so. He insists that he just needs to give his new life a try and see how it goes. She lets him slide on that—emotionally, they're already too far apart for her to turn this into a real fight—and his argument sounds as convincing in the moment as most of his grifts. But we know much more than Kim about what he's doing, and what he's in the process of becoming. If his decision to tear up the therapist's number was inspired by seeing how little help Howard's shrink has been, Jimmy also understands on some level that turning his gaze inward will get in the way of his big and exciting plans. A Jimmy who goes into therapy—and who is honest with his therapist—would be forced to acknowledge the moral realities of that piñata stunt. A Jimmy who has been cut loose in different ways by the two people who inspired him to become a lawyer doesn't have to answer to anyone, including himself. He can do what he wants, take what he wants, and have a blast doing it. It's the kind of life Chuck pulled him away from when he got him the mailroom job, and it's the kind of diabolical power—Slippin' Jimmy with a law degree—that Chuck always feared.

SEASON 4, EPISODE 7
WRITTEN BY ALISON TATLOCK
DIRECTED BY DEBORAH CHOW

"Something Stupid"

"You do your thing, I'll do mine." —**Jimmy**

Jimmy's legal suspension began midway through Season 3, which means we have now been through more than an entire season's worth of *Saul* episodes without our main character being able to practice his chosen profession. That is a lot, even for a series that's happiest when it's moving slowly, and that has only covered two months of that suspension prior to "Something Stupid."

A time jump had to happen sooner or later, or else the series risked Jimmy not becoming Saul until Bob Odenkirk needed a walker to get around. That jump* finally occurs† in the brilliant opening montage of "Something Stupid,"‡ as we follow Jimmy and Kim through roughly nine months where they keep moving further apart, even as they always seem to be side by side. This idea is conveyed in an elegantly simple yet unmistakable way: from the moment the image of Jimmy and Kim brushing their teeth together splits into two images of them doing it on different days, there is a thick black line running vertically down the middle of the screen, whether we are watching Jimmy and Kim separately or together. Occasionally, one of them crosses this artificial barrier— Jimmy pours Kim some wine with dinner, Kim throws her leg over Jimmy's body while they sleep—but for the most part it literalizes the respectful barrier they have created between one another.

They are friends, and roommates, and presumably still lovers, but they are going in different directions. She's kicking ass and taking names in her new job at S&C (and in doing public defender work when she's not busy unpacking

---

* The time jump also allows Hector to make small progress in his recovery from the stroke. Here, we see Gus as inwardly sadistic and outwardly benevolent as he can be, as he quietly revels in the discovery that Hector's mind is intact, then sends the impressive Dr. Bruckner on her way before she can further help her patient, ensuring Gus's nemesis will remain a prisoner of his own body. Gus's barely concealed smile is one of Esposito's best moments since his return to the role.

† Super Lab construction, meanwhile, has progressed a lot more than Hector, but not as much as Mike, Werner, or the frustrated crew members like Kai would have hoped by now. Even with the time jump, we're still several years away from Walt's cancer diagnosis, and thus from the Lab being fully operational. So delays will have to be baked into the process.

‡ The montage is accompanied by a cover of the episode's title tune (most famous as a Frank and Nancy Sinatra duet) by the band Lola Marsh, commissioned by *Saul* music supervisor Thomas Golubic. It's an excellent music episode overall, with Burl Ives's "Big Rock Candy Mountain" accompanying Werner's crew through another day of drudgery.

trophies from each new Mesa Verde branch), while he and Huell have a thriving (and mostly legal) operation selling burners to the greater Albuquerque criminal community. He is now using Saul Goodman as an ongoing work name—which helps explain why he'll use it as a lawyer, since it's how so many potential clients will know him—and there are moments where the Jimmy McGill part of him barely seems present.

When the montage begins, they are positioned either shoulder to shoulder or directly facing one another. As it moves along, more and more often they are presented facing opposite directions. The montage ends with another instance of the split screen showing two halves of the same moment, as Kim and Jimmy sleep with their backs pointed at each other, each perched so close to the edge of the bed that there's room for another adult human to lie comfortably between them. But even this feels like an illusion, because when she turns off her lamp, her side goes pitch black while his doesn't, as he opens his eyes. Though they're in the same place at the same time, it feels like two people in very different states of reality.

The whole thing is spectacular, on par with the "Street Life" montage from "Quite a Ride" (which, like this episode, was edited by Skip MacDonald). It advances plot and theme, even as it's enormously entertaining to watch, and it sets us up for an hour where Jimmy and Kim seem on the verge of having the split we've all feared was coming. (Or maybe hoped for, since we wouldn't wish a life with Saul Goodman on Kim.)

With the cast off her arm, Kim can finally tie her trademark power ponytail again, and her abilities and grounding within Albuquerque's legitimate legal community seem at their strongest. When Jimmy comes to her late in the hour with a complicated, very Saul Goodman strategy for discrediting the plainclothes cop who arrested Huell for assault, Rhea Seehorn has this marvelous look on her face, like Kim is listening to a foreign language she can't even identify, let alone translate. It's not just that their careers are on such divergent trajectories, but that their philosophies are.

Earlier in the show's run, there were moments where their styles overlapped just enough that they made sense as quasi-partners. Now? Now Jimmy's the guy who makes a scene at Kim's work party—talking up a much more lavish company retreat than Rich Schweikart is interested in paying for, just because Jimmy's bored and resentful of this place for stealing away his partner—that she has to endure with a forced smile on her face. And their relationship is now so tentative that she no longer cares enough to really scold him about it, simply griping, "Well, that was something," before allowing him to turn on the car radio for the awkward drive home. Nor does she raise much of a fuss when he tells her about the burner business while asking her to defend

Huell's assault case, though she's obviously thrown by the news that he's been doing this for months without telling her. But it's not until she tries to negotiate a lighter plea deal with the DA that the reality of who and what her boyfriend has become really hits home, as her opposing counsel describes Jimmy as a "scumbag disbarred lawyer who peddles drop phones to criminals." It's an overstatement (Jimmy is suspended, not disbarred), but largely accurate, and the cold hard slap of reality that Kim may need to realize it's time for them to part ways personally, as well as professionally.

Or is it? Jimmy seems on the verge of pulling some kind of Saul Goodman stunt to prevent Huell (who has no interest in doing even a brief prison stretch) from turning fugitive. But Kim, rather than make a futile attempt to change Huell's mind, abruptly decides to visit an office supply store, where she loads her shopping cart with enough markers and pens to make an entire third-grade class art show. Her plan won't be revealed until the next episode, but at a minimum it suggests the kind of out-of-the-box thinking that made Kim and Jimmy such a good match in the first place, before the war with Chuck and its fatal aftermath started pushing them apart.

All she says, before the credits roll, is, "I have a better way." That applies to whatever her scheme is regarding Huell, but it also sounds like a phrase Kim should be applying to Jimmy's life and career in general. We know where the Saul Goodman way leads, and we unfortunately know that he's going to follow it. But it's nice to imagine, for however long Jimmy and Kim are still together—or, for that matter, for however long Jimmy McGill as we know him continues to exist—the timeline diverging,* and Jimmy coming to understand that Kim really does have the better way, and that if he can follow it, the barrier between them over the last nine months will fall away.

---

*   Vince Gilligan ran into *Fargo* creator Noah Hawley midway through the show's run, and Hawley gave him a pitch for the remainder of the series: "He never becomes Saul Goodman. He just goes on as Jimmy McGill, and that's the show."

SEASON 4, EPISODE 8
WRITTEN BY GORDON SMITH
DIRECTED BY JIM MCKAY

"Coushatta"

"Let's do it again." —**Kim**

Prequels are not generally designed to feature big mysteries. With this one, we know exactly what Jimmy McGill will become, and how the stories of Mike Ehrmantraut, Gus Fring, and most of the other cartel characters will end.

But then there's Kim Wexler.

Kim's not the only *Better Call Saul* character whose ultimate fate we don't know. But with all due respect to Nacho and Howard and Dr. Caldera, she's special. For all the initial fan enthusiasm to spend more time with Mike, to get more quickly from Jimmy to Saul, etc., Kim has become perhaps the most universally popular character across either this show or *Breaking Bad*. The question of what would become of Chuck was fascinating. But it was never nearly as fraught because viewers hated Chuck, even as they appreciated his importance to Jimmy's story. Kim, even more than Jimmy McGill himself, is the reason no one's been in a hurry to get to Saul. The assumption is that Saul Goodman has no room in his life for someone like Kim Wexler. So the show keeps kicking Jimmy's transformation, and what it will do to their relationship, down the road. And we all go along with it because we don't want to lose Kim, and don't want the mystery of where she is during *Breaking Bad* to be solved.

For a while, Season 4 seemed ready to answer the uncomfortable question in about as painless a manner as was possible. Kim would not die, it looked like, nor anything else too awful. Instead, it seemed as if we were being set up for her career and personality to evolve in a way that would prove incompatible with the man we know Jimmy will become. Sad, but not a crushing tragedy. It was the best of a universally bad group of potential outcomes.

So leave it to this week's installment, "Coushatta," to reverse field on what Kim wants—and, in the process, reopen all sorts of frightening possibilities for what could happen to her.

When the episode begins, Jimmy and Kim are operating as they have for most of the season: together in practical terms, apart in emotional ones. She drops him off at the bus station for the long trip to the eponymous Louisiana community, acting like he's a semi-estranged friend she has reluctantly agreed to give a ride to while his car is in the shop. She's more comfortable working alone to the sounds of Stereolab on her headphones than she is talking to him about the plan. Even Jimmy, who has a weakness for buying into his own bullshit some of the time, can recognize that this marriage—as Mrs. Nguyen mistakes the relationship for—is on the rocks, and it's his own fault. He and we are both prepped for the idea that Kim will bail Jimmy and Huell out of one last mess, and then rightfully get on with her life as a responsible, mostly law-abiding adult.

Fortunately for Jimmy—and unfortunately for Kim—this is not at all what happens.

Instead, she is so caught up in the thrill of running a masterful short con on Suzanne from the DA's office that her regular job in banking law starts to feel even more painfully dull than before. She's zoning out in meetings with Kevin and Paige and trying to chase that feeling by admiring that tequila bottle cap souvenir from her days as Giselle St. Claire. Earlier, when Suzanne caves and offers Huell a plea deal with no prison time attached, Kim practically tackles Jimmy with her kiss, she's so turned on by it all.* And when Jimmy is busy checking out another potential office space—this time in *a* strip mall, but not *the* strip mall that will one day be home to Saul, Francesca, and the inflatable Statue of Liberty—Kim shows up unannounced to express her desire for a sequel.

This is a very far cry from the fun-loving but ultimately sensible woman who enjoyed scamming Ken Wins out of a big bar tab, but who was aghast to learn that Jimmy manufactured evidence of Daniel Wormald doing a crybaby squat. That video wasn't a patch on all the laws Jimmy broke in the process of convincing Suzanne that Huell had an entire community rallying to his defense. (Gordon Smith's script even makes a point of having Jimmy list most of them right before that kiss, so we can understand the stakes involved.) Yet instead of turning her off even more, this one excites her—at first for sex, and then for the prospect of the next hustle.

This is incredibly dangerous territory for the writers to have Kim visit. It would be bad enough if she was doing this out of some kind of misplaced but understandable loyalty to Jimmy: *I love him, and if I want us to stay together, I have to become more like him.* It's very clearly not that. She does care for him, but she's developed a thirst for the con itself, not just the con man who taught her how to run a grift. She needs Jimmy to make these stunts work, and it does

---

* If at times it seems odd that Jimmy and Kim are so rarely physical with one another onscreen, this is why. A moment like that kiss, and the acknowledgment afterward that they had celebratory sex, has so much more impact if it was previously rare even when times were relatively good between these two.

add spice to their relationship, but it's the victory itself, and the method by which it was achieved, that's pulling at her most strongly.

Already this season, we've seen Kim endanger her most important professional relationship because she was distracted by a pro bono client. That would be bad but ultimately salvageable since she wouldn't really miss Mesa Verde anywhere but in her wallet. (And Kim has never come across as particularly money-hungry, beyond making sure bills get paid.) But if she's redeveloped a taste for cons—and, in particular, cons that tie into her work as a representative of the New Mexico bar—then that has the potential to blow up in ugly, reputation-ruining, career-ending fashion.

If that happens, it will be because of Kim's relationship with Jimmy, but it will also be of her own choosing. That feels like a bigger, more painful tragedy than if she were to become an innocent victim of a Saul Goodman scheme, or even if she were to somehow become collateral damage of Saul's time working with drug dealers.

Speaking of which, we catch up with Nacho post–time jump, now running the old Salamanca crew (with Domingo filling his old slot at El Michoacáno), living in a fancy house with two eager-to-please female junkies. But it's all a facade as he saves cash in preparation to skip town with his father and a pair of fake IDs. And a huge monkey wrench gets thrown into that plan with the arrival of Lalo (Tony Dalton),* another Salamanca cousin who seems shrewder and more calculating than the others.

As we've discussed, when Walt and Jesse take Saul out into the desert in his first *Breaking Bad* appearance, he assumes they're from the cartel, and tries to lay the blame on Ignacio for whatever it is they think he's done. But when he realizes that his kidnappers are a couple of white guys, he's relieved to know that Lalo didn't send them, in a tone suggesting Saul is utterly terrified of this man. But because this is the only mention of him on *Breaking Bad,*† the *Saul* writers have as wide a degree of latitude with him as they do with Kim and the other characters who are original to this show.

In interviews when *Saul* was originally airing, both Rhea Seehorn and Bob Odenkirk speculated that perhaps Saul and Kim are a happy couple during the events of *Breaking Bad,* and we just never hear about her because Saul rightfully has no interest in telling his criminal associates about her. Maybe "Let's do it again" is the first step toward them fully accepting one another for

---

* Born in Texas, Dalton spent most of his early career working in Mexican films and TV series, including a stint risking life and limb in a *Jackass*-esque show called *No Te Equivoques.*
† It's such a *Breaking Bad* deep cut that when Vince Gilligan triumphantly announced at a press conference that Season 4 would introduce Lalo, the assembled television reporters—including yours truly, I have to admit—were all confused and had to Google the name later.

who they are and what they love to do, and that they will somehow make it work despite being on wildly different professional tracks. It doesn't seem likely, though, because the Saul who was fleeing Albuquerque in "Granite State" (and in the flashbacks from this show's "Quite a Ride") did not act like a man who was leaving someone important behind.

So Kim has to be out of the picture eventually, which has long been the biggest mystery *Better Call Saul* has to offer. And it's one that we're inching closer to solving, unfortunately.

SEASON 4, EPISODE 9
WRITTEN BY GENNIFER HUTCHISON
DIRECTED BY THOMAS SCHNAUZ

"Wiedersehen"

"Jimmy, you are always down." —**Kim**

Jimmy makes two mistakes at his bar reinstatement hearing in "Wieder-sehen." The more obvious one, which Kim calls him out for, is that he never once mentions Chuck. The three lawyers hearing his case very clearly want him to say something kind about his late, professionally great brother, and it never even occurs to Jimmy to do it. When Kim brings up Chuck during their argument on the parking garage roof, he's surprised by the very idea. He argues, rightly, that citing Chuck as an inspiration would have been the height of insincerity, given how their relationship wound up, and would have only lived down to the panel's assumptions about him.

The more important mistake, it seems, comes a few moments earlier in the interview. One of the panelists asks what the law means to Jimmy, and it's clear from the look on his face, and the long pause before he begins fully answering, that this has never occurred to him, either. This is him failing to invoke Chuck in spirit as much as name. Chuck, for all his many flaws, wouldn't have had to think for a second to answer this question, because it was the one that defined his life. To Chuck, the law meant everything. *Was* everything. Chuck saw a beauty in the law, a fundamental value in it. Jimmy never has. He began studying as a means to an end: to impress his brother, and to get closer to the woman he liked. He eventually came to see the power of his new profession: that he could use his way with people to help them, rather than swindle them, and that this felt good. But even as he was building up his solo practice, there was still this sense that he viewed the law not as *the* thing, but the thing that would get him to the next thing.* He wanted that shared office with Kim. He wanted respect from Chuck—and, when that proved impossible, he wanted to become rich and famous enough to fill up that particular emotional hole. He's a lawyer because there were lawyers in his life that he cared about. But the law itself doesn't hold the weight for him that it did for Chuck, or that it still mostly does for Kim. So Jimmy improvises, which he's always been great at. He spins the tale of his embarrassing correspondence school and his

---

* To paraphrase the great period drama *Halt and Catch Fire*, whose run on AMC overlapped with *Saul*'s.

struggles to enter the profession. And he even, in a roundabout way, sings the praises of the law by talking about the people he's helped, which does matter to him on some level. But the speech, while eloquent, doesn't really answer the panelist's question, and Jimmy's surprise at it in the first place speaks as much to why the group rejects him for reinstatement as his non-mention of Chuck.

However much Chuck's judgmental attitude pushed his brother down the Saul Goodman road,* there is also something fundamentally broken and dishonest within Jimmy that made him forge the Mesa Verde documents, that made him film Daniel Wormald wiggling around in a pie, that encouraged him to take all the legal and ethical shortcuts he's been opting for since the series began. Even the purest possible version of Jimmy McGill is at best on the morally sketchy end of the profession. And that's a Jimmy who hasn't pled guilty to the crimes he committed busting into Chuck's house to destroy the cassette tape. An indignant, infuriated Jimmy tells Kim that he "did everything right," and that he can't believe the board wouldn't reinstate him. But knowing what we know about Jimmy's past, let alone Saul's future, are they being unfair to do it? Or do they recognize a slightly more rational version of what Chuck saw: a charming guy whom their profession is nonetheless probably safer without, given his past misdeeds?

"Wiedersehen" makes the board's case even before Jimmy inadvertently does. We open up with Kim and Jimmy pulling off another caper, this time to swap out the plans for Mesa Verde's Lubbock branch with the slightly larger version Kevin now wants to build. It's a vintage Slippin' Jimmy grift with props (crutches, a bottle of milk) and backstory (Kim claims to be a single mom, with Jimmy as her idiot brother-turned-nanny Bill) designed to make her more sympathetic to Shirley the records clerk, and to keep Shirley suitably distracted when it's time for Kim to get the revised plans stamped and officially logged in the archives. This is not the kind of stunt any lawyer should be pulling, and especially a prominent and respected one like Kim Wexler. But just being around Jimmy and running lower-stakes schemes with him has made her excited to play his games.

After leaving Lubbock, the partners get to talking again, and the show eases back a bit on the idea of Kim permanently breaking bad. "I think we should only use our powers for good," she says, in a tone suggesting she doesn't

---

*   Meanwhile, things are getting messy over in cartel world. Werner's homesickness endangers the whole project when he figures out how to escape the luxurious prison where he and his team have to live. And Lalo—who gives Tio Hector his iconic hotel bell in a visit to the nursing home—is quickly proving to be a very different kind of Salamanca: patient, clever, even charming, where the other members of the family we've met are either unreasonable hotheads, single-minded brutes, or both. Gus can tell this will be a more difficult foe to dispatch, and he's clearly not happy about it.

plan to make a habit of these schemes. But as Jimmy points out, getting this larger branch built doesn't really qualify, especially since Kim successfully talked Kevin off that ledge in the previous episode. There was no reason to do it, except that Kim wanted to. She's just not ready to replace Marco as Jimmy's full-time partner in crime.

And it's her reluctance to be his partner in any official way outside the bedroom that turns their post-hearing discussion from uncomfortable to downright nasty. As she tries to look for a way to undo the damage done by that interview, Jimmy decides that Kim will, like his brother, always see him as Slippin' Jimmy, and vents, "That's why we don't have an office!" Kim rightly calls him out on this silliness, listing the many, many, *many* times when she has risked her reputation and more to help him, but he's too worked up to consider this. "You get a little bored with your life, come down and roll around in the dirt with Slippin' Jimmy," he sneers.

That the fight gets this heated is, in a way, a healthy sign for their relationship. Earlier in the season, they were so distant that Kim didn't even bother scolding him about the scene he made at the office party. Now, they're invested enough again in one another that they can get this angry and say these cruel things. And sure enough, after he silently packs to move out, he instead makes peace by admitting how badly he messed up, and that he still wants to be a lawyer.

"Well, we can start with that," Kim says, her voice sadly cracking as she recognizes how tenuous this all is—romantically and professionally both—and how their lives could fall apart at any moment because Jimmy can't stop being Jimmy.

Jimmy still wants to be a lawyer. Should he be? Based on what we know is coming, certainly not. But the world around him is also encouraging him to give in to his worst instincts, whether it's from fights (first with Chuck, now with the legal establishment as a whole) or Kim's periodic desire to play Giselle. Already, Jimmy is considering how to deal with a client base who knows him as Saul Goodman—"That's just details," Kim argues—but a smooth reinstatement could have set him back on the path to being a criminal lawyer, but not a *criminal* lawyer. His back is against the wall again, and the longer it stays there, the greater the likelihood that any desire of his to impress or even appease the legal community vanishes like Werner into the New Mexico desert.

We know Jimmy will get his law license back, and sooner rather than later. God help everyone around him when he does.

SEASON 4, EPISODE 10
WRITTEN BY PETER GOULD & THOMAS SCHNAUZ
DIRECTED BY ADAM BERNSTEIN

"Winner"

"You made a mistake, and they are never forgetting it. As far as they're concerned, your mistake is just—it's who you are. And it's all you are." —**Jimmy**

Saul Goodman has officially arrived.

But s'all's not good, man.

"Winner" takes us to a moment we all once assumed would arrive much sooner than it did. Back then, the audience, the writers, and Kim Wexler hadn't all fallen in love with Jimmy McGill. Saul Goodman was fun . . . and inevitable. Who, we might have wondered back then, could possibly have wanted to watch a Saul show where he wasn't even really Saul? But then Jimmy charmed the pants off of all of us, and *Better Call Saul* became not a *Breaking Bad* bonus feature, but a kind of parallel tragedy to the original show. Walter White was a man the world believed to be good, only for circumstance, arrogance, and sheer force of will to reveal the monster that was always hiding underneath that beige wardrobe. Jimmy McGill, on the other hand, was a man the world believed to be bad, despite his tremendous capacity for empathy and self-sacrifice. The world's ongoing skepticism, coupled with his own abundant flaws, inspired him to live down to everyone's lowest expectations of him. Like Walt's transformation into Heisenberg, Jimmy becoming Saul isn't something to be raced through, and we are all very fortunate that the creative team realized this as the show went along.

The finale concludes with Jimmy adopting Saul as his professional moniker with the New Mexico Bar Association, following through on his observation in the previous episode that it's the name most of his potential client base knows him by. But he's been periodically channeling Saul's worst impulses ever since his reinstatement got rejected the first time.

The hour is primarily one more Viktor and Giselle con. Kim appears to set aside all other work to arrange an elaborate and expensive ($23,000 alone to rename the law library reading room) series of plays designed to spread the word about Jimmy's continued grief over the loss of Chuck. We open with a flashback to the day Jimmy became an attorney in the first place, with Chuck convincingly feigning enthusiasm about the whole affair. The brothers wind up on stage that evening doing a karaoke rendition of ABBA's "Winner Takes It All." It's funny, of course, particularly when the reluctant Chuck seizes the mic from his little brother to show off his superior pipes.* But it's also profoundly sad, not only because of how things would wind up between the siblings, but because the duet shows how close they *could* have been. If Chuck could have accepted Jimmy's transformation as the sincere thing it was intended to be, maybe Jimmy winds up working at HHM (or, as he wanted to call it for symmetry's sake, HHMM), he helps Chuck through to the other side of his illness, and the two become the good team Jimmy often dreamed about. Chuck did, as he often insisted, love his brother—just not in the pure, completely unforgiving way that Jimmy may have required. Chuck doesn't want to stay for karaoke, but he does, and he has a great time. He doesn't want to spend the night at Jimmy's little apartment, but he does because he knows his brother needs—and deserves—a big breakfast the next morning. For that matter, he is aghast at the idea of Slippin' Jimmy with a law degree, but he stands up and acts proud at the bar ceremony. It's a great day and night between the brothers, in a lifetime when they were at odds more often than not. But you look at the two of them lying side by side in the bed and softly reprising the ABBA song, and you wish, as Jimmy often did, that it could have been like this all the time.

But things went in different directions for both of them, tragically. So the Jimmy who cries against Chuck's enormous headstone, or who hides out from the reading room dedication guests, or who takes that long pause while reading Chuck's letter to the appeals board, is performing emotions he no longer feels. The part of him capable of grief or guilt over Chuck died in Kim's living room in this season's premiere. The earlier scenes are presented to us transparently as cons: Jimmy is counting to himself and muttering "watermelon pickles" (a phrase background actors in movies use to simulate crowd noise) at the cemetery, and both there and at the reception, he checks in with Kim about the process of fooling these saps into believing that he's sad. As a potent contrast, we see Jimmy fulfilling his role on the board for Chuck's new scholarship and arguing vigorously in favor of a young female candidate whom the other board members dismissively refer to as "the shoplifter." Jimmy's speech on behalf of someone who made mistakes, but tried to move past them, could be read as one more bit of playacting in this elaborate charade to convince the entire Albuquerque legal community of his sincerity and goodness. But we also know how much this very issue has plagued him—how it's the reason his brother could never accept him as a lawyer, resulting in all that followed. Howard, who has always had a soft spot for Jimmy, is impressed by the speech, but not enough of the board is, and the girl doesn't get the scholarship. Jimmy then makes a point

---

* It's just a shame the brothers don't stay on stage long enough for a meta installment of Jimmy Loves Movies, where they wind up dusting on "Big Bottom" or some other Spinal Tap song.

of tracking her down outside the HHM building to give her the kind of advice he feels she needs to absorb: "Screw them. Remember: the winner takes it all." He has taken this perfect moment with his brother and transformed it into part of his justification for becoming everything Chuck would despise. It's unclear whether his message fully sinks in, or if she looks back at Jimmy on her way to the bus just because she's confused by him. But after, he goes to his car and cries for real—ugly tears, muffled "no"s, and everything else Bob Odenkirk can beautifully do to distinguish this from Jimmy the hustler—not over the loss of his brother, but over his understanding that the world will always look at him as the mistake, no matter what he does.

It's that understanding that leads to the masterful performance he gives to the appeals board in the season's climax. It's convincing enough to fool the viewer as much as the board. When he pauses in the middle of reading the letter, after the part about how happy their mother was when baby Jimmy came home from the hospital, it seems as if Jimmy is for the first time truly understanding the weight of that sentiment, and how Chuck spent so much of his life fighting a losing battle to be loved as much as his troublemaking kid brother. He puts the letter away and appears to speak from the heart, delivering the eulogy he couldn't bring himself to give at the funeral, visibly moving not only the board, but Kim, who cared for both McGills and is deeply touched at the notion that Jimmy has made peace with Chuck in death, if not in life. (It's Odenkirk's big moment of oratory, but it's Rhea Seehorn's response that really sells it to the audience.)

In the hallway after, while Kim is still floating on air over the way that, she believes, Jimmy has turned the grift into something real, Jimmy casually (and inadvertently cruelly) reveals that it was just another act. Kim's face falls, as much at how oblivious Jimmy is to her disappointment as at the realization of the lie itself. Just as it never occurred to him to talk about Chuck at the initial bar hearing, the thought that Kim could have believed this new speech never enters his mind. Jimmy wants Kim to be exactly like him, but she's not. She gets turned on by the cons but isn't consumed by them. She doesn't have a chip on her shoulder about her modest background. She has taken shortcuts and outright cheated the system, but these things come as a last resort to her, where for Jimmy, they're a first impulse that he can only sometimes resist.

One of the key passages of Jimmy's speech finds him promising that if he's reinstated, "I'll do everything in my power to be worthy of the name McGill." When he gets confirmation that he's won, one of the first things he does is to announce his plan to work under a different name entirely—the one he was using when we met him. To Jimmy, this is no big deal: just an expeditious way to attract clients who met him when he was selling burner phones to them. But it's him running away from his brother's legacy only moments after a tribute to Chuck saved him, and it's him furthering the transformation we've known was coming since the series began. He leaves Kim in the hallway, looking very small and very confused about who this man is in front of her. She was his partner in this particular crime, but in the end, she looks like just another victim of a scheme by Slippin' Jimmy—or, as he'll be known professionally from now on, by Saul Goodman.

While Jimmy is continuing his transformation into Saul, the rest of the episode offers a parallel story where Mike fully enters the criminal world by killing Werner on Gus's orders. The construction of the Super Lab proves to be a red herring. Kai and the other workers are sent home and the job is left unfinished, with Gus scowling mightily when Gale suggests he might be able to do a rudimentary cook in this primitive Batcave-like structure. We are, as we knew from the flashback at the start of *Breaking Bad* Season 4, years away from the Lab being completed and operational. So the story is really about Mike's own evolution from antihero to pure villain.

Mike has been a criminal for some time now, but the man we met at the start of the series wouldn't have shot Werner in cold blood. Mike did security jobs, and he stole drug money, but there was a time when he went out of his way to avoid murdering even unapologetic criminals like Tuco, or the cartel truck driver he hijacked.* Here, he is still favoring nonviolent (and simpler) solutions whenever possible, like the delightful, quintessentially Ehrmantraut moment where he takes the gum, not the gun, out of the glove compartment to trap Lalo inside a parking lot just long enough to shake his tail. He even seems on the verge of convincing Gus to let Werner live, and it's only the tenacity of Lalo that dooms his friend. (A Salamanca knowing the name of his Lab's engineer is too big a risk for the Chicken Man to take.)

If the Super Lab scenes at times felt like filler earlier in the season, the payoff is more than worth it for the moment where Mike has to accept the fact that his friend has to die, and Mike has to be the one to kill him. (The look in Jonathan Banks's eyes after the phone call with Gus is his most powerful moment on the show since he cried over his son way back in "Five-O.") A half-measure won't do, not anymore. When Mike takes Werner out into the desert, it's a mirror of the discussion Jimmy and Kim will have a few scenes later after

---

* Years later, when Mike is plotting to rob a freight train with Walt and Jesse, he suggests that the only way to pull it off would require them to murder the two innocent engineers on board. "I have done this long enough to know," he explains, "that there are two kinds of heists: those where the guys get away with it, and those that leave witnesses." That older Mike is a much more effective criminal than the one from the early *Saul* seasons, but he has lost a key part of himself along the way.

the appeal hearing. Werner, like Kim, is having one conversation—where he believes the only thing he has to plead for is his conjugal visit—while his friend is having a different, far colder one altogether. It's a brutal sequence, as circumstances force Werner to yell at his wife in the last time she will ever hear his voice. Yet despite that, he respects Mike enough, and is a gentle enough soul, that he lets his homicidal pal off the hook by pretending to walk off and look at the stars—sparing Mike from having to look him in the eye as he pulls the trigger.

Mike ends this particular phase of the story having learned an important, if painful, lesson about the things he'll have to do in this new life he's chosen. And he ends it clearly owing Gus, after his own indulgence of Werner ruined this expensive, important project. Now he has a huge debt to repay, and Werner's death erases any doubt as to who and what he has become.

With both Mike and Jimmy, we began the series knowing the kinds of men they would be within a few years. Jimmy had a lot further to go emotionally to become Saul than Mike had to in order to become Gus's henchman. But among the things *Better Call Saul* has done so masterfully is to make their pre–*Breaking Bad* incarnations so appealing, and so much more vulnerable than the guys who worked with Walt and Jesse, that the inevitable instead became agonizing. Once, we might have rooted for either or both of them to appear with—to paraphrase Jimmy at karaoke with Kim—their full powers unleashed. Now, it's happened. It's where we all knew the story was heading, and the way it's played out has been incredible. But forgive me for feeling like Kim standing in that hallway after Jimmy gives her the double point, wondering exactly how we got here, and wishing there was some way to undo what just happened.

SEASON 5, EPISODE 1
WRITTEN BY PETER GOULD
DIRECTED BY BRONWEN HUGHES

"Magic Man"

"See, this is why this works. I go too far, and you pull me back." —**Jimmy**

Jimmy McGill.

Saul Goodman.

Gene Takovic.

One man, three names. Or is it three different men rightly using three different names?

Going back to when we first met Saul on *Breaking Bad*, Bob Odenkirk has been playing the character under multiple aliases. (And that's not even counting Viktor, of Viktor and Giselle fame.) *Saul* began with poor Gene trudging through his lonely, paranoid days at Cinnabon, then introduced us to Jimmy McGill, who turned out to be something more complicated than a pre-comb-over Saul Goodman. Though he began using Saul Goodman as a work name while producing commercials and selling drop phones, he was still clearly the Jimmy we had come to know and love. It wasn't until midway through last season that we briefly saw the true Saul Goodman, frantically preparing to exit his Albuquerque life near the end of the events of *Breaking Bad*.

So what separates these three, exactly? How much does it matter? And when will Jimmy McGill fully become Saul Goodman in this series' present?

Gene is easy to carve off from the other two. Gene values survival above all else and has divested himself of anything that might get him identified as Saul or Jimmy, even though those character traits were what once made his life worth living. We only glimpse him for a few minutes at the start of each season, but we can see how painfully empty his time in Omaha is, and how simultaneously thrilled and terrified he feels whenever he lets one of his old identities peek out for a moment.

We know Saul relatively well from the other show. The Saul Goodman we meet in *Breaking Bad* Season 2 is a blithely ruthless individual, willing to sell out anyone and everyone who threatens him, and baffled that his most important clients aren't prepared to do the same. He's not a monster to the degree that Walt or Tuco or Gus is, but he is someone who cares about getting and keeping what he feels entitled to above anything else. He is a fairly two-dimensional (if very entertaining) character, and those dimensions are selfish ones.

Jimmy, though? Jimmy contains multitudes. He is a survivor like Gene and has done some terrible things in the name of self-preservation (and, occasionally, in the name of protecting people he cares about like Kim). And he is a con man at heart like Saul, often finding his greatest pleasure in getting over on his social superiors. But he's also more empathetic and fundamentally kind. He took real pleasure in talking with his elder-care law clients. He was a devoted caretaker to Chuck, despite how obviously his brother disapproved of him. His instincts still tend toward chicanery and other shortcuts, but there is a goodness and capacity for shame in him that's utterly absent from Saul on *Breaking Bad.*

Throughout the run of *Better Call Saul* to this point, it's been pretty easy to keep the three iterations separate. Gene is Gene. Jimmy is Jimmy. Saul is Saul. That's even how the writers refer to them in the scripts; even when Jimmy was calling himself Saul in recent seasons, the scripts still referred to him as Jimmy. The "Ozymandias"-era teaser from "Quite a Ride" was the only time so far the dialogue markers and stage directions used the name Saul.

We are at a crossroads now, though. Season 4 concluded with Jimmy deciding to practice law under the Goodman name. Peter Gould told me at the time that they considered the current status quo to be Jimmy using the new name as a marketing strategy, rather than the full transformation, and that in the scripts, "My guess is that we'll call him Jimmy as long as Kim does."

Kim does, indeed, keep calling him Jimmy in this episode, though the first time we see them together, she's still absorbing the implications of his professional name change. And later, while he and Kim are exchanging gifts, he even refers to Saul in the third person, as if he is a separate being—or, at least, a character that movie fan Jimmy McGill has chosen to play. So as far as Kim, Jimmy, and the scripts are concerned, he's still Jimmy McGill. But is he really?

As I watched "Magic Man" the first time, I found myself unconsciously referring to him as Saul in my notes almost as often as I called him Jimmy—not just in scenes where he's presenting himself as an attorney, but at times when he's just chatting with Kim. He's certainly not gone the full Goodman yet, but there's something more cavalier in his manner. Or, at least, there's something more unnerving at seeing Chuck McGill's worst fears realized as his brother goes full Slippin' Jimmy on the Albuquerque legal community. It's not that Jimmy was the most ethical and prim lawyer back in his Sandpiper days, but there was still a restraint to his behavior and his bearing that seems largely gone. Heck, he even introduces his criminal law practice to his low-life drop phone clients by erecting a carnival tent in a parking lot.* It's all an act, and yet

---

* Jimmy also uses a hotel bell to signal the entrance of each new potential client, and such a bell of course conjures thoughts of Hector Salamanca. As is often the case with *Saul*, the episode's plottier sections take place over on the cartel side of things, which for the moment remains entirely disconnected from Jimmy/Saul's legal career. Tony Dalton was made a cast regular for this season, and Lalo remains an enormous headache for both Nacho and Gus. He's as tenacious as the other

more and more, the act and the man seem indistinguishable. If it walks like a Goodman, talks like a Goodman, and calls itself Goodman, how far can it really be from being a Goodman?

In that same scene where he speaks of Saul in the third person, after all, he does the same for Jimmy, telling Kim, "I can't go back to being Jimmy McGill. Jimmy McGill the lawyer is always going to be Chuck McGill's loser brother. I'm done with that." He sees it as a reputation issue, and maybe his explanation sways Kim in the moment. But we know that the name represents something much worse than a fresh start and a cry for respect that he didn't feel he could get as Jimmy.

Jimmy's early days as attorney Saul are rougher around the edges than the *Breaking Bad* era strip mall operation with Francesca. He puts on a big show in the parking lot for potential clients (with Huell to provide both security and evidence of his legal genius), and he even brings back his film crew pals to stage a scene involving hapless prosecutor Bill Oakley (Peter Diseth) in an attempt to recruit even more clients. But he's not quite a master salesman in the parking lot and has to fall back on the 50 percent off promotion he had previously told Kim he wouldn't use. And even his scam impulses remain frequently altruistic. When Kim's pro bono client Bobby refuses to take a generous plea deal over her strong recommendation, Jimmy suggests tricking him into it with a bit of improv theater like the one he just ran on Bill. Kim has hustled free drinks out of Ken Wins, and even kept Huell out of prison through deception, but this seems a bridge too far for her. "I'm not scamming my clients," she insists, sounding offended at the mere idea.

And then she does it anyway—just without telling Jimmy about it. She hates herself for the deception, but her compassion for her clients is ultimately stronger than her sense of professional ethics, and she's also been around Slippin' Jimmy too long to be immune to his way of thinking. The episode's present-day action opens with Jimmy taking a big step toward becoming Saul Goodman for real—and celebrating that transformation. But it ends with Kim catching her breath in a courthouse stairwell, aware that she is transforming, too, and in ways she's not at all pleased about.

Salamancas, but he's also smarter and more patient than Hector or (especially) Tuco. Gus goes to a lot of trouble to portray the late Werner Ziegler as a troublemaking employee who was killed for stealing from Gus's meth supply, but Lalo sees right through the whole charade, and is pleased to finally get a look at the mysterious Michael. As for Mike, he has had enough of being part of the Fring organization in the wake of killing Werner. It's an understandable response on a character level, given how close he and Werner became last season and how much it pained him to have to execute his friend. But since we know Mike is destined to be Gus's right-hand man, and soon, it's one of those periodic moments where the series seems to be going in narrative circles to prevent characters from turning into their *Breaking Bad* selves too soon.

Earlier in the premiere, she gives Jimmy a monogrammed briefcase with his real initials, which he insists he can still use as Saul Goodman, since he'll tell people that JMM stands for "Justice Matters Most." And she also gives him a "World's 2nd Best Lawyer Again" travel mug, a sequel to the one she gifted him back in Season 2. Both presents are meant for Jimmy McGill, but Jimmy is well on his way to being Saul, and then Gene. We know it, and if Kim obviously doesn't know it in that detail, she can at least see that something is happening here beyond a name change.

Speaking of Gene from Cinnabon, this season's opening visit with the mustachioed fugitive picks up moments after we left him in the Season 4 premiere, as he panics over realizing that Jeff the cab driver (Don Harvey) recognized him as Saul Goodman. He goes straight to DEFCON-2, packing a bag and his stash of diamonds and hiding out at a truck stop until he finds out whether the authorities have been alerted to his true identity. When it seems safe, he returns home and to work, only for Jeff to confront him at the mall and demand to hear Saul's infamous catchphrase. Worse, Jeff makes clear that this won't be their last encounter. ("Little rusty, but you'll do better next time.") Now we're in full panic mode, which includes a call to the vacuum repair shop back in Albuquerque where the unflappable disappearance expert, Ed, is still hard at work.* For a moment, it seems like Gene's story—and, thus, the story of *Better Call Saul*—will conclude with him adopting yet another name and persona. But as Ed begins giving him instructions about where and when to meet, Gene comes to a decision.

"I've changed my mind," he tells Ed. "I'm gonna fix it myself."

"Myself," he says.

Myself.

To which self is he referring?

We don't know Gene nearly as well as Jimmy or Saul, but this seems very uncharacteristic of someone determined to be human wallpaper. It feels much more the kind of move we'd see from the guy we've watched for most of the previous four seasons, or at least from the guy Gene was immediately before moving to Omaha. Jimmy and Saul are both fighters, and it appears our man has decided to be true to his former selves, rather than continuing to cower as this shadow figure circumstance has turned him into.

---

* Initially, the show was just going to put Ed's voice on the other end of the phone line. But as serendipity had it, Robert Forster was filming his scenes for the *Breaking Bad* sequel movie *El Camino* a few months before "Magic Man" was to be shot, and producer Melissa Bernstein realized they had an opportunity to put Forster on camera for both at the same time. Forster died the day *El Camino* was released, and "Magic Man" concludes with a dedication to him.

Saul Goodman isn't really a separate person from Jimmy McGill, obviously, any more than Heisenberg was from Walter White. They are just their characters' respective darkest natures being given free rein—in both cases, out of wounded pride as much as anything else. And Gene Takovic is the same guy, too, even if he's had to disguise himself emotionally as much as physically. But each represents choices this one man made along the way, at great cost to himself and others.

AMC announced shortly before Season 5 debuted that the sixth season would also be the final one. "Magic Man" essentially begins the endgame for all things *Better Call Saul*, which in the moment feels like it will conclude both Jimmy's and Gene's stories with each of them turning into Saul Goodman.

SEASON 5, EPISODE 2
WRITTEN BY ALISON TATLOCK
DIRECTED BY NORBERTO BARBA

"50% Off"

"Mr. Varga. Long time, no see." —**Jimmy**

The very first episode of *Better Call Saul* ends with Tuco Salamanca sticking a
gun in Jimmy McGill's face and pulling him into his grandmother's house.
That cliffhanger, and Tuco's violent shenanigans in the ensuing episode,
created the impression that Jimmy and his favorite parking lot attendant Mike
would soon be regularly caught up in cartel business, and that Saul Goodman
was only a little bit down the road. But as we know, the writers decided to go in
a different direction with Jimmy, and that change of heart had ripple effects
throughout the rest of the show. Nacho, who would have been a link between
Jimmy and the drug world, wound up appearing in fewer than half of Season
1's episodes, and has vanished from the show for stretches in later years.
Jimmy and Mike worked together on a few extra-legal capers early on. But as
Jimmy got caught up in the Sandpiper case, his relationship with Kim, his feud
with Chuck, and many other things having nothing to do with the local meth
trade, Mike was sent into that world on his own. And as a result, *Better Call
Saul* essentially became two largely unconnected series operating under the
same title: the Jimmy McGill story and the Mike Ehrmantraut one. (Maybe we
call that *No Half-Measures?*)

Some of this may have been necessary even if Jimmy had set up Saul
Goodman's criminal law practice earlier in the series since the creative
team was bound by the facts of *Breaking Bad*. On that show, for instance, Saul
didn't personally know Gus, and seemed to have no idea that his investigator
Mike was really Gus's right-hand man. So some split between one story and
the other would have been necessary no matter the timeline. It's just been
extremely pronounced this way. At times, it can be a best of both worlds situation, offering both subtle, layered character drama in the Jimmy half and lots
of intrigue, suspense, and *Breaking Bad* fan service in the Mike half. But at
other times, it's felt like the Jimmy show is the one that everyone realized they
wanted to make, while the Mike show is the one that the creators understood
that they had to make. Both are about how their central characters got from
Point A to Point B. But because we know so much about the characters on the
drug side of things going in, and so little about Kim, Chuck, Howard, and even
Saul/Jimmy himself, the Jimmy show has much more room to maneuver on

that path than the Mike one does. *No Half-Measures* has to travel along a very narrow, straight line, where *Better Call Saul* can have more fun taking the scenic route.

And the closer we've gotten to the events of *Breaking Bad*, the more that the Mike show risks feeling like a very expensive set of footnotes, answering questions big and small from the parent series: *Who built the Super Lab? What put Hector in the wheelchair?* Or, this week, *How did Krazy-8 get his nickname?** The level of craft and care of everyone involved is so high that filling in these blanks is still extremely entertaining, even poignant as we've gotten to know Mike and Nacho so well. But the series' two halves have felt separate and decidedly unequal for a while now on a dramatic level.

The separation goes away, at least temporarily, with the conclusion of "50% Off." For the first time since waaaaay back in Season 1's "Hero," Jimmy and Nacho share a scene together, as Nacho collects Jimmy as part of whatever Lalo has planned for the recently incarcerated Domingo. Coming so close to the end credits, it's more a portent of things to come than a scene, but it's also one that feels inevitable. We know from his first appearance on *Breaking Bad* that Saul was entangled with both Nacho and Lalo. So that has to be addressed here, just as much as the odd matter of Mike posing as Saul's investigator even while he's really working for Gus. And with so little time left in the series, it's time to start turning those two disparate shows back into a unified one.

That will have to wait for the next episode, though. "50% Off" is named after Jimmy's promotional campaign, which the meth heads in the teaser use to justify an epic petty crime spree. But the title also seems to acknowledge that fifty percent of this show has been off to one side, and fifty percent off to the other. And that structure continues at least for this one last episode before Jimmy gets drawn back into the world we all know so well.

For Jimmy, that means getting the hang of his new criminal law practice, but also trying to smooth things over with Kim as it becomes clear how not on board she is with Saul Goodman. The work half is easier. He's still not the Saul that Walt and Jesse hired—among other things, his tentative slogan is the less catchy "Speedy Justice For You"—but otherwise seems in complete command of the courthouse and his already long list of clients, with a mix of genuine legal skill and some Slippin' Jimmy tactics. When, for instance, Suzanne Ericsen declines his offer to parley early on the many cases they have in common, Jimmy bribes a custodian to trap their elevator between floors long enough for a plea bargain lightning round.

---

* An unconfident Domingo folds with a winning poker hand featuring three 8s. Lalo, amused to win on a bluff, dubs his underling "*Ocho Loco*," a moniker that will stick for the rest of Domingo's short life.

Kim proves the harder sell. She's the one person who knows Jimmy well enough to understand the full implications of this change in professional name, specialty, and all-around persona, and to be troubled by it. (Suzanne and Bill Oakley never had a very high opinion of Jimmy to begin with.) Jimmy takes her to see an impressive house for sale, a familiar move for him, akin to the downtown high-rise office he wanted to rent for their theoretical law practice. Things are not great between them at the moment—even his invitation is phrased as, "If we go right now, it'll be over like that"—but as they explore the house and contemplate a hypothetical future together, the fundamental warmth between them begins to thaw the ice that's starting to build up regarding Saul Goodman and his many shenanigans. When Kim turns on the master bathroom's shower while Jimmy is standing in it, it doesn't solve their problems, but the prank is at least a reminder that she still really likes him, despite his many flaws.

Things are a lot messier, and simply busier, over on the cartel side of things this week, with Lalo and Gus trying to outmaneuver each other, while Nacho is as usual caught in the middle. And while Mike is out of the game at the moment, his mind and heart are very much stuck in it.

For a character the series once had little room for, Nacho has in many ways turned into the heart of the cartel scenes. Where Mike and Gus both arrived here with (breaking) baggage, Nacho is a blank slate. Plot-wise, he can be whatever the show needs him to be. But there's also no unavoidable destination he needs to arrive at on an emotional level, which has given the writers and Michael Mando a lot more to work with as Nacho fights for mere survival. Here, he has to employ some acrobatic, Pinkman-esque derring-do to secure the stash house's drugs before the cops can find it—and, more importantly, to impress Lalo enough to win his trust. We're practically at a David Mamet level of games within games here, where Nacho has to be more loyal to Gus (who has threatened to murder Manuel Varga as leverage) even as Lalo thinks the opposite is true. But Mando's sweaty desperation makes the whole thing clear and taut. And the ongoing presence of Hector—whose mind remains sharp, even as his body is a prison—means the Lalo/Gus feud doesn't feel like a wild mismatch, even though we know the Chicken Man still has higher to fly before the bell tolls for him.

The current state of play doesn't involve Mike, who is once again testing out retirement. It does not go well, as Mike's attempt to finish Kaylee's treehouse leads to him screaming at his adorable granddaughter for the sin of making him feel guilty about Matty—and, by extension, about Werner. It's ugly to watch him vent his own self-loathing on this little girl, but it's also a mark of how lost Mike is right now. He has moved in and out of the drug game over these four-plus seasons, and it never seems to benefit him in any way but his bank account. And given what we know about his cash down the road, well . . . it would be nice if he could just keep adding on to that treehouse instead.

Jimmy crossed paths with Mike much more recently than with Nacho. But their interactions have grown sparser and less frequent the longer *Better Call Saul* has been around. "50% Off" concludes with an overdue Jimmy and Nacho reunion. When Jimmy and Mike team up again, the series will feel close to whole, but also that much closer to the sad fates that await both of them as a result of their partnership.

SEASON 5, EPISODE 3
WRITTEN BY ANN CHERKIS
DIRECTED BY MICHAEL MORRIS

"The Guy for This"

"When you're in, you're in." —**Nacho**

After "50% Off" reunited Jimmy and Nacho, "The Guy for This" doesn't so much break down the wall between the show's worlds as it relocates it a bit, so that Jimmy is for the moment on the cartel side, while Kim is largely holding down the law side on her own.

The episode is keenly aware of this shift, and the impact it's having on our heroine and antihero. Kim reacts to Jimmy's rising professional fortunes as if he has invited a third person into their relationship without her permission; when he declares that Saul just had his best day yet, Kim grouses, "Huh. Good for Saul." But the hour also smartly links them through the same basic dilemma. Both have convinced themselves they can do exactly what they want professionally, and both are rudely reminded of the limits of their power. Jimmy's money is coming from a drug kingpin, and Kim's from a bank, and both find themselves forced to do unsavory things for clients who won't take no for an answer.

Kim thought she had arranged the perfect balance of financial and emotional fulfillment by joining Schweikart & Cokely. Their associates would do most of the heavy lifting on Mesa Verde, leaving Kim free to pursue her more soul-nurturing criminal defense work. But as Rich Schweikart gently but pointedly reminds her, Mesa Verde keeps the lights on at the firm, not her pro bono clients. So, when Mesa Verde's new call center in Tucumcari hits a roadblock in the form of a stubborn local resident named Everett Acker,* Kim has no choice but to put her do-gooding on hold so she can kick an old man out of the house he built and has lived in for thirty years.

This is an unpleasant task, and the spiritual opposite of what Kim has been trying to do with the law. Mesa Verde is legally in the right to claim the land based on the lease Acker signed in 1974, and as Kim points out, all the other neighbors took the nominal payout the bank offered them to move. But legally right and morally right aren't necessarily the same thing, and Kim feels like trash trying to bribe Acker into leaving. She soon turns on him after he

---

* Acker is played by Barry Corbin, a veteran character actor who had a long TV stint as the mayor on *Northern Exposure* and has had a varied film career ranging from *WarGames* to *No Country for Old Men* to *Killers of the Flower Moon.*

dismisses her as a soulless rich woman, but it's not until their next encounter that we understand what a vulnerable spot that insult hit. When she returns to Acker's house later on to help him pack and find a new house, she lays bare the past she and the show have kept hidden from us until now: she grew up so poor that her family was constantly skipping out on landlords in the middle of the night. It's a biographical detail that fits everything we've seen about Kim as a striver, as a champion of the powerless, and as someone who can move in the sphere of someone like Rich without ever seeming totally comfortable there. But Acker doesn't know Kim like we do, and assumes her words are just more lies, sending her off by contemptuously asking, "You'll say anything to get what you want, won't you?"

Jimmy assumes the danger he's in is of a more physical kind than what Kim endures. We pick up right where we left off, with Jimmy being taken for an involuntary ride by Nacho.* Jimmy understandably believes this is some long-delayed punishment related to the incident involving Tuco, his grandmother, and the skater twins, and is briefly relieved to learn that Tuco's cousin Lalo wants to hire him as a Krazy-8's lawyer. But his alarm bells go off when he finds out that his task is to feed Domingo information to hand to the authorities that will hurt Gus. This is, at minimum, highly unethical, on top of entangling him with criminals far more dangerous than his current client base. Whether it's because he still has some professional standards, or is simply afraid of an ongoing relationship with the Salamanca family, Jimmy's desperate attempt to avoid taking the job is perhaps the clearest sign so far this season that he remains Saul Goodman in professional name only.

But Lalo, as we have seen, doesn't believe in the concept of "no."[†] And soon the man who would be Saul finds himself in the criminal courts building, making nice with Domingo and coaching him through the play they will soon perform for law enforcement. Since this is a con job more than it is a legal job, Jimmy of course proves a natural at it, even as his audience turns

---

* It's an excellent Nacho episode overall. He's doing his best to play both sides against the middle, here earning Lalo's trust in a way that will hurt Gus, by giving the DEA (via Domingo) the locations of some Fring organization dead drops. But the whole thing remains a prison for him, and for his father. Mr. Varga swings by his son's swanky new house to tell him about an offer on the family business. Unlike the one Mesa Verde makes for Mr. Acker's house, it's extremely lucrative—which makes Mr. Varga mistrust it just as much as Acker mistrusts Kim.

† Mike, meanwhile, is in pure destructive guilt mode as a result of Lalo's presence forcing him to kill Werner. At the bar where he once took Werner for a night out, he notices the Sydney Opera House postcard that inspired Werner to tell the story of how his father helped build it. It's a painful reminder of the friend he murdered, and Mike pleads with the bartender to take it off the wall. The gesture doesn't salve him for long, and on his drunken walk home, he breaks the arm of one of the young toughs who tries to mug him, then looks almost disappointed when none of his friends want to try their luck with him.

out to be a pair of DEA agents we know painfully well: Hank Schrader and Steve Gomez.

The *Saul* producers announced the return of actors Dean Norris and Steven Michael Quezada before Season 5 began, realizing that surprise isn't the be-all, end-all for this kind of show. Still, Hank gets one hell of an introduction. First we see a very familiar beer gut enter the frame. Then Hank's and Steve's silhouettes are moving together, out of focus. Then we can see the back of Hank's head—the shape distinctive, even if he's one of many bald *Breaking Bad*-ies—and finally his badge, before Hank himself comes into focus. If it's not exactly the shark from *Jaws* appearing piecemeal before Roy Scheider finally gets a look at it, it's still a buildup that captures his import to the parent show, while also making it clear to the subsection of the audience who only watches *Saul* that these guys are Kind of a Big Deal.

One of the most notable improvements between the first two *Breaking Bad* seasons was the depth the show gave Hank, who was a two-dimensional macho blowhard in most of his early appearances. Some of that onscreen transformation can be ascribed to the events Hank went through in Season 2 (killing Tuco, witnessing horrible violence in El Paso). But it's not hard to write off his initial characterization as his brother-in-law's view of him. Until Walt began cooking meth, he wasn't particularly close to Hank, and perhaps never glimpsed the depth lurking beneath the bluster. For the moment, we're seeing Hank in that swaggering alpha male mode, but it's only a brief scene that's about getting Jimmy entangled in the war between Lalo and Gus. Hank and Gomez make sense as unwitting players in that war, not only because they're the local men with badges we know best, but because it was established on *Breaking Bad* that Krazy-8 was their informant. Like the building of the Super Lab or Domingo's nickname, it's not necessarily a piece of franchise lore in crucial need of explanation. But in this case, it feels like the fan service and the storytelling are working hand in hand.

For Jimmy, it's a victory, but perhaps a pyrrhic one. He makes a chunk of cash in a single day,* and he impresses Lalo. But now he's a part of this thing that is very dangerous to body and spirit. The episode opens with a classically Heisenbergian vignette about the ice cream cone Jimmy had to abandon on the sidewalk when Nacho came for him. In intense close-up, we see one ant after another emerge from the cracks in the concrete to take advantage of this unexpected bounty of sugar. Like Hank's gut, the symbolism's hard to miss: Jimmy

---

*   Even this provides more evidence that Jimmy isn't really Saul yet: he completely lowballs himself with Lalo, asking for the paltry sum of $7,925, which is much less than even the cash Lalo has on his person. He'll have a stronger grasp of both his own worth and that of drug dealers by the time he meets Walt and Jesse.

has cast aside something sweet (a relatively honest legal career like the one he had before the war with Chuck) for something destructive, and he's as oblivi-. ous to the carnage he's starting to cause as the passersby on the street are to what's happening down at ant level. Later, Jimmy returns to the same curb to find the ice cream somehow still there after all this time. He tries shooing away the bugs, before walking off himself. Like his protests with Lalo, there's a brief stab at something more decent, but increasingly he is becoming true to his new persona.

Still, he's Jimmy McGill at heart, and he and Kim are, for the moment, still more of a match than they aren't. Jimmy returns from his long day with Nacho and Lalo to find Kim drinking on the apartment balcony. She's cold to him and quickly returns to her work. But when she finishes the long drive back from Tucumcari, now it's Jimmy waiting for her on the balcony, ready to share a smoke and get her the drink she so obviously needs. They say nothing, because Jimmy knows her well enough to understand that what she needs right now is for her boyfriend to be there for her. He goofs around, pretending to drop one of the bottles, and in the process inspires her to hurl hers into the parking lot, and then another, and another, as Jimmy joins in. Again, a mess is being made, but this time, it's a mess that makes Kim Wexler feel better. She and Jimmy are basically starring in two separate shows at the moment, but occasionally they can meet in the middle and briefly remind each other, and us, of why they belonged together in the first place, and how much it'll hurt whenever they're fully apart.

SEASON 5, EPISODE 4
WRITTEN AND DIRECTED BY GORDON SMITH

"Namaste"

"Yesterday was bad. Today, I'm gonna fix it." —**Kim**

The main action of "Namaste" picks up the morning after "The Guy for This" ended. Kim and Jimmy are hung over from their night of drunken vandalism, and as they head out for work, Kim is struck by the sight of all the broken bottles they tossed from the balcony the night before. In the previous episode, Jimmy discovered the mess he'd made by dropping his ice cream cone on the curb but shrugged it off and walked away, so it's not surprising that he tells Kim to let the building association handle things in their parking lot. But after Jimmy has peeled out in his Esteem for another day as Saul Goodman, Kim grabs a broom and, in her tailored suit and pumps, opts to literally clean up her own mess, even as she's working the phone in hopes of metaphorically doing the same regarding Mr. Acker.

As much as Kim loves Jimmy, and as willing as she is at times to swim in murky ethical waters with him, she's ultimately a much more responsible and compassionate person than he is. She doesn't have to do either of these tasks. As Jimmy says, someone else will sweep up the glass, while her legal responsibility is to Mesa Verde, not this stubborn old man who repeatedly insulted her. But she knows both of these problems ultimately fall on her, and she won't be happy unless she pushes the broom herself.

Kim's not the only one in cleaning mode throughout "Namaste." And like her, the other characters discover that some messes don't want to go away, no matter how hard you sweep or scrub.

The other literal cleaning job happens over at Los Pollos Hermanos, where Gus's loyal assistant manager Lyle winds up staying long after his shift is done, working his fingers raw with steel wool as he attempts to scrub the deep fryer to his boss's satisfaction. Poor Lyle has no way of knowing about Gus's other life as the Chicken Man of Albuquerque, nor that this concern over the fryer is how Gus deals with his anxiety as he waits to see if Victor and Tyrus can complete the con job that Nacho has set up with Hank* and Gomez. It's a striking sequence, and not just for the way Lyle's mundane task is

---

* Hank and Gomez's final scene in this one recontextualizes some of Hank's early bluster on *Breaking Bad*. When it's just Hank and Steve talking, Hank can clearly tell something isn't quite right about this operation and is disappointed that they only arrested small fish. But then he turns to all the agents and cops who participated in the operation and is the swaggering good ol' boy we first met

contrasted with the much higher stakes of Victor leading a DEA task force on a semi-wild goose chase. This feels like the first time on *Better Call Saul*—and one of the few times in Giancarlo Esposito's entire time playing the role—where we are seeing Gus Fring sweat. He is so used to being master of all he surveys—even when he is playing subordinate to the Salamancas or Juan Bolsa, he is clearly manipulating events—that he seems almost startlingly vulnerable as he sits in his office and waits for the text, taking out all his mounting frustration on Lyle.

Mike belatedly tries to repair the damage he caused when he yelled at Kaylee back in "50% Off," going to Stacey's house and asking to watch his granddaughter again. But he never even gets inside the door, as his daughter-in-law gently but firmly suggests that this emotional wound needs more time to heal, and that Mike should use that time to get back to himself. "Get back to myself," Mike repeats, in a somber tone suggesting that such a fate is the worst thing anyone can ask of him. The Mike scenes so far this season have been effectively threading a storytelling needle. On the one hand, the show needed to sideline Mike for a bit so he wouldn't be involved in the escalating Gus/Lalo tensions, and so he'd be professionally unencumbered when he wakes up in that odd compound at the end of the episode. But it doesn't feel like spinning wheels because Jonathan Banks is just that good at playing Mike's pain (listen to the break in his voice when Mike assures Stacey that he'll be okay), and because it's a genuine and important character arc. We are nearing Mike's last chance to not go into business with Gus Fring, which we know will end poorly for both of them. Last season, it seemed more that Mike fell into the Super Lab job than that he made an active choice to join the team. So it matters that we're seeing him try to get away, and that it is not going at all well for him. Without work, and with Kaylee understandably shaken by their last encounter, Mike has nothing to tune out thoughts of Werner, or Matty, so he opts to pick a fight with the same crew he so easily took down in the previous episode, eager for the physical punishment they give him. He wakes up a disaster, but he wants to be one. (If anything, he looks disappointed to be waking up at all, having failed at suicide-by-punk.)

After his dalliance with the Salamancas last week, Jimmy is on more comfortable terrain landing the junkies from "50% Off" as his new clients and running a short con in court by having a lookalike sit in for a defendant to discredit an eyewitness. But he also takes a lunch with Howard Hamlin and discovers that Howard wants to belatedly clean up the mess he created years

---

on the parent show—a character he has learned to play very well to work in this world, even if he's really much more thoughtful.

before by letting Chuck talk him out of hiring Jimmy to be an HHM associate. This is a very different Howard from the broken man Jimmy had to give a tough-love speech to in last season's "Piñata." The firm is doing well again, Howard is loving life and embodying the vanity license plate that gives "Namaste" its title.* He is genuinely curious about Jimmy's new identity as Saul Goodman, asking the question that defines the series: "If he's not Jimmy McGill, who is he? What's he about?" Jimmy gives him a song and dance about David vs Goliath, but Howard correctly notes that he could play that role under his real name.

Despite all the bad blood between them—much, but not all, of it Chuck's fault—Howard wants to bring Jimmy into the fold, eager to have the guy he once dubbed Charlie Hustle working cases for HHM. We know from Season 2 that Jimmy is temperamentally unsuited to work at such a place—he even mentions Cliff Main while Howard is making his sales pitch—but like Mike's attempt to enjoy retirement, this is something of a last chance for Jimmy before he goes full Saul. He could take the offer, have security and even the satisfaction of knowing the position would make Chuck roll over in his grave. But the reasons for wanting that job are long gone. Chuck's dead, Kim's at another firm—and Jimmy is in willful denial about how much she dislikes Saul Goodman—and hanging out his own shingle gives Jimmy the freedom to pull courtroom stunts that Howard would never allow.

But Jimmy isn't just uninterested in the job Howard is dangling in front of him. He is *offended* to see how well Howard is doing emotionally since that encounter in the men's room. Chuck's death broke both of them, but where Jimmy had to turn himself into a largely new person to survive it, Howard over time has managed to revert back into the guy he used to be. His interest in hiring Jimmy, and living up to the ideals Jimmy argued for in the Season 4 finale, is genuine. We know he's always liked Jimmy, and that he's basically a well-meaning guy. But his ability to achieve inner peace marks him as someone worthy of Jimmy's contempt. And on his long drive home from meeting with Mr. Acker—a little guy being stepped on by a Goliath that Howard's firm used to represent—Jimmy is inspired to stop at a secondhand store in search of tools of mayhem. We see this visit out of context, as the episode's teaser, unsure why Jimmy needs a heavy object and for what purpose. But it's not until the episode's almost over that we learn those used bowling balls were purchased for Jimmy to hurl over the gate to Howard's mansion, as projectiles aimed at the car that stirred up all of Jimmy's old anger and class resentment. No good

---

* Technically, it reads "NAMAST3."

deed goes unpunished, and Howard's well-meaning offer to his mentor's kid brother leads to this act of vandalism.

Jimmy winds up visiting Acker only after Kim tries and fails to convince Kevin to try an alternate location for the Tucumcari call center. This is dangerous ground she is treading on. Acker is not her client; Mesa Verde is. And Rich Schweikart knows who Kim's boyfriend is, though he may not yet know that Saul Goodman and Jimmy McGill are more or less the same person. There are many ways in which this gambit could absolutely blow up on her, creating a mess she won't be able to clean up without losing her cushy job.

Maybe this is what she wants, though. She comes into the courtroom to watch Jimmy work and is there to witness the chicanery with the defendant's lookalike. She's amused but unfazed, and she sits quietly in the gallery for a long time while Jimmy gets scolded in the judge's chambers. She knows who he is and how he conducts himself now. And he is what she needs in order to do right by Mr. Acker. Kim's mostly a straight arrow, but she has a weakness for Jimmy, for his mindset of taking shortcuts with the law, and for underdogs. She's long been impatient with Mesa Verde, and this stunt with getting Jimmy to represent Acker seems as much getting out from under that job as it is about helping an old man on the verge of losing the house he built for himself. It is her way of throwing a bowling ball in the direction of a rich man with whom she no longer wants to associate.

Because sometimes, the only way to fix one mess is to make a bigger one.

SEASON 5, EPISODE 5
WRITTEN BY HEATHER MARION
DIRECTED BY JIM MCKAY

"Dedicado a Max"

"It seems to me that you are at a crossroads." —**Gus**

Throughout the run of *Better Call Saul*, Kim Wexler and Mike Ehrmantraut have represented two very different paths for our main character. Kim is the path we want Jimmy to stay on; Mike is the path we unfortunately know he will take. Because those paths diverge so wildly, the two characters have yet to meet through four and a half seasons of the show.

Midway through "Dedicado a Max," we come as close as we ever have to Jimmy's once and future partners sharing a scene, as Kim is listening in on Jimmy's side of a phone call to Mike. The call is played for laughs, as Mike has no time for Jimmy's nonsense* while he's recuperating down in Mexico. (Jonathan Banks's weary delivery of "I'm in a tunnel" is a thing of deadpan comic beauty.)

The moment for Mike to take on work with Jimmy/Saul isn't here yet, nor is there any evidence so far that he and Kim might ever speak. But the near-intersection between the two of them comes in an episode where both are faced with the same question: Should they retreat into a safe and honest life, or to push into more reckless and potentially exciting territory? And in both cases, they seem to opt for recklessness.

The hour does a more thorough and convincing job of detailing how Kim reaches this point than it does for Mike. Much of her half of the episode plays out in charming caper fashion, as Kim and Jimmy run a series of elaborate short cons right under the nose of Mesa Verde,† because Kevin mistakenly believes that the chief scammer is Everett Acker, and not his favorite attorney. It's been a recurring theme of Kim's relationship with Jimmy that they seem at their happiest and most connected whenever she's willing to step over onto his

---

* With Mike out of town (and uninterested), Jimmy asks Dr. Caldera for another investigator, and winds up with the bearded, intense, "Mr. X"—aka the loudmouth (played by Steven Ogg) whom Mike easily disarmed back in Season 1's "Pimento." The character was never referred to by name in the earlier episode, though the script called him Sobchak, since writer Thomas Schnauz had John Goodman from *The Big Lebowski* in mind when he wrote it. The original plan in this episode was to have Bill Burr reprise his *Breaking Bad* role as Huell's partner Kuby. But Burr was unavailable, so Ogg got to come back.

† Jimmy Loves Movies: we see him spreading the slightly radioactive smoke detector residue onto Acker's property with the same method Ashley-Pitt used to dispose of tunnel dirt in *The Great Escape*: bags of the stuff hidden inside his pants, to be opened and released as he walks around, his own footsteps blending the new and old particles together.

side of the ethical line. Here, we see this play out with the delightful scene where Jimmy encourages Kim to role play as Kevin so he can properly enjoy the story of her latest grift. Kim's Kevin impression is pretty broad, but within moments, Jimmy is expertly playing Kim,* and then it veers into a sex game without any warning at all.

Ultimately, though, Kim isn't doing this to feel closer to Jimmy. She's doing it because she's mad at Kevin, at Rich, at Mesa Verde, and even at herself for not disentangling from this mess sooner. She may not consciously be trying to sabotage her job at the firm, or her status as the bank's top lawyer, but her fury and her need to control things has led her onto some very shaky ground. Rich sees through Kim's puppeteering,† and tries to quietly assign her to other cases to protect both her and the firm. Instead, it inspires a public scene from Kim that could have easily resulted in her dismissal. Even if her anger begins as trying to protect Acker and the scheme by staying on the case, she takes it way too far when she continues the fight out in the hallway in front of half the firm. This is no longer Kim the ice-cold manipulator, but Kim the hot mess.

Even Jimmy knows she is taking this too far. Like Rich in that hallway, he tries giving Kim every possible chance to give up once it seems like they've run out of maneuvering room to save Acker's house. For once, Jimmy is being the responsible one, while Kim can't let go of the need to win and get over on her superiors. As entertaining as it is to watch her and Jimmy whenever they're in cahoots, when even he is advising her to stop, she has placed herself in an incredibly risky position.

Where Kim makes a clear choice at her own professional crossroads, the episode technically ends with Mike still considering between the two paths Gus presents him: going back to civilian life and marinating in guilt and anger, or signing up for Gus's cold war against the Salamancas. We obviously know that he'll choose Gus, but "Dedicado a Max" doesn't lay out a hugely convincing case for that.

We discover that the village he woke up in at the end of the previous episode, constructed by Gus as a charitable tribute to his late partner Max, is a day's drive south of the El Paso–Juárez border. Mike's injuries heal up with some help from Gus's doctor.‡ It's a nice place, and Mike fits in well there once

---

* It's a great comic setup for a moment later in the episode when Kim makes the same hand gesture at Rich that Jimmy so perfectly used while copying her.

† Going all the way back to Howard seeing through Jimmy's billboard stunt in "Hero," *Saul* has made sure to treat powerful characters in the lawyer world as if they're smart enough to have earned their positions. It would defy credulity if everyone at this level—a clever cookie like Rich most of all—was hoodwinked by Kim.

‡ Years later, remember, the same physician (last seen procuring the "yea big" packet of drugs for Mike back in Season 3's "Sunk Costs") will patch up the bullet wound Mike received during Gus's grand revenge on Don Eladio. Mike's impatient to get home that time, too.

he accepts the idea of staying for a bit. He can enjoy watching children play even while he's estranged from Kaylee, and he can put his bountiful home repair skills to good use. The longer he stays, the more content he seems with this kind of life.

Instead, Gus arrives and meets him at the fountain bearing Max's name. He presents himself as a relatively good and moral drug dealer—more artfully than Walter White will in a few years, but still deeply hypocritical—that Mike would do well to work alongside. And he frames the war in terms Mike can also appreciate: as revenge. Mike still owes the Salamancas for the murdered Samaritan, and it was Lalo's tenacity that led to Werner having to be executed rather than sent home. It's not a bad point for Gus to make in his favor. But the case against just going home to Kaylee and Stacey doesn't entirely ring true. Mike's in a bad way right now, but that's in large part fallout from the job he already took for Gus. Which seems more likely from this point: Mike stays a civilian, and within weeks or maybe months he is regularly playing with his granddaughter again, or Mike goes to work for Gus and never has to do anything that will linger emotionally when he's around his family? These are odds that should be easy for Mike to measure in favor of rejecting Gus, yet the episode seems designed to explain why he would instead accept the offer. Yes, Gus has built this nice place in the middle of nowhere, but he will be asking Mike to murder people—even if they're bad people. The potential for it to bleed onto Kaylee (metaphorically, if not literally) just seems way too high. His time in the village feels more like a pleasant interlude than a strong dramatic argument for taking him one big step along the way to the guy he is on *Breaking Bad.*

Rhea Seehorn and Jonathan Banks have such abundant, amusing chemistry whenever they appear in public to discuss the show that it's only natural to root for Kim and Mike to meet. For a long time, though, it felt like they couldn't possibly come into contact, because Jimmy would be moving away from Kim's world and toward Mike's. Now, though, Kim's parallel path seems in danger of taking a sharp turn toward Mike's, and suddenly the prospect of seeing them share a scene doesn't feel so fun anymore.

SEASON 5, EPISODE 6
WRITTEN BY THOMAS SCHNAUZ
DIRECTED BY MICHAEL MORRIS

"Wexler v. Goodman"

"I don't believe you. You don't believe yourself. It is a lie. You lie. I lie. This has to end! I cannot keep living like this!" —**Kim**

What happens to Kim?

This is the biggest question left for *Better Call Saul*. Arguably, it's the most important question of the entire series. There have been smaller mysteries solved (why Jimmy changed his name, Mike's reasons for teaming with Gus*), and there are a few other dangling plot and character threads in need of tying off before the series ends, particularly involving Nacho and Lalo. But we know how this story ends for Jimmy, Mike, Gus, and several other characters—and that it won't be a good ending for any of them. Kim, though? Her future is a riddle wrapped inside an enigma, and one that's as much about defining Saul Goodman's story on *Breaking Bad* as about concluding her own arc on this series. Does she die? Is her career ruined by her association with Jimmy? Do the two of them just drift apart? Does Saul Goodman go home every night to Kim Wexler?

The unnervingly titled "Wexler v. Goodman" seems to suggest one ending for Kim—and much earlier than any of us might have wanted—before veering off in a far more troubling direction. First, though, it provides us a fuller picture of Kim's origin story. The teaser takes us back to her childhood in Nebraska, where she's lingering outside her middle school long after her mother should have picked her up from band practice. She's so young and looks extra vulnerable standing next to that huge cello case. But even as a grown woman, Kim's strength has always been more mental and emotional than physical. She wouldn't win a fistfight with one of the Cousins, but she wouldn't act intimidated by them, either. She's nervous that her mother is so late to pick her up, but also smart and strong-willed enough once she does arrive to recognize what a mistake it would be to get into a car driven by a drunk woman. So, she sets off to walk the three miles to their house, over her mother's wounded

---

* Mike is now firmly back on Team Pollos, using his Dave Clark alias (previously deployed in the *Breaking Bad* Season 5 premiere, when he had to find out what happened to Gus's laptop) to set up Lalo to be arrested for murdering the TravelWire clerk last season. But in attempting another nonviolent half-measure like he opted for with Lalo's cousin, it seems that Mike still has some steps to walk down before he's fully the guy we met on the other show.

protests. She doesn't pause, doesn't look back; she knows what she needs to do, however hard it may be, and she does it. The scene matches up not only with what Kim told Everett Acker about her childhood, but with the woman we've seen that girl become. Kim wants to take on everything herself because she spent her formative years being taught that this was the only way she could expect anything to get done and done right.

The teaser also speaks to the reasons she's drawn to Jimmy: both her mother and her boyfriend are addicts, where one can't resist booze and the other can't resist a good con. He is never happier than when he's running a play, as we see in the joy on his face as he directs the fake commercials he plans to use to blackmail Kevin. When Kim, chastened by her argument with Rich in "Dedicado a Max," decides to call off the play and arrange a modest settlement for Acker, Jimmy's disappointment is much more about not getting to finish the grift than it is about the potential money involved.

"It's just not worth it," Kim insists, and Jimmy reluctantly agrees in the moment. And for a few minutes afterward, we get glimpses of the more responsible and decent guy that he's capable of being. He agrees to cancel the plan and clean up the nail salon before Mrs. Nguyen opens in the morning. When next we see him, he's declining a freebie offered by two sex workers as an extra thank you for his legal work, and even expressing concern that they're going right back to their jobs. But then his mischievous, damn-the-man side takes over, and it occurs to him to instead hire them for another emotional attack on Howard Hamlin. While Jimmy's old nemesis Cliff Main watches in dismay, the prostitutes pretend that Howard is a regular client, in debt to their pimp Joe Dog.[*]

Jimmy's pleasure in seeing one rich swell taken down a peg inspires him to keep going, and to resurrect the various schemes he and Kim had planned to deploy against Kevin. We know it's coming long before Kim does, which only makes her stunned reaction in the Schweikart & Cokely conference room that much more painful. Jimmy gets exactly what they originally wanted—Acker keeps his house and gets some cash, and Kevin even has to pay extra for the rights to the Mesa Verde logo—but it's not at all what Kim is looking for by this point. As she will say later on in the discomfort of their apartment, "You made me the sucker—again."

As she arrives home, Jimmy is plucking away at "Smoke on the Water" on the guitar—his old partner Marco's favorite song. The show uses it as a sign of when Jimmy is getting close to being Saul Goodman in more than name. Kim

---

[*] Patrick Fabian's indignant delivery of "Joe Dog" and "tugboat" is hilarious. Howard is mostly comic relief at the moment, but he's very effective comic relief.

doesn't know the importance of the song, but she recognizes that the man who pulled this stunt is very different from the one she wants to build a life with. And for a few agonizing moments, it seems like the episode will end with their relationship torn asunder, and Jimmy with no more obstacles toward going full Goodman.

But that would be too abrupt an exit for the show's most loved character, especially with nearly a season and a half of the series to go. Instead, the episode ends with a reminder that Kim is an addict, too; her weakness just happens to be for lovable but damaged people like her boyfriend and occasional partner in crime. So even though she has just spent several minutes clearly articulating why she can't trust Jimmy, and that they are better off going their separate ways, she concludes the episode by suggesting, "Or maybe we get married."

It is a *terrible* idea. Even Kim seems to know it. This is not a romantic proposal in any way, but the brainstorm of a defeated woman who recognizes that for once, she's too weak to pick up her cello and walk away. She's going to hop in and ride along until they're run off the road. As someone deeply invested in the life of this fictional character turning out okay, it's something I don't want to see. But as a masochist who loves this show and its predecessor most when they're at their ugliest and most punishing, it's hard not to root for the chance to see how Seehorn, Odenkirk, and company play out the car wreck that's clearly coming.

How Rhea Seehorn Became the MVP of *Better Call Saul*

[This story originally appeared on RollingStone.com on March 25, 2020]

Rhea Seehorn only came out to Hollywood so she could watch *The Sopranos*.

In the spring of 2003, Seehorn was nearly a decade into her acting career, largely in East Coast theater productions. The work was fulfilling, but low-paying. While all her friends had been raving for years about HBO's epic mob drama, Seehorn hadn't seen it; she couldn't afford cable. So when her agent called her—while Seehorn was cleaning toilets for her day job as a receptionist at a Brooklyn construction site—to say she had gotten an audition for an ABC sitcom, her biggest concern was whether the studio would put her up in a hotel for the night.

"I thought, 'It comes with a trip to L.A., and I finally get to watch *The Sopranos*? Let's do it,'" she recalls now.

As it turned out, Seehorn didn't get to see any of Tony and Carmela on that trip. The audition—for *I'm With Her*, a series loosely based on the relationship between the sitcom writer Chris Henchy and the actress Brooke Shields, where Seehorn would be reading for the actress character's sister—was moved up to first thing in the morning after she arrived in town. She staggered into the studio still wearing the clothes she'd barely slept in, clueless about how to behave in this setting (she started eating a bagel before being told the food was meant for the executives), and did a five-minute riff as a character she had invented. She got the part, and moved to L.A.—and eventually got cable, thanks to the bigger paycheck.

Seehorn has been working steadily ever since, in other sitcoms like *Whitney*, lighthearted dramas like *The Starter Wife* and *Franklin & Bash*, and now in her breakout role as Jimmy McGill's conscience/girlfriend Kim Wexler on *Better Call Saul*—among the very best of the complex cable dramas that *The Sopranos* made possible. Throughout, her career has been equal parts art and practicality, not just in the dirty jobs she had to take, like the one at the construction site, to make it happen, but in how she builds her characters out of rigorous study and questioning, finding intense power in extreme subtlety.

Seehorn's work ethic is the reason Kim Wexler has evolved from a person for whom the show's creators had no concrete plan, beyond giving Jimmy (Bob Odenkirk) a confidante, into the heart of the series, and the reason they drastically changed their original intentions about when and how Jimmy would become Saul Goodman. Kim has gone from afterthought to one of the most beloved characters on either *Better Call Saul* or *Breaking Bad.*

"She just brings so much depth, and there's so much thought and so much intelligence to every moment that she plays," says *Saul* co-creator Peter Gould. "She's able to play all the ideas between the words and make them ring and sing. She's just fascinating to watch. You want to know what's going on between those ears."

Born Deborah Rhea Seehorn, she began using her middle name—pronounced "Ray," after the man who introduced her parents to one another—because "the Deborahs and Debbies that I knew or saw on TV always seemed to be really attractive cheerleaders, and it was not my lane at all in school," Seehorn says. "I just remember feeling a disassociation with the name, from a very early age."* Her mother was an executive assistant, mostly for the Navy, while her father was a counterintelligence agent for the Naval Investigative Service. His work led the family to move around a lot during Seehorn's childhood, including postings in Japan, Arizona, and Virginia.

"I never saw pictures, but you would hear stories," she says of her father. "He was in Russia before the Iron Curtain came down, and apparently [posed as] a woman at one point."

There's more than a bit of acting to that kind of work, though Seehorn and her dad never got to bond over the shared experience. He died when she was eighteen, at a time when she assumed she was going to be a painter. In college at George Mason University in Fairfax, Virginia, she was required to take an elective outside of her visual arts program, and tried an acting class.

"Thank God it wasn't a feel-good, let's just lie on the floor, feel how we feel about ourselves class," she recalls. "It was all craft. It was practical aesthetics, a handbook for actors—here's how you break down a script, this is what an objective is, this is an obstacle. I was in such heaven that I never looked back after that."

At the time, she was forty-five pounds heavier than she is now, with a jet-black crew cut. She couldn't imagine a world in which she would ever get to act on television, but thought the stage would be a good place for her. Her acting teacher, Lynnie Raybuck, encouraged her to check out the theater scene in nearby Washington, D.C., and soon Seehorn was offering to tackle any odd job that might get her noticed as someone who was both passionate and a hard worker.

---

* Her sister is the only person to still call her Debbie "to bug the crap out of me, but that's what sisters do." Many fans mispronounce her name "RHEE-uh," like *Cheers* star Rhea Perlman; Seehorn is too polite and happy to meet them to offer a correction.

"I volunteered to usher at Woolly Mammoth [Theatre Company] for a year," she says. "I volunteered for stage-running crew, box office, anything to make that bridge between academic and professional, so that I could learn professional things, be around professional people, show that I was willing to put in the hours. Also, when I got out for auditions, I'm not knocking on a door of someone who's never seen me before. They've seen me making the disgusting fried eggs for a play that lasted all summer."

Eventually, she was getting significant theater roles (and rave reviews). She took odd jobs to pay the bills, like clerking at a record store or doing home repair using whatever knowledge she could glean by reading the how-to books at Home Depot. ("I learned how to re-caulk a bathtub after I had already told the guy that I could do it," she says, admitting her work "was OK; it wasn't great.") A good source of income in those days was to appear in industrial films that corporations used to train their employees; in one, Seehorn played a woman calling in to an AT&T hotline because the concept of voicemail confused her—"Like, I can't understand how to hang up the phone; it's insane." (She's heard from friends in the area that another—in which she teaches bartenders and waitresses how to deal with drunk customers—is still being used all these years later.)

She auditioned for what few film and TV productions were happening in the region: her first TV role was in an episode of the Baltimore-based *Homicide: Life on the Street*. But even though her physical appearance had changed from her college days, that world still seemed at odds with how she saw herself.

"By then I was a twenty-five-year-old blonde, so I would get sent in for the ingenue," she says, "but I would go at it as a character actor. I can't just play the guy's girlfriend. If the most interesting thing about me is my boyfriend, I'm not going to get the part, because I would add all this subtext of like, 'No, no, no. There has to be something going on with her. Was she abused? Why is she just standing there?' I didn't get parts for a while because of that."

Seehorn had grown up idolizing Bea Arthur for playing brassy, no-bullshit women in sitcoms like *Maude* and *Golden Girls*. Starting with *I'm With Her*—where her character, Cheri Baldzikowski, was skeptical bordering on contemptuous of her sister's new civilian boyfriend—she found herself playing younger versions of Bea Arthur parts in one sitcom after another. "I got typecast as something that I was very proud of," she says, "which was this very wry, sarcastic, knowing [woman]." Most of the shows were canceled quickly—NBC's *Whitney*, at two seasons, was her longest full-time gig pre-*Saul*—and some never aired at all, but the jobs kept coming, and Seehorn kept enjoying them.

When you enter the business in a sitcom, though, the business sees you as a sitcom actor. Chances to audition for dramatic roles proved few and far between. One of the few casting directors willing to think outside the box with her was Sharon Bialy, who was intrigued by Seehorn's theater resume, because, she says, "so many of the shows I do require an actor who can handle language well." Bialy and her co-workers Sherry Thomas and Russell Scott frequently brought in Seehorn to read for more serious parts. Shortly before *Better Call Saul* went into pre-production, Seehorn lost out on two different jobs she badly wanted where Bialy was doing the casting. Bialy reached out with a message of encouragement.

"I just remember saying—and I've never said this to an actor before—'It didn't work out, but there's something coming up that I know will be the right job for you,'" Bialy says. "And I never say that, because you can never predict what will happen. But I had already read the pilot for *Better Call Saul*, and I just had an instinct that she would be great for the role. I said, 'Just be patient. Hang in there.'"

There wasn't much to Kim in that pilot, where she appears in only two scenes, with a couple of lines; Gould and Vince Gilligan hadn't given the character much thought. As Gould puts it, "We knew there should be a woman in Jimmy's life, somebody who was certainly as much a friend as anything else. That was about as much as we knew, that these two people had a history, and that it was a complicated history." For the audition, to preserve secrecy on a high-profile project, they invented a couple of fake scenes: one about a cop who discovers her younger sister has left college (for which the cop is still giving her money) and become a crack-addicted prostitute; the other about a woman who has found success after leaving her small hometown, then runs into an old friend whom she may or may not have dated in the past. Seehorn impressed enough that Bialy told her then and there about the real character, and after a confused, profane response (according to Bialy, she said, "Wait, she's not a cop? She doesn't have a sister? What the fuck?"), they kept going. "One of the important components is how quickly the actor can take the adjustment and shape it into something else," says Bialy. "That's what Rhea was able to do in the next take. It didn't take her five takes; she got it immediately."

Though many of the *Saul* writers had worked together on *Breaking Bad*, they struggled mightily to figure out what the spin-off should be in terms of story and tone, and how to use the characters who had never appeared on the parent show. *Breaking Bad* alum Gennifer Hutchison recalls a lot of early debate in the writers' room over how Kim felt about Jimmy's con-man side. In her script for the show's fourth episode, "Hero," Hutchison wrote a moment where Kim privately smiles in response to a Jimmy scheme that had outraged her boss, Howard Hamlin. ("Publicity stunt or not," the stage directions read, "she liked it.") With so little material early on, Seehorn had to invent a backstory and motivations in her head to make the character make sense to her, and over the years, many of those early ideas proved consistent with what the show gradually revealed about Kim. (This speaks to Seehorn's instincts, but also to the writers watching what she was doing and following her lead.) Even before she got the "Hero" script, she had decided that it was more interesting if Kim was attracted to Jimmy in part because of his occasional criminal impulses rather than in spite of them. Director Colin Bucksey had her try a series of smiles—some big, some barely perceptible. "On a scale of one to ten, ten being the biggest smile," Seehorn says, "I think he picked one of my fours."

Though Gilligan and Gould weren't sure at the script stage if the smile would stay, Seehorn's performance unlocked the character—and, in many ways, the show—for them.

"The way she played it just felt so right that it gave us a strong feeling for where we were going with her," says Gould.

The creators had assumed that Jimmy would become Saul fairly quickly, and ended that first season with Jimmy in the car after blowing off a job interview that Kim had arranged for him, a wicked grin on his face that *Breaking Bad* fans would recognize. It was only after the season was in the can that it occurred to Gould what a bad spot Jimmy was putting Kim in by ignoring this great opportunity she had arranged. ("We started saying, 'Wait, did he just leave her high and dry?'" he explains.) The Season 2 premiere revealed that Jimmy actually had gone to the meeting for her sake, and he would eventually take the job to impress her.

"That started changing the course of the story," says Gould. "The emotional connection between these two characters had a gravitational pull that started twisting the whole story around. Right now, a lot of what happened on the show revolves around this very complicated—and I think very adult, in its own way—relationship between those two."

That need for Jimmy, and for the show, to pay Kim the respect she'd earned by that point radically altered Saul in multiple ways. It slowed Jimmy's transformation into the scoundrel Saul Goodman to a measured pace that more closely parallels the tragic moral descent of Saul's most infamous client, Walter White. And it forced the creative team to essentially split the series in two, with Jimmy and Kim on one side and all the drug dealers on the other.

These changes remind Gilligan, only on a grander scale, of when he abandoned his initial plan on *Breaking Bad* to kill off Jesse Pinkman early in Season 1. "Thank God, we got as lucky with Rhea as we did with Aaron Paul," he says. "But this is different, because Jesse, God bless him, he and Walt were not really equals in their character dynamic. But these two characters are definitely equals, and most of the time, Kim is Jimmy's better—certainly his better angel."

That it was a silent, barely perceptible reaction that proved the Rosetta stone for Kim, and for *Better Call Saul*, feels appropriate. Seehorn's work throughout the series isn't flashy. Kim is a control freak who keeps her emotions as tightly coiled as her signature power ponytail. Yet it's clear throughout the show how she feels about Jimmy, about her co-workers, and about whatever mess she has found herself in. Seehorn trained herself to be a character actor at an age when no one envisioned her as such; those long-honed instincts to be understated and real are paying off fantastically in this role.

The only downside to such incredible but nuanced work is that Seehorn has yet to be recognized for it by her peers. Where Odenkirk, Jonathan Banks, Giancarlo Esposito, and Michael McKean have all received Emmy nominations for the show, Seehorn is 0-for-4 to date.

"I think she's been robbed," laments Sharon Bialy. "I think one of the reasons is her work is so seamless and honest and beautiful. It's not showy. She just serves the writing. That kind of talent often goes unnoticed, because it's so seamless. And I hope for the final seasons, people wake up."

In the meantime, the rigorous training continues. Seehorn has never shared a scene with Banks, Esposito, or several of her other co-stars, yet she goes to the set to watch all of their scenes, even if she's not working that day. For the moment, the cartel stories have nothing to do with what's happening to Kim, yet she finds them very informative to what she has to play.

"It's a very specific tone of show," she explains. "For me, it sits just outside of realism and naturalism. There's something kind of poetic about the way people shift in their speech or the way events unfold. I like that music in my ear as much as possible between my work. It's not about me staying in character and walking around making people call me Kim; but completely removing myself from set and then going right into a scene the next morning is not as easy for me as it is for some actors. So, it's selfish. And then I'm also just getting a free acting lesson. Jonathan and Giancarlo, when I watch their scenes, they teach me how to use the camera in a way that I didn't come into this series understanding as much as I'm aspiring to now. Sometimes, when Kim has intimate moments, I used to turn away from the camera, because I do treat the camera as another person that's there, and the audience is often my confidant in the scenes, because Kim can be very silent and withholding. And I'll watch Jonathan and ask him questions. Or I'll ask Giancarlo, 'How do you invite the camera into the most private of moments without looking showy or without looking deliberate?'"

One of the more unsavory, and completely unintended, aspects of *Breaking Bad* was how a segment of that show's audience turned viciously against Walt's wife Skyler. On paper, she was the sympathetic figure in the story, but to some viewers, she was the nag who was trying to keep Walt from embracing his inner badass. *Better Call Saul* has even more explicitly positioned Kim as the woman who is keeping Jimmy from becoming Saul Goodman, yet it's hard to find fans of the show who feel anything but adoration and protective feelings for her.* Like a lot of things about the series, the change in response goes back to Kim's secret smile, and to the feelings behind it. Kim enjoys Slippin' Jimmy the grifter almost as much as the audience does, after all.

"She's actually not telling him, 'You should be what I want you to be,'" Seehorn argues of Kim. "She's telling him, 'That's not what you said you wanted to be. I'm trying to help you be what you said you wanted to be.' And then, secondly, as often as she's warning him or slowing down his trajectory, she's also the audience's point of view about what's charming and funny and loving and sweet about him."

Kim is crucial to the series in another way. The fates of most of the cartel characters are already locked in, and if we don't know exactly how Jimmy's post–*Breaking Bad* exile as Omaha shopping mall Cinnabon manager Gene will end, most of his story has also already been written. That leaves Kim's future as the great mystery of *Better Call Saul*. Does she die? Does Jimmy ruin her career? In the most recent episode (spoiler), Kim proposed marriage as a last-ditch effort to save their flagging relationship; is there a chance that when Saul Goodman went home from helping Walt and Jesse launder their money, Kim was there waiting for him? Or, for that matter, could Nebraska native Kim wander into Gene's Cinnabon to give these star-crossed lovers an improbable happily-ever-after?

"What's going to happen to Kim?" Gould wonders. "That's maybe the biggest question we've got now. Kim and Nacho, but Kim is the one I'm worried about. I think there's still a lot of hope for Kim Wexler."

Seehorn binged all of *Breaking Bad* shortly after that show ended, and mostly doesn't play fan-girl on the set. (Though when a scene in the fourth season took place in Saul Goodman's famous office, she couldn't resist posing for some photos of herself at his desk.) Early on, she spent a lot of time asking the same questions about Kim that we all have. The answers didn't exist at that point—"We see about three inches down the road at any particular moment," Gould admits—and she ultimately realized that finding out would

---

* Hard, but not impossible. Some viewers are only in it for the *Breaking Bad*-adjacent material, and Seehorn has occasionally heard secondhand from people who say that they can't wait until Kim dies.

be counterproductive, since her performance would be influenced by things that Kim didn't yet know.

While reminding me several times throughout our conversation that she can't technically say whether Kim will still be a regular character for the sixth and final season, Seehorn says of the eventual end of her time on the series, "I'm sad. I can't think that I'm not sad about it. It's the best part I've ever played, and I will miss that experience, and I will miss all the people on it. But I've made my peace as far as however I'm going out—it's going to be the smartest way she could have possibly gone out. I trust them with her."

"It's funny how the character grew on us, and the actress, God knows, grew on us," Gilligan says. "We just love her to pieces. She's adorable, she's funny as hell, she's a good person, and she's smart as a whip. And she helps center the show for me. That's saying a lot, because every main actor on this show could carry their own TV show, but Rhea, she's something else. She's really special."

The praise is nice, but in many ways, Seehorn still feels like that jet-lagged young woman from seventeen years ago, stumbling into an audition with sheet marks on her face and no idea where she was or what she was supposed to do.

"When you're twenty-some years into your career, [it's a lot] to have a role that is challenging and every season becomes more challenging," she says. "This season, I had scenes where I was like, 'This might be the day when everybody finds out that I can't act. The jig might be up today.' Just because it's an incredible gift to have writing like Peter and Vince's, and then have people that are that smart and care that much about the storytelling go, 'You're the person that can pull this scene off. It's you.'" Even after all this time, she says, "You're like, 'Are you sure?'"

SEASON 5, EPISODE 7
WRITTEN BY ALISON TATLOCK
DIRECTED BY MELISSA BERNSTEIN

"JMM"

"But, do you want to be a 'Friend of the Cartel'?" —**Kim**

The letters that form the title of "JMM" are expanded three different ways in the episode. First, they are the initials of James Morgan McGill, whose full name is recited by the judge marrying Jimmy and Kim in a brisk civil ceremony. Second, they are the slogan Jimmy coined for himself—"Justice Matters Most"—when Kim gave him the monogrammed briefcase after he had already changed his professional name. It's a lame motto—in public, Jimmy has already moved beyond it to the "Speedy Justice For You" catchphrase—and one that Lalo suggests could be improved to our third version: Just. Make. Money.

We know that Jimmy will eventually use this show's title as his tagline, but that's for the benefit of potential clients. Lalo's suggestion, on the other hand, is the whole ethos of Saul Goodman.

Just. Make. Money.

Don't worry about the law. Don't worry about ethics. Don't worry about who gets hurt, and maybe don't even worry about danger to yourself if the upside is big enough.

Just. Make. Money.

It's a phrase so completely, unquestionably Saul Goodman that it feels appropriate that it would be presented in an episode that gives us our first real glimpse of Saul in this series' present-day action.

Jimmy has used the alias off and on for years, but it was just that. Even this season, operating in public under that name, wearing the suits and working the bluetooth headset, he has still been much closer to the Jimmy McGill we know and love than the Saul we thought we knew so well on *Breaking Bad*. But in two different remarkable moments in "JMM," Jimmy goes away so the real Saul can come out to play. It is not a permanent transformation yet, but the man ranting at Howard Hamlin in the halls of the courthouse seems poised to take over for good—or, rather, for bad—and soon.

Saul's outburst is one bookend of a fantastic episode that begins, like it ends, in and around a courtroom. We open on a semi-happy occasion: the wedding of Kim and Jimmy, as she so foolishly proposed at the end of "Wexler v. Goodman." As Jimmy explains to Huell (on hand as a witness), it's less a cause for celebration than it is a legal arrangement to create spousal privilege, and he looks visibly uncomfortable as the judge takes them through the ceremony. At minimum, he knows this isn't the wedding Kim Wexler deserves,* nor the reason they should be getting married. Deep down, he surely suspects that this will go badly for Kim, and that she doesn't deserve that, either. But facing him is a woman who does not seem disappointed by the circumstances in which she finds herself. Kim's face isn't exactly glowing, but her eyes are clearly smiling— Rhea Seehorn, you may have heard, is a talented performer—her voice breaks ever so slightly but unmistakably when she says, "I do," and then she looks genuinely happy at being told that they are now husband and wife. Jimmy assumed she had a dream wedding in mind when she was twelve. But we saw in the previous episode's teaser what Kim had to think about at that age. And we know her well enough to recognize that even though this surely will end in tears, or worse, all Kim needs is an honest relationship with the man she loves, and she believes this hare-brained scheme will give her that.

And it does that—at least for now. In the hour's opening moments, she explains—like a lawyer negotiating a contract—that what matters most to her isn't justice, but open communication. If Jimmy provides full disclosure, she believes, the rest will sort itself out. When the newlyweds are in bed together that night—with a full day's work sandwiched between the wedding and this non-honeymoon—he at first opts against telling her that Lalo is his client. But there's enough of Jimmy McGill still at the wheel for him to pause and fess up, including about Lalo's offer to make him into a Friend of the Cartel.

Kim has just had a triumphant day over in the ever-shrinking part of the series having nothing to do with the manufacture and distribution of illegal drugs. She and Rich attempt to patch things up with Mesa Verde, and when Kevin seems dismissive of them—and particularly of Kim, for having the poor judgment to date the man who made a fool of everyone in his office at that moment—she decides to push back. Even though she knows that she created this entire fiasco—and broke her legal obligation to put her client's best interests ahead of anyone else's—she calls out Kevin for all the times he ignored her advice in the whole affair with Everett Acker and suggests their relationship can't continue with that dynamic. It's Kim deploying some chicanery of her own—even if Kevin was pig-headed in the situation she created—but it also seems to be her finally doing what she set out to when she swept up the broken glass in the parking lot. She has cleaned up her own mess, and perhaps made things better for everyone in the long run. (At a minimum, she has for Acker and for Olivia Bitsui, the artist whose photograph was used as the Mesa Verde

---

* They don't even get a chance to have a celebratory lunch afterward, because her schedule is booked.

logo.) It's a moment so satisfying it—like so many Kim scenes—suggests that this creative team could produce a thoroughly entertaining show about banking and real estate law, so long as she was the main character in it.

But Kim isn't the main character in a show about banking and real estate law. She's the romantic partner and conscience of the main character on a show about losing your moral compass and breaking as badly as anyone in this universe not named Heisenberg can. As Jimmy tells her about Lalo and his offer, it's as if she's getting her first glimpse of the other half of the show. It is clearly not a glimpse she enjoys, but it is for the moment a temporary one, as Jimmy assures her he would have no interest in being the cartel's friend even if it was possible to bail out Lalo, which it doesn't seem to be.

But fate—or, rather, Jimmy's once and future partner Mike*—has other plans. Team Pollos† realizes that an incarcerated Lalo is still a danger to the operation, and that Mike's half-measure with the librarian has to be undone in favor of a more permanent solution.‡ Which means Lalo has to make bail—potentially cementing the cartel's friendship with Saul Goodman in the process.

This is a fascinating turn of events, given what we know about Saul and Mike's relationship on *Breaking Bad*, and what little we saw of Saul's pre-Heisenberg business. Saul seemed to believe that Mike was his investigator/fixer, and acted shocked to find out he had another, more powerful employer the whole time. And while Saul was near the top of the Albuquerque shyster food chain, he also didn't seem like a significant player in the drug world when we met him. That's why he's so eager to play Tom Hagen to Walt's Vito Corleone.

Whatever happens next with Lalo and the cartel, this at a minimum reframes Saul and Walt's relationship as a do-over for Saul, rather than his first attempt at playing on this level. And in the meantime, Mike and Jimmy's

---

* Mike offers a belated—and necessary—explanation for why he's thrown in his lot with Gus Fring. When Stacey notes that he's seemed more at peace lately, Mike tells her, "Decided to play the cards I was dealt." It's not so much that his stay in Mexico convinced Mike of Gus's relative altruism, but that it gave him time to clear his head and accept that he was already in too deep with these people to cleanly walk away. This way, he gets some measure of control—which is more than poor Nacho has—and it's clear that he's a trusted employee. For the moment, that's enough.

† As Mike and Gus prepare their endgame with Lalo, in the meantime they have to make Nacho look good, which means Nacho and Gus work together to blow up a Los Pollos Hermanos location down in Los Lunas. Gus's use of one of his chickens as a delayed fuse—letting it slowly heat up until the accumulated grease slides it down the hot plate and into the fryer grease—is damn near Heisenbergian in its deployment of the materials on hand.

‡ Before he and Nacho play arson, Gus first has to travel to Madrigal headquarters to inform both Lydia and her boss Peter Schuler about the state of things. Lydia is awestruck by Gus's confidence and brains, while Herr Schuler—introduced, as he was on *Breaking Bad*, while dipping fried potatoes into sauce—is understandably tying himself up in knots over the danger he has placed himself and the company in by agreeing to back Gus and the construction of the Super Lab. Also? Gus removing his jacket and shoes before entering Schuler's adjoining hotel room briefly makes him seem like an evil Mister Rogers.

reunion fundamentally alters the trajectory of Jimmy's deal with Lalo and sets up the clearest sign yet that Saul Goodman's ascension is nearly complete.

Before the judge comes in to hear Jimmy's argument about witness tampering,* Jimmy is distracted by the sight of the grieving relatives of Fred Whalen in the gallery. Lalo has forgotten the name of the man he killed and is only concerned with pulling off this latest con, while Jimmy looks genuinely wracked with guilt over what he is about to do to this poor family.

And then we get the first of the remarkable moments: like a horrifying magic trick, the transformation just happens. One moment, we are watching Jimmy McGill, lost in melancholy as he sits at the defense table, the sound of the courtroom fading into a dull roar; the next, Saul Goodman is standing up before the court, passionately arguing to arrange the freedom of the monster he knows he's representing. There is nothing in between, as if Jimmy went into one of those fugue states Walt once talked about, and out came the true, irrepressible Saul.

Whatever the reason, the next scene suggests Jimmy hasn't completely vanished yet. Outside the courtroom, he peeks around a corner to watch Whalen's family absorb the news that Lalo has made bail. Of all the pictures to tell a thousand words over the course of this show and its predecessor, the shot of Jimmy's face half-reflected in the marble wall is perhaps the most stunning and eloquent. The half face and its reflection should form a whole, but they don't because of the angle. There is the light side of Jimmy McGill, and the dark side of Saul Goodman, but together they add up to less than the sum of their parts, because something is missing from Saul—something whose absence will enable Walter White to rain death, destruction, and heartache down on a whole lot of people in the coming years.

But still, you can see the part of Jimmy who hasn't been fully submerged yet. And that's when we get to the second remarkable moment. Howard breaks Jimmy out of his spell and asks yet again about the job offer he made. Like Rich Schweikart seeing through what Kim and Jimmy were doing, Howard is not stupid. He has figured out that bad things started happening to him as a result of his lunch with Jimmy, and he is there to rescind the offer. Jimmy McGill tries to play dumb and deflect Howard's suspicion, but when Howard says, "Jimmy, I'm sorry you're in pain," it is unmistakably Saul Goodman who answers him, shouting at the top of his lungs about how small Howard seems compared to the man he believes he is destined to become as a Friend of the Cartel.

---

* Tim Roberts, the dismayed lead investigator on the Lalo case, was an old buddy of Hank's on *Breaking Bad*. Among other things, he helped look for Walt when he went missing thanks to Tuco and was later assigned to Gale's murder.

The first time we saw Jimmy and Howard in a room together, Jimmy was jokingly acting out the "primal forces of nature" monologue from *Network*. Here, Saul seems to be playing it for real, screaming, "I travel in worlds you can't even imagine! You can't conceive what I'm capable of! I'm like a god in human clothing! *Lightning bolts shoot from my fingertips!*"

This is the *Better Call Saul* equivalent of Walt's famous "I Am The One Who Knocks!" speech—only cranked up to 11 in volume and colorful rhetoric. Saul is a better talker than Walt, but he also needs to sell himself more than Walt did in that moment with Skyler. (And Walt was already trying way too hard to intimidate her.) Walt had by this point in *Breaking Bad* knocked for several of his enemies, where the time for lightning to shoot from Saul's fingertips is still to come. But you can sense it in the not-too-distant future, just like real lightning is visible well before you hear the accompanying sound of thunder. Like Walt's speech, it's spectacular as the words emerge from Saul's mouth, but also instantly sad. (Even Jimmy seems to recognize this, given the way all the air goes out of him once Howard is out of sight.) We know where those words will lead him, and we also know the pain and insecurity that's prompted them in the first place. Walter White killed a lot of people to show the world how powerful he was; Saul Goodman's going to help him for the same goddamn reason.

Yet as incredible as the picture of Jimmy's bifurcated face is, as unsettling as the lightning bolts rant is, it's hard to let go of that abrupt cut from Jimmy in the chair to Saul on his feet. In many ways, this is the scene the entire series has been building up to, and the crucial part of it occurs off camera. Why do you suppose that happened? Maybe the show's creative team knew that Bob Odenkirk would get to play a similar Jimmy/Saul switch only moments later in the argument with Howard and wanted to save it for the episode's climax. Maybe the vehemence of Jimmy's response to Howard was so much more blatantly a Saul Goodman scene that all involved felt it was the one they had to show.

But maybe it's less about story than about sentiment, and about how Peter Gould, Vince Gilligan, and everyone else found themselves surprised by how much they loved Jimmy McGill, and how little they wanted to let him become Saul—even though the design of the show as a prequel gave them no choice in the matter. I think back to a conversation I had with *The Sopranos* creator David Chase,* about the choice to deliberately pan up from the scene of a treasured character's murder right before the fatal shots were fired. Chase thought

---

* For another fine title from Abrams Books, *The Sopranos Sessions*, still available wherever books are sold.

about the question for a long time, then admitted that he had grown really fond of the character, and that even though he'd written her into a position where he had no choice but to kill her off, he had the director move the camera at the last moment out of "a feeling I had that I didn't want to see that."

Is he Saul for good(man) now? This series has offered too many false alarms before now to say for sure. But it's easy to look at that hard cut in the same way: as a moment that Gould and company were forced to write, but one they didn't actually want to see.

I can't blame them.

SEASON 5, EPISODE 8
WRITTEN BY GORDON SMITH
DIRECTED BY VINCE GILLIGAN

"Bagman"

"That's the price." —**Jimmy**

If "JMM" gave us the *Better Call Saul* equivalent of Walter White's "I Am The One Who Knocks!" speech, then "Bagman" is a spiritual prequel to one of the best *Breaking Bad* episodes of all, Season 2's "4 Days Out." Once again, we have the show's two male leads in a fight for survival in the desert after unexpected circumstances knock their vehicle out of commission, and getting on each other's nerves along the way. The context is very different, as is the degree of danger, since Jimmy and Mike are not only battling the elements but trying to evade the one bandit who survived Mike's sniper fire. And in each case, our antihero saves the day by playing to his strengths. For Walter White, it's his intelligence; for Jimmy McGill, it's his facility with a con and his utter belief that he can scam anybody.

"4 Days Out" has long had a reputation as the best episode you can show a non–*Breaking Bad* viewer to try to convert them, because it's as standalone as a drama like that is capable of being. Saul pops up early on to discuss the state of Walt's finances, and potentially bad new developments with Walt's cancer hang over the whole hour, but for the most part it is a wild, fun, gorgeously shot standalone adventure that showcases the enormous chemistry between Bryan Cranston and Aaron Paul. It doesn't get too mired in the darkness that ultimately characterized that series (though Walt's response to the cancer being in remission provides a taste of it), but in some ways it's an even better sales tool for the uninitiated than the pilot episode.

"Bagman" wouldn't work nearly as well for someone who had never watched *Better Call Saul*. But this is a feature, not a bug. It's thrilling, scary, and at times darkly hilarious to watch Jimmy and Mike attempt to get out of the desert alive with all of Lalo's cash intact. The episode's power, though, ultimately comes from precisely when it's happening in the story of Jimmy's transformation into Saul Goodman, from the already precarious state of his marriage to Kim, and from our knowledge of what the space blanket truly means. It's not as instantly quotable as "4 Days Out"—though the sight of Jimmy drinking his own urine instantly became a meme—but it's a more emotionally potent experience.

Event-wise, "Bagman" is a pretty straightforward episode. Jimmy goes to pick up the money, he gets attacked by bandits, Mike saves him, and then the two have to find a way to get back to civilization without being killed by the guy who got away. The only characters of note are Jimmy, Mike, Kim, and Lalo, with both the bandits and the Cousins (who bring Jimmy the cash and then head back home) functioning as plot devices. There are no subplots, no check-ins with Mesa Verde or Nacho's dad or how Lyle feels about a sister workplace exploding. Once Jimmy and Mike's ordeal begins, we only leave the desert to see Kim asking Lalo for help finding her husband. It is this story and only this story being told. It's just being told at a staggering level of execution.

Vince Gilligan largely stepped away from the middle *Saul* seasons to make *El Camino* and develop other projects, but he still helped develop each season's story arcs during this period, and he still directed one episode per season. It was luck of the draw that he got "Bagman," as episodes are often assigned to writers and directors before anyone knows what will be in them. So it's kismet that the franchise's best director of desert scenes wound up with the chance to shoot the hell out of an hour set almost entirely in the harsh, bright, dusty terrain. Gilligan and director of photography Marshall Adams have never worked better together, with one spectacular composition after another. Even before the true misadventure begins, we have Jimmy's legs framing the arrival of the Cousins' car, followed by his head as a mirror of sorts to show how Leonel and Marco move in unison on either side of it. There is that beautiful god's-eye view shot of Mike walking around the bodies of the men he has killed to save Jimmy and the cash. "JMM" ended with Jimmy telling Howard about the lightning bolts he can shoot from his fingertips; this shot reveals him for the tiny, powerless speck he is in this world. Even when the screen isn't shimmering from the heat, Gilligan and Adams make you feel the discomfort in every minute of every scene. And we haven't even gotten to the jaw-dropping moment in the climax where Jimmy stands in the middle of a road as the bandit's truck flips over and over toward him in the aftermath of Mike's sniper shot. Where Gus or the Cousins might have kept moving without flinching in such a circumstance, Jimmy is rooted to that spot, too exhausted and terrified to take another step, cowering as he waits to see if this thing falls on top of him in spite of Mike's best efforts. It's incredible.

But Gilligan has always been just as good with character as with visuals, and he and Gordon Smith do a masterful job of making this more than just a physical ordeal, but an emotional one. If the real Saul Goodman finally bubbled up to the surface in "JMM," then the desert heat and the indignities that accompany it go a long way toward forging him into a permanent, unyielding shape.

After a teaser where the Cousins gather the bail money from a Salamanca warehouse, we cut to Lalo in an interview room at the jail, his bare feet propped up as he enjoys reading a news account from Los Lunas of the destruction of that town's Los Pollos Hermanos. (He's oblivious to the fact that both the restaurant's fiery end and his impending bail are the result of Gus Fring's plan to erase him from the planet.) He then explains to Jimmy how to find the well where the Cousins will hand over the cash—it's a potent reminder of his attention to detail that he knows the exact mileage along the dirt road—and explains that his lawyer's anonymity in the drug game makes him the ideal courier for such a valuable package. Jimmy instantly recognizes that this is a terrible idea, and he's on the verge of walking away, but two things seem to stop him. The first is Lalo's indifferent, almost chipper tone, which suggests that the cartel can just as easily find another "friend" if this is too much trouble for Saul Goodman, Esq. The second is an impulse that we've seen drive Jimmy in the past under various names: there is money to be had—big money—and he'd be a fool not to try for it. So where he drastically undervalued himself the first time Lalo employed his services, here Jimmy asks for a cool $100,000 commission. We know from seeing the warehouse vault that Lalo could easily pay Jimmy 20 percent of the cash, or 100 percent, without putting an appreciable crimp in his operating funds, but it's nonetheless a number that makes it worth our man's while.

"That's the price," he tells Lalo, unaware of just how big a price he in turn will pay for that $100,000.

We then come home to Kim and Jimmy's apartment, where he springs on her the friend-of-the-cartel news she's been bracing for, only worse because of the insane thing he's doing in order to achieve that status. Jimmy tries downplaying the risk, but Kim isn't one of Jimmy's marks. The only times he's ever been able to fool her (like with his speech about Chuck to get his suspension lifted) have been when she wanted to be fooled. Not here. Not now. This development rightly terrifies her, and she lays out her feelings as plainly as she can: "I don't like this. I don't want you to do it." Every word of that second sentence bursts out of her in a pained staccato, sounding as much like the lonely twelve-year-old girl with the cello and the alcoholic mom as it does the grown woman who has made a new family with a different kind of addict. He hugs her and assures her that things will be fine, but she's no longer listening, as she starts to realize how this story will likely end for the both of them.

From there, we're in the desert, for the aforementioned handoff with the Cousins (which begins with a gorgeous shot from underneath the water in the well), followed by Jimmy driving north as he sings a variation of "99 Bottles of Beer" about the fortune in the Esteem's trunk. That's when the ambush happens, followed by the counter-ambush by Mike the sniper. The scene at first keeps secret the identity of Jimmy's savior, but who else could it be? This is

Mike finally operating at the level of power we witnessed a few times on *Breaking Bad*, taking out a half-dozen heavily armed men all by himself. But as he will later admit to Jimmy, he should have brought more guys to run surveillance. Mike's overconfidence results in the destruction of his truck as well as the escape of one of the bandits, and puts him and a shell-shocked Jimmy in the front seat of the bullet-riddled Esteem, trying and failing to get back to civilization before it dies on them.

Though Saul Goodman drove a Cadillac on *Breaking Bad*, the Esteem has been Jimmy McGill's signature vehicle—an ugly, mismatched old junker that causes people to underrate its driver. In helping Mike push the inoperable car into a ravine—and realizing that a stray round destroyed the World's 2nd Best Lawyer Again travel mug—he's saying goodbye to a part of himself. He can get a much nicer car with part of the commission, but bit by bit, the things that clearly differentiated Jimmy from Saul are falling away from him.

Then we're into a full-on endurance challenge for our two unlikely partners, with Mike forcing Jimmy to carry both bags of money. Jimmy is still too stunned from almost dying, and Mike too taciturn, as always, for it to be the gabfest Walt and Jesse had under similar conditions. Still, the two go through a lot together over the course of these two days, in a manner that would seem to fly in the face of their relationship on *Breaking Bad*. For that matter, the Jimmy/Saul who makes himself bait in the episode's climax seems far removed from the Saul who was desperately pleading for his life and blaming Ignacio when Walt and Jesse took him into the desert in his first appearance.

Or maybe it all fits together. When I interviewed Peter Gould at the end of Season 4, he said this of what he had in mind when he wrote that original desert scene where Saul mentioned both Lalo and Ignacio:

> We wanted to indicate that Saul Goodman had been in life-and-death situations before, and he had left a trail of people who were angry at him, who maybe he's done wrong. And also that he might have some cartel connections, which of course becomes important on *Breaking Bad*.

The "life-and-death situations" part of that quote is the more interesting one. We've seen Saul in danger before on this show, going all the way back to another Salamanca-inspired trip to the desert in the second episode ever. He kept a cool head then, and he mostly does throughout "Bagman," understanding right away that he needs to give these guys access to his trunk, and eventually figuring out that the only way to get their pursuer off their tail is to play bait so Mike can kill the guy. Our man is an actor, and he could very easily have been playing a role for Walt and Jesse.

And returning to the question of exactly why Gus Fring's right-hand man would have a side job working for a shyster he doesn't even seem to like, "Bagman" suggests another possible explanation. Mike, as we know, is a man who believes in paying karmic debts he owes. He's the one who puppeteered Jimmy into arranging bail for Lalo, and Jimmy goes through a horrible ordeal as a result. And at the same time, Mike is witness to Jimmy's unexpected burst of bravery with the space blanket, and is impressed by that. Maybe it's as simple as Mike developing a grudging respect for the guy, while also feeling like he owes him for putting Jimmy in danger—and for whatever blowback is to come with Kim.

This is more of a transformative episode for Jimmy than for Mike, but Mike still gets one of its most emotional scenes, where he explains to his traveling companion why he is still trying to get home, and why he has associated himself with such deadly criminals. "I have people waiting for me," he says. "They don't know what I do, they never will. They're protected. But I do what I do so they can have a better life. And if I live or if I die, it really doesn't make a difference to me, as long as they have what they need. So when it is my time to go, I will go knowing I did everything I could for them." It's a great speech, delivered with gravity but also vulnerability by Jonathan Banks, and made all the more poignant by us knowing how badly Mike will fail Kaylee and Stacey in the end. And thanks in part to Jimmy, Mike will get to make it home to them again.

Earlier, Mike is dismayed to learn that Jimmy has told Kim about the money pickup, fearing that she will tell the police, or at least a friend or a relative, and then he'll have another loose end to reluctantly tie up. He, of course, has never met Kim, and doesn't know her like Jimmy or we do. She has no one else—no family to whom she's still connected, no friends we've ever met, and no coworkers she would trust with this information—and is smart enough to know how badly things would go if she spoke to law enforcement. So her only option, once Jimmy fails to come home that night, is to go see the man who sent him on the trip. And as Lalo re-enters the interview room to find this impressive woman waiting for him, the final barrier between the Jimmy show and the Mike show crumbles for good. She seems in greater peril in that moment than Jimmy does during the ambush. It's not just that we know he will survive for years to come, but that he chose this path, whereas Kim has been reluctantly dragged along. This is not her world, and she has much more to lose by entering it than Slippin' Jimmy does. And she doesn't even get anything out of this risk since Lalo refuses to tell her where to look for her husband. "If he's alive, he'll show," Lalo reasons. Kim starts to complete the thought for him by saying, "And if he's . . ." But it hurts too much to ponder, and her voice is already shattered and empty on the "he's." For the moment, she gets nothing out of the encounter but more pain and fear. But now Lalo Salamanca knows she exists, and that she's also a lawyer, and this sure does not feel like it will be their only encounter, does it?

While Mike and Jimmy are discussing Kim and making camp, Mike takes out a space blanket to keep warm in the desert's midnight chill. He offers Jimmy a spare, not realizing the metaphorical weight this object has for the brother of the late Chuck McGill. For Jimmy, that thing practically *is* Chuck: a shiny symbol of all his brother tried to deny him, and of the folly of trying to live as a straight arrow. He'd rather shiver against a rock than find physical comfort in that accursed sheet of mylar.

Eventually, the weight of the duffel bags and the physical impact of being out in the heat with so little hydration seems too much for Jimmy to take. Mike talks about his family to encourage a collapsed, defeated Jimmy to stand up and keep moving, but it's the return of the bandit's truck that does the job. Jimmy rises, gathers the space blanket around his shoulders, and starts trudging toward the road. At first, it seems as if he is now following Chuck's lead, wrapping himself in that ridiculous-looking thing before committing suicide. Instead, he surprises Mike by telling him to have his rifle ready, and we realize he's using a con man's favorite trick: misdirection. Because when civilized thought and alternators and travel mugs and everything in his life have failed him, Jimmy McGill still knows how to put on a good hustle, and still believes he can outthink any opponent.

And he does. Mike makes the shot on the second try, the truck rolls off to the side before it gets close to Jimmy, and our heroes live to bicker another day. Jimmy sits in the road with his head in his hands, clearly on the verge of tears if only his body was capable of producing liquid after two days under the sun's anvil. And then Saul takes a long, defiant swig of his own pee—a mortification for being stupid enough to come out here, as much as it is a life-preserving means of rehydrating—then stands up and gets moving, not even pausing to let Mike take the lead. He is a Friend of the Cartel now. He has paid one hell of a price to accomplish that, but he is alive, and his chapped lips and other injuries will heal right along with his wounded ego. If the lightning isn't quite at his fingertips yet, he still has other powers at his command.

What an hour from everyone involved, but especially from Bob Odenkirk. These last few episodes have been huge in terms of the series' primary character arc, and he's been more than up to that challenge. We've long passed the point where his gifts as a dramatic actor are surprising, but the sheer, utterly raw physicality of what he does here seems beyond anything he's done in the past, even at what until now seemed like his very best.

The episode's final shot could be read as one more *Breaking Bad* callback, or as something uniquely *Better Call Saul*. As Jimmy resumes his march up the road, the space blanket flutters away. Is this an homage to the khakis Walter White lost in his very first episode? Is it meant to be one of the last remnants of James Morgan McGill floating off into the unknown, no longer a concern of Saul Goodman's? Or is it just the latest example of *Better Call Saul* managing to do fan service and exquisite character work at the exact same time?

It's not fair to compare an episode from the stretch run of a series' penultimate season to one from another series that hadn't fully figured itself out yet. And "4 Days Out" and "Bagman" are ultimately trying to accomplish different things in terms of tone and characterization. This is the episode any *Better Call Saul* fan can point to, not as a tool to convert the skeptics, but as a symbol of how the spin-off came to rival the original, by finding more emotionally complex routes through seemingly familiar territory, and by operating at a level of craft that can at times surpass the best of *Breaking Bad*. It's not something even the most optimistic *Saul* fans could have anticipated when the show began—or even when this fifth season began.

Yet here we are. What a pisser.

SEASON 5, EPISODE 9
WRITTEN AND DIRECTED BY THOMAS SCHNAUZ

"Bad Choice Road"

"I just want to hear the story." —**Lalo**

So do we need to start referring to Kim Wexler as "The One Who Mocks"?

"Bad Choice Road" begins with a sequel to the great montage from last season's "Something Stupid." Again, a cover of the Sinatra song plays as we see Jimmy and Kim in split screen. Back then, the device was used to illustrate the growing emotional distance between them; here, it's emphasizing the physical distance, as he and Mike finish the desert trek they began in "Bagman," while Kim frets back in the apartment. Occasionally, their movements are in sync, but in wildly different circumstances, like when she enjoys a clean glass of water from the kitchen sink while he has to swallow more of his own pee. The original montage concluded with its separate images merging back together, even as Jimmy's and Kim's lives kept drifting further apart. Here, the image is never whole because our leads are in separate locations. But by the end of this fantastic episode, the two halves of *Better Call Saul* itself, long kept apart, finally merge into one thrilling, terrifying story.

Jimmy and Kim have separately met with Lalo at the jail in recent episodes. But when he enters their home, armed with a gun and a smile, any distinction between the cartel and civilian aspects of the show ceases to exist. Earlier in the episode, Kim quits Schweikart & Cokely,* and Mesa Verde, because banking law now bores her. It feels like the series has, in the process, left behind nearly all interest in noncriminal life. Mike warns Jimmy about the bad road he has gone down, and how impossible it will be to get off it. Jimmy will later mangle the lesson in attempting to convince Kim that she's made a terrible mistake by quitting her lucrative job, but it's already too late for her, and him, and *Better Call Saul*. Everyone's gone down Bad Choice Road now, and there's no turning back.

Where "Bagman" was focused almost entirely on Jimmy and Mike's painful desert odyssey, "Bad Choice Road" is a pretty traditionally structured episode until that long climactic sequence in and around the apartment. We catch up with nearly all the cast (save Howard, who at the moment exists as a symbol of the life that Jimmy and the series are both running from) and advance various subplots. Gus figures out that the bandits were hired by Juan

---

*   On her way out of the S&C offices, Kim makes sure to grab the fancy tequila stopper from the first adventure of Viktor and Giselle.

Bolsa, who seems very displeased by the thought of Lalo getting out of jail and returning to Mexico. Mike tries to negotiate Nacho's release from Gus's control—or, failing that, for the safety of Manuel Varga—but the Chicken Man is unyielding in his belief that Nacho is too treacherous to be managed through anything but fear.* Lalo says goodbye to Hector, trying to assure the frail and bitter old man that he'll be back once the heat dies down, but his final gaze at his uncle (who is participating silently in a nursing home birthday celebration, looking ridiculous and sad in a party hat) suggests he knows this is the last time they'll see each other. Kim quits the firm, and Jimmy even appears in court on behalf of a client, though the only thing we see is the awkward aftermath, as Bill Oakley taunts him for snatching defeat from the jaws of victory.

Jimmy's off his game because he is understandably traumatized by what he did and saw in the desert. He's moving slower due to the severe sunburn, but he also seems to be thinking slower. Familiar sounds like Kim running the juicer now remind him of gunshots and explosions. He's lying to Kim about what really happened, unaware that she's already seen the bullet hole in the travel mug, and is dismayed to realize that the only person he can talk to about it is Mike. When he sits in Mike's sedan, he seems genuinely shaken by the thought of those dead men, even after Mike argues that it was a kill-or-be-killed situation. Memories of Fred Whalen's murder trouble him more, and even Mike's hints that Lalo will soon be taken care of upset him. Despite events of recent episodes, Jimmy McGill in this episode seems incredibly far from being Saul Goodman, who in his very first appearance was advising Walter White to murder an underling.

Mike assures Jimmy that he will move past this in time, and with Lalo heading toward a permanent end, it seems for a moment that Jimmy has a chance to return his world to something resembling normal. But the combination of fate, Kim, and Lalo has other plans for him.

Lalo again proves much smarter than anyone wants him to be, realizing that he and Nacho didn't pass Jimmy's broken-down car on the drive to the well to meet the Cousins. So he orders Nacho to take him north in search of it and is observant enough to notice the tracks Mike and Jimmy left when they pushed it into the ravine. Lalo seems impossibly powerful in this sequence, even making a casual leap from the ravine's edge onto the overturned vehicle below. In that moment, it's hard not to wish that we got to see this guy face Saul Goodman's most infamous client because he has all the most dangerous qualities of Walt's enemies—the physical threat of Tuco or the Cousins, plus a

---

* If you consider the history of the series, Gus has a point. Nacho previously asked Mike to kill Tuco and later poisoned Hector. Trying to murder a difficult boss is his go-to move.

perceptiveness and grasp of strategy that can be Fringesque, minus being as blinded by revenge as either Gus or Hector—wrapped in one grinning, tenacious package. Alas, we know that won't happen.

Instead, we get something even more marvelous, and largely unexpected: Lalo getting verbally pantsed by our heroine, our adored, the great Kim Wexler.

When Jimmy finds out that Kim has quit her job,* he assumes she's overreacting to his near-death experience. His desert odyssey did influence her decision, but not in the way he thinks. While she's alarmed by the possibility of his dying out there (and finally lets herself cry when he calls to say he's alive), it feels more like she could have taken a day and a half off from work for a more mundane reason and still felt the same lack of connection and interest upon returning. She doesn't want to be this person anymore—and hasn't for most of this season. The gamesmanship about Everett Acker's house was as much Kim subconsciously trying to escape a job she had grown to hate as it was her trying to do right by a cranky old man.

That said, Jimmy's peril, and the ensuing lies he tells her about it, puts her on an emotional journey that perhaps helps ready her for Lalo's arrival at the apartment door. She knows he's lying to her about what really happened, and even confronts him about it. But news that Lalo met his wife rightly terrifies Jimmy and makes him keep lying even when she assures him she won't judge him. At another time in their relationship, this would drive a wedge between them. But the fight that led to her marriage proposal fundamentally changed—or maybe just broke—something in Kim. Now, she just wants Jimmy, and will keep making concessions to allow the relationship to continue. Even knowing that someone shot at him, and that he won't tell her about it, seems like something she quickly learns to compartmentalize. When they finally fight in their apartment, it's not over what happened in the desert, but about Jimmy's response to her leaving the firm.

They don't get to take that argument to its conclusion, though, because suddenly Mike is making a frantic call to Jimmy, and Lalo is standing in their doorway, unnervingly relaxed and upbeat as usual. They have no choice but to let him in, and as he crosses the threshold, Kim unequivocally passes over into the same world that's home to Mike, Gus, the Cousins, and, eventually, Heisenberg.

---

* If you listen carefully to the movie Jimmy attempts to watch with Kim prior to her returning to work, it's the Cary Grant/Rosalind Russell/Howard Hawks classic *His Girl Friday*, which is about a woman who keeps returning to a relationship she knows is deeply unhealthy for her, with a man whose charm and wild professional lifestyle she ultimately can't resist.

Between the argument about the law firm and Lalo's pop-in, the apartment sequence runs about sixteen minutes. This is an eternity for a single television scene, even a bifurcated one like this.* On the one hand, it feels endless, because Lalo as usual is a dog with a bone and keeps making Jimmy tell the story over and over, teasing out new details each time even as he doesn't believe his attorney. The longer it goes, the tenser everything feels, as does the sheer wrongness of Kim being present for it.

But on the other hand, the sequence somehow also seems to fly by, because it's so exciting and sharp. Soon, we are cutting between the apartment itself and the view through Mike's sniper scope on the roof of another building in the development. But before Mike has to decide whether to take the shot, then deal with the messy clean-up such an act would entail, Kim literally steps in his path and saves the goddamn day, scolding Lalo as if he were just another annoying, mercurial client like Kevin from Mesa Verde. She raises reasonable doubt about the bullet holes by ascribing them to local vandals, then points out how shaky Lalo's operation must be if he has to task Saul Goodman with transporting this amount of cash.

"If you don't trust your men with your money," she tells him, summing up her simple but firm closing argument, "you have bigger problems than if you trust Saul Goodman," then advises him, "Jesus, get your shit together!" Whether or not Lalo believes Jimmy, Kim successfully refocuses his anger toward a target south of the border. He leaves, allowing her, Jimmy, and Mike to all exhale, even though none are particularly at ease with what just happened—and what almost happened next.

It's a knockout performance (by both Kim and Rhea Seehorn), and one suggesting Kim could do just fine working on Jimmy's side of the street if she wanted to. Earlier, Jimmy admonishes her for visiting Lalo: "You don't see Lalo. I see Lalo, okay? I'm in the game. You're not in the game." We don't want her in the game because we know how the game ends for everybody in this world, Jimmy/Saul/Gene included. But, protective as we are of Kim, that amazing scene manages to conjure seductive visions of her playing that game, at least for a while.

---

* In the episode's original airings, there were more frequent ad breaks than usual in its first half in order to allow the final act to run that long without commercial interruption.

SEASON 5, EPISODE 10
WRITTEN BY PETER GOULD & ARIEL LEVINE
DIRECTED BY PETER GOULD

"Something Unforgivable"

"Am I bad for you?" —**Jimmy**

What if we've been looking at this all wrong?

We've assumed for a long time that Jimmy McGill would become the true Saul Goodman—not the guy wearing his clothes and using his name, but the amoral bastard who facilitated Walter White's rise to power—out of bitterness over how Chuck and the legal establishment treated him, and/or as a response to however things seemed likely to end with Kim. The series has been framed as an inescapable tragedy in which a roguish but mostly good person gradually becomes a monster due to the world's expectations for him. Kim, as much as we've grown to love and respect her, would be collateral damage in any version of this story.

"Something Unforgivable," though, suggests that something else may have been happening this whole time, and in the process offers an entirely new path for the sixth and final season.

Because if anyone talks and acts like Saul Goodman by the end of this finale, it's Kim Wexler.

Before we get to that alarming note, plus a thrilling shoot-out at Lalo's compound down in Chihuahua, "Something Unforgivable" is a deliberately less intense experience than the last few episodes. We pick up right where "Bad Choice Road" left off, with a shaken Jimmy and Kim making sure that Lalo has left the vicinity. After a quick phone check-in with Mike, Jimmy allows himself to exhale, an action that several characters will repeat throughout the hour, including Mike after Jimmy leaves his house and Kim after being told that Lalo won't be troubling them again. Even people who don't literally exhale are metaphorically doing it, with Lalo heading south to follow Kim's advice and put his house in order. It's as if Peter Gould realized that he needed to ease back after placing his characters in such physical and emotional jeopardy the last few episodes. It's the calm after the storm, and it gives everyone a chance to reflect and figure out who and what they've become.

For Lalo, this respite is a chance to re-ingratiate himself with Don Eladio, while officially presenting Nacho as the new man in charge north of the border. He doesn't know the details of what Gus and Juan Bolsa have been doing to take him out of the game, but he's aware that the Salamancas have been supplanted by the hated Chicken Man as the cartel's favorites. He can't be in direct confrontation with Gus anymore, but his return to Mexico has the advantage of giving him face time with the man in charge, whom he knows is impressed by the kind of grand gestures at which Lalo specializes. In this case, it's putting a small fortune inside a red Ferrari like the one that Tom Selleck drove on *Magnum, P.I.* and handing the keys to Don Eladio, who looks like a kid at Christmas.

If Lalo is in his element with Eladio and among the staff at his compound, Nacho is very much on edge, especially once he gets a call from Gus's hired killers alerting him to the plan for that night. Still, Nacho is a survivor and a thinker, and he puts on a good show for the big boss, spinning a business plan that involves pitting biker gangs against one another so the cartel can take over their territory. Would this actually work if Nacho were to make it back to Albuquerque and run the operation? It doesn't really matter, because all he has to do in the moment is convince Eladio that he's a smarter and more reliable manager than Tuco. Mission accomplished.

Lalo's irrepressible charm in those early Mexico scenes could lull us into thinking he's let his guard down enough to allow Gus's assassination plan to work. But by this point it's clear that he's as superhuman in his own way as Gus or the Cousins. Nacho is alarmed to find Lalo awake by the fire when he attempts to let the gunmen in through the back gate, and Lalo suggests that his own difficulty sleeping is another kind of superpower, allowing him to get the big thinking done while his enemies and allies slumber. Nacho's improvised kitchen fire provides a momentary distraction,* especially since Lalo assumes it's the fault of his youngest and most irresponsible bodyguard, Ciro. But his Spidey sense again kicks in quickly enough for him to use Ciro as a human shield against the first wave of bullets from the hitmen, and from there he has the home field advantage on top of his prodigious gifts with violence. He has a tunnel under the house, because of course he does,† and suckers his opponents into following him into it, even as he has looped back around to the entrance to shoot them while they're crawling ducks. Nacho slips away in the chaos, but he's hundreds of miles from home, with no allies, and an enraged Lalo will surely realize that Nacho isn't lying dead like his favorite cook. It's a crackerjack sequence, with all the action clear even though it takes place in the middle

---

* His resourcefulness also shows itself when he uses tin snips and an aluminum can to pick the lock on Lalo's back gate. It's a bit of gadgeteering worthy of MacGyver—or, for that matter, Mike Ehrmantraut.

† Lalo has more than a bit in common with El Chapo, including this helpful architectural feature at his home base.

of the night, and it goes even further toward building up Lalo as a huge threat to almost all of our remaining characters as we head into the final season.

It's also the first time a *Better Call Saul* season has ended so far narratively from Jimmy. Previous finales have either closed with scenes featuring him or (in the case of Chuck's suicide) ones that are much more emotionally connected to him than Lalo kicking ass and taking names. Perhaps it's Gould and Ariel Levine's way of showing how much the cartel story has taken over the entire series, and how close Jimmy is to being part of it full-time. Or maybe it's because they realized that the final scene with Jimmy and Kim is so much of a mirror of Season 4's conclusion that they didn't want to hang a lamp on it too much by placing it last.

In that final Season 4 scene, Kim is taken aback to realize that Jimmy was faking the emotions in his speech about Chuck, and that he has opted to practice law under a new name. Jimmy, oblivious to her distress, smiles and does a double point as he says, "It's all good, man" and walks off, with the camera pulling away from Kim, making her seem very small, alone, and vulnerable. Here, we get that scene in reverse. Now it's Jimmy who's startled, this time by Kim's plan to wreck Howard's career to speed up the Sandpiper settlement and use the money to set up a pro bono defense practice. Now it's Kim who seems utterly unaware that she and her partner aren't on the same spiritual page, and the double point is taken to the next level by Kim miming a pair of finger guns and making a show of blowing away the smoke from the barrels, like she's a cowboy in one of the old movies Jimmy loves to watch. Now it's Jimmy from whom the camera retreats, leaving him looking tiny and isolated, and not the least bit like the Saul Goodman who seemed to be taking control back in "JMM."

The finale goes the extra mile in setting Jimmy up to feel shocked in that moment. He and Kim arrive at their fancy hotel hideout together, but almost immediately are on separate pages. He wants to hide from Lalo, and maybe enjoy some amenities in the process; she wants to go to court, where she asks Grant from the public defender's office* to give her more overflow cases. He goes to confront Mike about the state of play; she laughs at Howard for talking about bowling balls and prostitutes only a few hours after her life was threatened by Lalo. They are not focusing on the same things at all, so Jimmy is at a particular disadvantage when Kim starts talking about the scam she'd like to run on Howard. She has already put Lalo in the rearview mirror, whereas it's all Jimmy's been thinking about.

---

* Played by comedian Roy Wood Jr.

She, of course, didn't nearly die in the desert, so all of this remains a bit more abstract to her, even after Lalo's house call. Or maybe this is just PTSD of a different stripe, and her shock over that conversation is pushing the darkest and most amoral aspects of her personality forward.

Or maybe it's something we've seen elsewhere in this universe, from the main character on the show that introduced Saul Goodman.

Think about what we know and have seen of Kim Wexler. She built herself a life and career out of nothing. She can convincingly move through the world of Howard Hamlin and Kevin Wachtell, but she's always had to conceal a degree of resentment of these rich and powerful men for whom good things seem to come so easily. She is better than her peers at almost any task to which she sets her mind. We saw with the stunt that kept Huell out of prison that Kim can be a cleverer con artist than Jimmy, and in verbally dismantling Lalo, she suggested that she might be a better Friend of the Cartel than him, too. And in the wake of an experience that could very well have killed her, but didn't, Kim finds herself contemplating doing something genuinely evil, even as she tells herself and her spouse that she would be doing it for a fundamentally good reason.

Sound like anyone we know who knocks?

The scene in the empty courtroom with Howard is unnerving because of how obviously correct he is about everything, even as she literally laughs it off. She placed a very bad bet on Jimmy McGill when she proposed marriage rather than a breakup, and she has no choice but to keep doubling down on that bet, throwing good money after bad to convince herself that she made the right choice.* Howard describes Jimmy as "someone who's not in control of himself," but he could just as easily be talking about Kim. And once again, his attempt to do a good deed looks like it will come back to bite him, terribly.

When Kim pitches the Sandpiper gambit to Jimmy, she's in her Kansas City Royals nightshirt. Her hair is down. She is utterly relaxed, and as far removed as she's capable of being from the controlled, coiffed, polished attorney that the rest of the world sees—that even Howard thought he was seeing when he pulled her aside to warn her about Jimmy.

Even Jimmy doesn't see it at first when she pitches the play to him. He repeatedly tries to dissuade her, first by suggesting it might be too difficult to pull off, which Kim greets with a priceless/terrifying smirk, because of course she can pull it off. Then he tries warning her about what it would mean for Howard, and in turn how that would make Kim feel, suggesting she wouldn't

---

* In case you'd forgotten the fallacy of the sunk cost that Kim discussed early in Season 3, she is acting it out right here.

possibly be okay with it in the cold light of day. And Kim Wexler, looking as serene, happy, and beautiful as she has at any point in the run of the series, replies, "Wouldn't I?"

As will be the case with her husband's future client, she has convinced herself that she will be doing an evil thing for a noble cause. But it sure seems like she is doing it for herself—that when she's pulling a con, she likes it, she's good at it, and she feels really . . . alive.

Kim has pulled Jimmy into the light on so many occasions over these five seasons, but he's also periodically pulled her into the dark. The assumption we had all along was that Jimmy would break bad in a way that would bring utter ruin, if not worse, to the woman he loves, and that he would embrace his inner Saul-ness in reaction to that. "Something Unforgivable," though, invites an entirely new line of questioning. What if Jimmy doesn't truly become Saul Goodman in response to a bad thing happening to Kim? What if he does it to prevent that bad thing from happening? What if he realizes that the only way he can scare her straight is to fulfill Chuck's prophecy (which Howard invokes earlier in this episode) and show her exactly how dangerous Slippin' Jimmy with a law degree is? What if the best thing Jimmy can possibly do before this show is over is to embrace the absolute worst part of himself?

Then again, does the woman who shoots the finger guns at Jimmy look like she wants to be saved?

"Wine and Roses" / "Carrot and Stick"*

"Wolves and sheep." —**Jimmy**

Every previous *Saul* season has begun in exactly the same way, with a black-and-white flash-forward to the lonely, paranoid life of Omaha mall Cinnabon manager Gene Takovic, aka Saul Goodman, aka Jimmy McGill. If this were just another year, we would certainly pick up right where we left off with Gene, as he told Ed that he would fix the problem with Jeff the cab driver himself. But this is not just another season; it is the conclusion of *Better Call Saul*, and, for now, the conclusion of Peter Gould and Vince Gilligan's time in the Heisenberg-verse. Barring some kind of sequel to *El Camino* where Jesse Pinkman[†] runs into trouble up in Alaska, Gene's misadventures are the chronological end of the story of this show and of *Breaking Bad*. So our return trip to Omaha can wait.

But "Wine and Roses" still finds a way to situate us in a world where Saul Goodman has become a fugitive from justice, even if the only glimpses of him in it are re-creations of his image. We appear to be somewhere within the events of "Granite State," the penultimate episode of the parent series. Saul has vanished after his favorite client was publicly outed as the Southwest's top meth distributor, and the authorities have sent a team of movers to catalog and pack up Saul's house. As Bob Odenkirk and Rhea Seehorn like to say whenever someone asks about Kim Wexler's fate, we never went home with Saul after he provided legal advice for Walt and Jesse, so we had no idea if he had a wife, or anything about how he was living. Here, we seem to get the answer to both—the latter in particular. Saul was *loaded*, living in an absurdly decorated mansion filled with suits, ties, shoes, statues and other expensive, if tacky, pieces of art. Director Michael Morris and longtime *Saul* director of photography Marshall Adams go to town exploring every garish corner of the place, starting with an

---

* AMC originally aired these episodes back-to-back on the same night, and they feel more like a supersize premiere than wholly separate installments. So, as happened back when Season 6 debuted, we'll talk about them together.

† We get a couple of different Jesse nods in these episodes: Jimmy meets Kim at the El Camino Dining Room, and later Kim uses magnets as a metaphor for how to play the Howard scam. We all know how much Mr. Pinkman loved magnets.

avalanche of neckties falling in the opening moment (transitioning us from Gene's usual monochrome look to the glorious color of Saul's heyday) all the way through Saul inevitably having a golden toilet. (As has been said about a famous con man of our own world, he is living a child's conception of what a rich person must be like.)

So why does the final season begin by showing us all this swag?* Maybe it's a way to continue the flash-forward tradition without getting back to Gene until we absolutely have to. Or maybe it's just about the very last trophy we see before the opening credits, which is also the first trophy that Jimmy McGill felt was worth keeping: the Zafiro Añejo tequila bottle cap from the inaugural adventure of Viktor and Giselle.

If *Better Call Saul* began as the story of how a shady but ultimately nice guy devolved into a cold and malevolent criminal/lawyer, it at some point has expanded into the story about how he pulled the love of his life down the moral rabbit hole with him. The Kim who was so mad about the crybaby squat video might not recognize the Kim of last season who was able to verbally spar with Lalo Salamanca, let alone the ruthless one we see here. In the Season 5 finale, Jimmy hoped that Kim was joking about wrecking Howard Hamlin's reputation in order to force an early Sandpiper settlement, and to use Jimmy's cut to finance her legal aid practice. These episodes make clear that it is not at all a joke, as Kim sets about perpetrating all kinds of extra-legal mischief, to her husband's increasing dismay.

The shape of Kim's plan becomes clear over the course of these two episodes: she and Jimmy will create the illusion that Howard has a drug problem, rendering enough doubt in Cliff Main to make him settle the case while he still can. This plays out first with Jimmy sneaking into the locker room at Howard and Cliff's country club—after first making a scene in front of baffled club manager Norm†—to put a bag of "cocaine" (really just baby powder) in Howard's locker. The scheme then expands in "Carrot and Stick" to involve Betsy and Craig Kettleman, whom we last saw back in Season 1, when their legal troubles over Craig's embezzlement from a local treasury prompted a war for their services between Jimmy and HHM. They are running a tax preparation service and are bitter about losing their comfortable upper-middle-class life—their kids now have to go to public school, Betsy whines to an unsympathetic Jimmy. Both their desperation and their past association with Howard make

---

* One of the more interesting items is brand-new to the series: a vintage paperback copy of H. G. Wells's *The Time Machine*, which we see again on Jimmy's end table in "Carrot and Stick."

† Guest star James Urbaniak, a marvelous straight man to Odenkirk.

them easy marks for the grift, as Jimmy expertly steers them toward Cliff to continue the lie about Howard's cocaine use.*

Betsy remains a shrewd enough operator to figure out the broad outline of how Jimmy used them, and why, which is when the titular carrot and stick come into play. Jimmy is willing to use some of the cash from Lalo to keep the Kettlemans quiet. Kim, though, figures out that they've been taking money off the top of all their elderly clients' tax rewards—once an embezzler, always an embezzler—and threatens to report them to the feds. Betsy caves and agrees to keep her mouth shut, but when Jimmy returns to the car at the end of the episode, Kim is annoyed to realize that he paid the Kettlemans anyway out of some sense of guilt over what he did to them before.

Earlier in "Wine and Roses," we see Kim consider Jimmy's travel mug with the bullet hole in it. This was a gift she gave him in more innocent times, and now it's something she casually tosses in the trash, a symbol of a life she assumes he is leaving behind. Yet somehow, at the beginning of this series' home stretch, Jimmy doesn't seem especially close to truly being Saul Goodman. He's suddenly the soft touch, while Kim is the hardened con artist. In both the teaser and a later scene at the courthouse—where Kim passes one of Jimmy's extra suits through the x-ray machine so a client can wear it—we see Saul's clothes independent from Jimmy's body. It is an identity he has put on, but one that doesn't entirely fit the man we are seeing in the show's present. If anything, it is almost as if Kim has become the real Saul Goodman and is using Jimmy as her front man. (Those suits might clash with her power ponytail, anyway.) We hear her describe an ideally vulgar office for Saul—once again thinking of Jimmy *as* Saul, and only correcting herself after—that is more or less exactly like the one we see him using on *Breaking Bad*. She is building the legend, and he is reluctantly going along for the ride.

Shortly before Kim tells Jimmy about her plans for this "cathedral of justice," he sees her speaking with a client and his mother, and utterly lights up at the sight of her being so dedicated and compassionate. (Bob Odenkirk: great dramatic actor!) *This* is the woman he fell in love with, and once upon a time it seemed as if she had fallen for the idealized version of Jimmy who was always slightly out of reach of the well-meaning but flawed real guy. Now, though, she seems all in on Saul as the guy for her, as both a lover and an aspirational figure,

---

* Jimmy accusing the country club of anti-Semitism—despite not being remotely Jewish but deliberately using a Jewish-sounding name for work—is the most amusing part of either episode. (It's one of the funniest things the show has given Bob Odenkirk to do in quite some time.) But a close second is Julie Ann Emery's delivery as Betsy mistakenly assumes that Jimmy is talking about Kim: "That awful woman with the ponytail was a cocaine addict?!?"

even as she is still able to compartmentalize the part of herself that cares so much about her clients. (Rhea Seehorn: also a great dramatic actor!)

It's remarkable to think that we have arrived at a moment where there are only eleven episodes left after "Carrot and Stick," and somehow Jimmy is nowhere near being Saul Goodman for real. He seemed close at times, but now he is backtracking, because of both his experiences with Lalo and what he has witnessed of his influence on Kim. Something unspeakably awful is lurking in his future, just to emotionally get him from this point to the guy who built a gaudy mansion on drug profits and explosive homicides—even worse than might have seemed necessary a season or two ago.

Though the Jimmy and Mike halves of the show intersected a lot in the later episodes of Season 5, they are largely separate here, other than perhaps the glimpse of a car following Jimmy and Kim as they leave the Kettlemans' office at the end of "Carrot and Stick." So we are temporarily back to not only two separate shows, but to the lawyer half being more compelling—or perhaps just easier to follow—than the cartel half.

We pick up only hours after the failed hit on Lalo at his compound. Both Nacho and Lalo are in the wind—Nacho trying to escape his obvious involvement in the assassination attempt, Lalo pretending to be dead while he figures out how to prove his suspicion that Gus was behind his latest brush with death. For Nacho, this means spending most of these episodes hiding out at a cheap motel connected to Gus's operation, justifiably paranoid that both sides want him dead. For Lalo, this means following through on a brutal, long in the works contingency plan where he has set up local civilian Mateo to be a plausible stand-in for his corpse. He has previously paid for Mateo's dental work, with Mateo not realizing that his teeth will now match Lalo's. And while Mateo's wife Sylvia is patching up Lalo's wounds from the fight with Gus's mercenaries, Lalo encourages Mateo to shave his beard into a mustache and soul patch look, much like Lalo's own. RIP, Mateo and Sylvia, and RIP, the obnoxious coyotes who decline Lalo's "Be nice" suggestion and refuse to refund his money once he realizes that the answers he seeks are south of the border rather than north.

As is often the case this early in a *Saul* season, the plot moves very slowly. It feels like the show devotes half of these episodes just to Nacho exploring his motel room and watching for people watching him. And then there's yet another long montage of Mike tearing apart someone's home (Nacho's, in this case) looking for useful clues. But in many ways, both this show and *Breaking Bad* are procedurals about people figuring their way out of impossible situations, and they tell those stories as well as they do by following every step along the path to escape. So, we have to understand the geography of that motel and its parking lot to appreciate Nacho's ability to get out of it, and to best follow the shoot-out he gets into with the Cousins.* And a "Mike dismantles things" montage is never less than incredibly watchable.

At the same time, it's difficult to keep up with all the moves and counter-moves at times, in part because Mike's agenda is not in lockstep with Gus's. Mike likes Nacho and feels bad that Gus has placed the kid in such a difficult position, while Gus has nothing but contempt for Ignacio Varga. Both men, though, do not want Nacho to become a live prisoner of the Salamancas, knowing that he would reveal their role in the botched assassination attempt. Mike replaces Nacho's safe with an identical one, and plants falsified evidence of a Peruvian wire transfer to draw attention away from Gus. (Mike also removes all traces of Nacho's dad, understanding that Manuel Varga is a complete innocent in all of this.) Mike's hope is that Nacho will simply get away, perhaps with his help, while understanding that death seems more likely. Gus, though, just wants Nacho dead. The whole thing is deliberately messy—we even see the meticulous Gus knock over a glass in one scene—but it's a lot to keep track of, especially now that Hector is feeling mentally strong enough to assist his nephews in all of this.

At one point in "Carrot and Stick," Jimmy proposes a way to have a fake client approach Cliff Main. Just as Walter White once questioned every detail of Jesse's plan to shoot Tuco, Kim picks this story apart as unworkable, insisting that they have to find a sweet spot where Cliff will take the meeting, but not the case. Similarly, *Better Call Saul* has to find a way at the start of every season to have things move relatively slowly, but never so slowly that it's boring. Though there are some bumps regarding Nacho's perilous circumstances, for the most part this double feature finds the same kind of sweet spot that the Kettlemans ultimately serve for Kim's plan.

That tequila stopper was once a treasured memory of a great night a man and a woman had together on the road to becoming a couple. Now it's just so much trash lying against the curb, and perhaps a symbol of the moment when Jimmy McGill began to ruin Kim Wexler's life as much as his own.

---

* Two Cousin echoes here: First, Leonel and Marco themselves went to America in a coyote truck back in *Breaking Bad* Season 3, and also left bodies in their wake. And second, Nacho attempts to drive his stolen truck in reverse at them, just as Hank uses his SUV as a weapon in the legendary "One Minute" shootout. Hank's vehicular aim just proves better than Nacho's does here.

SEASON 6, EPISODE 3
WRITTEN AND DIRECTED BY GORDON SMITH

"Rock and Hard Place"

"Adios, Papa." —**Nacho**

The writers of both *Breaking Bad* and *Better Call Saul* are proud to admit how much each show was made up as it went along, and how many aspects of each were happy accidents. Jesse Pinkman was supposed to die within a few episodes of introducing Walter White to the Albuquerque drug scene, for instance; then Vince Gilligan got to watch Aaron Paul at work.

Few characters in either series are more symbolic of that improvisational quality than Nacho Varga. As we all know, Nacho only exists at all because in Saul Goodman's first appearance on *Breaking Bad*, he mentioned the names "Ignacio" and "Lalo" to Walt and Jesse when they dragged him out to the desert to scare him. So when Gilligan and Gould decided many years later to do a Saul prequel series, they had to come up with an Ignacio to explain why Saul would name-check him in such a tense moment. The funny thing is, that never quite happened. The initial plan was for Nacho and Jimmy to be frequent antagonists in Season 1, but, as we know, that plan also included Jimmy's move into the strip mall office before the first finale. As the creative team fell in love with the nicer version of Jimmy McGill, Nacho became an early storytelling casualty, disappearing from the narrative for long stretches.

But Nacho stuck around because Gould and everyone else liked Michael Mando's work, for obvious reasons, and because they clearly liked having someone on the cartel end of things who didn't fit neatly into the franchise's preexisting archetypes. Nacho started out as Tuco's sidekick, but he was never as volatile as Tuco, nor did he have the swagger of any of the Salamancas. There was an understated certainty similar to Mike's—it's one of the reasons the two of them got along so well, and why Mike has been willing to stick his neck out for the kid—but Nacho has generally come across as a scrapper more eager to get out of other people's messes than to seek power for himself.

He was a fun and fascinating character to watch for five-plus seasons, even if he was not at all what was planned at the start. He started interacting a lot with Mike, Hector, Lalo, and eventually Gus, and never really made his way back to Jimmy (other than some brief interactions last season when Lalo needed a defense attorney). Instead, his story comes to a tragic, powerful, and ultimately fitting end in "Rock and Hard Place."

Having escaped the Cousins in the motel parking lot shoot-out, he continues to elude them by demonstrating the ability to hold his breath while submerged in a pool of oil at the bottom of an abandoned tanker truck. (Nacho is not as clever or talented as some, but he has willpower for days.) He understands, though, that he has only earned himself a reprieve and not a commutation of the death sentence Gus arranged for him. After a final, painfully muted phone call with Manuel Varga—the father oblivious that this will be their final conversation, the son unable to think of anything else*—he contacts Mike and offers a deal, where he will sell whatever story Gus wants, then die, so long as his dad is left out of this ugly business. Gus and Mike are at extreme loggerheads on everything—Tyrus is literally holding a gun on Mike when he takes Nacho's call, just to ensure Mike's affection for Ignacio doesn't interfere with the boss's plans—but it's an acceptable compromise. Mike has Nacho smuggled over the border, lets him enjoy a final meal—and a final drink to take some of the sting out of the beating he has to deliver to make the whole scam look real—and talks him through exactly how things will go with Hector and Juan Bolsa. In discovering the shards of the glass Gus broke in "Carrot and Stick," Nacho comes up with his own tweak to the plan, but otherwise goes along. Juan offers him the choice between a good death and a bad one, and Nacho picks the best death possible for himself—one where he finally gets to tell all those Salamancas just what he thinks of them, gets to take credit for what he did to put Hector in that wheelchair, and then blows his own brains out before the Cousins or anyone else is able to wound him and set him up for torture. (For that matter, he spares Mike the sniper from the unfortunate task of having to kill him.) The Cousins help Hector riddle his corpse with bullets afterward, but a dead man can't be hurt anymore.

It's one hell of a farewell, and both the scene and the episode as a whole serve as a reminder of why the show worked so hard to keep Nacho in play even when there didn't seem to be any necessary plot function for him. Mando is *fantastic* throughout—so tired, so defeated, and yet so insistent about ending things on something resembling his own terms if he can. It is a tour de force, particularly the phone call sequence and Nacho staring down the Salamancas for the last time.

Nacho is the only character out there in the desert that we never saw on *Breaking Bad*, and thus the only one who could possibly die. There should be no tension at all. But the emotions of Gordon Smith's script and direction are so

---

*   Nacho never met Werner Ziegler, but it turns out the two had more in common than being professional acquaintances of Mike.

potent that twists and turns feel beside the point, even as Nacho's impending death takes up the bulk of the hour.

The rest of it advances Kim and Jimmy's scam against Howard slightly—this time with a jaunty, classical music-scored caper where Huell and a friend copy the keys to the Namaste-mobile while Howard is out to lunch—and finally gives Kim some pause regarding Jimmy's brief Friend of the Cartel phase. Thanks to Jimmy's verbal slip in "Wine and Roses," Suzanne from the DA's office is dismayed to realize they had Lalo Salamanca in custody and let him get out on bail because he was using a fake name. She attempts to get to Lalo's attorney through the allegedly more respectable Kim, suggesting that if Jimmy was also fooled by the "Jorge De Guzman" alias, then he has the right to waive attorney-client privilege and tell the authorities everything he knows. Kim responds to the news with shock, but not the kind Suzanne assumes. Kim is mainly startled to be reminded of that whole dangerous escapade, since she has thrown herself so thoroughly into the Howard sting. Whether or not she rushed into such a sketchy idea in response to the trauma of being threatened by Lalo, she was able to put that all out of her mind, until Suzanne brings it rushing back. And she ultimately frames Suzanne's offer to Jimmy in a way intended to make it easier for him to say no: "Do you want to be a friend of the cartel, or do you want to be a rat?"

Earlier, while Jimmy is paying off Huell and his accomplice, our favorite pickpocket asks Jimmy why he is continuing to do criminal stuff like this now that he has a successful and legitimate life as an attorney. Jimmy borrows Kim's line about how they will be doing a lot of good for a lot of people: both the Sandpiper victims who might not live to see the class action suit play out at normal speed, and the potential future clients of Kim's pro bono defense firm. But you can see that even Jimmy has lost sight of that a bit—that, as always, he is caught up in the game itself, and not really thinking about the potential damage he could cause to himself or others.

It's a much more cavalier attitude than Jimmy's occasional associate Nacho Varga was allowed to have over the years. Nacho and Jimmy didn't get to interact as much as anyone had intended. But you have to think that the hustling part of Nacho would be impressed, or at least ruefully amused, to know that Saul Goodman—who may or may not even know he's dead—will invoke his name to get out of unexpected trouble years later. This obviously was never the plan for Nacho, but he long ago learned what happens to men who try to plan anything.

SEASON 6, EPISODE 4
WRITTEN BY ANN CHERKIS
DIRECTED BY RHEA SEEHORN

"Hit and Run"

"You think we're wicked?" —**Kim**

More than Gus Fring's arrival, more than the inevitable appearances of Walt and Jesse—which the *Saul* creative team officially announced before the final season premiered—there is one intersection between the *Breaking Bad* and *Better Call Saul* stories that fans have been eagerly anticipating over all others, and we finally get it here in "Hit and Run."

I refer, of course, to our glimpse of the first meeting between Jimmy and Spooge.

Wait, what? No. Amusing as it is to see Spooge—who memorably robbed Jesse in *Breaking Bad* Season 2, then was part of Jesse's all-day ordeal in that show's classic episode "Peekaboo"—in slightly better days, the meeting to which I am referring is, of course, Kim Wexler and Mike Ehrmantraut.

Rhea Seehorn* and Jonathan Banks worked on the same show for years— and have clear affection for one another—but they had never shared a scene together before this episode. It's a combination that's easy to get excited about for a couple of reasons. The first is that, even more than Kim's encounters with Lalo, this would permanently glue the series' two fractured halves back together, because Mike is an important part of Jimmy's future, whereas Lalo is out of the picture by the time Walt and Jesse do their first cook together. The second is that Kim and Mike, like Nacho and Mike, were so obviously kindred spirits that it would have been a shame if they could never hang out together. Both are no-frills, low-ego people who don't need the world to know how good they are at everything. It's not hard to imagine a low-stakes sitcom spin-off of the show that's just them meeting for drinks at the El Camino every night to swap stories about Jimmy, for Mike to complain about Gus wanting his mercenaries to also be up to Pollos Hermanos standards, etc.

---

* What a nice coincidence that the episode Seehorn got assigned to direct—the first directing credit to her name at the time, other than a short film called *How Not to Buy a Couch*—was the episode where she and Banks have their first on-camera interaction. Vince Gilligan got the chance to direct a couple of latter-era *X-Files* episodes, and he kept paying that forward on Heisenberg-verse shows, giving writers (Peter Gould included), crew members, producers, and actors like Seehorn chances to get behind the camera. It's like he was running a small filmmaking school in addition to making great TV.

The two do not exactly get to shoot the breeze here. As is always the case these days when Mike reaches across the dividing line between cartel world and lawyer world, it is an emergency. Lalo is in the wind—not dead, as Kim believed as recently as the previous episode—and the cars that have been following Kim are not from the Salamancas, but from the Fring organization.* It is Mike's guys keeping tabs on anyone Lalo might try to contact as the next phase of his war against the Chicken Man. And by confronting two of said guys, Kim has messed everything up, and placed herself and her husband in greater danger. It is a scene dripping with tension—look at how Kim has started to shake by the time Mike leaves the restaurant—and yet also understated and lovely in the way you would hope for these two when they finally got to speak. Mike is plainspoken and circumspect like always, but with the gentle tone he saves for people who did not enter this world by choice. When, for instance, she oversteps by asking about his employer, he quietly reminds her, "I said I would answer anything I *can*." It is all that needs to be said, especially to a sharp cookie like Kim Wexler, Esq. And when she understandably wonders why Mike has come to her, rather than to the man with whom he has worked off and on for years, he speaks for the *Saul* fan base and pays her the ultimate Mike compliment: "Because I think you're made of sterner stuff."

Perhaps the most striking part of the conversation comes right at the end, when Kim realizes that this is *not* the first time they've met, even if it's the first such meeting we are privileged to witness. She remembers his stint working in the courthouse parking lot, and says, "You're the attendant."

"I was," Mike replies. Again, it is the minimal amount of words necessary to get the point across. It is startling for Kim to realize that this powerful and dangerous man in front of her was once an innocuous guy she said brief hellos to every day on her way into court. But then, the friendly attorney the attendant likely nodded back at is not really the person standing in front of Mike Ehrmantraut, fixer for a would-be kingpin, either. That Kim was a grinder, perfectly content to work within the larger machine of HHM, who assumed she would spend her career doing corporate law and certainly wouldn't be up to half the shady stuff she has been masterminding over these last few seasons.

---

* After the previous, extremely cartel-heavy episode, the pendulum here swings back almost entirely to lawyer world. Gus is hiding out in his civilian identity, though we see that he is so paranoid that he owns a second house in his neighborhood, with an underground tunnel connecting the two. 1213 Jefferson Street (where he will later host Walter White for a meal) is the front, but he conducts business out of the other one, while a middle-aged couple pose as its owners, bicycling in unison through the neighborhood and behaving very judgmentally about their neighbors' choice in house paint colors. With Nacho dead, Hector appeased, and Lalo still in the wind, there's not much for Gus and Mike to do but wait and argue about whether two years as a McDonald's short-order cook qualifies one to work for Los Pollos Hermanos.

What was it that Mike's future business partner once said to his chemistry class? Oh, that's right: "Growth, decay, transformation! It's fascinating, really."

Have Kim and Mike transformed from the people introduced in the *Saul* series premiere? Absolutely. But has it been growth, decay, or some combination of the two? Certainly, both wield far more power than they did at the start, but that power has come at some cost. Mike has gotten good people killed, and sometimes committed the deed himself. Kim has moved away from everything she seemed to believe about the importance of following the rules. Yes, she can verbally outmaneuver a man like Lalo Salamanca, but how did she get to the point where such a thing would even be necessary?

Kim recognizing Mike as the parking attendant is also notable because of what the episode has to say about the Jimmy from that era versus the ever-so-increasingly Saul Goodman we are watching now. After declining Suzanne Ericsen's offer to rat on Lalo, Jimmy returns to the courthouse to find that now he is being treated like an outcast. He once had the whole building wired, making up in sheer interpersonal skill what he lacked in legal acumen compared to people like Kim or his big brother. Many scenes here echo things we saw Jimmy doing in that very first episode: trying to charm the court clerk into rescheduling a hearing, or attempting to schmooze with Bill Oakley at the vending machine. But the clerk, Bill, the security guards, and everyone else look at Jimmy with utter contempt. Whatever chicanery he got up to in previous seasons, he was still lovable ol' Jimmy McGill, who colored outside the lines but was at least attempting to re-create the basic image. You might roll your eyes at him, might scold him, might even complain to a judge or the bar about his behavior. But ultimately, you would grab a beer with him at the end of a long day. *That's just Jimmy, you know?* Now, though, he has a different name and has done (to borrow Kim's phrasing) something unforgivable in brazenly helping a monster like Lalo escape custody. He is a pariah to all the people whose affection and respect he sought for so long.

But when life gives him lemons, Saul Goodman serves cucumber water instead. Word about the Lalo stunt has spread not only among the courthouse staff, but to criminals like Spooge. If Jimmy could get a *Salamanca* out of jail, imagine what he might be able to do for people much lower on the most wanted list! He is so in demand, so quickly, that his new would-be client base takes up most of the nail salon, much to the displeasure of Mrs. Nguyen. It is, in fact, the last straw for Jimmy's landlady, who kicks him out of the back office he's used off and on throughout the series. But this only provides the impetus for Jimmy to finally track down that potential "cathedral of justice" Kim talked about in the season premiere. And wouldn't you know it, said cathedral happens to be located inside a very familiar-looking strip mall!

We are now getting very close to the Saul Goodman we know. He's got the suits. He's got the rep among Albuquerque's hoodlum demographic. And now he has the office. He still needs the slogan that gives this show its title, needs to bring Francesca back into the fold, and needs to get the Caddy with the "LWYRUP" vanity plates. (Oh, and Mike for some reason has to decide to moonlight as his investigator.) But Peter Gould and company have basically brought Jimmy up to speed on a professional level. Is he Saul Goodman spiritually, though? Even a couple of episodes ago, after all, he seemed to be turning into the soft touch who wasn't comfortable with Kim's ruthless schemes. Here, though, he's so caught up in the grifter fun-and-games with Howard—which includes Jimmy getting back into the custom-made Howard-style suit (and garish spray tan) he had made for the billboard stunt in Season 1*—that whatever qualms he had in "Carrot and Stick" feel like distant memories.

And he responds to the legal establishment's rejection by acting like he never wanted to be part of their club to begin with and basking in the warm, slightly sticky embrace of Spooge and friends. When he tells Kim about his reception at the courthouse and being evicted by Mrs. Nguyen, she assumes he has had a bad day. To Jimmy, though—or maybe Saul?—this was a great day. He has become almost everything Chuck once feared he would be, though he does not quite seem like the kind of man who would casually suggest that Walt and Jesse have Badger killed to solve their problems. But it's getting late early.

Whatever Kim and Mike have transformed into, there is no question that Jimmy is on the path to decay. He has come a long way from the guy who used to sleep at the nail salon, but not exactly in the manner he might have liked. He doesn't have a care in the world, while Kim is now the one looking over her shoulder, mindful of what Mike told her, and the mess they are all now in together.

---

* Spooge is not the only *Breaking Bad* alum to resurface here. This stage of the Howard plan brings in Jesse's old friend Wendy the sex worker, who goes for a ride in the Namaste-mobile with the disguised Jimmy, so that it can appear Howard is tossing a prostitute out of his car in full view of Cliff Main. It all goes off perfectly—better than planned, in a way. Cliff is so impressed by Kim's pitch for the pro bono defense firm—which she initially tells him about just as the pretense for their sidewalk cafe meeting—that he offers to open doors for her. She still needs Jimmy's cut of the Sandpiper settlement to fund the operation, but it seems like she might have been able to pull off a version of her plan without destroying Howard's reputation in the process.

SEASON 6, EPISODE 5
WRITTEN BY ALISON TATLOCK
DIRECTED BY MELISSA BERNSTEIN

"Black and Blue"

*"You're right: I do have a problem. Just not the problem you think.
I have a Jimmy McGill problem."* **—Howard**

After the historic meeting between Kim and Mike, it would be easy to assume that the legal and cartel halves of *Better Call Saul* would begin merging more and more in these final episodes. There is a built-in limit to that, though, since Saul does not seem to know know Gus circa his introduction on *Breaking Bad*. The stories may intersect periodically, but they are still somewhat in parallel—in "Black and Blue," parallel in theme as much as in plot advancement. Specifically, we have Gus Fring and Howard Hamlin. They are the two characters who are the clearest symbols of whether we are in cartel world or lawyer world, and they spend "Black and Blue" faced with similar problems: their livelihoods are both being threatened by familiar opponents about whom they can do precious little at the moment.

Gus has known for a while that Lalo is trouble, but these last several episodes have been agonizing for him with their lack of new information. He has already been getting sloppy—recall the broken glass in his office that Nacho eventually made use of—and here we see him paranoid and distracted even while doing the routine business of managing Los Pollos Hermanos. Gus Fring is *never* distracted, least of all when he's performing his cover job, and it's a sign of just how rattled he is by the smartest Salamanca's ongoing absence.

Where Mike has assumed Lalo will go after someone in Albuquerque, Lalo instead makes his presence felt in, of all places, Germany—aka the homeland of the late Werner Ziegler. Lalo is going through Werner—or, rather, through his widow Margarethe—to find the proof he needs that Gus has been acting against the cartel's interests. The episode opens with a short film about the creation of a glass trophy with a slide rule inside—the sort of thing the meticulous yet old-school Werner would no doubt have enjoyed—and it closes with a tense scene where Lalo escapes the house with the thing right before Margarethe finds him. (This is better news for Margarethe than for Lalo, since he simply would have killed her if he couldn't climb out the window, once again demonstrating Spider-Man levels of agility.) The episode leaves ambiguity about what Lalo's whole game is, but we are long past the point where we should doubt any plan this guy sets in motion.

As with many cartel stories on *Saul*, the show is scrambling around the prequel problem. We know that Lalo is doomed to fail, because Juan Bolsa and Don Eladio remain utterly blind to Gus's true intentions until the Chicken Man kills them. The fun has to be in exactly how Gus triumphs. Here we see that he has discovered the same itch that Lalo is trying to scratch. The Super Lab has been a key part in his plan to overthrow the cartel, and Lalo has for the moment ruined that part of the plan. So Gus has Mike take him to the dig site, less to look for clues than to plant a weapon for what he assumes will be an eventual showdown with Lalo beneath the old laundromat.*

Lalo's specter hangs over the lawyer world scenes to a degree. Kim is up in the middle of the night barricading the apartment door in case the bad man returns. She talked her way out of trouble with him once, but understandably doesn't believe she can do it a second time. And perhaps more interestingly, she does not want to burden Jimmy† with the knowledge that their tormentor is still alive, nor that she has finally met his old friend Mike. Is this a kindness she is doing to her husband? Or does she worry that infecting him with this paranoia will make it more difficult for him to stay on task with Howard? As hard-edged as Kim has become, it could be either one.

Regardless of her motivations, Kim's plan appears to hit a snag—or does it?—when Cliff Main confronts Howard about all the shady things he's witnessed over these last few episodes. Once again, Howard is astute enough to realize that Jimmy is coming after him, even if he can't grasp his frenemy's motivations for trying to discredit him. As with Lalo versus Gus, it's more fun when both sides of the duel are smart and aware of what's happening. But in this case, it's fair to wonder exactly how much of an advantage Howard has just gained. He still doesn't recognize that Kim, not Jimmy, is the true architect of his misfortune, for instance. But more importantly, neither Kim nor Jimmy seems all that troubled by the news that he is onto them—as if this was either an expected part of the plan, or even a necessary one. As Howard points out,

---

* This inspiration does not come out of nowhere. Gus gets distracted after mentioning Los Pollos Hermanos' signature spice curls to a customer, because in Season 5 he pitched that menu addition to the Madrigal executives. Madrigal leads to thoughts of Germany, Germany leads to thoughts of Werner, Werner leads to the dig site as one of his few areas of vulnerability in relation to the cartel, etc.

† Another piece of the Saul Goodman professional puzzle comes into place with the return of Tina Parker as Francesca. She has not been watching the last two seasons of *Better Call Saul*, and thus is surprised by all the changes: a new office, no Kim, Jimmy is practicing law under a new name and has swapped out his lovable elder-law clients for a bunch of sketchy criminal defendants. Yet she is able to turn this uncertain new situation to her advantage, wheedling the maximum possible salary out of Jimmy (plus a "signing bonus" of the cash he has in his wallet) and making sure she has a say in decorating this space once the toilet is gone. We know from *Breaking Bad* that beneath that sweet demeanor lurks an absolute hustler, and she and her boss remain well-matched.

they did not really bother to cover their tracks: Jimmy already used sex workers against him, and Kim was Cliff's coffee date for the incident with Wendy. They had to know this was possible, perhaps likely, even if they couldn't guarantee exactly when Cliff might confront Howard.*

Howard hires a private investigator to tail Jimmy, but first he opts to take out his aggression in a more direct way: by luring Jimmy to his boxing gym for a few rounds. It is, on one level, another example of Howard naively trying to appeal to Jimmy's better nature, hoping that once confronted, the man he dubbed "Charlie Hustle" will back down from whatever nonsense he's attempting. Mainly, though, he wants to beat the crap out of this guy, and he does just that, in a fight impressive for just how clumsy and unglamorous it is. This is not a *Rocky* bout, but two middle-aged men who specialize in brains rather than brawn. Howard has more training than Jimmy does, though, and he also has more desire to win, whereas Jimmy only steps into the ring in the first place out of guilt—as Kim will later remind him, "You know what's coming next." And what's coming next has to be a whole lot worse than what we've seen so far.

Gus knows Lalo is coming for him, and perhaps even by what route. And he has the weight of franchise history behind him, even if Lalo appears to be in control right now. Howard Hamlin, on the other hand, is one of the few remaining characters to never appear on *Breaking Bad*. Almost anything could happen to him between now and the series finale, and it does not seem like good things are in store, even now that he knows that Jimmy is scheming against him. Knowledge is power in the Heisenberg-verse, but even knowledge can only take you so far when you're not the title character and your opponent is.

---

* Interestingly, Cliff chooses to do it after witnessing Howard in a moment of professional triumph, heading off a potential uprising from all the Sandpiper clients who are eager to settle the case while they're still alive to enjoy the money. Cliff notices that Howard is full of nervous energy while watching Erin try and fail to calm the clients, and it's possible he reads Howard's performance as something fueled by cocaine as much as by his innate charm.

SEASON 6, EPISODE 6
WRITTEN BY ARIEL LEVINE
DIRECTED BY GIANCARLO ESPOSITO

"Axe and Grind"

"Relax. You got away with it." —**Kim's mom**

What happens to Kim?

This was the question I posed regarding the previous *Saul* episode to feature young Kim (still played here by Katie Beth Hall, with her hair pulled partially back, but not yet in the full power ponytail) and Kim's mom (Beth Hoyt, who still looks and sounds uncannily like Rhea Seehorn). That episode, "Wexler v. Goodman," opened with young Kim walking away from her drunken mother rather than getting into a car with her. It closed with the adult Kim explaining in great detail why she had every good reason to break up with Jimmy, only for her to declare at the last moment that perhaps they should get married instead. It was Kim's weakness for hustlers and damaged people winning out over her understanding of what is good, for both her and the world at large.

"Axe and Grind" begins a bit differently, though it ends on a similar note. We are back in Nebraska, only this time Kim is the one in trouble, rather than her mom. She has been caught shoplifting a pair of earrings from Svensen's department store. This is wildly out of character for her as a girl, which even the store manager, Mr. Pearson, can tell. Kim's squeaky-clean presentation, along with Pearson being charmed by (and/or attracted to) her mom, gets her out of the jam. And her mom even re-steals the earrings for Kim, after raising such a fuss in Pearson's office about making Kim pay for them.

Much like the "Wexler v. Goodman" flashback, this is hugely informative about who Kim is now. She did not make a habit of stealing back then, but she also learned that you can get away with doing bad things if you are a good and forceful enough talker. It is a leap from Kim's mom hustling the store manager to Kim doing the same to Lalo Salamanca,* but one of degree rather than kind. And we've seen plenty of instances in past episodes where Kim has stretched the limits of the law and her own personal ethics simply because she could,

---

* Lalo's German odyssey pits him against Casper, one of the members of Werner's team at the dig site. Casper has the right idea to get the hell away from this confident interloper, but he takes it too easy on Lalo, striking him with the back of his axe, rather than the blade with which he had just chopped so much wood. That half-measure costs Casper his foot, and quite possibly his life, as he becomes the latest person who just isn't as calm or as ruthless as Lalo when violence is in the offing.

from keeping Huell out of prison to the sting she and Jimmy were preparing against Kevin last season. With *Breaking Bad*, a big question was whether it was a show about a good man who turned evil due to a fatal diagnosis, or about a man whose true nature only fully manifested itself under extreme circumstances. The latter interpretation always made more sense, as there were too many glimpses of a pre-cancer Walt acting just as aggrieved and entitled as the great and powerful Heisenberg. *Better Call Saul*, meanwhile, has at times created the illusion that it is the story of the incorrigible Slippin' Jimmy McGill dragging the pure and noble Kim Wexler into the sewer with him. But even before she proposed the current scam against Howard Hamlin, it was clear that Kim really enjoyed the grift, and that she was capable of being even more ruthless about it than Jimmy has ever been.

All of which brings us to the present-day action of "Axe and Grind." Our happily married couple are preparing for D-Day against Howard.* More pieces of the plan present themselves, from an otherwise harmless drug that can temporarily make Jimmy—and, down the road, Howard—seem as high as a kite,[†] to some faked photos cooked up with the help of Jimmy's favorite film crew, to Jimmy having phone access to the Sandpiper mediation call. The operation seems to be running smoothly, and Jimmy and Kim spend the night before D-Day picnicking outside the HHM offices that will soon be put in turmoil by their scheme.

At the same time, some major professional good fortune is coming Kim's way. Cliff Main comes to Albuquerque to watch Kim in action, as she doggedly tears apart the legal justification for the search of her client's vehicle. Outside the courtroom, he tells her that a prestigious foundation that funds criminal justice reform programs is looking to move into the southwest, and that he thinks Kim is a great candidate to work with them. There is a hitch, but it is a small one: the lunch meeting in Santa Fe with the foundation is on D-Day. But as Jimmy points out, the plan at this stage does not need Kim to be physically or mentally present for its final act . . .

---

*   We also learn that Howard's life is already plenty wrecked without Kim and Jimmy's help. He is living in his guest house, and it appears his marriage to Cheryl (Sandrine Holt) now exists in name only, though the two remain cordial with one another. Howard goes out of his way to prepare a beautiful morning coffee for Cheryl with a peace sign in the foam—displaying a meticulous, cleanliness-focused approach suggesting he and Gus Fring would get along well—and Cheryl barely looks at the thing before pouring it into a travel mug. (And, to Howard's dismay, she blithely spills some onto the countertop.)

†   The drug is provided by Dr. Caldera, who has grown tired of this lucrative but stress-inducing side hustle and is planning to sell his coded black book and get back to caring for pets full-time. We already know who's going to buy it, since it's one of the items being cataloged at Saul's house in the flash-forward opening sequence of "Wine and Roses."

. . . or, at least, it doesn't until Jimmy runs into the mediator at a liquor store (while attempting to buy another bottle of Zafiro Añejo to celebrate with Kim) and sees that the man's left arm is in a sling and cast, when the doppelgänger in the faked photos is uninjured. It is too big a change, Jimmy believes, to recover from at this last minute, and he is prepared to give up, regroup, and find another way to get at Howard down the road.

To Kim, this should not matter. The alleged reason she came up with this scam was to fund her plans for a high-powered criminal defense firm for indigent clients. But her own good work and connections seem to be making that a reality, with or without the Sandpiper money. All she has to do is keep driving to Santa Fe and speak as clearly and passionately to the foundation people as we know she can, and her plan is secured. Howard, Sandpiper, the mediator—all of that is largely beside the point. (Kim might still need some start-up money of her own, but there are other ways to get that, starting with the duffel bag full of cash Jimmy got from Lalo.) Just stay in the car, go to the meeting, and so much good can be done.

But we all know that Kim has other reasons for this beyond her desire to do good. She wants to hit back at Howard for being so patronizing with her in the Season 5 finale. And she can no longer resist the high of a good con. Ultimately, those two feelings outweigh her nobler instincts. After a few moments of Kim thinking—and few actors anywhere are more exciting to watch think than Rhea Seehorn—she declares, "It happens today," before she drives over the highway median and heads back down the hill toward Albuquerque, Jimmy, Howard, and the scheme she can't let go of, no matter how much she should.

It's a sequence reminiscent in some ways of events at the end of this show's first season and the start of its second, which also involved Cliff Main and Santa Fe. Way back when, Kim arranged a meeting between Jimmy and Cliff regarding Sandpiper and a potential job at Davis and Main. Jimmy instead drove away from it, too consumed with his own fondness for a life of crime, only to change his mind a day or two later and take the job. He didn't literally make a U-turn back then, but this is the same basic idea in reverse. In that case, the straight life did not suit Jimmy, and he found a way out of Davis and Main. Kim, meanwhile, has been straining against the limitations of the straight life for most of this series' run, and here she breaks free of its shackles altogether. Whatever happens to her next, there is no simple way to undo the choice she makes here. Cliff has gone out on a limb for her; there will surely not be a second meeting with the foundation. She is putting everything into her quest to ruin Howard and get a kick out of it while doing so. This does not seem likely to end well for her, with her soul and/or career hanging very much in the balance.

We want Kim to come out of this okay, both because she is such an endearing character and because she is practically the only person left who can. But the Heisenberg-verse is not a place that has typically allowed for happy endings. And if a bad one comes for Kim, we unfortunately can't call her an innocent bystander anymore. She earned her happy ending, then took a one-hundred-eighty-degree turn away from it. She is more her mother's daughter, more her husband's wife, than she would want to admit, and she is driving into a whole lot of trouble now.

What happens to Kim? I want it to be something good, but I fear that it will be anything but.

SEASON 6, EPISODE 7
WRITTEN AND DIRECTED BY THOMAS SCHNAUZ

"Plan and Execution"

"You're perfect for each other. You have a piece missing." —**Howard**

Early in "Plan and Execution," a young HHM associate named Cary is so startled to find Howard Hamlin waiting in the conference room, well ahead of the planned mediation with the Sandpiper defense team, he spills part of a tray of soda cans he was carrying to restock the minifridge. Howard reminds his anxious employee that the dropped cans are at risk of exploding but teaches him a simple trick to calm them down: simply place each can on a table and rotate it along its axis, and the centrifugal force will make the dreaded bubbles go away.

Howard is, we know, a meticulous person bordering on control freak. This notion of being able to contain something you know is supposed to explode is very much him. For that matter, it is very much Chuck McGill, who taught Howard this particular hack. But life is not something as easily controlled as pivoting a soda can atop a table, as Chuck tragically learned in his later years, his legacy so forgotten that a kid like Cary has never even heard of the man who put the M into HHM.

Chuck thought he could control everything until he couldn't, and then kept trying even after that, until his brother ruthlessly showed him otherwise. Similarly, when the Sandpiper mediation blows up in Howard's face as a result of Kim and Jimmy's chicanery, Howard still thinks he can get all the fizzy contents back into the can, even as Cliff Main keeps explaining that this mess has already spilled all over their case, and that their only choice is to settle with Rich Schweikart.

As this is happening, "Plan and Execution" has faked us into thinking that the can that is Lalo will not explode during this hour. The episode begins with a sequence detailing Lalo's elaborate yet invisible method for spying on the laundry, until he can find a way in to show Don Eladio proof that Gus is trying to build his own drug lab. After that, though, we are in lawyer world for a very long time—or in the cracked mirror version of lawyer world that we get to periodically glimpse whenever Jimmy and/or Kim are in the midst of some chicanery. It takes so long to return to Lalo that a viewer would not be blamed for forgetting he'd even been in the teaser—or, at least, for assuming that his latest maneuver against Gus would remain in the background while the primary focus is on the conclusion of this elaborate Sandpiper con.

But once shaken up, cartel world isn't able to keep itself from exploding any more than a soda can is. And in this case, the episode concludes with cartel world spraying itself all over lawyer world—or, to be blunt, with Howard's brains spraying themselves all over the wall and rug in Kim and Jimmy's apartment.

But this is all part of the short con that "Plan and Execution" is playing on its audience. Once Lalo vanishes after the opening credits, this all seems like a lark, with Dave Porter conjuring up some of his jauntiest caper music of the series' entire run, Jimmy and Kim both running around a lot, and the revelation that Howard's "private eye," Genidowski, has really been working for Jimmy this whole time. TV writers like to refer to overly complicated jokes or story ideas as "sweaty." Between Jimmy and Kim's sprinting and Howard suffering the effects of Dr. Caldera's drug, the whole scheme is both figuratively and literally sweaty, even though it all works out as planned. Howard swallows the bait about Jimmy bribing Judge Casimiro, makes an embarrassing scene during the mediation, and the contact high he received from the tainted photos only makes things look worse. As always, Howard is smart enough after the fact to recognize every single move Kim and Jimmy have made. But as an exasperated Cliff points out, it's too late to matter. The damage is done, and they have to take Rich's deal ASAP.

If you're a fan of Jimmy and Kim schemes, if you're eager to see a smug rich guy like Howard taken down a peg, and/or if you're rooting for Sandpiper plaintiffs like Irene to get paid while they're still alive to enjoy the money, then this all plays out incredibly well. If, on the other hand, you are concerned about the state of Jimmy's soul—and even more about Kim's—then there's not a lot of pleasure to be taken from seeing the con go so smoothly.

When Jimmy points out to Kim that she still has time to make it to the lunch in Santa Fe if she drives really fast, she replies, "Jimmy, this is where I need to be." Getting her criminal defense practice up and running—the alleged reason for this whole complicated and cruel plan—is no longer even a thought in her head. As Howard will point out later, in one of the most cogent and pointed moments of his too-brief life, she is doing it for fun, and boy is she having some here.

This late in the series, though, there is no time for simple, consequence-free hijinks. There has to be a cost, just like Walt and Jesse couldn't pull off the train heist in the "Dead Freight" episode of the final *Breaking Bad* season without Todd killing Drew Sharp. (Both Drew and Howard die for the same minor sin: being in the wrong place at the wrongest possible time.) It has seemed for a while like the cost would be Kim's dream of providing high-value defenses to low-income clients. But whatever happens with that, Howard himself is a cost: a human being who was not without his own foibles, but who was also generous and open-minded enough to encourage both Kim and Jimmy in their quests to transcend their backgrounds and become attorneys. All of this happened because Howard attempted to be kind, in his own way, to both of them: offering Jimmy a job at HHM, and warning Kim that her husband would get her into trouble down the road. He never could have imagined that the former action would result in bowling balls being tossed at his car, let alone that the latter would so deeply offend Kim that it would inspire this entire plot against him. When Kim first pitched the idea to Jimmy, she suggested that they would have to make it look like Howard had done "something unforgivable." But in the end, she is the one who did exactly that. There is no undoing any of this—no bringing back Howard's life, or even his reputation—and she and Jimmy will have to live with the bloody memories of what they set in motion. What we see of Saul Goodman on *Breaking Bad* suggests that his only way to cope moving forward was to compartmentalize and essentially turn off the part of his brain that would be troubled by something like this.*

Can Kim do the same? Would she even want to? Howard verbally cuts both of them down to size before Lalo shows up. If he's too judgmental in certain areas—Jimmy is not soulless, but bad luck and the skepticism of people like Chuck have repeatedly prompted his worst instincts to rise to the surface—he's right with the notion that there is no justifying what they did, especially when their primary goal was not the money, but the high of pulling it off. We see how tense they are while listening in to the conference call, but by the time the mediator has walked out, Rich has reduced his offer, and Cliff is trying to make the settlement sound like a good thing to the plaintiffs on the phone, Jimmy and Kim are already fooling around on the couch. This has all been a huge turn-on for them, the collateral damage not even worth considering.

Shortly after the make-out session, we are witness to a rare sight: Lalo Salamanca utterly losing his cool. He has called Hector to check in and update him on the plan to expose the Super Lab site to Don Eladio, only to realize that Gus's people have the nursing home phones bugged. Everything he has carefully worked on since surviving the assassination attempt has just gone up in flames, and he well and truly throws a tantrum down there in his little home away from home in the sewer. By the time he arrives in the apartment, though—a gust of wind ominously rattling a candle each time there is movement in the place—he

---

* The utterly raw horror with which Bob Odenkirk and Rhea Seehorn play the closing minutes, particularly after Lalo shoots Howard, is quite something. Would you believe that neither of them won an Emmy for their work on this show? For that matter, would you believe *Better Call Saul* as a whole won **zero** Emmys out of fifty-three nominations across six seasons, setting a record that should be an embarrassment to every Emmy voter out there? Peter Gould has some thoughts on this; see page 297.

is back to being the cool, lethal cucumber we know so well, while Jimmy and Kim are the terrified ones, and Howard is confused and then scared, but not scared enough to do anything. (Nine times out of ten, Lalo is able to kill people simply because they couldn't possibly conceive of him doing it.)

It is an incredibly dark note to end any episode on, never mind one that, at the time it first aired, led into a six-week break before the remaining episodes began to air. "Plan and Execution" leaves a lot up in the air regarding how much more Jimmy and Kim can be hurt by stray rounds from Lalo and Gus's war, as well as what will happen to Lalo.

Howard Hamlin, though? Howard spent his whole life looking perfect even though he felt anything but. When Cary is envious to hear Howard describe Chuck as the best legal mind he ever knew, Howard admits that maybe there are more important things in life. Like Chuck, Howard thought he could outwit Slippin' Jimmy. And like Chuck, Howard's life instead ended in dire fashion. He should not have been in that apartment, should never have had to cross paths with Lalo Salamanca. But he was, and he did, and now he's gone.

The audience understands at this point that Lalo can't win, and the show is clearly playing with this understanding. He seems so impossibly smart and capable that it's enough to make the viewer at least wonder if the rest of the story might unfold differently—that somehow, this is not going to lead us to the events of *Breaking Bad* as we know it. Or perhaps that's just something worth wishing for, since the only two major characters remaining whom we do not know for sure are alive during the events of *Breaking Bad* are Lalo . . . and Kim.

SEASON 6, EPISODE 8
WRITTEN BY GORDON SMITH
DIRECTED BY VINCE GILLIGAN

"Point and Shoot"

"Big talk. You done?" —**Lalo**
"No. Not yet." —**Gus**

Both *Better Call Saul* and *Breaking Bad* have well-deserved reputations for their narrative patience. Major events tend not to happen until the creative team has slowly but surely laid all the groundwork necessary for these events to make sense and have the maximum possible emotional impact. But the shows do not always take their time with this kind of thing. Tuco Salamanca, who seemed like he would be the main villain of *Breaking Bad* Season 2, instead died in that season's second episode. Nacho Varga killed himself in this season's second episode, when it appeared at one point like he might be a significant part of the series' endgame.

And now Lalo Salamanca—who certainly seemed like he would be the story engine for most of this final season—is dead and buried with five episodes still to go.

Why would *Better Call Saul* do it this way? Why get rid of the absurdly charismatic Tony Dalton—who was already absent from a good chunk of the season, while Lalo was laying low and pursuing a new angle against Gus—with multiple episodes remaining, and no real chance for him to play the role again? Why eliminate the last significant plot point of the cartel half of the show, since there really aren't any outstanding questions about what happens to Gus and Mike between now and when they're introduced on the parent series?

The answer seems to come down to what kind of story *Better Call Saul* is ultimately telling, and how much of the remaining time is needed in which to tell it.

If *Saul* is primarily a show about filling in historical gaps from *Breaking Bad,* and/or one that's most interested in the cartel—or even equally interested in cartel world and lawyer world—then killing Lalo so early seems an odd choice. If, on the other hand, the show is primarily about the emotional journey of its title character—how he gets from the man horrified to see Howard Hamlin's corpse being loaded into a fridge to the man who blithely suggests that Walt and Jesse just murder Badger—then it makes all the sense in the world. Because as great an addition to the Heisenberg-verse as Lalo turned out to be, he was ultimately a tool for that journey, and not someone who absolutely had to be around through the end of it.

And either way, there's the math. There are five episodes left, and so much left to be resolved, most notably what happens to Kim and the fate of Gene from Cinnabon. For *Better Call Saul* to properly deal with that meant that Lalo Salamanca simply ran out of road. Funny as he was, scary as he was, entertaining as hell as he was, he was unfortunately a character who could not survive the events of this series, because the things Gus does on *Breaking Bad* would be impossible with Lalo still in any way in the picture. So he had to go, and earlier than we might have assumed.

And regardless of the timing, "Point and Shoot" is a pretty spectacular episode of television. Lalo does not go quietly, and *Better Call Saul* for the most part treats his demise with the respect he has earned.

"Point and Shoot" begins with a flash-forward showing how Mike and his guys have staged things to make it look like Howard drowned in the Pacific Ocean while high, his body never to be recovered. It is, like so many Vince Gilligan–directed teasers, simultaneously beautiful and cruel, the surf looking beautiful even as one of Howard's shoes floats in it, the sand looking calm even amid the footprints, the trademark "NAMAST3" license plate taunting us with the implication of how and why this scene has been created by Mike.

From there, we are right back in the apartment, only seconds after we left our favorite legal married couple cowering in horror, fear, and self-loathing from the sight of Lalo murdering their old boss. Throughout his tenure on the show, one of Lalo's defining traits has been his ability to keep his head when all about him are losing theirs. Rarely has that contrast between predator and prey been starker than in this opening scene. Lalo usually deals either with completely oblivious innocents who aren't aware of the threat he poses until it's far too late, or with hardened criminals who simply underestimate his ruthlessness. Jimmy and Kim are neither. Both knew Lalo well enough to be terrified of him long before he murdered Howard. Both fancy themselves cold and calculating grifters, but they're not prepared to play on the level at which Lalo and Mike exist. They know enough to understand that Lalo could kill either or both of them at any moment, even as he converses with them like he barely has a care in the world. It's an acting clinic from all three performers,[*] but especially from Rhea Seehorn, who is practically vibrating throughout the

---

[*] This scene actually had to be filmed in two pieces, weeks apart. During a break in initially shooting the episode, Bob Odenkirk suffered a serious heart attack, where his heart stopped beating for eighteen minutes. When Odenkirk was finally healthy enough to return to work, filming largely moved on to the next episode, "Fun and Games," and it wasn't until later that this part of "Point and Shoot" could be completed. More on this on page 300.

sequence as Kim tries to reassemble all the shattered pieces of the person she thought she was for her entire life minus the preceding five minutes.*

One of the best choices Gordon Smith's script makes is to let both Lalo and Gus be exceedingly clever without needing them to unnecessarily spell it out to anyone who might be listening. As Lalo explains that he wants Jimmy to walk up to Gus's house and shoot him, a viewer could be forgiven for assuming Lalo is taking the longest of long shots and sending in an assassin who would never arouse Gus's suspicions, and whose potential death wouldn't trouble him at all. But whether you understand in that moment that Lalo is using Jimmy— and then Kim, when Jimmy convinces him to send her instead in hopes of saving her life—to draw Mike's forces away from the laundromat, or only later once we see him parked across the street, it is intensely satisfying to recognize his tactical smarts at work. The same goes for Gus's phone conversation with Kim after Mike inevitably foils her half-hearted assassination attempt.[†] When Gus is dumbstruck to hear that Jimmy talked Lalo out of his original plan, it could briefly play as if he is impressed that *anyone* has the ability to change Lalo's mind about anything, and that he perhaps wishes to enlist Jimmy's help in defeating his rival. Instead, it's Gus thinking through the real implication of Kim's words, recognizing that not even Slippin' Jimmy McGill—about whom Mike must have told him so much as Jimmy kept intersecting with the cartel— could actually talk Lalo into deviating from a plan. He realizes that Lalo must have agreed because the would-be hit was not the plan at all, but a distraction from the real plan. And because Gus has assumed for a while that Lalo would find his way to the Super Lab dig site, he immediately understands what the real plan must be.

This is a relatively compact episode, with most of the action taking place within the span of a couple of hours. Lalo sends Kim to shoot Gus, breaks into the laundromat while most of Mike's guys are away, takes Gus prisoner, records footage of the Super Lab to show Don Eladio, then gets shot with the pistol Gus hid in the treads of the digger. But the tension throughout is agonizing and exquisite, as are the performances by a group of actors who have to say much more with their expressions and body language than they do with dialogue.

---

* There's also the riveting sequence where Kim is stopped at a red light beside an Albuquerque PD patrol car, simultaneously afraid the cops will notice her and desperate to ask them for help. Director Gilligan and director of photography Paul Donachie shoot it with Seehorn out of focus, trusting that her body language will read even as the shot is centered on the two officers.

† Kim's armed walk up to Gus's door is a deliberate echo of Walt trying the same thing in the "Thirty-Eight Snub" episode of *Breaking Bad*. They even park in the same spot on Gus's street. Kim gets all the way to the door, though, where Tyrus calls to tell Walt to go home before he's even made it to the curb.

Gus shooting Lalo is perhaps the one point at which the episode falters. In general, Gilligan and the series' other directors have used *Saul* as a master class of how to film scenes in darkness—say, any of Jimmy's visits to Chuck's candlelit home, or Mike killing Werner out in the desert at night—that are nonetheless easy to see and understand. This sequence is not one of the better examples of that: watched on your average mid-priced smart TV, it's nearly as black as the infamous *Game of Thrones* episode where the White Walkers came to Winterfell and nobody in the audience could see what was happening.

But the sequences immediately before and after Gus goes for his hidden pistol more than make up for any visual muddiness, and/or plausibility questions about Gus's aim with a small gun in pitch blackness. The sheer joy that Lalo takes as he parades Gus through the Super Lab, sure that he has won the war and will return to Mexico in triumph, is a fitting final example of Lalo the irrepressible showman. And that in turn prompts a vicious and flowery monologue from Gus about how he really feels about Don Eladio and the rest of the cartel. When Gus finally gets to complete his master plan by poisoning Don Eladio in the *Breaking Bad* episode "Salud," there is no opportunity for him to express such sentiments; he's too busy vomiting up his share of the poisoned drink. So even though it is for a recording that none of its intended audience will ever see—and is really just a delaying tactic so Gus can circle around to the power cables and briefly plunge the room into darkness—it nonetheless feels emotionally satisfying to Gus, and to the viewer, that he gets to open up for once and say what's on his mind.

And after Gus flicks on some emergency lights and goes to confirm that his shots rang true, Lalo Salamanca dies laughing. Of course he does. Perhaps he is laughing at himself for finally underestimating an opponent. Perhaps he finds some humor in the improbable manner and location of his death. Perhaps his mind is completely elsewhere, his colorful life flashing before his eyes as blood oozes out of his chest and throat. Whatever the reason, it is the right note on which to say goodbye to a man who was so often amused by the situations in which he found himself, and by the people he met along the way. Hell, maybe now that he knows he has lost to Gus, and that Gus will likely carry out the rest of his scheme against his oblivious bosses, Lalo can finally take some pleasure in having gotten to spend time in the company of such a skilled and smart adversary.

Or maybe as he passes through the veil that separates this world from whatever comes after it, Lalo gets a glimpse of the dark joke that concludes the episode. After catching up with the four surviving main characters in the aftermath—Gus gets stitched up and calmly places Lyle in charge of Los Pollos Hermanos for a few days, and Mike gives Jimmy and Kim their marching orders while his guys clean up the bloody mess Lalo left in their apartment—we see Mike and Tyrus back at the Super Lab site, Tyrus using the digger to create a hole deep enough to bury the bodies of both Lalo and poor Howard. They will lie there together for years, maybe forever,* and the protagonists of *Breaking Bad* are going to get up to a lot of wacky and sometimes violent antics directly above their corpses.[†] Howard was not Lalo's final victim—several of Gus and Mike's soldiers are killed at the laundromat—but he is the last victim we have any investment in, and there's an odd poetry in seeing these avatars of cartel world and lawyer world laid to rest together.

At the apartment, Mike has told Jimmy and Kim to simply go back to their lives and act like everything is normal: "Today, you're Meryl Streep and Laurence Olivier." But can they? Jimmy has been more directly connected to violence in the past and demonstrated the ability to cut himself off from feelings of trauma and guilt. The whole feud with Howard, after all, only started as Jimmy's way of displacing the shame he felt for his role in Chuck's death. We know he can move on from this because we've seen him do it in his past, and we've seen him do it in his future: the Saul Goodman of *Breaking Bad* seems completely cut off from any emotion beyond the joy he takes from the life he's built for himself.

Like Jimmy, Kim is still in shock as Mike tells them what to do. But it feels like there's another layer to hers. Jimmy is horrified, still afraid of Lalo even after Mike strongly implies that he's dead for real this time.[‡] Kim, though, seems not just horrified, but ashamed. She did this. All of this. She came up with the idea to destroy Howard's reputation. She went to visit Lalo in jail. She is responsible for both of those men being in her apartment at the same time. (Jimmy holds some responsibility as well, but just as Kim believes she can and

---

* After Walt and Jesse burn the Lab down at the end of *Breaking Bad* Season 4, the DEA gets to explore the ruins, but nobody seems interested in digging up the foundations of the place. When I asked Gordon Smith about this, he said, "I think maybe they would just leave them there forever, unless for some reason they got some information that something is buried there. Why would you dig up the floor? It's a question of what you do with a condemned Super Lab? I don't really know what the EPA rules are for conflagrations in mega Super Labs."

† The next time you watch "Fly," the classic/divisive episode where Walt and Jesse chase a pesky insect around the Lab, good luck not thinking about what's right beneath their feet.

‡ This helps explain why Saul seems so relieved to learn that Walt and Jesse were not sent by Lalo, even though that abduction happens years after Lalo Salamanca was seen by anyone. Jimmy was already told once that Lalo died, and then the man was standing in his living room attaching a silencer to a pistol. Fool me once, shame on you. Fool me twice after I've been traumatized for life? Shame on me. Also, before Lalo puts the gag on Jimmy earlier in the episode, Lalo refers to Nacho by his real name, prompting Jimmy to attempt to put the blame on poor Ignacio, even saying it the same way he does to Walt and Jesse. Whether or not he learns in between that Nacho is dead, it becomes almost a sense memory thing for Saul when he thinks he's run into trouble with the cartel again.

should do any job herself, she also believes that if something was going to be stopped, she's the one who should have stopped it.) How, she seems to be wondering in this moment, did she become this person? How did she allow her life to take her to a point where she was on the verge of trying to assassinate a stranger? The woman sitting on the edge of this bed, barely able to pay attention to the instructions she's being given, is not someone whom the Kim Wexler at the start of the series would tolerate, or even recognize. How much of that Kim is left in this one, and how much longer will this Kim be able to stand who and what she has become?

As much fun as it was to watch Lalo stalk his way around town over the last few seasons, all the important questions that need to be answered in this final season revolve around Jimmy and Kim, and what happens to them in both body and spirit. Lalo Salamanca is dead, but *Better Call Saul* still has plenty of story left to tell in these last five hours.

SEASON 6, EPISODE 9
WRITTEN BY ANN CHERKIS
DIRECTED BY MICHAEL MORRIS

"Fun and Games"

"End of an era." —**Rich Schweikart**

"Fun and Games" brings us the moment that, before *Better Call Saul* debuted, all of us expected to come much sooner, and many of us really wanted: the full, unequivocal Saul Goodman in the series' present-day action. Bad comb-over, bluetooth, Caddy with "LWYRUP" license plate, utter lack of shame—the works.

Only by now, it is the moment none of us wants, and certainly not in the way that the series chooses to give it to us. Because to say hello to Saul Goodman means saying goodbye to our pal Jimmy McGill. And, even more bleakly, it means saying goodbye to Kim Wexler. Why would we have ever rooted for such a thing?

Despite knowing it was coming, it is a moment for which we were not prepared. *Better Call Saul* has done too good a job making us invest in Jimmy, and in Kim. It has teased us often in the past with the notion that Jimmy had finally gone full Saul. But, as it turns out, it wasn't when he began practicing law under that name. And it wasn't when he defended Lalo in court, even if Saul got to slip out for a few moments there. With so little time left before the finale, and so much to be dealt with in that time, Jimmy's complete transformation into Saul—not just the name, not just the tacky suits, but the empty shell of a man with no conscience and no remorse—was an inevitability. But it was an inevitability we tried putting out of our heads, because of the line it would draw between the show we've watched for these five-plus seasons and the one we remember so well for introducing Saul, Mike, and Gus.

"Fun and Games" draws that line as explicitly as it possibly can. Like that sequence during Lalo's defense in "JMM," one moment we are watching Jimmy McGill, and the next we are seeing Saul Goodman. Now, though, it is not a temporary outburst, but the permanent transformation. And it happens because Kim walks out of Jimmy's life.

The proper introduction of Saul feels shocking because of the deliberately abrupt time jump—modeled on the famous *2001: A Space Odyssey* edit of a prehistoric bone turning into a spaceship.* One moment, Jimmy is listening

---

* Saul, like Jimmy, loves to quote movies. So of course his proper introduction is inspired by an iconic movie moment.

to Kim pack up her stuff as she prepares to leave him. The next, Saul is waking up in bed in his garish mansion after a night with a sex worker—a deeply felt relationship replaced by a transactional one, and a complicated man replaced by a deliberate self-caricature.

But Saul's long-delayed arrival is shocking because so much of "Fun and Games" to that point acts like it wants to live up to its title as best it can under the current narrative circumstances. It does not start out like an episode that will be saying goodbye to our central characters as we knew them, and to the point in time at which we've been following them. It seems like a prototypical calm-after-the-storm story, giving both the characters and audience a chance to catch their breath before the endgame.

It is, in other words, one more Slippin' Jimmy confidence trick—albeit one that results in Jimmy himself vanishing.

The episode begins with a montage of three of our four surviving characters going about their business on the morning after Howard Hamlin and Lalo Salamanca were murdered and buried in a hole together. Mike is still cleaning up the crime scene at the apartment, and Jimmy and Kim are applying their very different approaches to criminal law. The scenes are shot and edited in a way that allows images from lawyer world to dissolve into ones from cartel world, and vice versa: coffee pouring from the courthouse vending machine becomes blood being squeezed out of a sponge, while Kim showing the jury a photo of her physically abused client turns into Mike studying a picture of the apartment pre-cleanup for comparison's sake. Like the shot of Lalo and Howard lying together in their eternal resting place, it is the *Saul* creative team using visual language to make clear that whatever separation once existed between the two worlds no longer exists. Mike finishes the cleanup job, and the spouses return home, but only to pack up to stay at a hotel because their home is not a place where they will be able to sleep that night. (Or ever, at least for Kim.)

From there, we follow Gus down to Mexico to be grilled by Don Eladio and Juan Bolsa regarding Hector's accusations of treachery against the Chicken Man. This turns out to be a show trial out of deference to the man Hector used to be, as we realize Lalo did too good a job of faking his own death following the botched hit on his compound. There is a charred corpse that matches his dental records (RIP, Mateo), and the only person Lalo spoke to after going on the run was his nonverbal uncle, whose faculties are no longer trusted by the head of the cartel. (After the Cousins wheel Hector away, Eladio even does a cruel impression of how Hector's face contorts post-stroke.) The scene is tense not because Gus is at any real risk of being discovered by Eladio or Juan at this stage of his plans, but because it feels like a storytelling thread is being tied off, for good. All six men gathered around Eladio's pool will be killed within a few years. With Lalo dead, Gus has already won. But he has also already lost, because his desire for a very specific kind of revenge—one where Hector Salamanca is forced to helplessly watch his nemesis destroy his family and organization—will ultimately be his own undoing.[*] But there is really no more to tell about this particular corner of the story . . .

. . . well, mostly. After he returns to his own home, opens the shutters to let daylight back in, and instructs Mike to resume construction on the Super Lab,[†] Gustavo Fring allows himself an indulgence, but only briefly. He heads to a local restaurant to enjoy both the wine and the chance to gently flirt with its charming sommelier, David.[‡]

"Hermanos," the *Breaking Bad* episode featuring the flashback where Hector murders Gus's partner Max, implied that Gus and Max were lovers—or, at least, established that Hector believed them to be. (Hector's gay panic was where his resentment of and suspicion toward the Chicken Man began.) *BB* never explicitly said this, and Giancarlo Esposito talked in the past about how he appreciated the ambiguity about how many layers existed within that partnership. Here, though, there is no mistaking Gus's feelings regarding David. It is a remarkable scene to witness because Esposito gets to play a Gus unlike any we have seen before on either series. To date, there have been three flavors of Gus: (1) The exceedingly polite local business owner who would love to offer you some of his signature spice curls; (2) The stoic, tight-lipped cartel executive; and (3) The avenging angel who will never get past that moment when Hector Salamanca put a bullet in Max's head. This man at the wine bar is very clearly the same as those, yet he is unlike any of them. He is . . . *enjoying* himself. He is reserved in speech, not because he is afraid to betray any weakness to potential enemies, but because he just wants to hear this beautiful man talk about wine. He is still precise in all things, as we see in the way he prepares to drink the expensive Côte Rôtie that David has poured for him. Yet he is almost unnervingly relaxed, relatively speaking, because of the pleasure he gets from being around the boy he likes.

The problem, as Inigo Montoya from *The Princess Bride* might tell you, is that when you devote your life to the revenge business, you have precious little room for anything else. When David steps away for a moment, Gus's contented

---

[*]   *DING! DING! DING!*

[†]   The show never gets around to explicitly showing Mike's elevation above Victor and Tyrus on the Pollos Hermanos org chart, but it's implied by this point. "We decided that Mike had proven himself invaluable by the end of *Better Call Saul*," says Peter Gould. "Tyrus probably ain't happy that he's been superseded."

[‡]   David is played by Reed Diamond, who left the ensemble of nineties cop drama *Homicide: Life on the Street* shortly before Esposito joined it. The two did share some scenes together in a *Homicide* reunion movie, and they have obvious chemistry here.

expression hardens into his more recognizable paranoid mask. Gus is a man in the midst of an elaborate, multiyear plot to destroy his enemies while making himself fabulously wealthy. Going any further than very occasional conversations with David (who implies he hasn't seen Gus in quite some time) would be dangerous for both of them. It is one thing for Hector to imply that Gus is gay, and another for anyone in the cartel to potentially find proof of it. And leaving institutional homophobia out of the equation, it is simply unfair of Gus to take on anyone as a romantic partner at a time such as this, because the possibility exists that they could wind up with a fate similar to Max's. (For that matter, given how Gus has turned his entire life into a quest to avenge Max's death, he might view getting involved with anyone else as a betrayal.) In the aftermath of vanquishing Lalo, Gus permits himself the smallest of celebrations, but that is all it can be. He leaves a generous tip on the bar and exits before David can return to tempt him further.

It's a lovely, terribly sad scene—almost by itself justifying Gus's prominence on a show where he was more boxed in as a character than anyone else in the ensemble. And, like the one at Don Eladio's pool, it plays as something of a coda to a story we've already watched. The larger tale of Gus Fring is complete. We know how he builds his empire and then how he lets Walter White topple the whole thing. There are no major plot questions to be answered, so instead he is given this final grace note before the series as a whole moves on to its next phase.

And boy, does it. Mike has a fraught conversation with Nacho's father Manuel about what happened to his son, that is itself an attempt to efficiently resolve old business,* and then we finally return to Jimmy and Kim. They are back in the familiar HHM atrium for Howard's memorial. Even before Rich Schweikart explains that the firm is renaming itself—all three name partners are now dead, after all—and downsizing to a smaller office elsewhere in Albuquerque, it feels like something important has been brought to an abrupt end. In a full-circle moment at the start of the sequence, Jimmy notices that building management finally got around to replacing the trash can he kicked after a

---

* This scene concludes Mike's own character arc on the series. For all the terrible things he has already done for Gus, there was still a part of him that couldn't let go of his days as a cop—couldn't fully accept that he had become an instrument of evil. When he promises Manuel that justice is coming for the Salamancas, it's to make himself feel good at least as much as it is meant for Manuel—and Manuel is not having it at all. The disapproving look he gives Mike as he tells him that this is not about justice, but never-ending revenge, hits Mike harder than all but a few things he's experienced through the run of the series. He tried to do right by Nacho, and largely failed. He tried to offer comforting words to Nacho's father and failed. He is a thug working for a kingpin. He can't deny it. Gus asking him to get back to work on the Super Lab is just a reminder of how he also failed his friend Werner, and then murdered him. By the time we first see him on *Breaking Bad*, Mike has let go of these illusions.

frustrating meeting with Howard way back in the series premiere. (The dented version was still in place as of the Season 4 finale.) Once inside the memorial, we get a glimpse of many of the key players from lawyer world, including Rich, Cliff Main, and Cheryl Hamlin. If the gang isn't all here, it is enough of a quorum for what turns out to be yet another goodbye to what this show was.

The whole event is, of course, excruciating for Jimmy and Kim, two of the three people most responsible for the death of the man being honored here. (The third is unable to attend but is otherwise *very* close to the deceased.) They cannot give Howard's widow closure on what actually happened. In fact, Kim makes things worse for her, deflecting Cheryl's understandable skepticism about her late husband's would-be drug use with an invented anecdote about walking in on Howard snorting a line in his office. In the process, she transmutes Cheryl's suspicions into self-loathing, sending the poor woman crying into the bathroom, under the belief that she failed to notice her own husband—even an estranged one—falling into addiction.

It is a necessary lie for Kim, and it is also the last straw. Down in the parking garage where she and Jimmy once shared a cigarette, Jimmy tries to put the whole Howard/Lalo affair behind them. Once again demonstrating his vast gift for compartmentalization, he tells his wife, "I know that was tough. But it's over now. I mean, really over. Let the healing begin." Kim leans in to give him a deep kiss, then wordlessly climbs into her own car and drives off, leaving him standing there, a bit puzzled by her reaction. He cannot possibly fathom what is already becoming clear to those of us watching, but she has just kissed him—and this entire life—goodbye.

Kim stops in court to explain that she has resigned from the New Mexico bar and left the legal profession altogether. In many ways, this is a greater tragedy than what follows between her and a confused, apoplectic, ultimately devastated Jimmy. Back in the apartment, dressed in casual clothes rather than her familiar tailored suits, she will tell him that she has had the time of her life with him. And that's true. But however much she loved Jimmy, she loved the law far more deeply. And all of it is ruined for her now. She can't be with him because of how many people get hurt in their wake. She can't practice law because it would remind her too much of Howard Hamlin, and about all the ethical rules she allowed herself to break because—as she will tell Jimmy, her voice so filled with self-loathing it's a wonder the sentence can get out at all—"I was having too much . . . *fun*." (That last word causes her so much agony, it's as if it emerged from her throat covered in razor wire.) Kim doesn't get to do the job she was born for. Her clients don't get the benefit of her skill and compassion. And it sure looks like Jimmy's cut of the Sandpiper settlement—the purported reason for the scam against Howard, even though we knew from the start Kim was motivated by something far less noble—goes into financing Saul's lavish new lifestyle, rather than funding criminal defense for the poor. It was all for nothing—less than nothing, given all the carnage Kim realizes they have left in their wake. They publicly humiliated Chuck in a way that fueled the worst aspects of his mental illness, ultimately making him feel like he'd be better off burning to death. They ruined Howard's reputation simply because they could, maneuvering him into a place where Lalo would kill him. They brought down HHM entirely. Again and again, they have done things that would have once seemed unthinkable to either or both of them, from Jimmy deliberately placing himself in an assassin's path (and chasing that experience with a warm gulp of his own piss) to Kim walking up to a stranger's front door with the intention of shooting him.

"You asked if you were bad for me," she tells her wounded spouse, recalling a conversation from early in the previous season finale. "That's not it. We are bad for each other."

The whole apartment scene is an absolute acting marvel from both Bob Odenkirk and Rhea Seehorn. He plays Jimmy as thunderstruck and irreparably wounded. She plays Kim as composed and controlled until she absolutely isn't, in that horrible moment when Jimmy tries to fix everything by reminding Kim that he loves her—the first time in the entire series that either of them has said this to the other on camera—and she replies, "I love you, too. But *so what?*" She is not saying it to be cruel. She is not attempting to dismiss his feelings as insincere, nor is she denying her own. She is just delivering the last closing statement of her life, and pointing out that their love has dire, at times fatal, consequences for other people, and the only way to prevent more pain is to get out now.

So a sobbing Kim walks back to the bedroom to resume packing. Jimmy stands there watching her. Both are shot from behind, and not just to give us one last look at Kim's trademark ponytail and Jimmy's familiar haircut. It is an exit for each of them—Kim walking offstage, Jimmy fading into Saul Goodman. Whatever comes next, this masterful hour of television says farewell to them as a couple, and to the versions of them we have known for so long.

Earlier, in the HHM lobby, Rich will say goodbye to Jimmy, before stopping to correct himself and address the man in front of him as Saul. This is another last in an episode full of them: the last time anyone in Albuquerque, or perhaps in the audience, will ever mistake the one identity for the other. Because what follows is Saul in all his glory: partying all night, working every minute of the day, barking orders through his earpiece at the increasingly bitter and cynical Francesca.

Again, we were meant to get here much sooner. Vince Gilligan and Peter Gould assumed they would be doing scenes set in Saul's "cathedral of justice" office by the end of the first season. Two things got in the way of that plan. First, they realized that they really liked Jimmy McGill, and wanted to spend more time with him. And second, they realized that they really liked Kim Wexler, and that a show where Jimmy raced into being Saul would not be doing right by Kim—assuming it still had room for her at all. So because their creators fell in love with them, these two characters got to fall in love with each other, and got to make the audience fall in love with them, too.

But so what?

Was it worth the joy these characters and their relationship gave us if this was where it was going to end? Given that we are not characters living in the Heisenberg-verse, I would argue that of course it was. The work Odenkirk, Seehorn, and their colleagues have done in building up Jimmy and Kim as both individuals and partners in romance and crime has been extraordinary. That it hurts to see these versions of them go, possibly forever, is part of the bargain you make when you begin a show like this. It wouldn't cause this much pain if it hadn't been so good for so long—if we hadn't, like Kim and Jimmy running their latest con, or even like Walter White and Jesse Pinkman exploiting the power of magnetism, been having so much *fun*.

And now we have left behind the show none of us expected, much less expected to care for as deeply as we have. In the past, when we arrived at these would-be crossroads, I often asked Peter Gould whether Jimmy had finally become Saul—and whether, as a reflection of this, the scripts now referred to him as such. As you know if you've been reading this far, Gould once told me, "My guess is that we'll call him Jimmy as long as Kim does."

Kim is gone now, and not coincidentally, in the very next scene after she walks out of our sight, the script explicitly refers to the man we are watching as Saul. He tried to be good for so long, and for so many reasons: to earn his brother's respect, to connect with his elderly clients, to impress Kim, and because doing good had the unexpected side benefit of making him feel good. Chuck is dead. The elder-law practice is long in the rearview, replaced by clients like Spooge. Nothing feels good anymore except Kim. Is it any wonder that, from our perspective as viewers, the instant Kim leaves, Saul materializes? She was the last thing standing in the way of his ascendance, and of the death of Jimmy McGill.

End of an era, indeed.

Better Call Saul Star Rhea Seehorn on Jimmy and Kim's "Alarming" and "Heartbreaking" Fight

[This story originally ran on RollingStone.com on July 18, 2022]

Did you know before you got this script that this would be how Kim and Jimmy's relationship ended?
No. No, I did not.

So what was your response to reading the script, getting through that scene, and then seeing that the very next scene is Saul Goodman?
It was alarming, and it was heartbreaking. I found it just an incredibly heartbreaking scene. Because it is not about two people falling out of love. They still love each other deeply. That scene is the first time we've heard them say "I love you," even though I personally think they've said it to each other often off-screen before. But to hear him say it for the first time in the show, and her response to be, "*So what?*"—and not in a flippant way, but her saying that it can't alter the erosion of who she is at this point. I just found it tragic and sad, and really interesting storytelling. We made a choice, when Bob and I were rehearsing with [director] Michael [Morris]. We spent a lot of time rehearsing it, and realized that we needed to have [director of photography] Marshall Adams and our camera ops come in because we wanted it to be relentless. I haven't seen it myself yet, but people that have seen versions have said, "I had to take a moment and walk around the block after it." It's what is going on in the scene, it's how it's performed, but it's also how it's being filmed in this breathless way. There's no escape from this argument, and it feels as overwhelming to the audience as the people doing it. It was important to us to keep that energy of "where's this going, where's this going, please don't go off a cliff," and then it goes off a cliff.

Back when you still allowed yourself to speculate on where Kim's story was going, had this scenario been one you considered?
No, not in its intricacies. But there's always the possibility of, "Does she leave him?" But I feel like it's a much more intelligent, intricate, and complex breakup. Sometimes, I can look at the scripts just as a fan, because I love the show, and I was like, "Oh, this would be more rewarding to me if I was a fan watching it." It's not that I'm storming out because, "I can't stand your shenanigans anymore!" It's complex. All the intelligence and morality and ethics

you've seen from Kim in earlier seasons leads to that moment where she's feeling, "I just can't keep eating myself alive." She can't figure out another way to molt the skin that she made for herself. And I didn't see all of that coming—not that kind of complexity, not that kind of pain. I think you almost could have predicted that she'd leave that relationship in anger. But it's beautiful.

How do you feel about the way the episode is structured so that Jimmy is watching her pack and then the very next thing we see is Saul Goodman, and the way it suggests that Kim was the only thing preventing him from becoming this person?
I found it just like a punch in the gut. [*laughs*] Very upsetting. I personally don't see it as only because of Kim that he becomes Saul. It's a series of events we've seen unfold, including events while he was growing up before we started watching the series. But you're right that she's last man standing in the way of it. But that is also a horrible tragedy. It makes me think about the Saul Goodman that we all thought was, at worst, a person with no conscience who's fine ordering hits on people and at best, a clown. And now I think that if I were to revisit *Breaking Bad* right now, I would find the character sad. I'll never not be able to see it as a tragic character now. It's so brilliant that they've managed to change your perspective on the show that already existed.

You've spent a lot of time with Jonathan Banks and Giancarlo Esposito over these years, but never on-camera before this season, when Kim finally interacted with Mike a few times and had a phone conversation with Gus. Would the experience have felt incomplete to you if one or both of those hadn't happened?
Incomplete? No. I am so far past where the needle on the dial says "complete." Given what I was given to do on this show, I won a long time ago. Right now, we're in full, happy cloud nine of what they allow me to do. But I am super, super grateful I got to do a scene with Jonathan. And not just because, as an actor, I would be remiss in not getting to play opposite, but also as those two characters. I really wanted to work on a scene that was Kim Wexler talking to Mike Ehrmantraut. And I got to direct him as well, and I got to direct Giancarlo in that episode.

Finally, you cannot say whether or not you'll be appearing on the show again. But if this is the last we see of Kim, can you reflect back upon what this experience has been like for you?
Like none other. I always said that if I wasn't an actor, I would have liked to be a psychologist. And I kind of got to be. The mental gymnastics of figuring out

this character that I just love—and I love how inscrutable she is so often. Following these very small cracks in the glaze of this vase has been so rewarding. Because they don't say plot should dictate character, they say character should dictate plot. Every time Kim shifted, it was shocking, and then it wasn't. You're like, "Oh, right, that's probably who she was." That has been so much fun, to work that hard on that level of detail of human behavior, so that you can afford yourself a story that you never saw coming. There is no bigger gift to an actor [than] to do a role like this.

And then you hand me my scene partner, with whom I spent most of seven years. Bob said this about me, and I one hundred percent can say it about him: he makes me a better actor. He makes me more present. He makes me want to stay up two more hours to work on this stuff. Not "makes," but he inspires you to! And then you get directors and showrunners who are great. It's an incredible feeling to be supported as a freelance person. And to have your heroes say, "Yeah, I think you can do it. Let's go." It's a support system like no other. And every single person there is in service of one thing: What's the smartest and most authentic story we can tell about these characters? And then let the audience be as smart as they are, and meet us where they're at. And they did, episode after episode.

SEASON 6, EPISODE 10
WRITTEN BY ALISON TATLOCK
DIRECTED BY MICHELLE MACLAREN

"Nippy"

"So after all that? A happy ending." —**Gene**

The opening title sequence for "Nippy" begins as one with which *Better Call Saul* viewers are quite familiar: Saul Goodman's "World's 2nd Greatest Lawyer" coffee mug* falling off his desk en route to shattering. But the mug's downward flight is interrupted this time. The videotape glitches, an old artifact from the days of VHS tapes warping with age (or heat, or cold, or pretty much any circumstance hazardous to a pretty fragile brand of physical media), and then it stops altogether, replaced by a blue video screen (itself familiar from the VCR age, particularly for homemade recordings) featuring this series' title and creator credits (both in the old-fashioned VHS mono font).

We are no longer, it seems, watching the same series we had for the previous fifty-nine episodes. The "[This] and [That]" title rubric from the rest of this season is gone. And rather than spend more time in Saul Goodman's heyday after the shocking time jump at the end of "Fun and Games," "Nippy" takes place entirely in the black-and-white world of Gene from Cinnabon.

After waiting so, so, so long to finally give us the real Saul as part of the narrative present, you would think the show would want to linger there while there's still time left to do so. Instead, it's startling to rush completely past that, to leave behind Kim, Mike, and Gus, and to make an extended stop in Omaha after previous seasons visited for only a few minutes apiece.

But if "Nippy" is not at all the episode we might have expected as the immediate follow-up to "Fun and Games," it's also an absolute romp, finding a charming way to merge the Gene and Jimmy personae while we're still recovering from the gut punch of waking up with Saul in bed last time.

As our first full Gene episode, "Nippy" features abundant callbacks to those earlier teasers. The episode, of course, requires Gene to find a way out of the grip that Jeff the cab driver† has on him. But there are frequent reminders

---

* You can view the shift from Kim's various "World's 2nd Best Lawyer" gag gifts to this as Saul mocking the ex-wife who abandoned him when he needed her most, or simply as a factual acknowledgment that the only attorney Saul felt was better than him has quit the profession altogether.

† Jeff looks very different this time, because actor Don Harvey was unavailable to reprise the role from the fourth and fifth season premieres and is replaced by Pat Healy. It's not an ideal situation, but a risk a show takes when a crucial role is played by an actor who appears only once per season, and thus isn't under contract to return whenever necessary. Healy also plays Jeff as more of a

of other Omaha segments. Nick the security guard, for instance, still remembers Gene telling the shoplifter to ask for a lawyer in the Season 3 teaser, and one of the glimpses of the garbage room during this episode's montages shows the "SG was here" message Gene scratched into the wall while trapped there at the start of Season 2.

But above all else, it is an hour that defies the stark black-and-white photography that has been a signature of the Gene timeline. It brings emotional color, thrills, and fun into the life of a man who believed he had forever denied himself these pleasures in return for staying out of prison. To get Jeff off his back, Gene has to embrace the parts of himself he thought he left behind in Albuquerque, acting as con man, master thief, and film producer all at the same time.

It's an utter gas. The great *Breaking Bad* director Michelle MacLaren returns for her third and final *Saul* outing, teamed with writer Alison Tatlock for a heist story that on one hand is lower-stakes than almost anything featured on either series so far—it's just a department store being hit for a few dozen items that will barely be missed—but on the other is so important because it allows Gene to stop hiding and embrace his old identities.

From the first black-and-white image, we can determine that we are in the Gene timeline. But then we get another curveball with the appearance of comedy legend Carol Burnett* as Marion. She is a prideful old lady who can get around just fine with her scooter and her grabber, thank you very much. But she is also an easy mark for the man who was once the most popular elder-law attorney in the greater Albuquerque area. He has moved some snow and slush around on her route back from the grocery store to stall out her scooter long enough for a vintage Jimmy McGill spiel about his missing (and wholly fictional) dog Nippy, lowering her defenses enough that she lets him push her up the slope, which in turn lets him cut a wire on the motor so she requires even more assistance. By the time Jeff comes home from work and is stunned to find the infamous Saul Goodman swapping stories and drinks with his mother, it's already all over. He's the true target of the scam, and he doesn't even realize it.

---

numbskull than the menacing Harvey version, who was so eager to hear Gene say Saul Goodman's catchphrase.

* You may recall from several seasons ago (and/or several hundred pages ago) that Chuck once invoked Burnett in a conversation with his wife Rebecca. So if the brothers McGill watched Carol Burnett, and if Gene did not instantly compliment Marion on her resemblance to Carol Burnett, it invites the question: What does the Heisenberg-verse version of Carol Burnett look like? When I asked Peter Gould about this during one of our Zooms, he stared at me for a long time—less confused by the question itself than that any rational human being would think to ask it—and finally said, "That's like a Zen koan. That's not a question that a mortal can answer. Like, what's moving, is it the flag or is it the wind? I don't know."

Gene's scheme comes, as any plan in this franchise must, in stages. Step 1: Befriend Marion as a way to put Jeff on the defensive, rather than leaving the cabbie feeling like he has the power in this relationship. Step 2: Convince Jeff that what he wants is not to blackmail Gene, but a chance to be part of "the game," leading the kind of glamorous and adventurous life Gene himself enjoyed as Saul Goodman. Step 3: Befriend mall security guards Nick and Frank,* then figure out how long eating a single Cinnabon might distract Frank from looking at the security monitors. Step 4: Pace out the distance between all the most valuable goods at Lancaster's department store and create a model for Jeff to use to rehearse a quick, carefully choreographed robbery that will go unnoticed long enough for the security videos to be automatically erased. Step 5: Arrange for Jeff to be smuggled into the Lancaster loading dock inside a delivery crate. Step 6: Hang with Frank like always while Jeff completes what is supposed to be a three-minute robbery, then arrange for Jeff's friend Buddy to pick up the loot crate in the morning while Jeff casually walks out after hiding out for the night in the bathroom.

There is, of course, a seventh step to the scheme, of which Jeff is unaware until after the theft is pulled off: Gene will use his knowledge of all the laws Jeff just broke as a way to neutralize the threat of Jeff exposing his identity, in a bit of "mutually assured destruction." It is very much a Jimmy McGill kind of solution, and a way to keep distinguishing him from the high school chemistry teacher he mentions while helping Jeff rehearse for the heist. Walt would have found a way to poison Jeff or blow him up real good, while Gene grifts him into submission.

All of this is presented with the panache you would expect from Team *Saul*, especially with MacLaren back behind the camera for the first time since early in Season 4. There are split screens, jaunty music—including a piece of Lalo Schifrin's score from the original *Mission: Impossible* TV show, called "Jim on the Move"—the security monitors being reflected in Gene's glasses, and other stylistic flourishes. When Gene makes Jeff run through the department store mock-up[†] again and again like he's Nathan Fielder in *The Rehearsal*, it is a reminder that Jimmy rarely seemed happier than when he was directing TV commercials. All the cons, all the courtroom appearances, all the brand-building stunts were ultimately a manifestation of James Morgan McGill the showman. Here, he is staging a performance for a pair of half-wits, but it's all he needs to do.

---

*   Frank is played by *Parks and Recreation* alum Jim O'Heir. Few actors on television are more convincing when they're enjoying foods that are bad for them.

†   Jimmy Loves Movies: his instructions to Jeff and Buddy during this sequence feature rhyming instructions in the vein of the final briefing from *The Dirty Dozen*.

Jimmy's skills as a performer prove even more necessary when the plan hits a snag, just as every Heisenberg-verse plan must at some point. In this case, it is Jeff slipping on a newly waxed spot on the department store floor and seemingly knocking himself out in the process. This is something of a callback itself, to when Chuck fell and hit his head while making a scene at the copy shop in the Season 2 finale. And it means that Gene has to keep Frank from turning back to the monitors even after the guard has spent three-plus minutes eating a Cinnabon with a knife and fork. So he fakes an emotional breakdown, talking about the empty life he has: both parents dead, brother dead, no wife, no children, no friends, no one to care about him if he were to die. Like so many of Jimmy McGill's performances—and Walter White's, for that matter—it is convincing because so much of it is rooted in truth. Gene cries more over the thought of his dead brother than Jimmy ever allowed himself to do in the immediate aftermath of Chuck's suicide. We know from Gene's past appearances that his existence in Omaha is as empty and lonely as he describes it to Frank. He is miserable—just slightly less miserable than he would be behind bars. He is able to hold Frank's attention long enough for Jeff to wake up, steal the remaining items on his list, and get to his men's room hiding place. But after, Gene has to stop to compose himself in a blind spot for the mall's security cameras. You can see his nerves are frazzled from the caper nearly going awry, but also from having to open up so many wounds he had been able to ignore for so long.

It's a masterful performance from Gene, and from Bob Odenkirk, who manages to play every layer of the pathos in that scene while also making it really funny when Gene tries to peer around Frank to look at the monitors even as he is continuing his sob story. Just a wonderful summation of so many of the things that he has been able to do in these overlapping roles across two shows.

The successful stalemate with Jeff seems to put a new bounce in Gene's step. He goes through work like he genuinely enjoys it, even losing track of when his lunch break is supposed to be as time flies while he's having fun. He allows himself the chance to visit the scene of the crime he so expertly orchestrated, and as he wanders around Lancaster's, he can't help but notice a gaudy shirt and necktie that he thinks would look great together. He even indulges himself by holding them up to himself in front of a mirror. He could buy them both, and a suit to go with them. But those are the clothes of the man he was, not the one he has had to become, so an indulgence is all it is. We conclude the episode with Gene drifting out of frame as the shirt and tie combo are the only parts of the image in focus. SG was here. And so was JMM.

SEASON 6, EPISODE 11
WRITTEN AND DIRECTED BY THOMAS SCHNAUZ

"Breaking Bad"

"She asked about me." —**Gene**

And here they finally are. Walter White and Jesse Pinkman. As the latter would say: "Yeah, bitch!"

Saul Goodman was introduced on a *Breaking Bad* episode titled "Better Call Saul," so it seems only fitting that the *Better Call Saul* episode presenting those same events from Saul's perspective should be titled "Breaking Bad." The hour finally brings us the promised cameos by Bryan Cranston and Aaron Paul as Walt and Jesse, and it shows the audience some of what Saul was thinking and doing when his new clients weren't around. But it's much less interested in presenting an alternate history of the Heisenberg era than in drawing parallels between the man Jimmy McGill had become by that point in his life and the man that Gene Takovic is rapidly letting himself become again.

Where "Nippy" took place entirely in Omaha, "Breaking Bad" splits its time between the black-and-white Gene world and the many colors—sometimes muted, sometimes garish—of Saul world circa *Breaking Bad* Season 2. We open with Saul lying on the floor of the RV* (the Crystal Ship, as Jesse likes to call it), a bag over his head as he is driven into the desert by men he assumes work for Lalo Salamanca. Then we are back in the Gene timeline, but in Albuquerque, catching up with a miserable Francesca, who now has to pay the bills managing a small apartment building occupied by pot-dealing morons. It is November 12, 2010, eight months since Gene began managing the Cinnabon, two months after the events of both the *Breaking Bad* finale and *El Camino,* and a few weeks after Gene and Jeff robbed the department store. It is also Jimmy McGill's fiftieth birthday, in a franchise where fiftieth birthdays tend to be important turning points for the protagonists. But more importantly, it is the date on which Saul and Francesca agreed—in the flash-forward teaser from Season 4's "Quite a Ride"†—that she would be waiting by a pay

---

* The original RV set from *Breaking Bad* was long gone, so, as this episode's writer/director Thomas Schnauz explains, "That sucker was (re)built from scratch. We had airbags that would lift it off the ground and shake it around as well."

† That "Quite a Ride" phone call was a point of contention in the writers' room—not to the degree of putting a machine gun in Walter White's trunk without having any idea why he would need it (which Vince Gilligan has called the biggest headache the writers made for themselves on *Breaking Bad*), but definitely a down-the-road problem the team had created for themselves. "It was added after we broke the episode in the writers' room," recalls Schnauz. "Peter and Ann [Cherkis] wrote that

phone for an important call.* The person on the other end of the line is our man, desperate for any good news from his old stomping grounds. Most of what Francesca (who is being paid for her time from some cash Saul buried before leaving town) has to offer is the bad kind: all of Saul's seemingly hidden assets have been seized, and with everyone else connected to Walt's exploits either dead or cooperating with authorities, Saul and Jesse are the two big targets remaining.†

There is one promising development Francesca reluctantly shares, out of the last residue of affection she still has for the man who originally hired her: Kim called to check up on her after Walt and Saul's exploits became very public, and she "asked if you were alive." This is an understandable question from a woman who once loved him, but Gene treats Kim's attempt for closure instead as an opening to reach out to her. She has apparently stuck to her decision to leave the law and is working for a sprinkler company in central Florida. We do not hear either end of the conversation Gene has when he calls the place, as Thomas Schnauz shoots it from outside the grimy roadside phone booth. But we can tell from Bob Odenkirk's performance that it goes very, very badly. (If Kim couldn't abide being with Jimmy after one person was killed, how do you think she reacted to the news that he had aided and abetted a drug kingpin

---

into the episode after the season was broken and decided we needed something. I don't know what they were thinking! When I saw it, I was like, 'What the hell is this?' Gordon [Smith] and the others joke that I was against the whole thing, and somehow it landed in my lap and I had to address it [here]."

* Speaking of that "Quite a Ride" teaser and phone calls, there is still that matter of which attorney's business card Saul gave to Francesca. Memories differ on what the original plan was. Ann Cherkis, who wrote "Quite a Ride," says she and Peter Gould never really discussed whose card it was. But Ariel Levine, who was the writers' assistant at the time (before becoming a full-fledged writer in later seasons), recalls that the initial plan was to show enough of the card that viewers could see it was Kim's. Before filming, she explains, it was decided to leave things ambiguous so the writers would have options for later. "We briefly played with the idea of revisiting the business card again in Season Five," Levine says, "and one of our pitches was that it could've been Howard's info! Another close call." With Howard dead and Kim out of the profession by this point, whose card was it? "It was most likely Schweikart's," says Gould.

† Vince Gilligan used El Camino to tie off one semi-loose Breaking Bad story thread by having Jesse hear a radio report clarifying that Walt definitely died from the gunshot wound. (Some fans had speculated that he somehow survived.) Schnauz uses Gene's conversation with Francesca to provide some more closure to the original series. We learn that the lottery ticket that Walt gave Skyler, featuring the GPS coordinates of Hank and Gomez's burial site, managed to get Skyler out of her legal trouble, as Walt had hoped. More amusingly, we find out that Huell made it home to Louisiana, getting off scot-free from his involvement in the criminal enterprise because Hank and Gomez left him illegally in a DEA safe house while they went off in their doomed pursuit of Walt. Breaking Bad fans used to jokingly wonder whether Huell just stayed in that safe house forever. "I hated breaking that illusion," says Schnauz. "I wanted to maybe keep that going. But we had to address that." Meanwhile, Schnauz had long wanted to establish that Daniel Wormald was the same "Danny" whom Saul mentioned on Breaking Bad as the trusted manager of Lazer Base, one of his many money-laundering front businesses. But that would have required a version of the show that spent much more time in the Walter White era than this did; instead, the best he could do was to have Gene ask Francesca about Danny.

with a high body count?) Gene's response—which includes screaming, slamming down the receiver, and kicking in some of the phone booth's glass exterior—suggests that a door has just been loudly slammed in his face.

Jimmy allowed himself to fully become Saul Goodman as a way to ease the pain after Kim walked out on him. And now Gene does the same thing when he realizes that his dream of one day reuniting with her has been dashed.

The caper from "Nippy" had a light, almost triumphant feeling to it. It wasn't so much Gene channeling Saul, even with the shirt-and-tie combo he modeled at the end, but Gene slippin' back to his more benign days as Jimmy. No damage was really done, other than to Frank's attempts to reduce his waistline. What happens after the Florida phone call is much darker. Saul is ascendant now, setting up a thorough, relentless identity theft scam with Jeff and Buddy. There is no larger purpose to this the way there was with the mall heist. Yes, Gene might want to rebuild some of the fortune the feds seized. But it's obvious that he's doing it because he needs the rush he got as Saul, as well as the ability to hurt other people to mask his own pain. As he tricks one sap after another with a very old hustle—pretending to get drunk with them when he's really draining each glass into a hot water bottle strapped to his belly—he revives his old *nom de scam* as Viktor. But this is a Viktor who does not have Kim's Giselle by his side, so there is no component of fun to be had. The cruelty is the point—even after he discovers that his latest mark, Mr. Lingk (Kevin Sussman), has an advanced form of cancer.

Though Gene briefly looks regretful on learning this, he still goes ahead with the plan as usual. He is furious to learn that Buddy couldn't go through with his end of the operation upon noticing Lingk's medication, which is similar to what Buddy's father took to battle cancer. It's not just that Gene, as he indignantly tells his underling, has a history with a cancer patient who was also an asshole—and that Lingk works as a convenient stand-in for the man Gene really wants to blame for his current circumstances, even though they are entirely a result of choices Saul Goodman made voluntarily. It's that Gene no longer cares who is hurt, or how, just so long as he has a means to shove down all of his own pain for as long as he can keep the grift humming. He fires Buddy and orders Jeff to drive him to Lingk's house, so blinded with anger that he once again smashes some glass, this time breaking into the house after Buddy removed the duct tape over the lock. It is utterly reckless and pointless, since the whole idea is to prevent the victims from realizing their information has been stolen until much, much later. But Saul Goodman—who Gene has become again in everything but name—doesn't care. He wants more. He *needs* more. And he needs it now.

Lingk's condition draws a line back to the episode's Albuquerque scenes circa "Better Call Saul," as we see that Saul knew about Walt's diagnosis even before Walt told him in "4 Days Out." But the reason the flashbacks are here—besides the opportunity to see Cranston and Paul play these roles together one last time, on a re-creation of the *Breaking Bad* set where they shared so many of their best scenes—is to underline what Gene is doing in 2010. After the bag has been removed from his head and he realizes that his abductor is "Mr. Mayhew," Saul is impressed to figure out that these two clowns are the ones responsible for the blue meth that has been causing such a stir in town. He could just take the money they are paying him to resolve the Badger situation and go back to what is clearly a very lucrative, enjoyable, and fairly safe life. But being Saul Goodman is an addiction, always creating the demand for bigger and more frequent highs. And in Heisenberg, he has found a man who can get him higher than he ever dreamed possible.

Schnauz loads the 2008 scenes with visual reminders of the original series: among others, the duct tape covering the bullet holes in the RV's door, the infamous red light of the RV from "4 Days Out," and Mike wearing sunglasses (like he did in his very first appearance) when he arrives in Saul's office. But the Cranston-Paul-Odenkirk interactions are the marquee event, and they live up to our anticipation. No, Paul does not look like an overgrown kid in his early twenties, even shot in darkness and with a beanie covering part of his head. But Jonathan Banks doesn't look like a middle-aged man anymore, either, and that's worked out just fine for his work on this series. The Cranston-Paul chemistry is as crackling as it's always been, and it's a treat to see once again how easily Walt gets annoyed with both Jesse and Saul, how eager Jesse is to show off his chemistry skills to anyone who will pay attention, and how resentful he in turn can get with Walt's high-handed demeanor. There's no big drama, because it would feel like a cheat to insert some new conflict for them that wasn't part of the step-by-step process we watched on *Breaking Bad*. But it's them back in their element one last time, and it's very, very good.

The more crucial flashback scene in many ways takes place back at Saul's office. He is lying on the floor using the Swing Master—which he purchases again in the Gene timeline in an attempt to get that ol' Saul Goodman feeling—when Mike arrives with new intel. This is yet another callback, as Saul was in the same position when Mike came to threaten him in "Full Measure"—a moment that's arguably the closest *Breaking Bad* ever came to suggesting Saul knew all along that his investigator really worked for someone else.

The new scene clarifies the true nature of their arrangement. Saul knows that Mike is in the primary employ of "He Who Shall Not Be Named." But Mike also takes some side work from Saul as a means of gathering intel on the Albuquerque criminal community, since Saul has purchased Dr. Caldera's little black book and is facilitating shady business on the side. More importantly, it does not attempt to retcon the nature of Saul's initial interactions with Walt.

We know, from the flashback at the start of *Breaking Bad* Season 4, that Gus was already interested in the blue meth because Gale wouldn't stop raving about it. But Saul's interest in working with Heisenberg is entirely his own. Even after Mike warns him that this guy is a reckless amateur who will endanger anyone foolish enough to work with him—advice Mike ultimately, and fatally, fails to take for himself—Saul can't let go of the idea. In Heisenberg, he sees a meal ticket. Attempting to be a Friend of the Cartel had nightmarish repercussions for Jimmy, including the death of Howard and the loss of Kim. But he has always been one to believe that the problem was never with the scheme, but its execution. This high school teacher does not seem to be the physical or tactical threat of a Lalo and is such a bumbler overall at this stage that Saul sees him as someone he can puppeteer into generating a large fortune for all involved.

And the idea works, for a while. But then Walt and Gus go to war, then Walt and Jesse do, then Walt and Hank, and Walt and the Neo-Nazis, and now the man who once called himself Saul Goodman lives alone in Omaha (and is back to paying sex workers), works in a shopping mall, and gets his kicks running short cons on well-to-do men in bars. It always ends in ruins, like the statue of Ozymandias that gave the best *Breaking Bad* episode its title, and that Saul unwittingly alludes to here when joking about him and his new criminal partners being buried in a sandstorm for a thousand years. He does not listen to Mike's counsel in the office, nor does he listen to Buddy and Jeff's attempts to tell him he is taking the current sting way too far.

The episode neatly transitions back and forth between the eras so that, for instance, Gene slamming the door of Jeff's cab turns into Saul closing the door of his Cadillac as he prepares to confront Walt at the school where he works. The most effective of these comes right after the Walt and Jesse scene. Walt finally gets the Crystal Ship running, but the camera lingers on the grave he and Jesse dug to scare Saul into cooperating, and that shot in turn dissolves into Gene lying awake in his bed—the two compositions blending together in a way that makes it look as if Gene is down at the bottom of that pit. He has metaphorically dug his own grave, despite ample warnings from Chuck, Kim, Mike, and now even Jeff. He is in a spiral entirely of his own making. He's wearing Marco's pinkie ring again (he put it back on to find courage for the department store heist), and otherwise donning the bland garb of Gene Takovic, but there is no one to blame here other than Jimmy McGill and the choice he made to become Saul Goodman.

That happy ending that Gene joked about with Marion in "Nippy" seems very far away right now, if not impossible.

SEASON 6, EPISODE 12
WRITTEN AND DIRECTED BY VINCE GILLIGAN

"Waterworks"

"This guy? Any good?" —Jesse
"When I knew him, he was." —Kim

In a different world, Kim Wexler and Jesse Pinkman should have never met. She was a high-powered civil attorney working, at different points, for two of Albuquerque's most prestigious firms; he was Cap'n Cook. In this one, they are linked not only by the fact that she once defended Jesse's friend Combo in juvenile court, but by their associations with Saul Goodman—associations that eventually destroyed any semblance of the life they once planned for themselves.

But they are linked in other ways, too. Both are characters for whom their creators had few plans: Vince Gilligan assumed Jesse would die a few episodes into *Breaking Bad*, while Peter Gould has bluntly said that he and Gilligan didn't give any deeper thought to developing Kim than deciding that "there should be a woman in Jimmy's life." (She only has two lines of dialogue in the *Better Call Saul* pilot.) And both gradually turned into the hearts of their respective series. It's only through Jesse that we begin to truly appreciate what a monster Walt is. Kim, for a long time, served the opposite function: her affection for Jimmy was so palpable that it made both the writers and the audience fall for him, too. And more recently, her reckless, addict-like behavior regarding Howard has put a spotlight on the extreme peril that comes from being around the charming but ultimately weak Jimmy. Jesse was the closest thing to a conscience Walt had; once their partnership dissolved, Walt's malevolence only grew. And as soon as Kim began packing to leave Jimmy, we jumped straight to him as the remorseless Saul Goodman.

Neither is innocent: Jesse was cooking meth before he ever reconnected with Walt, and by the end of the marriage, Kim was the one ruthlessly pushing the confidence schemes, not Jimmy. But both suffer horrible fates as a result of their respective partnerships: Jesse by spending months as Todd's meth slave, Kim by feeling like she has no choice but to quit the career she was so good at and loved so much.

Both eventually get far away—Jesse to Alaska, Kim to Central Florida—and both ultimately take responsibility for their actions. One of the final scenes in *El Camino* is Jesse giving Ed the vacuum salesman a letter to mail to Brock, no doubt explaining why Brock got sick and why Brock's mother was murdered.

(And also that her murderer will never hurt anyone again.) And in "Water-works," Kim takes Gene's taunts about turning herself in seriously, as she travels back to Albuquerque to tell both Howard's widow Cheryl and the authorities what really happened to her former boss.

Before that, we get an extended glimpse of Kim's life as a catalogs and brochures specialist for Palm Coast Sprinklers. These scenes are taking place contemporaneously with what her ex has been up to in her home state, so they are shot in the same stark black and white of all the Gene scenes. The cinematography choice is fitting, though, because her life is as bleached of color as his is. She is less of a loner, because she has no need to hide from the cops, so she has a boyfriend, Glen, and a group of other friends both at home (even if perhaps via Glen and his buddies) and the office. And she is dedicated to the job she does because Kim Wexler is not built to half-ass anything. But it is a deliberately boring life. Glen is nice but dull, the friends kind but banal—her lunch group at work seems positively agog at the idea of people using illegal drugs, while Kim once verbally pantsed Lalo Salamanca—and the job unchallenging. Gilligan, writing and directing his final episode of the series, deliberately lingers on random bits of office monotony, like two colleagues sharing a three-hole punch across their cubicle divider.*

It is better than the life she left the Midwest to avoid, but not by a ton: she's not a cashier at the Hinky Dinky, but her boyfriend brings her Miracle Whip instead of mayonnaise from the Winn-Dixie. And it is a very deliberate choice. Even if she was insistent on never returning to the law, there is other work she could have chosen that would take advantage of some of the skills and connections she developed in Albuquerque. She doesn't want any of that. Perhaps it is penance for Howard, and for whatever role she feels she played in turning Jimmy into Saul. Or perhaps it is a way of white-knuckling her way through her addiction to flimflammery; there are fewer temptations in an existence this vanilla.†

---

* Like Thomas Schnauz in the previous episode, Gilligan loads "Waterworks" with callbacks to moments from throughout the series. Saul tosses a rubber ball off the wall and tries various trick shots, just like he did as Jimmy while working in the empty cell phone store. When Kim goes back to the courthouse, she passes Mike's old parking booth—now fully automated—and lingers by the picnic tables where she and Jimmy sat right before their wedding. Gene being trapped in the bedroom when Mr. Lingk wakes up evokes Lalo being stuck in Werner Ziegler's home office when his widow unexpectedly returned to the house. (Gene does not possess Lalo's superhuman jumping abilities, and thus can't just leap down to the first floor.) And when Gene awaits Jeff's call from the police station, he waves his fingers at the burner phone, magician-style, in the same manner we saw Jimmy do when he was desperate for business back in the show's earliest days.

† Not only has Kim abandoned her familiar coiffure, with darker hair and bangs, but her wardrobe is night and day from her Albuquerque ensemble. Gone are the tailored suits and stilettos, replaced by denim skirts and white sneakers. Even when she goes to her old stomping grounds at the county

So by the time we finally get to hear Gene's fateful phone call with Kim, we understand the life she has and the reasons why. The previous episode implied that he didn't go full Saul until after the call ended so badly. But almost from the start, it's Saul in that phone booth, ugly and hurt and prepared to hurt Kim for not giving him what he wants out of the conversation. The longer she remains silent, the more he brags about eluding the authorities. When she suggests that he turn himself in, he dismisses her as a hypocrite, given the role that Kim played in getting Howard killed, and how she has remained silent about it for all these years.

Gene is not wrong about that, but he is wrong about everything that follows. Where he uses the conversation as an excuse to go on a grifting rampage, she uses it as a wake-up call to fly back to Albuquerque and do the right thing. As a bitter Cheryl recognizes, there is minimal risk of prison time for a crime where there is no physical evidence, and no living witness other than Kim's fugitive ex-husband. But whatever catharsis Kim gets from finally admitting her guilt, and from returning to the life she cost herself, is not enough.

Several times in this episode, Gilligan just lets the camera linger on Rhea Seehorn's incredibly expressive face. On the phone with Gene, she looks like a wild animal that's been cornered and can't figure a way out, and then she just looks tired of him and all of it, in a manner similar to how she'll look when she departs Saul's office in the flashback sequence.* And on the airport shuttle bus in the 2010 timeline, the camera again just holds on Seehorn as Kim considers everything she has done, and everything it has cost her and the people around her. Kim has so often been in complete command of her own emotions, and the *Saul* directors have long learned to trust Seehorn's ability to say crucial things about that character through extremely subtle shifts in expression. This starts out like that, as Kim's mask of composure cracks ever so slightly. But as the shuttle rolls along, the cracks become bigger and bigger, until finally they burst, and

---

courthouse, it's in a pair of sensible pumps with a chunky heel. But as she waits for the elevator, she spots a bright young defense lawyer basically sporting her old wardrobe—and her trademark power ponytail, but in brown—and helping an indigent client get dressed up for court, as we so often saw Kim doing in this show's later seasons. She screwed everything up for herself, but there are other idealistic defense lawyers out there, at least. And even more than the style shift, Kim's indecisiveness regarding Tammy's birthday cake flavor is a symbol of how much she has changed. Kim Wexler, attorney at law, tended to make choices quickly and stick to them, even if they wound up harming her or others later.

* As Kim is leaving the office, Saul refers to Francesca as "Sweet Cheeks." This fits with some of the gross nicknames he used for her on *Breaking Bad* but doesn't really match what we saw of the decidedly non-misogynist Jimmy McGill over the bulk of this series. Presented here, though, it starts to make some sense. It's part of the horrible defense mechanism he has built for himself to cope with the loss of Kim: if she won't have him, then he will make himself so disgusting to her that she will feel as upset as he does. Poor Francesca is just collateral damage in this unhealthy attempt at self-medicating.

the titular waterworks of the episode's title—not the sprinkler company, and not the downpour she and Jesse try to avoid—come flowing out of her. It's all too much for her, and it's everything this show has built to for her over these six seasons. It's awful, and it's incredible.

The episode then returns to Omaha to show Gene taking things too far with Mr. Lingk—stealing trophies and preparing to knock out the cancer patient with the urn containing the remains of his dog, Rusty—and then for the slapstick of a panicked Jeff crashing his cab into a parked car in front of two police officers who were just on meal break. But then we dial back to the final legal matter of Wexler v. Goodman, as Kim signs the divorce papers, makes a beeline away from the amoral asshole she just ceased to be married to, and finds herself under the strip mall awning next to her spiritual cousin from that other show.

Jesse is only there because his buddy Emilio—aka Walter White's first murder victim—has come to Saul seeking legal representation. (In the "Better Call Saul" episode of *Breaking Bad,* Jesse tells Walt that Saul got Emilio out of trouble on two different occasions, despite the cops having him dead to rights.) Like Kim's various interactions with Saul and/or Gene in this episode, she says very little, just waiting for the nicotine to kick in and hoping that the rain will stop before she has to listen to too much of this kid bragging about ways for criminals to evade the justice system. She believed passionately in her work as a public defender, but guys like Jesse, Emilio, and Combo are the dark side of that work—the ones who present an ongoing danger to others each time a lawyer like Kim or Saul gets them off. And she really can't stand listening to the future Mr. Driscoll praise the chicanery of the man she hopes to never see again.

Will she see him again? Again, while talking with Cheryl, Kim acknowledges that Jimmy/Saul/Gene is the only one who can corroborate her story. These last two episodes established that he is desperate to see her again, and that he responds to her understandable refusal to do so in the worst possible ways. And this installment concludes with Jeff's mother Marion ratting Gene out to the authorities* in a manner that could well bring him back to the scene of his many crimes. Under those circumstances, would he be willing to put Kim into a legal jackpot just as an excuse to see her again?

It's unclear. The man who could brain Mr. Lingk with Rusty's ashes, or the one who could harm and tie up a helpless old lady, would almost certainly be game for something that nasty. But Gene is spared the first decision when

---

* As the great Russian playwright Anton Chekhov once wrote, if you show an elderly woman learning how to find cat videos on the internet in episode 11, then she has to be able to bust our protagonist via Ask Jeeves in episode 12.

Lingk falls asleep again, and then he deliberately chooses not to do the second. He has allowed himself to become and do so many terrible things in the years since Kim told him, "I love you. But *so what*?" But there are apparently limits even to that. Somewhere buried deep beneath that mustache, those glasses, and that wispy hair, there still exists a part of Jimmy McGill, who took such pleasure being around senior citizens, and who once sacrificed an early payday from Sandpiper because he felt guilty about taking away Irene Landry's friends at the retirement home. There is just enough of that guy left to hand the Life Alert fob back to Marion, come what may, and then Gene Takovic is off and running into the snowy daylight, with no one to help him* and a whole lot of people eager to bring him to justice.

When Jesse asks Kim if Saul is any good, he is only referring to Mr. Goodman's legal skills. Those, he has in abundance. It's everything else he gradually became so bad at.

But now all those bad deeds are catching up to him. When the show established that Kim was from Nebraska, it was easy to hope that she would one day turn up in the mall for some kind of low-key Happily Ever After. But this dark fictional universe that Gilligan created has something of a moral compass to it. Bad things happen to characters who do not deserve it, but characters who deserve bad things inevitably get what is coming to them. The sins Jimmy McGill and Kim Wexler committed together on this show are enough to bar either of them from the pearly gates of this particular cosmology, never mind the ones Jimmy committed as Saul Goodman.

We've gotten to watch them at their best and at their worst for so many years now, and almost all of it has been riveting, up through and including "Waterworks."

---

* Even if he wanted to call Ed, Robert Forster had passed away by this point.

"It's Time to Do Something New": *Better Call Saul* Co-Creator Vince Gilligan on His Final Episode as Writer-Director

---

[This story originally ran on RollingStone.com on August 8, 2022]

You and Peter always say that you can only see two inches in front of your face as the show is being plotted. So at what point and how did you figure out what was going to happen to Kim?

The same way we always did. We just work out two inches ahead of our noses. I think it could have gone any which way, but there probably also was an element of us being loath to kill off her character. There were so many elements of this story that were preordained. You can't kill off Jimmy McGill in his own show, you can't kill off any character whom we know the fate of from *Breaking Bad*. But with Kim, the sky was the limit. I guess it just didn't feel right to kill her off. That was probably never on the table, honestly. We certainly kept silently smiling while people stopped us on the street and said, "You're not gonna kill Kim, are you?" We let people think that maybe we would, but none of us wanted to do it. But figuring out where she wound up, it was in little baby steps, little fits and starts, like every other bit of plotting we do.

This is the last time you got to direct Rhea Seehorn in this role. In a lot of this episode, you're just letting the camera linger on her face as she's reacting to things, including that great scene where she breaks down on the airport shuttle bus. What was it like working with her one last time as this character?

It was great! I love Rhea. Rhea is just wonderful. And the camera loves her as much as I do. Just getting those shots, on that actual moving bus, was a challenge. It was a real rental-car shuttle moving around on a loop within sight of the Albuquerque airport. We just locked down four cameras and let them roll, and I sat there trying to get as much out of her eye line as I could. We did two takes. We didn't even need two. But I'm the anxious type, and I was gonna have more than one take. I think we used the second one, but she was just as brilliant as the first one.

These episodes take place after *Breaking Bad* and after *El Camino*. As of now, they are the chronological end of this story. Do you see this as it for this fictional universe, or could you imagine revisiting it?

I can definitely imagine revisiting it. Selfishly, I'd like to do so, to keep this thing going. But without naming any names, I look around at some of the worlds, the universes, the stories that I love, whether they're on TV or in the movies. And I think there's a certain point, and it's hard to define, where you've done too much in the same universe. Just leave it alone. And some universes are much bigger and more elastic. Ours is a very small one, Albuquerque, New Mexico, versus some of these worlds and series of movies and TV shows. The main thing I'm scared of is becoming too much of a one-trick pony. Yes, I could do more with this universe. And maybe someday I will, especially if I fail at everything that comes next. Then I'll come crawling back. But right now, whether there's more room to grow or not—and there probably is—I feel like it's time to do something new.

Having basically just done these shows and *El Camino* for more than fifteen years, how does it feel to be coming to the end of that?
It's funny. A lot of people have been asking me lately, and it hasn't really hit me. The end of *Breaking Bad* was very much a bright line, a clear delineation. I remember being on the set on the last day, and everybody was very emotional. That was a great many years ago. It's been fifteen years now, and that was only year six or something like that, and that felt more momentous, more monumental. It's perhaps not a satisfying answer. Perhaps it hasn't hit me yet. I think it's hit Peter, I think it's hit the writers and the actors. Maybe it'll be a delayed reaction. I hope it won't be quite as intense and quite as public as what Kim goes through on that rental-car shuttle. But maybe it's like the reaction she has, after six years, crying for Howard Hamlin and whatever else she's crying for—her lost soul. I hope I'm home alone if that happens.

SEASON 6, EPISODE 13
WRITTEN AND DIRECTED BY PETER GOULD

"Saul Gone"

"Where do I see it ending? With me on top, like always." —**Saul**

James Morgan McGill and Walter Hartwell White join forces one final time midway through "Saul Gone." They are hiding out in the vacuum store's basement circa the "Granite State" episode of *Breaking Bad*, each of them waiting for Ed to smuggle them away to their new lives under assumed identities. Their conversation is a reminder of Walt's arrogance, as well as his contempt for Saul: when Saul suggests he could have sued Gray Matter on Walt's behalf, Walt dismisses him as the last attorney he ever would have employed for such a task. He would snort in disbelief if you were to tell him that the man he knows as Saul Goodman once kicked off a successful multimillion-dollar class action suit against another corporation on behalf of defenseless senior citizens.

Mostly, though, the conversation is there as part of a running dialogue throughout the era-spanning series finale. As he explicitly does with Mike in the opening prologue (set immediately after the events of "Bagman"), and as Chuck (in a flashback set shortly before the series began) implicitly tries to do with Jimmy, Saul asks Walt what he might change if he had a time machine. Walt the scientific snob calls this out for what it is, as an opportunity to consider regrets. Walt begins to admit that he erred in leaving Gray Matter, but as always, everything bad that ever happened to him is someone else's fault, and Gretchen and Elliott were "artfully maneuvering" him out of his own company.* The best that Saul can come up with for himself is a slip-and-fall that permanently injured his knee. A disgusted Walt takes the measure of his attorney and says, "So you were always like this."

This could be the *Better Call Saul* version of the best and most important scene from the *Breaking Bad* finale, "Felina," where Walt finally admitted to Skyler that he did all of these monstrous things not out of concern for his family, but because he liked doing them, was good at them, and that they made him feel alive. In that moment, Vince Gilligan was definitively acknowledging that circumstances didn't transform Mr. Chips into Scarface, but rather revealed that Scarface had always been lurking just below the surface. Much

---

* I also imagine they might disagree on what percentage of their discoveries were Walt's versus their own.

like Chuck, Walt decides in this scene that Jimmy/Saul/Gene* has always been an amoral huckster, no matter how he has tried to present himself to others over the years.

"Saul Gone" has other elements in common with "Felina." It also brings its protagonist back to Albuquerque for a confrontation with his bitter former spouse, and it allows him to undo some of the damage he left in his wake when he skipped town after "Ozymandias." Tonally and thematically, though, it's something else entirely. For one, it's more muted than "Felina," with the biggest fireworks here being verbal ones at Saul's sentencing hearing, compared to the remote-controlled machine gun Walt used to kill Uncle Jack and the Neo-Nazis. But more importantly, the sacrifice our protagonist makes here, and what it ultimately says about him and his journey, couldn't be more different.

Walt ends *Breaking Bad* entirely on his own terms. He knows he has very little time left to live, and he accomplishes everything that is still within his power: leaving money behind for Flynn and Holly, getting Skyler out of legal trouble, allowing Marie Schrader and Blanca Gomez to properly bury their murdered husbands, and killing off Jack, Lydia, and most everyone remaining who once wronged him. He frees Jesse, too, though that wasn't part of his initial plan, and then he dies relatively quickly from a bullet wound rather than the prolonged indignity of spending time in prison while the cancer tears through what's left of his body. While he confesses his true motivation to Skyler, he nonetheless gets to die as he lived for a year and change, master of all he surveys.

Saul Goodman is presented with a much tougher choice. He has successfully pulled off one final con, maneuvering the federal prosecutors into giving him a sweetheart deal by explaining that, should his case go to trial, he'd likely be able to sway at least one juror by presenting all of his crimes as things he did out of fear of what Walt, Jesse, and their many accomplices would have done had he not played along. To the horror and disbelief of Marie (still less than a year removed from her husband's disappearance, and only a few months from his body being found in the desert), he will serve seven and a half years in a cushy federal prison. He may have lost his entire fortune, but no doubt he will

---

* Throughout the episode, Odenkirk does a spectacular job maneuvering through his character's three main personae, particularly when Jimmy decides during the hearing to seize control of the wheel and throw Saul out into traffic. There's also that terrific scene in the Omaha jail where Gene spots the "My lawyer will ream yr ass" message carved into the cinderblock wall, and can't stop himself from laughing, Joker-style, as he fully reverts to Saul Goodman, the sort of lawyer who also reamed asses on behalf of his clients.

be able to leverage his infamy to build a new one upon his release. 'S'all good, man, right?

But in trying to embarrass the feds some more—and get some tasty ice cream served to him weekly in lockup—he learns about the statement Kim gave the DA about Howard's murder. Worse, he realizes that he goaded her into it during his telephone call during "Waterworks," and as poor, put-upon Bill Oakley tells him on the flight back to New Mexico, Cheryl Hamlin is likely to sue Kim for all she's worth.

So Jimmy McGill decides to cast off the hollow greed of Saul Goodman, as well as the naked desperation for freedom of Gene Takovic, and make a genuine sacrifice to get what he really wants. He will offer a true accounting of his crimes, no matter how much it extends his sentence (which goes from 7.5 years to 86), in the hope that Kim will stop hating him.

In an episode filled with callbacks and flashbacks,* the sentencing hearing is particularly designed to evoke all things *Better Call Saul*. Jimmy whispers one last "It's showtime!" before launching into a version of his performance before the New Mexico Bar Association in "Winner" at the end of Season 4. He is playing up his guilt and shame, less because it is the right thing to do for Marie, for Blanca Gomez, and for all the other people he allowed to be hurt by aiding and abetting Walt for those amazing and terrible sixteen months, than because he thinks it is what Kim wants to hear. But as a dismayed Bill tries to get his confession stricken from the record, Jimmy looks back at Kim and sees—as he did on the faces of the Bar Association lawyers as he prepared to read from Chuck's letter—that what he had planned is not going to be enough. He has to go much deeper. But in this case, it is not an act. He talks about his guilt over Howard's murder, and notes that while Kim left town, "I'm the one who ran away." He let his every good instinct recede as a way to blot out the

---

* Like Vince Gilligan and Thomas Schnauz did in the two previous episodes, Gould includes old references galore in this farewell to the Heisenberg-verse. On the *Better Call Saul* end of things, we get to see the space blanket and other detritus from "Bagman," with the blanket doubling as another reminder of Chuck. Jimmy's suggestion to Mike that they just split the $7 million recalls their discussion from the end of Season 1 about why they didn't hang on to the embezzled cash they took off the Kettlemans. (Their time travel conversation also has an implicit callback to Mike's "bad choice road" philosophy, as the thing he'd most like to undo is the day he took his first bribe as a cop.) In Montrose, Jimmy gets to put his Cinnabon skills to use by baking bread in the prison kitchen. And from the *Breaking Bad* end, we not only get to see Marie again, but finally see Steve Gomez's widow Blanca, whom he mentioned a few times in passing on both series. In court, Saul wears a ribbon on his suit that is almost certainly the blue memorial ribbon he began sporting in the wake of the plane crash Walt inadvertently caused at the end of *Breaking Bad* Season 2. And before labeling the Gray Matter situation as his greatest regret, Walt first looks at the expensive watch Jesse gave him for his fifty-first birthday, silently understanding that what he did to Jesse (including his very recent decision to leave him to be killed by the Neo-Nazis) is far worse than whatever version of the Gretchen and Elliott story he is telling himself right now.

pain of Kim's exit, Howard's murder, Chuck's suicide, and everyone else injured by the unbridled power of Slippin' Jimmy with a law degree. Physically, he stayed in Albuquerque, but he let what was left of his soul go on walkabout. We know—and, more importantly, Kim knows—that he is not faking it precisely because he doesn't turn on the waterworks the way he did in "Winner," or at other times we've seen him lie for his own gain. He is saying these things because he believes them, and because he finally understands that he needs to say them out loud, as much for himself as for the woman he still loves. And as the judge refers to him again as Mr. Goodman, he insists, "The name's McGill. I'm James McGill."

It is an incredible, beautiful sequence, precisely because of the patience Peter Gould and company have demonstrated over the years, and because of their trust in their performers to say a whole lot with very little. As stunning as Kim's weepy meltdown was in "Waterworks," what Rhea Seehorn does at the end of the sentencing hearing hits even harder. It is just the tiniest, tiniest hint of a smile—really, more of a relaxing of the stone face she has been giving her ex-husband until this moment—and yet it is everything. Seehorn is just that great at these micro expressions, and the series has painstakingly established the context for why she would need to hear him say these words, in this way, before forgiving him. It's all he needs to see, and all we need to know.

Does Jimmy's stunt with the judge get Kim out of legal danger from Cheryl? Gould opts not to answer the question within the episode, though he offered some thoughts on the subject in an interview he did with me at the time.* But we already know that Kim has gotten the closest thing to a happy ending that her sins would allow her within the moral universe of these two series. Before Suzanne Ericsen calls to warn her that Saul may be implicating her in new crimes—really, just his way of ensuring he will physically see her at least one more time, and that she will be present to witness his act of contrition—we see her leave work early to volunteer at a Central Florida Legal Aid office. She has denied herself the ability to practice law as part of her elaborate, deliberately colorless penance for Howard's death. But confessing to the DA and to Cheryl has eased some of that guilt, and she realizes that she still has

---

* "No, I don't [think Jimmy's actions get Kim out of trouble with Cheryl]," Gould told me. "I think that Kim is on her own journey, and I think he knows that. He does feel bad about what's happening with Cheryl. But I don't think Kim would like it if Jimmy pulled some maneuver that protected her from Cheryl. He doesn't save her; *she* saves her. They're done with saving each other by this time. What he sees is that she had the courage to face what she's done. And she did something that I don't think Jimmy/Gene ever thought she would do, which is not only to turn herself in, but actually to sit across from Cheryl Hamlin, who they both lied to disgustingly, and be a hundred percent truthful."

the opportunity to help people. Maybe at some point she will see if the Florida Bar Association will allow her in after all the things she did in New Mexico, or maybe she'll just continue to help out there in between her catalog and brochure job at Palm Coast Sprinklers. But she is at least adjacent to the kind of work that gave her the greatest satisfaction, and the Kim who is staying well after dark to do filing looks far more alive than the woman we saw going through the motions in "Waterworks."

She does get to take advantage of her legal career at least one more time, by using her old New Mexico bar card (with no expiration date) to pose as Jimmy's lawyer for a more intimate conversation than if they were speaking through prison glass. Like the first significant scene they shared in the *Better Call Saul* series premiere, very little is said out loud, but they lean against a wall lit diagonally, film noir–style, as they share a cigarette. (And the flame of the lighter and the cigarette are the only color allowed into the Jimmy/Kim timeline in the episode.)

In many ways, it is not what Saul Goodman might have wanted when the police caught him in a dumpster.* He jokes with Kim about reducing his sentence with good behavior, but he will never breathe free air again. He may not even see her again after she turns to look at him one last time on her way out of ADX Montrose penitentiary. But by coming to see him, and sharing a final cigarette with him, she gives him more than he could have hoped for—and in nearly all ways, more than he deserves. (Marie, brought expertly back to life by Betsy Brandt after nearly a decade away from the role, certainly wouldn't want Saul Goodman to enjoy a second of happiness.) But as we see on Jimmy's face while he watches her go, it's enough.

And that is ultimately the key difference between this show and the one preceding it, even though Gould, Vince Gilligan, Bob Odenkirk, and so many other people worked on both. Walter White goes out in a blaze of glory, a testament to a series that operated on a near-operatic level of emotion and carnage so much of the time. Jimmy McGill's big final moments involve a shared cigarette and silent glances, as befitting a show whose emotional highs and lows—especially in Jimmy and Kim's half of the series—tended to be on the subtler end of things.

Although he died midway through the series, it would not be a proper *Saul* finale without one last appearance by Chuck, who turns up in the episode's last flashback, right after the sentencing hearing. So often in the early years of the show, we would see Jimmy reach out to his brother for approval, or just connection, only to be slapped down by Chuck's pathological superiority complex

---

* Another callback, to Jimmy dumpster-diving for the shredded Sandpiper documents.

at work. But we also saw periodic moments showing that Chuck did love Jimmy in his own way, even though he was, as Jimmy describes him to the judge here, "limited." This scene is the inverse of many of those previous Jimmy/Chuck conversations: for once, it's Chuck who is palpably trying to make a connection, and Jimmy who seems baffled by the very idea. Jimmy will bring Chuck his groceries and his newspapers out of sibling loyalty and love, but the thought of just making small talk, or telling his esteemed brother about his latest lowlife clients, makes as much sense to him as the mere idea of Jimmy being a lawyer does to Chuck.

It is one of those moments where a time machine would be very handy, and not just because Chuck has a paperback copy of H. G. Wells's *The Time Machine* that will later appear on both Jimmy's nightstand and among Saul's possessions being cataloged in the Season 6 premiere. As we've talked about throughout the run of this wonderful show, Chuck's suspicions about Jimmy became a self-fulfilling prophecy, where his determination to stop his brother instead set Jimmy down the path to becoming Saul Goodman. But maybe if Jimmy traveled back to this particular evening for a do-over, he might stay, might tell Chuck about his life, and his cases, and might begin forging an emotional bond with his big brother running deeper than a sense of obligation and shared history. Maybe in that timeline, Chuck doesn't stand in the way of Jimmy joining HHM to work Sandpiper, the brothers don't go to war over Mesa Verde and the destroyed cassette tape, Jimmy doesn't get Chuck's malpractice insurance canceled out of spite, Chuck continues to find better ways to cope with his mental illness, and on and on.

It's not likely, because people usually are who they are; you can even read Chuck's comments about going back and changing your path as a gentle way of encouraging Jimmy to stop practicing law. But it's possible, because some people do have the capacity for change. Whether or not Saul's most notorious client was one of those people, Walt did tell his students that he thought of chemistry as the study of change: "Growth. Decay. Transformation." Over the course of this prequel, we've seen Jimmy McGill go through all of those phases. He was in the process of growing up when we met him, before things with Chuck, Howard, Mike,* Lalo, and more led him to allow himself to decay into Saul Goodman, before transforming into Gene Takovic just to stay alive and free, then finding a way to turn back into Jimmy at the end. He is not a good man in

---

* "Fun and Games" really was the end of cartel world as we knew it. Although Jonathan Banks returned for a couple of cameos, Mike's character arc on this series came to a conclusion with Mr. Varga scolding him about revenge versus justice, while Gus did not appear again after abruptly leaving his unofficial date with David the sommelier. No matter how exciting the cartel stories could be, this was ultimately Jimmy and Kim's show, and the final season was structured to reflect that.

any kind of black-and-white moral accounting. As he tells the judge, most of Walt's crimes would not have been possible without Saul helping to run the operation. And even as the sweeter, gentler Jimmy McGill, he perpetrated some truly heinous things, often just for the satisfaction of doing them. But there are good impulses within him, enough for him to do the right thing here at the end, despite enormous personal cost.

So while Walt may be correct that time travel is scientifically impossible, he is wrong in his assessment of his least favorite attorney. Saul Goodman has *not* always been this way, nor is he condemned to remain this way. That has been the key question, and the central tension, throughout this show. Because we enter the series having already seen the events of *Breaking Bad*, we assume Jimmy is doomed to lose this inner battle. In the end, though, he wins just enough to be worthy of one more smoke with Kim, before he has to go back to the punishment he has more than earned under any and every name.

Before we get to the lighting of cigarettes, though, we see our man riding the bus to his new supermax home. He is at peace with his choices, and seemingly unafraid of where he's going. Soon, he is shown that his confidence was correct, as his fellow prisoners begin to recognize him from his ubiquitous commercials. He is not only a minor celebrity among the incarcerated set, but a hero: a guy who would defend any criminal for any offense, without shame or judgment, and do shockingly well at helping them to evade the consequences of their actions. When we see him at Montrose, everyone calls him Saul and everyone seems to like him. Whether he is offering free legal advice or not, it appears he will do just fine behind bars.

As those prisoners realize they are in the presence of legal greatness of a sort, one of them leads them all in a celebratory chant: "BETTER CALL SAUL! BETTER CALL SAUL! BETTER CALL SAUL!" It's a reference to the man Jimmy McGill has chosen to stop being. But it's also something of a valedictory for the show built improbably around Jimmy. *Breaking Bad* periodically liked to quote Walt Whitman, and Walter White had a boundless capacity to celebrate himself in the worst possible ways. Our title character here had his own flair for self-promotion, though Jimmy's was often borne more out of insecurity or desperation, whereas Saul's was a coping mechanism to keep convincing himself that his new life was better than the one that had Kim in it. Here, though, this celebration of self feels wholly deserved. As a spin-off of a perfect series, built around a character who barely had two dimensions, let alone three, *Better Call Saul* had no business being good, never mind becoming a show where fans can legitimately question whether it's better than *Breaking Bad*. To have come so improbably far over these six seasons, to have done so many things so well over those years, and to facilitate so many absolutely dynamite performances by Bob Odenkirk, Rhea Seehorn, Jonathan Banks, and everyone else, has the show not earned the right to toot its own horn here at the end?

As Saul once told Francesca, it's been quite a ride. We may not see its like again for quite some time. Enjoy the feeling while it lingers.

BETTER CALL SAUL! BETTER CALL SAUL! BETTER CALL SAUL!

A Closing Argument*
with Peter Gould

In late 2023 and early 2024, Peter Gould sat down for a pair of lengthy new interviews to revisit the Saul experience one more time. While we had spoken often over the years, all but a couple of those conversations were done in a rush (15 minutes, 20 at most) while he was doing a full day of press, while he was in the midst of still making the show, when he didn't know what was coming next, and/or had to be vague in answering many questions. With the series finished, with no secrets left to guard, and with the benefit of not having to rush through each question and answer, we got to dig deep into everything, including story pitches that never got made, Bob Odenkirk's heart attack during filming of the final season, the series setting an Emmy record for futility, and more.

Any conversation with Peter Gould about Better Call Saul must, of course, start with a conversation about "Better Call Saul," the Breaking Bad episode that introduced our hero, right?

When the "Better Call Saul" episode was proposed, what was the concept in the room? Did you expect the character to have any legs? Or was he someone who would maybe be around for only half a season?

We were at that point in the show where we were on a course that we had not expected. We thought that Walt and Jesse were going to be working for Tuco. And then, as you know, we found out that Tuco is not available to us.† So, Tuco is killed early in Season Two. And now, they're out on their own. We started thinking about what are the problems that you have if you're a novice drug dealer trying to move all that meth. And one of the basic problems was, what happens if one of your guys gets arrested? So, of course, we've already got Badger. And, the thought was, *Who would be the lawyer here?*

And, at this point—I'll speak for myself—I didn't fully understand the tone of the show. I don't think anybody understood it except for Vince. I think this was Vince feeling out what the show was going to be going forward. So we came up with this idea of this character. And first, in the room, we had a lot of ideas that were crazier even than what we ended up doing. There was one pitch where, when he got paid, he would put the money into a pneumatic tube that

---

* Okay, so this is much more of a conversation than an argument. Please allow one last self-indulgent courtroom reference, your honors.

† Raymond Cruz was on loan from his day job on *The Closer*, and the TNT cop drama needed him back at work sooner than expected. Hence, Hank kills Tuco.

went straight to the bank. There were all kinds of crazy pitches like that. And we were just having fun with the character. And I remember, Vince came in with the name Saul Good. And then, one of the other writers said, "Saul Goodman." And then, one of the writers said, "What about 'LWYRUP' as a license plate?" And so, these started clinging to each other right away.

Really, his creation was all in service of Walt's story. We weren't thinking, *Here's an independent character who's going to have a life of his own.* We thought, *How does this serve Walt's story? And how is he different from the other characters we've seen?* He enjoys himself. He's very transactional. He's not violent, obviously. And all those things came, I think, in the architecture of just where we were in the story. Did we think he was going to have a future? Well, I'll tell you, personally, as I was writing the episode, I got very nervous. I got scared, because I was worried that we were going to break the show by making a character that was too silly—that he was going to be just too big for what I thought was a very grounded show. Grounded in its own way, let's put it that way.

And, my fear was actually enhanced when we had our first notes call with an executive who will remain nameless. Vince and I were on a conference call, and the question came up, basically, "We don't like this character. Could we start again and come up with a different story for this episode?"

Wow.
And Vince said, "No." He was strongly advocating for the script and for the character. And, to their credit, the person or persons on the call backed down, because they had to trust Vince. But, you can think about what an alternative universe would be where we had had to throw that episode out. And as it was, that season we ended up shutting down briefly, because we ran out of scripts— which never happened again, I'm happy to report. But that was probably the most stressful season of either show, for me, anyway. I lost a lot of sleep over it. There's actually a scene in that episode between Hank and Walt, where Hank talks about his insomnia. And that's literally lifted from what was going on in my life at that moment. Although, I had not shot Tuco. So, I was nervous about letting everybody down, especially Vince.

How did you come to Bob? Were you looking at a bunch of different people? Were you primarily considering comedians?
There were a few ideas that were thrown around. My wife actually made a list for me. I was telling her about the character and she made a list. And both she and [casting directors] Sharon Bialy and Sherry Thomas came up with a list, and Bob was at the top of all of them. I will say, and I've never said this before,

the one name that I remember being mentioned in addition to Bob's, was actually Michael McKean.

Wow again.

So, again, alternate universe. Vince and I get on the phone with Bob and Bob says, "I know the show's great." I don't think he would admit he hadn't watched it at that point—like most people. And, he said, "How can I do that? I'm not Jewish at all." And then, Vince explained that he was masquerading as a Jewish person for the clients, to give him more credibility with the underworld, in other words. Bob was always polite and very nice about it. But I didn't know if he was going to do it or not. And he did, and I was so excited because of all the people in the room, I was maybe the biggest *Mr. Show* fan.

Bob likes to tell the story about how, while filming his first *Breaking Bad* episode, a guy on the crew said he wanted to be hired for the eventual Saul spin-off. At what point in the making of *Breaking Bad* did the idea of a Saul spin-off actually become a thing you guys were talking about?

I remember Bob coming up to me during the shooting of that first episode. He said, "You guys are going to kill me off pretty fast, right?" And I said, "Bob, we built this whole set that's your office. I think you might be around for a little bit." Because we didn't have the money to build sets that we weren't going to keep using.

[With the spin-off], it was a gradual thing. Whenever we came up with something in the room that was just too silly, occasionally someone said, "Well, that's for the spin-off." I really restrained myself from thinking about it too much, because it seemed too good to be true. I was having such a great time on *Breaking Bad*, I felt like you just couldn't have a better situation. And I also just felt I had been around for a while in Hollywood, and I'd had my struggles. And, the fact that I was on a show that was so great, and it was so rewarding to work with a group and with Vince, it seemed too good to be true. So I didn't want to press my luck. But then, really, in the final season of *Breaking Bad*, Vince said to me, "Would you be interested in working with me on a spin-off?" And I said, "Absolutely. Absolutely." But keep in mind that I was just one of a group of very, very brilliant writer-producers in that room. And there were a lot of really special people in that room. And I didn't feel like I was any more special than anybody else. So the fact that Vince wanted to work with me on this, it meant an awful lot. And the fact that we created the character together obviously had played into that.

But even during that final season, we would pitch Saul Goodman getting killed. Absolutely. And, if it had been the right move for *Breaking Bad*, we would've killed that character. So, the spin-off couldn't be real until we had the whole story of *Breaking Bad* finished, because it's completely possible that the piece that would've made the finale of *Breaking Bad* work would be killing Saul Goodman. We would've done it in a New York minute. We would've done it right away. But then, in post, that was when Vince and I started talking more seriously about it.

When Vince and I spoke about the development process, he admitted that, after a little while, he really started banging his head against the wall and wondering why he ever thought this was a good idea for a TV show. Did you have any of these similar moments of self-doubt?

Oh, absolutely. Because the show had no obvious motor, at least when you start out. He's a lawyer, and he wants money, and he's got a sleazy side. And, where's the story? His goal was a little bit ephemeral to us at first. It was really hard to figure out. It was like doing the Rubik's Cube from hell because we had all the things that we'd established on *Breaking Bad*, and also, are people going to take to this character? In the moment, it always seems impossible. And, the other thing is, people loved *Breaking Bad* so much that it was like, "How is this ever going to be in the running?"

[*On our Zoom, Gould notices that I have a poster of the 1988 Robert De Niro/Charles Grodin buddy action comedy* Midnight Run *hanging on the wall behind me.*]

Your poster reminded me of something, because literally Vince and I were sitting down and we were going to have a conference call with the studio and the network. And one of the things we asked ourselves, "Who from *Breaking Bad* could we have back?" And, I think we both felt like, "Oh, well, wait a minute, [Jonathan] Banks." And there were a bunch of reasons for that. One of which was, you have a laconic character and a talkative character, and that just seems to work as a pair. But the other thing is, your poster over your shoulder is *Midnight Run*, which is one of my all-time favorite movies, and I just felt like, that's how these two archetypes could get together. And I think I pitched probably just to Vince at the time, "What if these two guys get stuck in the desert and they're handcuffed to each other?" And, that image for some reason really spoke to me, and I think spoke to all of us, and it just took us, whatever it was, forty, fifty episodes to get to it.

Saul on *Breaking Bad* is a wonderful character, but also a fairly thin character. He's at peace with himself. There's no inner conflict there. Was that one of the challenges you were struggling with as well—how to build a show around someone like that?

That was the thing we had to crack first. And this was Bob's hesitation about it too. Vince and I had lunch with Bob, and that was his question: "Well, what is there to this guy?" And, the way I approach a lot of this stuff is problem solving. And, I think, that was the origin of Chuck. And once you see, "Well, wait a minute. Yeah, this is the face he presents to the world: Saul Goodman. But there's this other thing going on too." And that was when we started talking about Chuck and the relationship between the two brothers. One of the things that we did really early on in the writers' room was we watched the movie *Crumb*, the brilliant Terry Zwigoff documentary about Robert Crumb and his brother.*

And that was very inspirational for us to think about the obligation that this Saul Goodman/Jimmy McGill character has to his older brother. That was really the origin of that. But, it was a struggle. I think one of the original ideas that I loved a lot was that he was going to be the Jerry Maguire for criminals. And we spent a lot of time on him putting criminal gangs together, and putting capers together, and being a little bit hands off. But when we came down to it, we had to give the guy skin in the game. Otherwise, there's no emotion to it.

You've said many times that you assumed by the end of the first season, Jimmy would at least be working in the strip mall office, if not calling himself Saul. At what point did you start to realize you weren't getting there that quickly?

That was in the first season. I think, part of the reason relates to your earlier question, because part of the reason we were looking forward to him being Saul in the office was we felt that that's when the clouds would part, and he's just doing fun scammy stuff for however long the show runs. And we were a hundred eighty degrees wrong about that.

I think it was pretty early on Season One when it just started getting more emotional, and we kept on asking ourselves, "Why has he become Saul Goodman?" We thought the answer would suddenly appear before us, and it just didn't. Why would this guy make this big switch? And not necessarily the name per se, which you could make a business argument for, but how could he become so emotionally detached from what's going on? How does he go from this tortured, good-hearted guy to being this happy-go-lucky criminal?

I think we thought it was a shorter journey, and then midway through the season it was, "Geez, we weren't anywhere near it." And, weirdly enough, what it reminds me of is *Breaking Bad*, because on that series we would always end up pitching, "Why doesn't Walt just go buy a gun and shoot so-and-so in the

---

* Crumb's older brother Charles, whose obsession with comics helped inspire Robert's career as a cartoonist, suffered from mental illness, and committed suicide in the early nineties.

head?" Constantly. And Vince would say, "This guy's just not ready for that yet." That was what we learned. And once we started seeing how vulnerable the character was, we started seeing that we could do more things.

Having said that, I think, at the end of the first season, when we broke it, and he says to Mike, "I know what stopped me. And you know what? It's never stopping me again," and he drives off, we could have, at that point, had him scouting the Saul Goodman office at the start of Season Two. And we could have said that his experience at the end of Season One—finding out that his brother was stabbing him in the back, of having his good old friend Marco die in his arms—was enough to set him off on this new trail. And then, the road to hell would be step-by-step. But what we found when we came back for Season Two was that there was a lot more going on between Jimmy and Kim than we thought. This shows you how the small decisions really set your course, because we said at the beginning of Season Two, "Well, what's he going to do next?" And it started bothering us that Kim had set up this meeting for a new job and he was just blowing her off. So, we felt like he had to go in, and then we started thinking, "Well, what's really going on between these two?" And that became the spine of a lot of the show.

So you're making the first season, he's not anywhere close to becoming Saul Goodman, he's practicing elder law, he's doing wills, he's setting up this class action at Sandpiper. Was there a point where you guys worried, "What show are we making? How did we get here?"
You know what? Not really, because we didn't tend to think in terms of what's the tone of the show, or what is the show conceptually? It was like, "Does this moment make sense? Does this move for the character make sense? Is this interesting to us? And does it advance our understanding of the character and how he's changing?" So, at that point, because of my experience on *Breaking Bad*, I think all of us felt like, "You know what? They've given us all this rope." Sony and AMC really were very supportive of whatever we were thinking. And so we thought, it would be kind of foolish for us to restrain ourselves. We're never going to have another opportunity like this. That's what I thought. And so, let's let the show guide us. And, the more we did that, the better the show got, I think.

You've often said that the big surprise of making the first season was how much you all came to like Jimmy. How and when did you start to realize that?
There are a couple places. One that comes to mind for me is in episode two. He's in this terrible situation with Tuco and Nacho and Tuco's guys, and these two

idiots who he's [inadvertently] provoked into crossing Tuco—the skate twins. He talks his way out of the trouble and could walk away. But instead, he comes back and takes his life into his own hands to do a defense for them, trying to tease out a version of mercy that will work for Tuco Salamanca. The fact that he turned around at that point felt semi-heroic in that moment. I really liked that. And also just the fact that he's got a crush on somebody who doesn't seem to reciprocate. Those are things that I think we can identify with really quickly. Yeah, I think we just really started enjoying the character once we started breaking those episodes.

At the time, the first season was reasonably well-received, but the response to "Five-O" versus the response to most of the other episodes that year was pretty stark. People were very excited. I remember at the time people saying things like, "Oh, this is the show I thought I was going to be getting. This is maybe the show that I want." Was there a part of you looking at that and saying, "Oh, maybe we should be leaning more in that direction?"

Not really. I mean, it just felt like that was only natural to explore Mike's background. I mean, I don't want to sound like I don't care about what people are saying, I think we all knew it was a great episode, but the DNA of the show was Bob's character. That's the DNA spiral that made it all work.

That was a way for us to highlight who Mike was and what his struggle was. And it started us down the path of having two parallel worlds. They were parallel for a lot longer than I expected. So, I never really thought, *Oh, we should be doing that.* It's interesting you said that, because the one that I remember people talking about at the time was the penultimate one with the big confrontation between Bob and Michael, where you find out what Chuck really thinks of Jimmy. I love "Five-O" too, but that was the one I remember people talking about the most. It was also one I was irritated to have to follow with the season finale.

I assume part of the whole point of Nacho was for the version of the show where he was going to become Saul very quickly, right? Because Michael [Mando] disappears for quite a while after you started getting deeper into elder law and Sandpiper.

I don't think we had a master plan for Nacho. We knew Michael was great. There is a version of the show where Tuco was a main character, but that wasn't going to work out for us again. And it took us a little while to start understanding [Nacho]. But the way it worked in my book is that it's a little musical where we started with telling the story of Jimmy, and then Mike comes in as an important character. And then Kim comes in, and then Nacho comes in. And they all become very, very important point-of-view characters, but they don't start that way. In the first episode, we're not seeing Mike's point of view at all. He's just the troll under the bridge.

In the Season Two premiere, you insert a scene into the middle of what we thought was a complete sequence in the Season One finale, so that Jimmy briefly goes to the Davis and Main meeting before driving away. I imagine that was all part of your realization that you didn't want him to screw over Kim.

Yeah, absolutely. We started exploring the relationship, and that was where we came up with a thing where he basically says, "If I take the job, is that going to enhance my chances with you?" And she says no. And then he leaves. And suddenly the decision that was just about *I'm a free bird now* has a lot more to do with Kim than it did before.

Tom Schnauz told me that there was a lot of disagreement in the room about whether or not, when Jimmy and Kim sleep together in the Season Two premiere, it was the first time. Where do you stand on that?

It could have been. Probably, yes. But if, say, we were working on a Season Seven and we wanted to do a flashback, I could picture a world where the two of them got together and had some fun with each other and she just said, "I'm sorry, but this is not what I want." In a way that could be just as painful. I'm always looking for the pain. That would be one option. Yeah, I could see it either way. I think for us in the room it was helpful to conceive of it as that being the first time, but I think we left our options open.

In hindsight, that's maybe among the most crucial episodes of the show. Because he starts doing the "Viktor with a K" routine, and she's into it.

Yes!

Skyler White didn't want Walt doing any of the stuff he did. And that, unfortunately, is part of why some fans had a terrible reaction to Skyler. Meanwhile, Kim loves the part of Jimmy that we all love. What was the process of figuring out what Kim's relationship to the shadier side of your leading man would be like?

Well, some of it's just thinking, *Well, what did we do before?* One of the most difficult things on *Breaking Bad* was to figure out why Skyler is still on the show. *Why doesn't she leave?* That was a constant struggle. Because we really wanted her on the show. We loved Anna, still do, and she contributed so much. But then we really had to drill down, because a lot of the time the logical thing for her to do would've been to walk out and get a divorce, the way she almost does.

For Kim, part of it is we wanted to zig when people expected us to zag. We have this character who's very restrained, who works in the law office, who seems really buttoned down. What's a different side of her? That was not a new invention in Season Two, that was really from the episode where Jimmy does that crazy stunt on the billboard. And back at HHM, Hamlin and everybody else is looking down at him and she's got this teeny little smile. It just felt like, *Okay*. Again, what I always go back to is, what did we do before and how does that affect where we're going?

Obviously, in hindsight, "Switch" is a hugely important episode because this is the beginning of their romantic relationship. And it's also Kim getting more into the con than she should. You couldn't see five, six years down the line and realize that they were going to get somebody killed this way eventually, but even at that stage, were you thinking at all about what the downside was of her playing Giselle St. Claire?
Yeah, this is very dangerous for Kim. We always had the idea that they worked in the mail room together earlier. And we asked ourselves what was happening in her career before. She's got a lot to lose. She's an up-and-coming lawyer, and now she's scamming at a bar. Yeah, one of the things I always ask is, "What does this character have to lose?" And I think you're right: that is really pivotal to the entire series. Because after that point, Kim has put certainly her career and her livelihood at stake a little bit, or she might. And Jimmy's got a lot to lose because he loves her. There's somebody who really appreciates him for who he is.

I've written a lot about how Chuck's distrust of Jimmy becomes a self-fulfilling prophecy.
Yes.

But here's what I've always wondered: If Chuck had gladly welcomed him into HHM when Jimmy passed the bar, or at least if he had allowed Jimmy to join the firm once he found the Sandpiper case, would Jimmy have been capable of having a long and happy career in elder law? Or do you think he ultimately was wired in a way where he was always going to sabotage that?
My God, that's the tragedy of it to me. I think if these brothers were able to see eye to eye, I don't know how much of this would've happened. I think Jimmy had a different path. I don't think he was genetically predestined to become

Saul Goodman the way he does. I think that it's a series of terrible decisions. And I don't think you can blame those decisions on anybody but him. But on the other hand, I think if Chuck had given his brother more of a benefit of the doubt, things could have gone differently. But I actually don't know that Jimmy earned that. I think you have to balance. I would not blame Chuck for who Jimmy becomes, because Jimmy certainly has earned his brother's distrust, and he continues to over and over again for very capricious reasons.

The titles of Season Two episodes create the whole "FRING'S BACK" anagram. When did you know for sure that Giancarlo would return so you could set that up, and the "Don't" note that Mike finds on his windshield in the Season Two finale?
This is an embarrassing story because we did talk about who wrote that note. And we thought, wouldn't it be cool for it to be Fring? And then as we ended the season, we reordered all the titles to make "Fring's back." But what we didn't do was tell Giancarlo that we had this idea! And this shows you how you can so easily underestimate the audience. They're frigging relentless. And this thing that we thought was going to be this tricky code that people would not figure out, almost as soon as the titles were released, they figured it out!

So we called Giancarlo in a hurry and pitched to him what we wanted to do and what we thought. And what he really wanted to know was, what is there to do with the character that we haven't done already? And we had thought about that a little bit, so we talked about it, and he trusted us, thank God. Because you can imagine, what if we hadn't gotten Giancarlo? Somebody else would've had to have written that note, and we would have this anagram in the titles that made no sense. Once again, we got lucky.

What would you have done if Giancarlo hadn't wanted to come back at all?
You know, it's a terrible thing to say, but we'd end each season running on fumes. So it was always, "Oh, that's a next season problem." And we would've tackled it then. God bless him, Giancarlo was willing to come back.

Okay, but now that you're not in the weeds and can look back, what would you have done? What would Mike's story have been without Gus, not just for Season Three, but for the rest of the series?
We would have pulled our hair out. It seems impossible, but I think we would have another journey through the underworld for Mike, and we would have alluded to Gus at the end. With Mike, we had a similar question to the one about what problem becoming Saul Goodman solves for Jimmy. Once we find out what happened to his son, due to Mike's criminal career, why on earth

would he ever get involved in crime again after that? We had a lot of work to do. It was more subtle. He doesn't change what he wears, or how he talks. But it changes what he does quite a bit. Probably, he would have become Jimmy's PI, and they might have worked together a little bit sooner. But I think we would have had to eventually have him walk into a Pollos Hermanos at the end of his journey.

But then you realize that, if we didn't have [Giancarlo], how on earth would we have gotten Tony Dalton into the show? It's the butterfly effect! Taking Giancarlo off the show kind of knocks three legs off the stool.

Giancarlo's wonderful on this show. You give him so many great things to do. But we're meeting him at a very different emotional place than we were meeting Jimmy and Mike. The equivalent version of Gus would be the one from either right before or right after Hector has killed Max. Whereas the Gus we meet in Season Three is basically the Gus we know from *Breaking Bad*—just a lot earlier on in the plan. As a character with less of an arc than the other two guys you were bringing over, was that complicated to write?
Absolutely, it was. And Giancarlo brought so much to it. Yeah, it called for a more subtle approach with the character. And you're absolutely right. It only made sense for him to be where he is in the show. It wouldn't have made sense for him to be a completely youthful, wide-eyed version of himself. We already did that with Jimmy. Sometimes you need a yardstick. Having said that, Giancarlo said something during *Breaking Bad*, on a panel: "Well, basically Gus Fring is a teacher." And at the time I remember walking out laughing, "He's a teacher, he's a teacher!" But you know what? He was really right, and that stayed with me. And that became one of the things that really helped us figure out the guy. That in addition to get revenge, he also is a mentor character to some of these other characters. And that really helped us a lot to think about how he got that way and his vulnerability, and his desire to re-create this golden relationship with Max.

At what point did you realize you were essentially making two shows?
Season Two, really. Season One, I thought we kept it balanced. It looked like they were going to converge. And then Season Two, the two worlds started to diverge more than we expected. I think we expected that Jimmy was going to be more involved with the underworld, and so he and Mike would dovetail. But then what ended up happening is we would say sometimes that we'd get two shows for the price of one. And so then Mike's world started running in parallel to Jimmy's. And it worried me tremendously. I was very concerned about it.

But I think looking back on it, it's effective, because when those worlds started to intersect, it had a lot more impact than if they had been constantly crossing over. The scene, for instance, where Lalo comes to Kim's apartment. I don't think that has the same impact if we'd been crossing those worlds the way I was originally expecting to.

And you accidentally wound up satisfying both constituencies: the audience that just wanted the cartel stuff, and the audience that really fell in love with Jimmy and Kim.
We would talk about that. I will say that in the room, for me personally, the underworld stuff came much more easily. The stakes were very clear, the transactions, the relationships were so clear, and Jimmy's world was always difficult. Difficult but rewarding.

I would've assumed it was the opposite, just because cartel world has so many more characters where we know what happens to them and how it happens, and the lawyer world has Kim and Chuck and Howard, and we don't know exactly how Jimmy becomes Saul. But it was the inverse of that?
For me it was, because the Jimmy side, it was all dependent on the psychology of the one character and what was going on with him. And he wasn't always easy to figure out. A little bit like Walt in that way.

But on the cartel side, did you have to stop and say, "Oh, wait, we have to do this, because this was established on *Breaking Bad*"?
Absolutely. Especially once you start bringing Hector in, and it's been established the Cousins don't come easily over the border, all that stuff. Because we've made a big deal out of them. In the future they have that magnificent entrance in *Breaking Bad*. How do the Cousins get from point A to point B? Why are the Cousins showing up? We know they live in Mexico. Why is Hector there? Well, we figured that out because of the Tuco thing. Sometimes we would think, *Oh, wouldn't it be fun to do this?* And then invariably someone in the room would say, "Oh, well, we can't because of this." And oftentimes it was Ariel Levine, who was absolutely the keeper of all the strands on both shows. She and a couple other folks in the office had a giant document of all the characters and props and everything. I never looked at this, but boy, it was really handy*.

---

* I asked Levine for some other instances where story ideas had to be abandoned because they conflicted with *Breaking Bad*. When Mike took his car to the chop shop in the Season Three premiere to look for the tracking device, she says, "We had several discussions in the room about whether

Over the course of the show, mainly on the cartel side, but to some degree on the lawyer side, you get to reveal the origins of all these iconic *Breaking Bad* things: how Hector winds up in the wheelchair and gets the hotel bell, where Jimmy gets the Statue of Liberty from, etc. Were there moments where you said, "This is fun for the fans, but are we overdoing it?"

I'll speak for myself; I was always a little suspicious of it. When that stuff came up, it was because it served the story. That's what I'm hoping. When Jimmy sees the Statue of Liberty, he's seeing what the Kettlemans are up to, and it's game recognizes game. And that was part of that story. Hector's bell, well, we know that Lalo loves his uncle, and he's going to visit him. Well, he should bring a present. What should he bring? Oh, well that makes sense. I'm sure from the outside, it looked like we were playing the greatest hits, but we were really trying not to. We were really focused on trying to make a show that could stand on its own. I was more interested in the things that called back to earlier events within *Better Call Saul*, like the Kettlemans. Things like that were even more exciting to me sometimes.

You just said that it wasn't always easy to figure out what was going on in Jimmy's head. Why was that?

He can be hard to read because he's so attentive to what everyone around him wants. And the person he's closest to, Kim Wexler, he feels protective of that relationship. I think he doesn't feel worthy of her. So there are things that he doesn't want to disclose to her, because he's worried she'll stop loving him. And I think he's also a complicated person who often acts from instinct. He's very, very smart, but he gives in to his instincts often. Those are all things that make him a little tricky to read. That particular season, it was very difficult because I think he was a mystery to himself. He really didn't feel what he knew he needed to feel because of what happened with Chuck. There have been many times in my life where some personally cataclysmic event happens and I think, *What's wrong with me? I'm not feeling a thing.* And then it hits me later, and

---

or not he could be at Old Joe's junkyard. In the end we decided against it because, in their scene in *Breaking Bad* episode 501, it felt like Mike and Joe hadn't met yet." While breaking the fifth *Saul* season, "We very briefly toyed with the idea that Gale might get in some legal trouble that could lead him to call Saul. For example, what if he were pulled over with a little weed—or even some meth-making supplies—in his possession?" They decided this would drastically alter his relationship with Gus, on top of the fact that Gale had a clean record when his murder was being investigated on *Breaking Bad*. And whenever the writers talked about spending more time in the Heisenberg years, there were lots of Kim pitches—including one where she would be revealed to be Judge Papadoumian, a character frequently mentioned on both shows, but never seen. "However, every time we thought about Kim being part of *Breaking Bad*-era Saul Goodman's life, it didn't feel right. Saul Goodman doesn't behave the way he does if Kim Wexler is in his life, so it felt like a continuity error at heart."

maybe that's because I'm so unevolved, but I feel like Jimmy maybe is unevolved in that way too. He's putting off the inevitable.

And why could Walt be hard to read on the other show?
Walt was different because whenever we lost touch with Walt's anger and his rage, we would get stuck. We'd just be thinking, *Well, this happens and this happens.* And then Vince would say, "Wait, wait, wait, where's Walt's head at? What's he thinking about?" That was the key phrase: Where's Walt's head at? Walt had such laser focus that he didn't have the time Jimmy does for self-reflection. I think the danger was always that Jimmy was going to wake up to how terrible his decisions were, to stop making them.

In the Season Three premiere, you've got about thirteen combined minutes across two scenes of Mike Ehrmantraut dismantling and putting stuff back together, with no dialogue. There'd been some of that in *Breaking Bad,* but not to this degree. And then you started doing that a lot. You said you were getting plenty of rope from Sony and AMC, but what gave you guys the confidence to say you could do this and that people would be interested, and it wouldn't seem self-indulgent or boring?
I think watching somebody who's good at what they do is fascinating. Process can be fascinating, it's something that we tend not to show in our entertainment. Mike is this relentless guy, and I think it's fascinating to watch him being relentless. There's no question that as time went on, we just had more and more nerve about this stuff. To me, cinematic storytelling doesn't mean production value necessarily. It means using the stuff that you've got in this medium we're working in to tell the story as creatively as you can. And that's a great example of doing just that. And Vince directed the hell out of it.

***Breaking Bad* would occasionally do montages, but they really became a *Saul* hallmark, whether it's Jimmy and Marco running scams in Cicero, Kim rolling calls in the stairwell, or Jimmy selling the burner phones. How did those get made? Would you go into an episode knowing there would be a montage, or was it something you worked out after the fact with the director, and with [editors Skip MacDonald, Chris McCaleb, and Kelley Dixon]?**
As time went on, I started coming up with some rules for myself about how you do a montage. But the first season, I don't think we really had all that. The one that I remember conceptually was the one that you mentioned at the end of Season One. We were in the writers' room, and I said, "Why don't we do this like a Vorkapich?" The famous montage expert, Slavko Vorkapich, who was an immigrant from [Serbia]. He came to the U.S. and he had trouble breaking in.

He made a short film and then he became the montage specialist. In the classic Hollywood movies, where you would have the Nazi boots trooping across maps of Europe and calendar pages falling and all that, he was the number one guy for that. And we're all film buffs, so I wanted to do one like that.

Then in Season Two, we had the one where Jimmy's trying to get fired, with the inflatable man. All we had was the idea that, okay, we're going to keep cutting to this inflatable man. And when we looked at it in the editing room, though no fault of the director, we realized we didn't have enough there. We went back and shot more pieces, and Kelly came up with all the little boxes moving around the screen, and she almost busted a gut doing. It was very complicated. And it turned out to be fantastic. That really taught me that we needed to go into the montages and have a concept: What's the way in? How does this start? What are we trying to accomplish with the montage? And is there a conceit to this montage?

The one that always stands out to me is "Something Stupid." We were sitting there going, "Okay, Jimmy is not practicing law. He's working in a cell phone store. In the previous episode, we have set him up selling cell phones, and meanwhile, Kim is doing more and more of this pro bono work, and we thought it was time to get that frigging cast off of Rhea Seehorn's arm. She's been very nice about it. But the cast has got to come off, and what's really going on between these two people?" We decided that Jimmy's got a sideline that he's not telling her about, and they're not doing anything together. There's no couple's activity that they've got going, so they're growing apart and the relationship is cooling down. And we thought, *What if there was just a line down the center of the screen and we do it as one big split screen?* That's a good conceit because now you've got an idea for what you can do with the whole sequence. And then we thought, *How do you begin it?* And it's, well, they're brushing their teeth and we'll keep going back to brushing their teeth. Deborah Chow directed that. The thing that was fascinating about it too is, how do you write that on the page? How do you put that over so the reader understands what the hell we're talking about, because we're in the writers' room and we're all waving our arms around and acting this thing out. How do you make sure that people who read it understand? So Alison Tatlock had to come up with a format to make it make sense.* And then Deborah Chow did this incredible board of what they were wearing. Stew Lyons, who was a producer on *Breaking Bad*, used to say,

---

* A sample, from Tatlock's script:
   ON THE LEFT: KIM'S CONDO - BEDROOM - NIGHT L11
   Files cluttering her bedside table, Kim lies in bed, asleep. Alone.

   R11 ON THE RIGHT: KIM'S CONDO - NIGHT R11
   Jimmy sits on the couch with CHIPS and DIP. He watches TV, a little checked out, absently rubbing his sore feet. Alone.

"Montage is French for 'overtime.'" The thing about montage is it can totally screw up your schedule. But the other trick to a montage is you limit it to locations you're already going to in the episode, so when you shoot a dialogue scene in the parking lot at the courthouse, then you grow and grab the montage piece of Jimmy and Kim doing whatever they're going to do in that same parking lot.

Chuck was a great character. How did he come to die after only three seasons?

Oh, we loved Chuck and we loved Michael McKean. I loved writing him. I loved watching him. It really happened while we were breaking that season because there was a fork in the road after "Chicanery." In that episode, Jimmy humiliates Chuck completely, and reveals him to be a man with a sickness. And this is a guy with incredible pride. At that point, what do we do with Chuck? Does he redouble his efforts to take Jimmy down? To stop him from being a lawyer? Or does something else happen? The definition of insanity is doing the same thing over and over again while expecting different results, and in my gut, I think, we felt like at a certain point, if Chuck keeps running after Jimmy, it becomes like the Road Runner. It's the world's greatest cartoon, but it's the same story every time, so we said, "Well, what if Chuck takes something from this? What if he realizes he has a little bit of self-reflection and says, 'I *am* sick,' and he starts to do something about it?" It was at that point we knew he wasn't going to be the same kind of opponent anymore.

And then it just naturally led to this storyline where this man with incredible pride tries to accept help for his mental health problem, but his pride ultimately won't let him fully heal himself. And it becomes the thing that happens at the end of the season. I remember saying to Vince, who was not in the room that year, "I think Chuck is going to die at the end of the season." And then later on I said, "Man, it's just awful to think about trying to do the show without Chuck and without Michael McKean." And Vince said, "Well, maybe you could put it off. Maybe keep him alive Season Four." And I just gritted my teeth because that's one of the things I learned from *Breaking Bad*. I loved the RV, and the RV gets crushed. I loved a lot of characters who died on *Breaking Bad*, and Vince was pretty ruthless about burning the bridges. And I felt like, *This is our bridge and let's see what Jimmy does if Chuck does this thing.* That was my first season as the complete package [solo] showrunner, and that was one of the biggest, most difficult story decisions that season.

In the Season Four premiere, Howard comes to the apartment and makes Jimmy realize that he's actually guilty of something worse than he thought he was, since the malpractice insurance thing is what really

ruined Chuck. And it seems like something in Jimmy breaks. He just compartmentalizes entirely, makes Howard be the one who feels guilty, and starts whistling and making coffee. That, to me, is the first real moment where, there was much more of a Saul Goodman response than a Jimmy McGill response.

I hadn't thought of it that way, but yeah, that does make sense. That season was particularly hard for Bob, I think, because Jimmy was a little impenetrable emotionally, certainly to Kim. And I think that was tricky.

How difficult was it making a season where he's not a lawyer for any of it, and where you had to do a time jump just to get to the end of his suspension?

It was difficult. And if we thought we were doing a law show, it would've been devastating. But it also led to some really fun, interesting stuff. And we loved the idea of him selling cell phones, since that drawer of phones was very important to him on *Breaking Bad*. It just inspired us to come up with the idea of him selling phones out of the store, because the guy is so entrepreneurial and creative that he's able to take even that job, which is not an interesting one, at least the way we portray it, and he makes it into something criminal.

Can you tell me more about why this seemed like a harder year than usual for Bob to get into Jimmy's head?

That was very tough for Bob, because Bob is an enlightened person. He understands himself pretty well, and he had to put himself in this other head. I think a strategic mistake we made writing the scripts was that we wrote some of the action lines from the perspective of how the viewer would regard what he's doing, like, "Why is he doing this?" But I think we needed to also give Bob more about what his internal monologue was in the action lines. Having said that, that's always tricky, because soon you end up with a script that looks like a phone book.

People like me were always asking you, "Wait, is he Saul *now*?" Were there moments in the room where you or the other writers were asking the same thing, well before Saul turns up for real near the end of the final season?

We knew we were dancing toward it, and I think the big moment for us when we said, "Oh, man, he's really Saul-ish right now," was when he ruins Mrs. Landry's life near the end of Season Three. But then he takes it back at the end of the season. But we constantly said, "Well, is he Saul yet?" The litmus test was, if he had clients, would he do what he does with Walt and say, in not so many words, that he's got to kill Jesse Pinkman? Would he do that right now? And we'd always go, "No, he wouldn't say that. He would desperately try to find another way. He wouldn't try to persuade one client to kill another." And we started despairing. "Well, when will he say that? What could it possibly be?" And then we started feeling, I think toward the end of Season Five, it had something to do with Kim and with losing Kim. Actually, it was during Season Five that we said, "Wait a minute. The right way for this to end is for the guy to be in prison. That feels right." That's what I remember, anyway.

The funny thing is, you spent barely any time with Saul Goodman. There's that teaser in Season Four. He wakes up after the time jump in "Fun and Games," and there's a little bit of him in "Waterworks" and in the finale, but there's probably less than a full episode with the "real" Saul. That's incredible in hindsight, given your expectations going in.
That's completely true. Yeah, we made the cheese soufflé with no cheese.

How did you end up going that way?
When it came down to it, we started realizing that there was going to be a time jump and he'd be Saul Goodman, how much are we going to have? And I think we had been through so much with the guy at that point that we understood what Saul Goodman was. He's an empty vessel in a certain way when he's Saul Goodman. He's playing a role.

Oh, here we go. I remembered another pitch. Originally, we were going to show Saul Goodman's home life, and one of the versions was that he'd get in the Cadillac and he'd drive to this nice neighborhood, pull his car in next to a BMW, and in the garage change out of his Saul Goodman suit and change into a black turtleneck and black jeans. And then he'd walk into his house and he's got a turntable and he's listening to jazz and he's got an overweight son. In other words, this guy lives a totally different life away from the spotlight. That was one of our original ideas, and it would've been really fun. But then it's a different show. It's about what happens when those two worlds are in conflict with each other, which is a lot like Walter White.

Getting back to the "Better Call Saul" episode script, you wrote, "It wasn't me, it was Ignacio!" and "Lalo didn't send you? No Lalo?" You've said many times you had no idea what either of those was going to be. When did you decide that you needed to introduce Lalo and explain that? And how did you come up with this absolutely wonderful character that Tony wound up playing?
This was a question right from the beginning because Bob was asking it. I think within the first couple of weeks that we were working together, he says,

"Are we going to see Lalo? What's the deal with Lalo? What happened between Saul and Lalo?" And we didn't know. But it was always on our mind. And Lalo shows up to fill a vacuum. The Salamancas, they don't have that deep a bench. Tuco goes down, and so here comes Tio, and Nacho becomes his second. And then he goes down. So Nacho's taking care of things for a bit. And then you get Lalo. I think we thought, *Well, we really want a different flavor of the cartel.* The Salamancas—the ones that we've seen, especially Hector and Tuco—they're real craggy, hardcore, angry guys. And what would it be like to have one Salamanca who's a little bit more carefree and enjoying himself? And we thought about Gus too. Who's a good foil for Gus? Gus is so restrained. Wouldn't it be fun to have a more exuberant character? And it all crystallized. A lot of the time you think about these things in general, and that only takes you so far. It crystallized when we thought about, *what's the first scene?* And we had this notion that everybody at the El Michoacáno is scared out of their minds. Nacho comes in, and they're all sitting in place, and there's this new character who's singing and cooking at the same time. And that tells you a lot about this guy. He's scary, but what he's doing while being scary is cooking. It felt like a great contrast with Nacho, who is so tortured and feels such an obligation to his father and is really trying to extract himself from these terrible decisions he made when he was younger. I think Nacho's an incredibly tragic character, because even when you first meet him, he's had it with the underworld. He'd much rather steal money from the Kettlemans than actually do any drug deals. And it's a slippery slope; he just ends up getting deeper and deeper and deeper. So that was the idea.

Then we saw auditions, and again, Bialy/Thomas, they brought us these wonderful actors. We saw Tony Dalton, and he just popped off the screen, and we said, "That's the guy. Don't shave the mustache." As soon as I saw Tony in that scene, I was thrilled. It's one of those moments where you go, "Oh, we've really got something here. This guy's great." It opened up a whole new arena for us to play in.

When you watch a prequel, you know the story is bound by certain things. At a certain point, I'm watching Lalo, and it's clear this guy cannot be alive during the events of *Breaking Bad*, because he would not have allowed Gus's plan to proceed the way it did. Yet I'm also thinking, *I like Lalo. I don't want him to die. I want him to be around forever. I wish he could have been on* Breaking Bad. Was there any point where you wished you had thought of the character sooner?

I was absolutely greedy for everything that we could have on *Better Call Saul*, believe me. But you don't know for sure that he's going to die. And also, this goes to a theory we've talked about many times, which is, it's not what happens, it's how it happens. Otherwise, no one would ever go see a play or a movie called *Napoleon*. You kind of know what's going to happen in the end. All you have to do is look at Wikipedia.

On the subject of being greedy, Lalo is offscreen for a good chunk of the final season while he's playing dead and plotting his next move against Gus. And then he dies with four episodes remaining. Were you ever tempted to try to get as much of Tony onscreen as possible that year?
That's really two questions, starting with why he's offscreen so much that season. My feeling was, it was good to have him offscreen because it was the threat. It's like a play, where everyone's talking about Lord So-and-So, and what Lord So-and-So is like, and what's he going to do when he shows up? It builds this anticipation. We knew that we were building up to this final confrontation between Lalo and Gus. So, I think that was really showmanship.

The other one is about him dying well before the end of the series. Again, I wanted it to be a funnel, where the story needed to be thinned out toward the end. It just felt like we wanted to have enough time to deal with Jimmy and Kim, and we wanted to go to Omaha. That's just the way the timing felt like it worked out because, ultimately, we wanted to end the show not as a cartel show or an action show. It was a show about a man's soul. It was a love story in a lot of ways. We needed the room to do that.

Nacho, meanwhile, dies in a scene where literally all the other people in the scene are people we know are alive on *Breaking Bad*. This should not be tense at all. Nacho is obviously going to die. But it's an incredible scene. Could you use that as an example of how you were able to tell all of these stories about characters whose fates we knew, that were preordained, and make them as tense and as exciting and as rich as they were?
I think you watch a movie moment by moment. I don't think you're always deducing where things are going to go. Or maybe you are, but I'm not. And Nacho, there is a world where he gets out of that. Part of the tension of the scene is that Mike was there with a high-powered rifle. For all we know, Mike's going to lay down a field of fire. Everybody else is going to duck down and Nacho's going to make a big run for it. Mike will take him in a car and drive him away. It could have happened that way. But it felt like that the ultimate thing for this character to do is to sacrifice himself for his father.

When you did that first Gene from Cinnabon teaser in the premiere, did you actually think that you were going to resolve this story after the events

of *Breaking Bad*? Or was it just that you wanted to give people a hint of where it was all going for Saul, before jumping back to before it all began?

I think we wanted to give a hint of where it was going. I don't think it was clear to us that there was a story in Omaha at that point. There really wasn't. If you think about it, the first two teasers about Gene in Omaha, they're kind of tone poems. The first one is just about regrets for the life that he left behind. And that was also a big thing for us. We had to keep saying to ourselves, "Well, whatever happens, when he's in Omaha, he still wants to be Saul Goodman." And that's what told us there had to be story there eventually. Even when he faints in the Season Three teaser, that potentially could have been something that stands by itself. The guy faints, and the next time you see him, if you ever do again, he's back to working in Cinnabon and he's just ten years older, or he is getting a gold watch from Cinnabon, or whatever it is. It's a self-contained little piece. But instead, what we did was we said, "Well, no, wait. Somebody recognizes him." And as soon as somebody recognizes him, then you know there's story there. What is he going to do?

But I know especially at the beginning, it was like, "Well, what are we going to do in Omaha?" And the answer was, "We don't know." One of the pitches was that he's in Omaha and you see him, and he takes a day off and he drives, and he drives to Lincoln. And he gets out of the car and he watches Kim, and she's got a house with a family and she's living her best life and he's just left out in the snow by himself eating out of a bag of McDonald's. And we thought we were going to do that for a while.

Pretty early on, we see that Kim sleeps in a Kansas City Royals shirt, and immediately people said, "Wait a minute. There's a Kansas City Royals affiliate in Omaha." And later on, you established that she was from Nebraska. People kept wondering if she was going to wander into the mall at some point. Was that something you were actually thinking of?

No. That was all in service of the pitch I just gave you, which was that she ends up going back home, and he knows she's there, but whether she knows where he is, I don't know. It seemed like a little bit of a long shot to have her walk into the mall and recognize him. That seemed a little bit crazy. We thought about it, though.

At what point did you realize that the story was not only going to end in the Gene timeline, but that you were going to spend multiple episodes there?

We started talking about that pretty early on. We said, "Wouldn't it be great to have a whole bunch of stuff in Omaha?" And I always had this idea that I would pitch but that we never did—and he's not my favorite person or my favorite director, but something that always stuck with me from D. W. Griffith's *Intolerance* is that it has four different storylines, and at the climax, they all intercut. I thought that was really fun, that there's this chase going on in four different time periods with different characters and they all get intercut. And I thought, *Wouldn't it be great if we could do that with Saul?* Saul's on the run, he's got trouble here in Albuquerque, and meanwhile he's under the gun up in Omaha. The closest we ever did to that was Tom's episode ["Breaking Bad"], and I think that's probably all to the good.

It goes back to what I said before. The more we thought about it, we thought, *Well, this guy still wants to be Saul. Is that where we want to leave him? Do we want to leave him at that point in life that all he's doing is wasting away, remembering the good times? Is that the right end?* And we thought, *Well, no, we've invested a lot in this character. We've invested a lot in Kim. Let's go forward and see what we can do.*

At the time, when we were working on the series finale, I was worried that it was almost too dark because we left him in prison, and I was delighted when people said it was a happy ending. And if it's a happy ending, I think it's because he finally gets out of his own way. That was what we realized we hadn't done. And there was no other way to do that because you saw what he was like in Omaha, and you saw what he was like when he left Albuquerque, so something had to happen in Omaha.

In the finale, there's the scene with him and Walt in Ed's basement, and Walt says, "So you were always like this." And for a minute, it feels like this is the version of the "Felina" scene where Walt says, "I did it for me."
Yes.

But then later on, you make clear, no, he was *not* always like this, and he does not always have to be like this. How much would you compare the arc of Jimmy descending into Saul versus Walt descending into Heisenberg? Do you see a lot of parallels there, or not ultimately?
It's a good question, because these guys both have a side to them that they're not using, and they both let their worst sides out. I think that's the thing that's similar about them. Jimmy never goes as far as Walt. Walt's such a fascinating, deep character, but I think he always had this giant chip on his shoulder. I think in both stories it's a little bit about giving in to your worst self, but also I don't believe "the fault is in our stars." I think that there's nothing that was fated about any of these things. And I don't think either one of these guys is a victim of circumstances. I think both shows are a portrait of what happens when you let your worst self make a series of bad decisions.

In both cases, the guy comes back to Albuquerque in the finale and undoes a lot of the problems he caused.
I hadn't thought of it that way. That's true.

But Walt dies and everyone still hates him, whereas Jimmy decides, *I'm going to take the rap. I'm going to go to prison like I should*. But Kim forgives him, and at least he gets to see her one more time. Again, it's not a happy ending, but it's a lot happier than "Felina." How did you decide that this is what Jimmy deserves after all that he has done?
Walt really gets what he wants, I think, in a lot of ways. Walt doesn't want to be in prison. Was his family liking him ever really that important to him? Maybe. But that went out the window pretty early on in the show. What does Jimmy want? What Jimmy wants isn't as tangible as what Walt wants. Here's the thing, I think they both want significance. And for Walt, it's like, "I'm going to leave the money to my family whether they like me or not, and they're never going to be able to get over that. And that's going to be my memorial." And Jimmy, I think he really wants people to like him. And most of all, he wants love. And I think he wants Kim's love.

In a weird way, they get at least part of what they want, or what they didn't know they wanted, at the end, but Jimmy's a more human scale–character. He never commits a murder. It's a more complex situation too because he's a bystander and he's an aider. He's not an instigator of violence, for the most part. I'm not sure I'm answering your question, but I think as we were working on it, which is probably the only thing I can really say authoritatively, we weren't thinking in terms of the two of them being parallel. And the only thing we would think about is, *Well, whatever it was, we did that with Walt. We can't do that with Jimmy.*

You and Vince co-created this character. You wrote the very first episode to feature him. You wound up running this show the whole time, whereas Vince came and went. Saul is ultimately your baby. Do you find yourself feeling more protective of him at the end as a result of that?
I wouldn't say I was more protective, but I wanted to be true to the guy. And I also identified with both those guys in my own writerly way. I think [Jimmy] has a lot in common with us in the writers' room. He's a movie buff. He's a romantic in a weird way. And he's also a lot like a writer in a lot of ways. So, yeah, I felt protective, but I didn't want to protect him from the consequences of his actions. As a dramatist, you can start liking your characters so much you want to give them an easy road, and that's really one of the great dangers of the work, is that you like the character, you like the actor who plays the character, so you're going to go easy on them. That was something that we had to fight on this show.

It certainly was something we fought with Jesse Pinkman because there was always the discussion of what does Jesse Pinkman deserve? What does Jimmy deserve, and does he get it or does he not get it? Because I think that's, I'm not saying that these shows or any show is a morality play, but I think that's one of the yardsticks that you measure drama by. One of the things that makes drama exciting is when there's an injustice. That's usually the jumping-off point.

Over the years, did you ever come close to having Walt and/or Jesse appear prior to when they finally did?
Something that was pitched constantly was that Kim has a case and Walt is called for jury duty. In one of the versions of the pitch, Kim strikes him from the jury pool and he gets a big chip on his shoulder. And he confronts her afterward: "Why would you strike me from the jury pool?" And they have a whole confrontation. So yeah, we were always thinking about, *Is there something fun that we could do with these guys?*

I'll speak for myself, but I think we were all trying to only use the *Breaking Bad* characters when it would really add to Jimmy's story. I felt like it was a lot that we brought Tuco back in the pilot. That was huge. And as soon as you start bringing in those characters, it became important that the show stand on its own without relying on them as a crutch and, as I said before, playing the greatest hits. I was proud that we waited because we wanted to work with all these people, and certainly Bryan and Aaron several times voiced their willingness to show up. It was very tempting, and it was, frankly, something the studio and the network would ask every so often. "Are they going to come back?" And we'd always say, "We're not quite ready for that."

That episode clarifies a number of things from *Breaking Bad*. One is that Jimmy got interested in Walt entirely on his own, even though Gus and Mike had been looking into him. It also sort of clarifies why Mike is working as Jimmy's investigator after he's got this hugely important and lucrative job working for Gus. But certainly you could have established that Jimmy is lying to Walt when he says, "I know a guy who knows a guy who knows another guy." How did you ultimately land on this as how you would deal with both?
We often asked ourselves, "Why is Mike working for Jimmy?" And we decided that Jimmy's got his fingers in the underworld, and so it's a way for Gus to know everything that's happening in Albuquerque and on the dark side of things. That's one of the fun things about going back to the show and asking questions. On *Breaking Bad*, we have Pollos Hermanos, there are two chickens. Well, who's

the other? Gus is one of the chicken brothers, who's the other chicken brother? And so we had the logo before we knew anything about Gus's past. And I think in this case, it's more of the same.

But were there ever points at which you started to wonder about whether Jimmy/Saul actually had any kind of relationship with Gus?

Yeah, we did wonder that. And it just felt like in the scope of our time, it was too heavy for him. Jimmy wasn't really ready to work with someone at Gus's scale. And why would Gus work with Jimmy? Believe me, I can't remember any specifics, but there were pitches where Jimmy helps him in some way. I think there was a pitch where Jimmy finds out about Gus, and he solicits his business and does all kinds of this and that to try to get into business with the guy because he's a whale. You can come up with all these fun ideas, but if the character's not ready for it, or if it's not expressing something about what's going on with the character, then it's a little bit of a dead end.

Right after Hector kills Max on *Breaking Bad*, Don Eladio alludes to Gus having been a big deal in Chile. That's all we ever learned about that. You were able to use this show to fill in a lot of blanks over the years. Is that something that was ever discussed as being worthy of explanation?

It was absolutely discussed. Every aspect of Gus's past was discussed. I have a theory, though, that you really don't want to cross every *t* and dot every *i*, because we're in collaboration with the audience's imagination. Who knows, this may be the basis for the next spin-off with Giancarlo. I don't know. But I feel like you want to be careful about how much you get into just making everything into answering every possible question. Because then you've got a world that has definite edges to it, and it's more interesting if the world goes off the edge of the screen.

One thing you did choose to answer, in the very last scene where Giancarlo is playing this character, is that yes, Gus is gay. He is smitten with Reed Diamond, and clearly Hector was right about Gus and Max's relationship. Giancarlo had said previously he liked the ambiguity, at least on *Breaking Bad*, that it was not spelled out. How did you decide you actually wanted to answer this, and this way?

It felt like it was definitely going to happen on *Better Call Saul*, because you're going to spend more time with the character. And this is part of who he is. I don't remember us coming up with any other version of that. But it felt good. And he's a horrible person, Gus Fring, but he's a tragic character because he's got this lost love. He ends up structuring his entire existence around revenge.

He's a little bit like the Count of Monte Cristo in a certain way—the worst version of the Count of Monte Cristo. The fact that he has a chance for a love connection and then he just can't bring himself to sully the memory of his lost love, I think it's tragic. If he spent more time with Reed, then maybe things would've gone very differently for Gustavo Fring.

If you think about it, the mistake is not seeking revenge, but insisting that Hector stay alive to watch everyone else die first. If he had just killed the guy, none of the other stuff would've happened!
That's a good point. It's a little bit parallel with Chuck. It's about ego.

Were there ever serious discussions about Kim dying?
Not really. Speaking for myself, I always thought there would have been something cheap and familiar about Kim's death causing Jimmy's change. Would have made her nothing more than a vehicle for his devolution. Never felt right to me.

"Fun and Games" is the last episode that follows the "This and That" title rubric from the final season. It's the last episode of the series with the traditional opening credits. It's the last episode with Gus, with any of the cartel characters, with an actual Mike storyline, as opposed to Mike cameoing in things going on with Jimmy and Saul. It's this unusual thing where the show we've been watching for fifty-nine episodes just *ends*, in a way. And then we get this four-episode epilogue where everything's structured differently, and we've said goodbye to one whole half of the show. How did you get there?
The show wasn't over. I think we were just responding to where the story took us, because we knew there was more to the story in Omaha. And we felt that once Kim has left Jimmy, that segment of the story, that is over. It's done. It felt like that's the moment where you jump forward. Again, we started with the question: What kind of problem does becoming Saul Goodman solve? We had no idea what the answer was. The clouds started to part in maybe Seasons Four and Five. *Okay, it has something to do with Kim. Kim's going to leave him. Why would Kim leave him?* And then we thought about all those things, and about his responsibility for a death, an extremely violent death in front of him. Kim's shared responsibility of that, that separates them. So then your question is, what happens after you've answered the question of the show?

Well, the other question of the show is, is this guy ever going to grow? Is Saul Goodman in end-state form? But we already knew that Saul Goodman was not in end-state form because we had set that at the beginning of the show. We said, "No, there's something there." And as time went on, we realized there was a story there in Omaha. So it just felt like, let's just go ahead and do Omaha because it's a different show and there are no subplots. And as we went on, we added this amazing cast and we started adding more point-of-view characters and having more parallel scenes with them. Ultimately, it felt like it should be a funnel, and we should go from talking about several people to just going back to our initial focus, which was Jimmy and the question surrounding him.

It felt right. And, to me, it actually felt ballsy. Let's just be like *2001: A Space Odyssey*. Let's cut ahead. Let's just go for it. And I always know that it might be good if I get a little nervous and scared, because I was absolutely worried about what people would think of it, and how it was going to go. And the fact that they bought into it made me happy. But I could tell from just talking to people and the response that it did throw people for a loop when suddenly they're in this black-and-white world with "Nippy." And not only just a black-and-white world, but a world where that episode has an endpoint* that doesn't leave any story open except for what's going on in this guy's head, which is taking the show back to the studs.

In hindsight, if you'd known you were going to be devoting the last four episodes largely to the 2010 timeline, would you have made the first Gene prologue black and white?
Oh, yeah. I was crazy about the black and white. I still am. And because we couldn't go to Omaha to film those—we would have had to use a whole different crew—the black and white really helped sell Albuquerque as Omaha.

[*Part of this conversation took place on January 16, 2024, one day after* Better Call Saul *was shut out at the 75th Primetime Emmy Awards, completing an absurd—and unflattering to Emmy voters—0-for-53 streak of Emmy nominations to wins over the life of the series. This shattered the previous record for Emmy series futility, when* Newhart *went 0-for-25 in the eighties.*[†]]

How did this happen? How did the Emmys so thoroughly fail you this way?
Look, if you get hung up on these awards, it's the quick way to insanity. It's like the ultimate version of social media. It's super alluring, it's really fun to win. It's a lot of delight, but I think our timing just wasn't great. To be honest with you, this year I was absolutely certain we weren't going to win, so it was much lower pressure on me. Before I started going to the Emmys, I'd be like, "Why

---

* My original take on "Nippy" was more or less, "Why are we getting the end of Gene's story when the show still has three episodes left to go?" Sometimes, I am bad at seeing the future.

† On the same night that *Saul* was blanked for the last time, *The Late Show with Stephen Colbert* nudged into second place, at 0-for-26.

would they be bummed out that they didn't win? Because you got nominated for this great award. It's amazing. Just enjoy the ride." And I would always be like, "What is her problem? What is his problem?" And then, I went myself the first time and you get all wound up because your category shows up. They show a little clip, your name is said, and then you think, *Oh, well, maybe . . . Is it possible?* You get all hyped up, and there's this rush of adrenaline, and then it's somebody else or another show. And there's a moment of delight and relaxation because you don't have to get up on television and talk. And then, soon after that, the "Ah, shit," kind of sets in.

But I've been through it enough at this point that I'm not too upset. I will say that the thing that makes me a little sad is that those of us who worked on *Breaking Bad*, especially in the writers' room, we had the privilege of getting a couple of Emmys for that, and that was wonderful.* But there are a lot of wonderful producers who were only on *Saul* and they didn't get statuettes, so that's a little sad to me. And also, I do believe that the work that was done is deserving of awards.

When you say it was bad timing, do you mean that you came on while *Game of Thrones* was still airing, and finished up while *Succession* was crushing everything? Or was there more?
I think that's something.† I think the rules of the voting changed a little bit. I don't have a great insight into this. And by the way, the two shows together were on for fifteen years. I think when you're a voter, sometimes you think, *Well, those folks have already gotten [their Emmys]; I'm more interested in rewarding something new than something that's been around for a while.* And I understand. Being an Emmy voter, I know how capricious it is. So, maybe we shouldn't take it quite so seriously.

But you know what? Critics gave us plenty of awards. We got a lot of critics' awards. So, where's the complaint? I'm kind of joking and I'm kind of not,

---

* Gould also recalled that Bryan Cranston brought his first *Breaking Bad* Emmy with him to work one day while filming a Season Two episode you may be familiar with, called "Better Call Saul." Gould and many other members of the cast and crew took turns posing for photos with it while seated on the famous bench with the Saul Goodman ad.

† In hindsight, the best shot at a win for either the show or Odenkirk was in 2017, when *Game of Thrones* took the year off. Instead, *The Handmaid's Tale* won over Emmy voters as the show of the moment, and *This Is Us* breakout star Sterling K. Brown won for drama lead actor. Odenkirk and Rhea Seehorn also seemed like they had a chance in 2022, since the final batch of Season Six episodes were airing while people were voting on that season's first half, so that "Saul Gone" and "Waterworks" would be in people's heads. (Anna Gunn had once benefited from this, winning for the penultimate group of *Breaking Bad* episodes in part because "Ozymandias" and the series finale debuted during that voting window.) Instead, Odenkirk lost to *Squid Game* star Lee Jung-jae, and voters chose to give *Ozark*'s Julia Garner a third trophy rather than recognizing Seehorn.

because your job is to watch everything on TV. And so, to get an award from the critics' organization, I would bet you that the average critic has watched more TV in a year than the average actor or showrunner or writer or editor, because we're all busy working on our own shows. So, anyway, that's my argument for today. As you can see, I'm [great] at making myself feel better.

The show is great no matter what. There's just the TV historian part of me that thinks, *Jesus, Rhea doesn't have an Emmy, Bob doesn't have an Emmy, Jonathan and Giancarlo don't have an Emmy across two shows. That's not okay.*

No, I'm with you. Look, I could be just as outraged as you, but I think the good thing about it is it's such an egregious oversight that it's sort of like the one that everybody talks about—*The Wire*. I mean there's no question that *The Wire* is one of the best television shows ever in history, in my mind, and they didn't even get the nominations.* So, it'd be great if we're in the *Guinness Book of World Records* for most snubs. I mean, that's something.

There were a few times over the run of *Breaking Bad* where a renewal came very late, and it felt like the show could have just ended abruptly. Were there ever moments in *Saul* where you worried about the future? Did AMC and Sony want to make fewer seasons than you did? More? Or about the same?

Breaking Bad was a very different process. But on *Saul*, we were in such a privileged position. I don't remember what season it was, but [then-AMC president] Charlie Collier called me, and he said, "I just want you to know we would like as many as you want to make. You tell me how many seasons you want to do and how many episodes, and we'll be delighted to take as many as you'll make." So ultimately, it was up to me. This was probably at the end of Season Three or Four. And it was on my mind that *Breaking Bad* had been sixty-two [episodes]. And I was like, "All right. We're going to do one more episode than *Breaking Bad*, just to prove that we can." And the truth is that there's no science to this. It's completely back of the back of the envelope. It's something where you just get the feeling like, "Okay, that's probably about right." And one of the things that we always think about is we don't want to overstay our welcome. Maybe we did, hopefully we didn't. But to overstay our welcome and to have people go, "Oh, that's still on?" So, I think it was the right number of episodes.

---

* *The Wire* was nominated twice—half as many times as the Jim Belushi sitcom *According to Jim* received.

Breaking Bad was much more fraught about the pickups. I remember being jealous of *Mad Men*, because whenever they had a *Mad Men* premiere party, they would have these enormous, wonderful events, and it would be announced at the party that they had been picked up for another season, and we never had that. Especially in the beginning, they would wait until the last possible second when the options on the actors were going to run out. And I don't think it had anything to do with them not liking the show or wanting to do more. I think it had to do with a lot of behind-the-scenes wrangling that was going on.

And on the flip side, were there ever moments where you thought you might be ready to finish the story sooner than expected?
No, not story-wise, because it was very simple: Is he Saul Goodman yet? We weren't there yet. But that's the story. In terms of me personally, there were moments when the job got really hard and I thought, *Oh, I don't know if I'm going to make it to the end.* Just the amount of physical stress, or, *Am I going to snap?* And all the little health problems that come up when you're under stress. So, yeah, there were times when I was like, *Oh boy, I don't know if I can make this and make it to the end.* And then, every season we just kind of get excited about it again and there you go.

I always thought there was a chance we'd fuck it up, though. There was no sense that we had a net below us. Right up to the last episode, I thought that maybe this isn't going to work for people.

While we're on the subject of health, we have to talk about Bob's heart attack. What was that day like for you?
I was back in L.A. Vince called me because he had been directing when it happened, and said, "Melissa [Bernstein] and I are in a car, we're following an ambulance. Bob collapsed on the set, and it really doesn't look good." My first instinct was to run to Albuquerque—I didn't, because there were plenty of people hovering around, worried. I helped out with coordinating getting Bob's family to Albuquerque, and Sony was fantastic with this.

After shutting down for a few days, we just had no idea what his status was going to be. I talked to his wife, Naomi. I spoke to Rhea Seehorn, and she was as upset as I've ever heard anybody. It was a great feeling of helplessness, of not knowing what was going to happen next. And then, pretty soon, amazingly enough, I don't remember exactly the timeline, but I was on the phone with Bob himself, and I could hear he was himself, but he wasn't remembering things quite right. He was in the room with Naomi and he said, "Peter, I have nothing to do here. Please send me a script so I can study up. I know you don't like to send them too early." And Naomi was off mic going, "No, no, you don't send him anything!" Because literally, the doctors said he needs to sit in a room lit by candlelight and he needs time to recover. Honest to God, we didn't know if we were going to have a show or if we were going to finish it. And it felt so completely irrelevant, because it's when you realize it's just a fucking piece of entertainment.

That was an awful time. Rosa Estrada was our medical advisor, and then she was in charge of all of our COVID stuff. And because she was there, that's one of the reasons he's alive today.

I spoke to her on the phone, and you're just talking to everybody, hoping that maybe talking about it's going to make you feel better, but just also being in incredible suspense and being very worried about Bob's family. That was the experience. And then bit by bit, I'd hear from him on the phone. I hadn't seen him. And then we'd hear, "The doctors say he might be able to come back at this point in time, but we're going to have to watch out for him." And so, Bob's doctors made some rules, and we made some rules about how he was going to work, because Bob is a workaholic. He's intense.

You think about *Better Call Saul*, he has five- or ten-page scenes, sometimes a couple of them a week. And he prepares like crazy for those. He knows all the dialogue. He knows all the beats. He's worked with the other actors before he gets to the set. We had to really think about how we were going to handle that.

I was in Albuquerque for when he came back. It was such a feeling to have him walk onto the stage, and the way he talked to the crew, and the emotional intelligence he had about what people were feeling. I think he was more worried about what everybody else was feeling than anything about himself. The first shot we did was the very first shot you see of him in the season, a little pickup from that scene in the hotel room where they wake up together. And it's a miracle, but it was very emotional. It was very tough for everybody.

Obviously, Bob's health, and the emotional well-being of his family, were all that really mattered at the beginning of this. But once you knew that he was going to live, but not necessarily how fully he would recover, did you, Vince, or anyone else allow yourselves to discuss what you would do if he couldn't come back? Or if he could come back, but in a very limited way?
Not really. Most of our conversations were, "What can we keep shooting right now?" And we got very lucky, because at that point in the season, suddenly you had a lot of material with Mike and with Gus, and we had some little pickups to do for previous episodes. So we were only down for three or four days, and then the crew was back to work and shooting.

But look, if he hadn't been himself . . . [*long pause*] It didn't really bear thinking about, but I will say, I think we would've just dropped the show. I think Sony would've had to take a terrible financial loss, because it would be an utterly incomplete story. And they were shooting the scene that comes immediately after Lalo has shot Howard. There's no rewriting to get around that. That's about all I can say. We were ready to dump the whole thing. I mean, I wasn't thinking about that. It's too complicated. It was too big to really kind of think it through. But I'm sure somebody deep in the bowels of Sony had to start doing some calculations about what kind of loss they'd have to take, and thank God it didn't happen.

Did you have to rewrite any of Bob's material for the remaining episodes because of the doctors' rules? I can't imagine him filming something like "Bagman" at this point.
Alan, we didn't change a damn thing. Writing-wise, we didn't change a thing and we didn't have to. If we had had something that was physically challenging, we would have had to figure out ways to shoot it so we would use more of a double.

The whole season was [filmed during] COVID. Because when we started the season, a lot of shows were coming back and what you heard in the business was, "Well, nobody can shoot a crowd scene. Everything's going to be two, three people in a room. You can't do this. You can't do that." And we said, "We're not going to suddenly do a season that doesn't feel like the rest of the show because of this. We can't lower our standards or change the way the story's told because of this external circumstance. We have to find a way around it."

So it was more about giving him breaks than giving him different material?
Yeah. And scheduling so that he didn't have too many consecutive big days. Bob was the one, he'd always, "Oh, I can stay. Let me stay. I can stay a little longer to finish this." But Melissa Bernstein and the rest of the producers just put the hammer down, and when the clock struck a certain hour, he turned back into a pumpkin and had to go home and relax. And as time went on, I actually think it was probably in some ways really good for everybody because it kept us, for the most part, from doing really something that the business is hopefully moving away from—doing crazy long hours.

When *Breaking Bad* started, basic cable was going through a creative renaissance. By the time *Saul* ended, nearly all of the most interesting scripted shows were being made for premium cable or streaming. And all

but the biggest streaming shows at the moment are lucky to make it to three seasons. Could something like either of your two shows, that tell complicated plot and character arcs over five or more seasons, get made today?

Possibly, but I think the odds are much more against it now than they were. My hope is that there's always going to be a big enough wedge of the audience that's interested in leaning forward to watch the TV instead of leaning back. I love both kinds of TV. I love the TV that just kind of washes over you, but I like it when you really have to watch to catch it. And my hope is that maybe the ratio changes, but we're still able to do both. Ironically enough, once you introduce advertising again [to ad-supported streaming tiers], I think that maybe at that point, a longer run of a show then becomes more useful. So we'll see.

What was the last scene of the series to be filmed?

The last thing we shot, and this is the genius of scheduling, was the last scene between Jimmy and Kim in the visiting room, smoking against the wall. It was the same day we shot Jimmy alone in the holding cell when he's got the Gene mustache. We shot little bits and pieces of other things. Then we got to that last scene, and the way I blocked it, at first, we wouldn't have been able to make the day. Marshall [Adams] and Melissa [Bernstein] suggested a blocking change to simplify it. They started to save the day. Then right toward the end it, we still weren't going to make the day. But Marshall did something that DPs almost never do: he figured out a way to shoot both Jimmy and Kim, their close-ups at the wall, at the same time, and he had to use a mirror to shoot the side facing Jimmy. We were able to shoot that simultaneously, which was just wonderful. It was wonderful for the schedule, but it also meant that all those little moments and exchanges between them were actually happening, and they weren't having to re-create the moment. That was, literally, the last thing that we shot.

How were Bob and Rhea doing at the end there? They get to share their final scene together, and then the experience is over. And how were you doing?

I think we were all exhausted, but sad and happy with what we had done. We all made speeches to the crew. We're all wearing masks, making speeches with a microphone. They did a fantastic job in that scene. There's very few words, but they found the beats, and I was so proud of it. I was so excited by what we had done.

Also, I was directing. So, when you're directing, all you're doing is thinking about, *Am I getting it?* I'm not thinking, *Oh, this is the end of the fifteen-year-long journey.* That didn't really land for me until much, much later, but there were, along the way, all these little moments, like saying goodbye to Carol Burnett when she left.

It was a really hard season to shoot, especially because of Bob's health, but also COVID and how ambitious the show was. It was just a really rough time—as rough as it could be with everybody being a good person. The really bad stuff happens if people are being shits to each other, and that never happened, but it was just physically and emotionally wearing. Having Carol come in when she did, toward the end after Bob had come back, just made everybody happy. She's a magical, magical person. She's so freaking smart about everything, and about people. She's just very perceptive, but also generous. [It was like] she gave us all Prozac, and she gave us a lift from being there and being on the set. Then when she left, right at the beginning of shooting the finale, a little joy left the room. But I think everybody was mostly feeling good and we were proud of what we'd done.

Do you think that when they look at each other as Kim is walking to the exit, that's the last they ever see of each other?
That sequence was not broken in the room. That was something I added as I was writing. What excited me about that was the sadness of it and the ambiguity of it. My hope and desire would be that the characters live on in the heads of the audience. So, a little bit of ambiguity is good.

In my mind, I could go back and forth, depends on what day you ask me. I find it hard to believe that she's done with him. He's in one of the most awful situations a human being can be in. Now having shot in a real prison, it's a dire, dire place. It's just awful, and it's terrible that we have to have them. She knows he's there. I find it hard to believe that she's not going to call him, send him a letter, send him some cash to buy cigarettes, whatever.

And I find it hard to believe that he's not going to make himself really useful to the other prisoners. It seems like he has already. He's found a place of equilibrium in there. But I find it hard to believe that she would just walk away forever and never have any contact with him. On the other hand, it would be a big leap to think that they could get involved romantically again. Maybe, but my mother used to say this, "Where there's life, there's hope."

One of the things I always say when people ask me which show do you think is better is that all of you who had worked on *Breaking Bad* and continued on to *Saul* had been telling these particular kinds of stories, in this production apparatus, in this location, working with each other for so long, that a lot of you were just simply better at the job by the time you got

to make *Better Call Saul*. So I love the "Four Days Out" episode of *Breaking Bad*, but, in terms of two guys stuck in the desert, "Bagman" is executed at a much, much higher level. Do you feel you guys had more of a hang of it this time around?

That's hard for me to say. I always had this feeling of safety on *Breaking Bad* because of Vince. Once we started, I just realized that, *Boy, I'm in the presence of a guy who really—this is going to come out great.* I really trusted him.

With *Better Call Saul*, I don't know if we got better at it. I mean, the crew certainly got better and better, but I think the truth is that they're really two different kinds of shows. If we had made *Better Call Saul* first, I don't think you would ever come up with *Breaking Bad* after *Better Call Saul*. First of all, I don't know if *Saul* would've gotten a second season if it had been a totally original show. But it wasn't just a brand extension. It was really its own animal. I think there's also just something leaner and cleaner about *Breaking Bad*. I think *Saul*, for better or for worse, it's more discursive. It's not always as propulsive as *Breaking Bad*, which is something I love about *Breaking Bad*, but I also love the way *Saul* is. It's really two different, but delicious, flavors, and it just depends which one are you in the mood for.

You are definitely right about one thing, which is the first season of any show is really tough. It's the hardest thing. I never had to show run the first season of a show, really, because with *Better Call Saul*, we already had the crew, we had most of the key cast already, so we had a big head start on that one. To that extent, I think you're right. I think we had gotten better at the job because we had a lot of advantages.

There's a lot of talk in the finale about time travel, and changes we wish we could make in our pasts. If I gave you a time machine and you could go back to *Breaking Bad*, or even to early *Better Call Saul*, and undo something that prevented you from telling a story here, what would you change?

This is a terrible answer, but I'd be tempted to take out the mention of Saul's ex-wives. It bugs me that we never really followed up on that, but what else would I do? It's like, as Orson Welles used to say, lack of limits is the enemy of art. Sometimes doing the crossword is easier than writing a poem—having constraints, like the timeline, was helpful. I was really taken by surprise when we realized how he wasn't really in Omaha as long as I would've liked. I would've liked to have had him working in Omaha for maybe a couple of years, at least. And I think when we actually broke down the timeline, it was maybe six months, and that never felt like enough time for me. But since we never explicitly said to the audience how long it was, it's just something you'd have to deduce.

There are things I would've loved to explore, like exactly how did the Disappearer set him up with this job? When he showed up, he's going to work at a Cinnabon. Presumably, this Gene Takovic identity has some kind of a backstory to it. I wanted to see more of him sweating and trying to learn all this stuff. I would've loved to have seen that. I wish we could have.

Now I'm going in the wrong direction because I'm just thinking of all the characters we would've loved to see—have Walter Jr. and Skyler on the show. But figuring out how they would ever have anything to do with Jimmy or with Saul, it just seemed like such a freaking stretch. I couldn't see it. There were just so many things we could have done with Kim, too. If Kim had stayed in Albuquerque and she hadn't had to leave when she did, she could have represented Skyler.* There are all kinds of possibilities that we could have played with, but in the end, I can't get too terribly upset about any of that.

When I interviewed Vince about his last episode, he said that he might eventually want to go back to this universe after he's finally allowed himself to do other things. If he did want to do it, would you? Or do you feel like you've done your time with this?
I'm not going to exclude that possibility. It was the best project ever—the most fun ever. I got used to running the show by myself, and there are other things I'm interested in doing. But if we came up with another spin-off that felt right and we could figure it out, that would be good, I think I'd be open to it. We tested our luck so much on this project. I really thought that it couldn't get any better than *Breaking Bad*, and then to do *Better Call Saul* and have it come out so well, are we really going to do another one and have it come out that well, or half that well? What you don't want is to throw the rest of the work into a poor light. And so it would really have to pass a very high bar.

Earlier, you pointed out that you couldn't think about the big picture while you were filming the series finale. As time passes and you've moved away from the practicality of making and editing the show, and you start to realize, _Okay, this was the last fifteen years of my life and it's over_, how does that feel?
I think I'm still figuring it out. You're talking to me the day after our very last Emmys, where I got to see a lot of the people who worked on the show. Most of the cast, I got to spend the day with. I just miss the people. I miss that situation. I'm not doing a show right now. I hope like hell that I get to do another TV show.

---

* Another abandoned story pitch had Marie going to Jimmy (or, depending on the timing, Saul) to get her out of a shoplifting charge before Hank found out.

I can't imagine that it's going to be the same kind of experience, though, because I don't think it gets any better than that.

Right now, I'll be honest, I'm missing the work. I'm feeling like, sometimes, *Did we have to end it? Couldn't we have done another couple of seasons before he ends up in Omaha?* But mostly, I just feel a satisfaction that it works for people, and that people are still watching it, and I'm hearing nice things about it. But I miss it. I miss going to Albuquerque. There's a big part of my life going there and going to those stages. And even on Vince's new show, I'm a consulting producer on that, but it's not at the same studio. The studio where we shot *Breaking Bad* is now the Netflix studio, and it's full of Netflix shows. So that's not where the new show is going to be filmed. It's a strange thing and I'm still getting my head around it.

I will say I think that the voices of the characters as embodied by those actors are going to be with me forever. I'm very sorry that I've written my last Jimmy McGill scene, my last Gus Fring scene, my last Mike Ehrmantraut scene. I probably have written the last of all those characters, but they still live on in my head.

Acknowledgments

If you read this book's predecessor, *Breaking Bad 101: The Complete Critical Companion*, you may recall the story of how I had to watch and review two of that show's final three episodes from a hospital bed, because my appendix ruptured hours before the airing of "Ozymandias."

Because life can have a cold sense of humor, I found myself writing this new book while periodically spending time in hospitals, dealing with long-delayed complications from that original surgery. While I wouldn't recommend such an encore, it did at least feel oddly familiar to again be watching and writing about events in the Heisenberg-verse while nurses were placing IVs, tests were being scheduled, etc.

Thank you to Eric Klopfer for having the conviction that *Better Call Saul* deserved a book of its own just as much as its predecessor. Thank you to Connor Leonard for shepherding this project, and helping me find the spot in the Venn diagram that would speak to both first-time viewers and *Saul* veterans. Thank you to my brilliant agent, Amy Williams, who has kept my authorial career in order while I've had to focus on health, family, and my day job over at *Rolling Stone*. Speaking of which, thank you to Sean Woods, David Fear, Lisa Tozzi, Alison Weinflash, and the rest of the gang at *RS*, as always, for giving me the flexibility to do another book in between writing columns, reporting features, and poking my head into the office now and again. Thank you to Dan Fienberg, Richard Rushfield, Keith Phipps, Brian Grubb, Brett Michael Dykes, and Maria Fontoura, who helped oversee and/or edit the original versions of these recaps when they first appeared online at various professional homes.

Thank you to everyone from both this show and *Breaking Bad* who have given so much of their time to answering my many questions going back to 2008. For this book, I'm particularly grateful to Tom Schnauz for acting as the franchise's institutional memory, responding quickly to every esoteric query I had, and hooking me up with other veterans of the writing staff who knew the few things that he didn't. Ariel Levine, Ann Cherkis, Alison Tatlock, Genn Hutchison, and others were eager to share details from their scripts. Rhea Seehorn as always delivered far more information and insight than I could have hoped to ask for. And Peter Gould provided as much time as necessary, even hopping on a lengthy Zoom the night after *Saul*'s final Emmy shutout, just because my deadline was closing in.

And thanks, as always, to my wonderful family for their unceasing love and support. Between the three of them, they've seen exactly one episode of either series (my wife was with me in the hospital for "Ozymandias"), so I can't drop references to space blankets, cocobolo desks, or *Ice Station Zebra* at dinner. But that's probably for the best, anyway.